This new book from the author of *Through the Maelstrom: A Red Army Soldier's War on the Eastern Front* reveals a bitter truth about that war, which has thrown neo-Stalinists in Russia today into a fury. A frontline veteran who survived the most savage and continuous fighting of the Second World War refutes one of the primary Soviet myths: that it was Stalin's "brilliant strategic mind" and his "invaluable contributions" that brought about the eventual victory. Partially relying on his own frontline experience in fighting from Rzhev 1942 to Königsburg 1945, the author argues that the Red Army emerged victorious from the war in spite of the Kremlin tyrant who never spared his soldiers' lives and who recognized only one strategy: to break the *Wehrmacht's* resistance by overloading it with the corpses of Red Army soldiers. He maintains that it was the people who won the war, but Stalin stole the mantle of victory and donned it himself after the war. Gorbachevsky goes on to argue that the Soviet regime and recent official Russian estimates deliberately understated the staggering true cost of that victory, and reveals the scandalous official mistreatment of returning prisoners of war; neglect of war invalids and disregard of the millions of soldiers' remains lying in shallow, unmarked, often fraternal graves and the millions more still listed as "missing in action" – all of which show the Stalinist system's disdain for human life.

I0892906

Boris Gorbachevsky was a Red Army veteran of three years of combat on the Eastern Front of the Second World War. Twice wounded, he rose to the rank of captain and was decorated with four orders and many medals for his service in campaigns that took him from Rzhev in 1942 to the shores of the Baltic and on to Czechoslovakia by war's end. He was a 1950 graduate of the Moscow Printing Institute where he worked for the next 40 years as an instructor, journalist and editor. He was the author of 24 books published in Russia - six of them children's books - and for 20 years served as the editor of the All-Union Institute of Scientific and Technical Information's monthly journal *Izdatel'skoe delo i poligrafiia* [*Publishing and Printing*].

In 1994 he moved to Rhode Island where for six years he published the State's sole Russian-language journal *Vestnik Rod-Ailenda.* In 2007 he published his memoirs in Russia, *Rzhevskaia Miasorubka* [*The Rzhev Slaughterhouse*], which were translated into English and published by the University Press of Kansas in 2008 under the title *Through the Maelstrom: A Red Army Soldier's War on the Eastern Front.* Unfortunately, Boris Gorbachevsky passed away before this book was published.

Stuart Britton is a freelance translator residing in Cedar Rapids, Iowa. He has been responsible for making available in the English language a growing list of historical titles by the "new wave" of Russian historians, who have access to previously classified archival records and who write more objectively about the Red Army's campaigns and battles on the Eastern Front of the Second World War. These titles include Valeriy Zamulin's award-winning book *Demolishing the Myth* (Helion, 2011), Lev Lopukhovsky's highly praised work, *The Viazma Catastrophe, 1941* (Helion, 2013), and Rostislav Aliev's study of the heroic stand by the defenders of the Brest Fortress, *The Siege of Brest 1941* (Pen & Sword, 2013). In addition, Mr. Britton has translated several memoirs by Red Army veterans, such as Petr Mikhin's *Guns Against the Reich* (Pen and Sword, 2010), Joseph Pilyushin's *Red Sniper on the Eastern Front* (Pen and Sword, 2010) and Vasiliy Krysov's *Panzer Destroyer* (Pen and Sword, 2010). Upcoming titles include a biography of Marshal K.K. Rokossovsky by Boris Sokolov, to be published by Helion.

GENERALISSIMO STALIN

THE MYTH OF STALIN AS A GREAT MILITARY STRATEGIST

A Red Army veteran reflects on Stalin's wartime leadership

Boris Gorbachevsky

Translated and edited by Stuart Britton

Helion & Company

Dedication

In cherished memory of my father - a friend and teacher. As an associate of Sergo Ordzhonikidze he fully experienced all the "charms" of the Stalinist regime - and it was only by chance that he wasn't shot by the NKVD. However, his love for the Motherland didn't break his loyalties and he dedicated himself to the building of Communism in all the critical sectors of industry wherever the Party sent him.

Helion & Company Limited
26 Willow Road
Solihull
West Midlands
B91 1UE
England
Tel. 0121 705 3393
Fax 0121 711 4075
Email: info@helion.co.uk
Website: www.helion.co.uk
Twitter: @helionbooks
Visit our blog http://blog.helion.co.uk/

Published by Helion & Company 2014

Designed and typeset by Great White Designs (www.greatwhitedesigns.com)
Cover designed by Farr out Publications, Wokingham, Berkshire
Printed by Lightning Source Limited, Milton Keynes, Buckinghamshire

Originally published as *Pobeda vopreki Stalina: Frontovik protiv stalinistov* (Moscow: Yauza, Eksmo, 2010).

ISBN 978-1-909384-25-5

British Library Cataloguing-in-Publication Data.
A catalogue record for this book is available from the British Library.

Contents

A Few Preliminary Words

The subject of "Stalin and the war" has long been a classic *sui generis*. Much has been said - even more has been written - both lies and apologies, but very little of the truth.

In this sustained dialog, the discussion of I.V. Stalin's military leadership occupies a special place. Obviously, this is explained by the fact that Stalin in the Second World War was a peer of both Roosevelt and Churchill; the Supreme Commander of the Red Army who correspondingly directed the *Stavka* of the Supreme High command. The guns had barely had time to fall silent when Stalin adroitly mounted the pedestal as "The Great Strategist and Commander". We'll note that already on 24 June 1945 in his speech at a parade to celebrate the victory, Zhukov called Stalin a "great commander" - under whose leadership the Red Army crushed Hitler's Germany. Thirty years later the Marshal [Zhukov] labeled his Supreme Commander a '*shtafirka*' - someone in the Russian army distant from military matters. Which can be believed? Khrushchev with a great deal of noise toppled the Generalissimo from his high pedestal. Brezhnev attempted to resurrect the cult of the "Great Commander", but failed. More than 65 years have passed since the Great Patriotic War - more than enough time it would seem to settle the matter, but that still hasn't happened.

In this book, I speak on this subject from a position of a former frontline veteran and captain of the Red Army - an eyewitness to and active participant in major military events of the Great Patriotic War. Of course, I don't claim to have a monopoly on the truth.

In my memoirs *Rzhevskaia miasorubka* [*The Rzhev Slaughterhouse*] published by Izdatel'stvo Iauza-EKSMO in 2007 and translated into English as *Through the Maelstrom: A Red Army Soldier's War on the Eastern Front* (University Press of Kansas, 2008), I spoke a bit about the Stalinist strategy, which for example turned the three major battles at Rzhev into a bloody slaughter. In this book, I am continuing this subject that I touched upon previously.

In response to the nightingale warbling of the palace historians about "the Great Commander", I will cite three of his most important strategic blunders: his bungling directives to the military districts on the first day of the war and his erroneous assumptions about the directions of the enemy's main attack - which in 1941 and 1942 placed the country on the verge of a catastrophe. No one has dared to rebut the mistakes in the 'strategist's' dictatorial thinking. How many human lives they cost only God knows, but He remains silent.

In fact, Stalin had no sort of basic war strategy. His strategy, such as it was, consisted of one cruel demand: "Fight at any cost!" This meant to fight without regard for human lives or losses in combat equipment. That's how the Red Army fought at Moscow; at Rzhev; on the Dnepr; at Königsberg and that's how it took Berlin. This was the essence of Stalin's command activity. He never left the confines of the Kremlin walls or of the *Stavka* – the commander never once traveled to the front. He was an "armchair commander". Unfortunately, to the present day the still-classified documents of the *Stavka* don't allow the full disclosure of the Supreme Commander's actions - including his role in the Stalingrad Operation.

If a military operation (there were more than 300 of them during the war) ended successfully Stalin took credit for it - yet on those occasions of failure, there would immediately follow reprisal after reprisal and a scapegoat would be found. Just think, more than 100 generals were executed during the war who took the rap for Stalin's blunders. Surprisingly, the failures in the battles for Rzhev became an exception to the Supreme Commander's rules; the main commanders there - including Konev and Zhukov - went unpunished. Incidentally, all this didn't prevent Stalin from obtaining a marshal's title.

Nevertheless, history has still recorded a small portion of the "Great Strategist's" activities. Remember: approximately 7 million soldiers and officers of the Red Army were killed during the war - of which 5 million were buried unknown in fraternal graves; approximately 5 million became prisoners of war - of which more than 2 million perished in German camps and almost as many in Soviet camps after the war; 2.5 million spent the rest of their lives as invalids - sharing a bitter fate in life conditions under Soviet power (in one of the chapters, their sad lot is discussed in more detail); 1.5 million of these soldiers and officers deserted (desertion from the ranks of the Red Army continued even in the victorious year of 1945) and around 1 million of them were shot by their own side - often without trial as a consequence of the Special Departments and SMERSH officers.

Finally, we'll talk about the historically unprecedented so-called "filtration" (a process that checked the loyalty of anyone returning from behind German lines or German captivity), which was conceived by Stalin back in 1941. During the war and after it more than 10 million men and women passed through checking in special camps of the Gulag type; former Soviet military prisoners - those men and women who escaped German encirclement - and all sorts of people who lived under German occupation and had breathed "enemy air".

Many didn't pass the checking; battered and beaten, they were forced to recant and to sign confessions to false charges and then went through stage after stage in Gulag camps or went straight to their executions. There is a lot of evidence testifying to this, which I will relay in this book. The latest estimates of the number of Soviet dead in the Great Patriotic War amount to 27 to 30 million people.

There it is - a far from complete inventory of the cost of victory as achieved by the "Great Strategist and Commander". Today, the champions of the Rus' - not without a nod to remembrance - make a lot of noise about the "battles where they had fought together"; glorify the great leader and call him the "Creator of Victory" - the symbol of the Fatherland! It makes one want to say: "Come to your senses, sirs! Was that the way it really was?" But I am confident that readers will be found who will ask (with or without irony) the reasonable question about the real creator of the victory and who will recall "Stalin's 10 Blows".[1]

The Belorussian historian Vladimir Beshanov wrote an accurate book, which talked in detail about the Red Army's battles with the foe, which Soviet propagandists baptized as "Stalin's 10 Blows". They actually were the best strikes against the enemy (1944-1945). However, the numbers of the Red Army's casualties in these offensives - cited by the author - are shocking. Once again fight at any cost not with skill, but with the advantage of numbers. Now the time has come to name the real creators of victory.

In the vicinity of Rzhev in the summer of 1942, our first division commander Andrei Filimonovich Kupriianov told us, his first troops, the following: In the autumn of 1941 he had brought 1,000 18-year-old cadets of the Omsk Military School, who had never before seen combat, to save Moscow. They all fell on the battlefields in front of Moscow. Back then, a total of thousands of cadets from 70 of the country's military schools were defending Moscow. At the cost of their lives, they saved the capital. Their exploits still wait for their chronicler.

THERE THEY ARE – THE CREATORS OF VICTORY!

What does the current generation know about the 400 soldiers who repeated Aleksandr Matrosov's sacrifice?[2] Among them was Sergeant Ivan Alekseev of the 220th Rifle Division. I personally knew this fellow.

THERE THEY ARE – THE CREATORS OF VICTORY!

How little we know about those heroes - those soldiers and officers - who for two months in the summer of 1941 held up the German offensive toward Moscow. How many of them gave up their lives there?

THERE THEY ARE – THE CREATORS OF VICTORY!

The simple Belorussian woman, Elena Mazanik - a partisan who assassinated Wilhelm Kuba, the Nazi gauleiter of occupied Belorussia - deserves high honor as a creator of victory. The list of the genuine creators of victory at the front and in the rear in the Great Patriotic War is endless.

I cannot overlook the simplistic view of the modern generation of Russians toward the role of the Allies in the joint struggle against Nazi Germany. They assert: "We would have won the war even without them!" No! German historians believe that they lost the war due to three reasons: they are the Allies' strategic bombing campaign; Lend-Lease; and the unexpectedly stubborn resistance of the Russians. That which has been said in the Soviet and later Russian press is far from the truth.

Several words about the "unexpected resistance of the Red Army", which according to some historians was supposedly not the case in 1941. The Germans suffered their heaviest losses during the war against the Red Army. In the victorious summer of 1941, the *Wehrmacht* still lost 742,000 soldiers and officers. In the preceding campaigns against Poland, France, Norway, Belgium, Holland, Denmark and in the Balkan countries Germany had lost a total of 418,805 of its soldiers. In order to put an end to the baseless talk about our Allies, I'll cite just one little-known example. While shipping military supplies to the Soviet Union under the terms of Lend-Lease, more than 6,000 American and British sailors lost their lives at sea.

THERE THEY ARE – THE CREATORS OF VICTORY!

After the war ended Stalin deceived the entire world, his own people and us – the frontline soldiers. He gave a deliberately and greatly understated number of those killed in the war. That's what the "Father of Peoples" did for the sake of his exaggerated fame as a "commander". Party bureaucrats promised repeatedly that the State would undertake an honest count of the dead, but this also became a lie. Twenty to 30 years later - convinced that they'd been deceived - veterans and the youth, the children and grandchildren of the fallen soldiers, took shovels into their hands. In recent years "searchers" (older schoolchildren, young workers and university students) have dug up tens of thousands of remains of Soviet soldiers from the fields of former battles and given them an honorable burial.

Then finally, I'll be remiss if I fail to say a few words about something else. An unforeseen event has taken place in Russia. Two Moscow publishers - Ast-Astrel' and Izdatel'stvo Iauza –EKSMO - literally in a single volley have issued Russian translations of more than 10 books by two authors: Mark Solonin - an aviation engineer from Samara - and the prominent American military historian David Glantz. They touch upon topics that were taboo until very recently. For example, there is Mark Solonin's study *22 Iunia ili kogda nachalas' Velikaia Otechestvennaia voina* [*22nd June, or when the Great Patriotic War began*] (Moscow: Izdatel'stvo Iauza-EKSMO, 2007) and David M. Glantz's *Krupneisheee porazhenie Zhukova: Katastrofa Krasnoi Armii v operatsii "Marsa" 1942* [*Zhukov's Greatest Defeat: The Red Army's Catastrophe in Operation Mars, 1942*] (Moscow: Izdatel'stvo Ast-Astrel', 2008).

The appearance of these books opens a new page in domestic military historical literature in Russia. They are serious books that grip the soul and demand deep reflection, which call for a re-thinking of many previously "irrefutable" truths. Russian military historiography had previously seen nothing like these books.

My young friend, if you want to find out how it was in actual fact in the years of the Great Patriotic War - how the Red Army won the war - read the authors that I have named. Their books, I have no doubt, will bring Russians to a better understanding of the subject "Stalin and the war".

"There is nothing higher than the truth."

F. M. Dostoevsky

1

In the Years of the Great Patriotic War ...

Personal impressions: Three stories that took place a week before the war - plus a bit more...

Several days prior to 22 June, I passed my final school exam. We were living at the time in the Moscow area in the wonderful historical village of Kuskovo not far from the capital. There were woods near our two-story wooden home. A little more distant was a magnificent park complex - the former estate of a famous nobleman from Catherine the Great's time - Count P. Sheremet'ev, whose palace had been splendidly preserved together with its exquisite fineries; its stunning inventory of paintings by Russian and foreign masters and its unique collection of 18th-century Russian porcelain. Next to the park was a lake dotted with tiny green islands - a swan sanctuary. It always made me happy to see them.

On the morning of 22 June I was bathing in the lake - enjoying the quiet, sunny summer Sunday and the warmth of the water. Approximately a week before, when I had returned home from Moscow and had shown my mother my diploma, after congratulating me she handed me a summons from the *voenkomat* [military enlistment center]. The next day I had passed through the medical commission and had learned that I was being assigned to the naval infantry. At that time the Red Army was in the process of forming the first battalions of the naval infantry. To my question to the military commissar about how I could be assigned to the Marines when I didn't even know how to swim, he laughed and replied: "They'll teach you!" After this, likely not for the first time, he told me the old anecdote about the man who didn't want to get in the water until he had learned how to swim. He ordered my head to be shaved and for me to come back on Monday the 23rd with my things.

I returned to the *voenkomat* on the appointed day. It was unrecognizable - noise; phone calls; people running; shouts and arguments. All the hallways and staircases were packed with young men. They were volunteers who were eager to get to the front. The military commissar stepped out and in a loud voice said to everyone: "Fellows, your turn will come. The war only started yesterday." It became known that the Presidium of the USSR Supreme Soviet had declared a mobilization of 13 age classes throughout the country's 14 military districts. As we understood, they were calling up people who had previous service in the Red Army. They sent all the volunteers, including me, back to our homes to wait for special instructions.

It is difficult to forget this "longest day" and the shortest night of the year. Especially noon ... At noon, my Papa, Mama and I were waiting for a speech by V. M. Molotov that had been announced. We were all seated around a small table and radio receiver - which at that time was a rarity in a Soviet family - and were waiting quietly for the hands on the clock to reach 12:00 ... Each word of the People's Commissar of Foreign Affairs pierced the soul, struck the heart and caused it to throb. To be honest, at the time I still didn't fully recognize the terrible disaster which was inundating the entire country in literally one moment. Why? Was it my youth or my blind faith in the Soviet press? I couldn't even conceive what was really happening: yesterday's friends had suddenly become mortal foes.

I was born in a time of peace. My generation knew about war only from books and films. The majority of both the books and films glorified the Red Army and the songs that we sang around the campfires in our Young Pioneer detachments depicted victorious exploits in battles with the enemy. I, like many other of my peers, couldn't immediately and fully grasp what had happened that morning of 22 June - moreover because for almost two years the government and press had been assuring the people that Germany was our best friend while the "American plutocrats and English subversives" were our most bitter foe. What had happened? Just a week ago TASS had denounced rumors that Germany was preparing to attack us as false ... Then suddenly?

After Molotov's radio address concluded, Mama and Papa were literally stupefied. Papa was smoking one cigarette after another. Mama, embracing me, was crying. Why? Although approximately 70 years have passed since that day, the first stern words of Molotov's speech have lingered in my memory: "Today at four o' clock in the morning without declaring any grievances against the Soviet Union - without a declaration of war - German forces attacked our country ..." The address ended in something like the following: "Our cause is just. The enemy will be crushed. Victory will be ours." And so forth ... How were we to take the lofty words that had been uttered?

Why had yesterday's friend, which had been the recipient of so many warm and cordial words from our side, suddenly attacked our country? Were there nevertheless any grievances or not? Did Germany attack us without a declaration of war? When would victory come? Why was our cause just? Questions and more questions were swirling around in my head - questions without any answers.

German grievances ... what is known about them? "Hitler's Declaration" appeared for the first time - to be honest in abbreviated form - in the West when the *New York Times* published it on 22 June 1941.

For the first time in 1986 the truth about the concentration of Soviet troops on the border appeared - that is, 45 years after the launching of Barbarossa. Only then did we find out that shortly before the German invasion more than 800,000 men had been secretly called up into the Red Army. This is official information, but here is my own personal testimony. Back in 1941 before the war - every day while waiting at a station for an electrical trolley to Moscow - I saw how the tracks were crowded with military troop trains. In May and in the first half of June, with each passing day their number increased. Through the open doors of the converted boxcars, soldiers swapped jokes. When one of the trains would first move out, the soldiers usually would part with words like: "Until we meet in Berlin!"

Millions of people, from Moscow to the far ends of the country - hearing the words of the People's Commissar of Foreign Affairs - avoided thinking of the fate of their fathers, husbands and sons with whom, as everyone understood, they would very soon part - and possibly forever. I often recalled two phrases that I heard on the street on that day: "There will be a lot of blood ..." and "I believe in Comrade Stalin". Additionally, in those first days of the war Soviet people would ask each other not as a joke, but in all seriousness: "Why aren't the German soldiers surrendering to the Red Army?" or: "Why hasn't the German working class risen up against Hitler?" or even: "How should we treat the Germans once the Red Army enters German territory?" Today, these questions sound amusing ... Yes, but back then the Soviet people had been brainwashed for so long about class solidarity and about the notion of a war with little blood on someone else's territory. We'll be forgiving to those who asked such naïve questions back in 1941.

What was happening in those same days on the border? I'll cite a letter to the *Izvestiia* newspaper written by the former frontline soldier Modest Markovich Markov:

> ...Two weeks before the war we were summoned to headquarters and given a lecture entitled: 'Germany - the Soviet Union's faithful friend'. We were told to park our tanks and to turn over all our ammunition to an artillery depot. I came running to the tank park at 0030. Aircraft were humming overhead. The mood of everyone was cheerful: maneuvers had begun. The first bombing attack was on the depot. There were shouts: 'These are concrete training bombs!' The second bombing run attacked the neighboring battalion. There were more shouts: 'Someone's been killed'; 'Someone's lost a leg!' Only then did we understand that this was war...[1]

A couple of more short letters:

> P. Cherniaev: "I was the Officer of the Day when it started. A clear sky with no clouds, but there was a rumble of thunder in the air. Their artillery was firing over us at Grodno. We had no weapons

> and the [enemy] pilots could see this. They were literally cutting us down with their wings. Light tanks were crushing soldiers almost without firing. But we didn't have anything to shoot, even at a sparrow. Regiment commander Chukamov had his legs taken off by a shell, but he had time to issue a command: 'Save yourselves, whoever can!' Only a handful of men were now still alive."[2]

S. Zubenko:

> Sergeant Volodia Kapustin was killed on the first day near Graevo. Gushing blood, he was trying to exonerate himself - saying that he couldn't have done more than he already did. His final words were: 'We weren't the ones that lost, not the privates ...'[3]

The radio waves were carrying hoarse voices - which often sounded like military commands - and the beating of drums; victorious fanfares boomed. Primarily, it was the sound of German speech in all of this radio noise. I managed to interpret and understand something of it. I had studied German in school. German troops had reached Minsk; were bursting into the Baltic republics and were heading toward Moscow, Leningrad and Kiev.

When I told Papa about what I had heard, he didn't believe me and asked again: "Perhaps there was something you didn't understand or you're mistaken about something?" I repeated what I had just said. He was terribly shaken and kept repeating: "How could this have happened? Where is the Red Army? How did Stalin allow such a thing?" He immediately asked me not to share this bad news with anyone else until there were official announcements about it. Soon thereafter, the authorities ordered all citizens to turn in their radio receivers. We kept the black loudspeaker, which was attached to the wall and kept on around the clock. Suddenly there would be an important report "In the latest hour". With agitation I would listen closely to the announcements of the *Sovinformburo* [Soviet Information Bureau], which had been created on the second day of the war. They would be transmitted twice a day - in the morning and evening -and then be repeated many times.

All of several days of combat operations passed, but the tone of the frontline summaries - no matter how they tried to polish them - was not soothing. First of all we were fighting on our own territory - not someone else's territory - something that Comrade Stalin had more than once assured us would be the case; secondly, like cinema stills, different areas of combat which millions of people were following closely, would appear in the reports and then disappear.

Take for example the seemingly joyful first summary report from the Soviet General Staff (which we now know was untrue):

> ...On 22 June 1941 regular troops of the German army attacked our border outposts on a front from the Baltic Sea to the Black Sea and - in the course of the first half of the day - we were hold-

> ing them back. In the second half of the day the German troops encountered forward units of the Red Army's field forces. After savage fighting the enemy was driven back with heavy losses. Only on the Grodno and Krystopol' directions did the enemy manage to achieve insignificant tactical successes and to occupy the minor towns of Kal'variia, Stoianuv and Tsekhanovets (the first two 15 kilometers and the latter 10 kilometers from the border).
>
> Enemy aviation attacked a number of our airfields and populated places, but everywhere received a decisive repulse from our fighters and anti-aircraft artillery, which inflicted large losses on the enemy. We downed 65 aircraft...

On the fourth day of the war, 26 June, Il'ia Ehrenburg's first article 'Hitler's Hordes' was published in the *Krasnaia zvezda* [*Red star*] newspaper. Thus began the creative path of the best publicist in the years of the war - a real favorite of the frontline troops. On 24 July, Konstantin Simonov's first poem '*Prezrenie k smerti*' ['*Contempt for death*'] appeared on the pages of the *Krasnaia zvezda*. On 6 August his second poem '*Sekret pobedy*' ['*Secret of victory*'] was published in the same newspaper. Thus began the creative path of one of the best frontline poets. I have recalled lines of this poem for my entire life: '*U khrabykh est' tol'ko bessmertie, smerti u khrabykh net!*' ['*The brave have only immortality, the brave have no death!*']

On the ninth day of the war, information about the four main directions – the Minsk, Lutsk, Novgorod-Volynsk and Baranovichi directions – appeared in the news. On the 20th day, already new directions were being announced: Polotsk, Bobruisk, Mogilev-Podol'sk. Always more new directions ... This was alarming; people's faces increasingly looked anxious and troubled. It became ever more difficult to grasp the bitter reality. The foe was pushing us ever back - ever closer to Moscow, Leningrad and Kiev. Where were our aircraft - about which the poets had written so colorfully - and our heroic "Red falcons" - about which songs had been sung?

Quite recently in many Palaces of Culture and factory clubs, people had attentively gazed upon colorful posters of the GLAVPUR [Main Political Directorate of the Red Army] and their hearts had been filled with pride. I should think so ... one artillery salvo from a Soviet division, as some of these posters maintained, was twice as powerful as the salvo from an enemy division. But which enemy ... can you guess? War happened. The artillerymen rolled out their cannons and a catastrophe occurred; their shells were literally blown sky-high by the rain of German bombs.

On 27 June, on the fifth day of the war, there appeared an announcement about the creation of the State Defense Committee. Henceforth, all the power in the country was concentrated in its hands. I. V. Stalin became the committee's chairman.

With each passing day of the war, people began to understand better what the disappearance of some directions and the appearance of new directions of German advance really meant ... The communiqués were so brief, illogical and unclear while the newspapers primarily trumpeted news of the first heroic pilot and the exploits of tankers who'd given a fitting rebuff to the aggressor. Meanwhile the aggressor had already occupied Belorussia, the Baltic republics, Moldavia and part of the Ukraine. How was it possible to comprehend all this?

The encirclement of entire armies, corps and divisions - and the capture of thousands and thousands of soldiers and officers - were being concealed from the public. Rumors about the tragic situation at the front were circulating in the air and people were intercepting them - asking each other one and the same question: "When would the turning point come?" Grains of the bitter truth about the Red Army's catastrophe that was happening were nevertheless slipping through into the society - and they were soul-chilling.

A more elastic terminology appeared in the press: "movement"; "penetrated"; "fought to the end"; "fell back to a new defensive line"; "successfully repulsing enemy attacks"; "shift of positions" and so forth. In the domestic historiography of the Great Patriotic War, a novel linguistic abstraction has long existed which supposedly explains away the first terrible period of the war as a "strategic defense". Do contemporary Russian historians really assume that this lie, like any other lie, having long legs will supersede the truth?

Bombs dropped on Moscow for the first time on 21 July. Within a week, old directions disappeared from the *Sovinformburo* communiqués: Polotsk, Pskov, Novgorod-Volynsk, Bobruisk, but there still remained the Smolensk axis. Again the inconceivable bewilderment and heavy pain in the heart ... The Zhitomir, Korosten' and Belaia Tserkov' directions disappeared. It became clear that Zhitomir, Korosten' and Belaia Tserkov' had fallen into German hands.

How did the Germans themselves assess the war's start? Now this is known. The first days were easy for them. The Chief of the *Wehrmacht's* General Staff, Franz Halder, makes this clear. Here is what he wrote in his war diary on 22 June 1941:

> ... Tactical surprise of the enemy has apparently been achieved along the entire front. All bridges across the Bug River, as on the entire river Frontier, were undefended and are in our hands intact. That the enemy was taken by surprise is evident from the facts that the troops were caught in their quarters; that planes on the airfields were covered up and that enemy groups faced with the unexpected development at the front inquired at their HQ in the rear what they should do. More effects of the surprise may be anticipated from the assaults of our armor, which have been ordered in all sectors. The Navy reports that the enemy seems to have been taken by surprise also in their zone of action. His reactions to the measures of the last few days were of a purely passive nature and he is now holding back his naval forces in ports - apparently in fear of mines.

> ...
>
> 1330. Op. sec.:
>
> a. Air Force reports 800 enemy aircraft destroyed ... Leningrad sea approaches mined without losses. Our own losses so far, 10 aircraft.
>
> b. AGp. Center reports wild flight on the Brest-Litovsk – Minsk road. Russian command organization in complete confusion.
>
> c. AGp. South reports that our patrols have crossed the Prut River between Galatz and Husi and Jassy without encountering any resistance. Bridges are in our hands.
>
> ...
>
> As a result of this tactical surprise, enemy resistance directly on the border was weak and disorganized ....
>
> After the initial shock, the enemy has turned to fight. ... Some sectors are deprived of high-echelon control. But quite apart from that, the impact of the shock is such that the Russian High Command could not be expected in the first few days to form a clear enough picture of the situation to make so far-reaching a decision. On top of everything, the command organization is too ponderous to effect swift operational regrouping in reaction to our attack...[4]

On the very first day of the war, I traveled into Moscow to visit my friend Mark Podobedov. His family, like my own, had moved to Moscow from Khar'kov shortly before the war. Mark and I went to the same school and were in the same class. Along my way into Moscow I walked up to the sole newspaper stand in Kuskovo and looked through the day's issue of *Pravda*. I couldn't believe my eyes and searched through all four pages again. The country's main Party newspaper looked so absurd. War had begun, but in the paper for 22 June there was not a single word about it.

The Podobedovs greeted me warmly. Everyone was speaking about the start of the war. No one could understand why Hitler had attacked Russia. It was suicidal for Germany! Mark's stepfather, who was already far from young and a religious man who had fought in the First World War, spitefully and openly declared: "The German invasion is God's punishment to the great sinner for his crimes. It will cost us dearly." Everyone understood who he had in mind when he mentioned the "great sinner". I didn't begin to debate him, though I couldn't clearly see how the simple people had sinned. The eldest son Zhenia - an engineer at an aircraft factory - said that in the next few days they would begin to move the plant to the East. The youngest son Mark suffered from chronic asthma and wasn't fit for the army. However, he was very bitter about the disaster and was planning to go dig anti-tank ditches.

Two days later I again went to Moscow. I went by the Komsomol City Committee on Arkhipov Street. There they added me to the list of Komsomol members who were volunteering for the task of constructing defensive lines around Moscow. Then I headed into the center of the city.

I walked along one of the city's main thoroughfares, Gor'kiy Street, from the city center to the Belorussian Station. There was increased security at the entrance to Red Square. Military patrols had appeared on the streets; the red Nazi flag with the black swastika in the center was no longer visible on the German Embassy and the Embassy itself was closed. Some people were loading heavy bags with sand and covering the large display windows of shops with them. Wherever you looked, the windows of apartment buildings wore crisscrossed paper strips in case of a bombing raid. The first signs indicating the way to bomb shelters had appeared. How strange it seemed: it was just the third day of the war, but the city was quickly adapting to new life conditions. How were things at the top – the same?

On Pushkin Square, kids were playing at war. I stopped and listened in on their chatter. It was just as it had always been before the war: the Blues and the Reds. The young boys were scouts and the girls were nurses. An agreement: "Keep away; don't kill the nurses." Would the Germans behave the same way?

I dropped by a bookstore. The poster bearing the slogan "Let Soviet-German friendship grow stronger" had disappeared and no others had yet taken its place. Apparently, they were waiting for instructions? On the other hand, books had appeared in the display windows about Russian commanders and Russian valor of yore. Primarily, I noticed people were buying up these books. One could see the first exhibition stands displaying caricatures and cartoons - the works of the talented artists Boris Efimov and the Kurkyniksy.[5] Today it is known that Joseph Goebbels had included them together with Il'ia Ehrenburg on the list of people subject to hanging - after the *Wehrmacht* victory, of course.

There were a lot of military men, as a rule, in fresh new uniforms. I still didn't understand military insignias of rank very well. March companies were passing by - heading primarily toward the Belorussian Station.

On Saturday evening, an old friend of my Papa's came to visit us in Kuskovo - a journalist named Khanaan Zatuchny. They had worked together in the past and my father was troubled over his friend's broken career and fate. It is worth a brief discussion. In 1937, Zatuchny had been the Chief Editor of the *Donetskaia Pravda* newspaper. On one summer evening a comrade, who was a staffer in the local branch of the NKVD, had called him at his office and asked him to step outside for a couple of minutes. Risking his own life, he informed Zatuchny that they would be coming for him that night. The chief editor didn't return to his editorial office. He secretly lived for more than three years in Moscow on Pokrovsky Street at his sister's residence. Meanwhile, those who had come for him left with empty hands and the target "got lost in the shuffle"...

On this evening, Zatuchny had much to tell us. He was better informed than any of us about the situation at the front. He gave the reasons for the Red Army's initial defeats. He also told us about the Germans' annihilation of the Jewish populations in the cities they had seized - a subject on which the Soviet press was silent from the first days of the war to the last.

Incidentally, we didn't know "who was who". For example, who was the army's top commissar or who was in charge of the press and the information agencies? We learned that Lev Zakharovich Mekhlis was the Chief of the Red Army's Main Political Directorate; that Lev Rovinsky was the Editor-in-Chief at the *Izvestiia* newspaper and that David Ortenburg was the Chief Editor at *Krasnaia zvezda.* Iakov Khavinson was the director of TASS and Solomon Lozovsky was the Deputy Director of the *Sovinformburo.* "A Jewish bouquet" Khanaan joked. There you have it, more fodder for Goebbels.

Before leaving, Khanaan told us he was leaving for Alma-Ata. He had married a woman from there - an assistant to the city's public prosecutor. She was promising to replace his domestic passport and he swore to live with her until the end of the war.

Papa asked Khanaan: "Aren't you afraid to wind up as her hostage if your life together doesn't work out?"

"I have no other choice," replied Khanaan. "I can't stay with my sister in Moscow any longer. It is risky. A harsh time of war is beginning."

As we parted, Khanaan expressed an optimistic view about the war's course: "Hitler doesn't know Stalin well. This Asian will put millions of peasants into soldier's greatcoats. This isn't the first time for him, and he'll drive the Führer into the grave ..."

In the first days of the war, verses by Lebedev-Kumach appeared in the press:

Arise, enormous country

Arise for mortal combat

With the fascist forces of darkness

With the accursed horde!

These verses, which came out under the title '*Sviashchennaia voina*' ['*Holy war*'], soon became the war's main song. Usually it was sung while standing like a hymn. That's how they referred to the war for a long time – as "holy"; "a people's war"; "Great"; "patriotic". The name "Great Patriotic War" appeared significantly later. It was applied to the war against the fascists for the first time only in an order from the Supreme Commander dated 1 November 1944.[6]

Two feats

At the beginning of July, my father was appointed as the director of a large construction project in the Urals in the city of Kyshtym. A graphite plant had to be constructed within seven months. At that time, graphite was used primarily in the manufacturing of artillery shells and in pencil production. Not much time would pass before graphite would be necessary for atomic reactors as well. In the initial stage of the war, some areas where graphite was extracted were already occupied by the Germans and others were under the threat of quickly falling into German hands.

With a permit, signed by the People's Commissar at the order of the State Defense Committee, Papa departed for the Urals with some assistants. At the end of July, Mama and I together with employees of the People's Commissariat of the Building Materials Industry (where Papa oversaw the extraction of non-metallic minerals) and their families set off in freight cars for Kyshtym. The train moved at slow speed and only arrived there in the middle of August.

What struck me most of all along the way? We were often passed by long trains with small grilled windows in the railcars. They were moving faster than we were, not to the West, but all to the East. From the little windows carried the sounds of loud shouts: "They're taking us to camps! They're taking us to camps!" the people were shouting. "We want to go to the front; to defend the Motherland! Let Stalin know, explain to him. He doesn't know." Then again: "We know, they're hauling us to camps, not to the front!"

Ambulance trains were often passing us. At stations where we halted side by side I tried to converse with the nurses and medics. I was trying to learn even a drop of truth about events at the front. However, everyone that I approached turned and walked away without answering my questions. Plainly, they'd been forbidden to engage in any conversations on these topics with onlookers.

Upon my very first encounter with the town of Kyshtym when we arrived I liked it. It was all green and clean surrounded by a large forest. There was a stream and the residents were kind and hardworking. Many of them were avid hunters, fishermen and went mushroom hunting. Papa prepared a spacious peasant pentagonal hut for us. I lived in it until December 1941, when I left for the army.

Having arrived in Kyshtym, the next day I went to the *voenkomat*. The commissar registered me and noting my middle education, promised to send me to a military school as soon as a place was open. Soon the moment arrived and I set off to join the Cheliabinsk Tank School. A medical board turned down my application to join the tankers. It turned out that I was color-blind (which until that time I didn't realize); that I was very flat-footed and had a weak heart. How many times I asked: "Take me, what difference does color-blindness make? There are no signal lights at the front!" The doctors flatly refused to hear me out and chucked me out into the corridor. I had liked the school. There was no sort of parade drill. They taught the students how to drive tanks, how to engage enemy tanks, how to cross water barriers in them and how to save themselves or the vehicle when necessary … They were sending students to the front in new tanks directly from the factory.

Returning to Kyshtym, I told the commissar about my failure. He calmed me down: "You weren't suitable for the tankers – you'll become an artilleryman; if you're not cut out to be a gunner, you'll command infantry; there is a lot to do in the army."

I was ordered to wait.

In September I went to work as a lathe operator's apprentice at an armament factory. It arose in Kyshtym as a special case, but at the same time it was typical for that heroic time when people at the front and in the rear were trying to save the Fatherland. Here's how it happened. About a month-and-a-half after the start of the war, 28 Jews arrived in Kyshtym. They were simple, modest people. Only some of them were religious. They had fled their native Kiev as the Germans were approaching the city.

Back in Kiev they had all worked at a factory that made beds. There were among them lathe operators, tool makers and metal workers. The factory produced metal beds with nickel-plated frames covered by interlaced wire mattress supports. The factory director was the 32-year-old engineer Lenia Umansky. He was a graduate of the Kiev Polytechnic Institute, where he had studied together with my cousin. Few Ukrainians had traveled to Kyshtym with them. Why? They were reasoning this way: "We aren't Jews. What do the German have against us?"

The energetic Lenia had managed to get hold of some platform cars and had loaded them with machine tools, hand tools, bundles of wire and even barrels of lubricants. There was almost not any room left on the cars. Nevertheless, all the workers and their families somehow managed to find places among the cargo. Lenia forbade bringing along family belongings, and allowed only foodstuffs. On the 19th day of their journey, the Kiev Jewish residents arrived in Cheliabinsk. They were sent along to Kyshtym.

On the day of their arrival - while the workers, wives and children unloaded the platform cars - Lenia headed off to see the First Secretary of the Party City Committee. He familiarized the Secretary with an idea that he had conceived along the way – to build a factory to produce shells for tanks. He laid a folder containing his plans and calculations on the Secretary's desk. Said Lenia: "We are asking little from the city: a small place, even better if it is an old, but furnished premise; 70 job permits and a housing permit for everyone that works at the factory."

A war was going on and anyone with the least bit of responsibility had to make decisions in a matter of days -or more likely, a matter of hours - and to find a way out of a most difficult situation. On the next day, the First Secretary tracked Lenia down and told him: "We've found accommodations – stables on an old stud farm. There's nothing else. Put them into shape. I hope you'll manage. All the rest that you requested, you'll receive. Good luck. Not each day, but each hour is precious: the Fatherland is in danger!"

First publicly stated by Stalin, in those days "The Fatherland is in danger!" became a unique, magical incantation - a watch-word and an expression of faith in victory not only at the front, but in the rear as well. We nodded off with it and went to sleep at night with it; we sent husbands and sons off to the front with it; together with it, partisan detachments made their way into the enemy rear and with it we went into battle.

Over two months 28 Kiev Jews, their wives, adolescent sons and 16 Russians from the Urals worked to clean the stables which had been built, as they joked back then, in the time of Ivan the Terrible out of large clumps of manure that were as hard as steel; put up some roofs that leaked here and there; renovated the stables into some really spacious accommodations; heated them; poured a concrete floor; set up the machine tools and added electricity and plumbing. There were a lot of difficulties. People from Cheliabinsk helped out.

Within a short time Lenia's deputy, Semen Tonkover had constructed a dining hall; some toilets (a luxury at the time); a shower room and a rabbit shed. He drove out to a state farm just outside the city and worked out a direct bartering system with it. The factory would repair the farm's tractors and seeding machines in exchange for the delivery of potatoes, onions and carrots from the farm. On the factory's first production day, the state farmers brought the factory workers a pig that weighed around 80 kilograms as a gift.

In November, military procurers arrived in Kyshtym in order to receive the first production run of solid-shot shell heads for tank guns. In the first month, they produced all of 100 of them. When I left the factory at the end of 1941 they were now working in two, 12-hour shifts each day to produce 1,200 shell heads. Multiply the given number by 30 days per month - they worked with no days off - and you get 36,000 shell heads per month. In 1942, as my Mama wrote to me at the front, the factory trebled its output. It was a marvel!

Despite the poor nutrition, the bad news from the front and the eternal worry over children and loved ones who were fighting at the front, the people quietly - at times gritting their teeth - carried out their duty; constantly searching for new reserves of strength in themselves and in others - and, what was quite surprising, finding them. Indeed, no one, not a single person, failed to believe what had been accomplished was a genuine feat. That's how the people thought of the workers and factories in the rear, as long as the Allies failed to open a Second Front. A noble goal, as history gives evidence, is capable of much. It is ready to engender a person with superhuman energy and to impart him or her with titanic strength. That's the way it was!

About my two cousins

I would like to demonstrate the role that fate plays in the life of a human using the example of my two cousins. A week before the war, I received the last letter from my cousin Mark. He had already been serving in the Red Army for more than a year. Mark's mother, who was my father's sister and my beloved Aunt Berta, was living in Kiev then. She persuaded the military commissar, who was a family acquaintance, to allow her son to serve in the Kiev Military District. She often traveled to visit her son at his unit. Mark received a few days' leave on several occasions to visit home. Suddenly, an order arrived. The division in which he served was urgently moved up closer to the border.

My other cousin, Igor', lived in Khar'kov with an aunt. His mother had passed away when he was only seven years old and his father, the Leningrad writer

Vladimirsky, when he found out in 1937 that a case was being prepared against him in "the Big House" (that is to say, in the NKVD), fearing arrest he had hanged himself. Igor' was called up for the army in 1940. There was no one left to utter a word on behalf of the poor conscript and he was sent to serve in the Far East where he fortunately spent the entire war; rose to the rank of senior lieutenant and took part in the Manchurian campaign against the Japanese in August 1945, which he survived. After the war he graduated from the Military Academy of Armored Forces and then commanded a tank regiment in the Ukraine as a colonel until his retirement from active service.

Mark's fate was different. Before the war, military censors didn't scrutinize soldiers' letters so closely. In his last letter, Mark told me about his unit, which was positioned not far from the border. He and his comrades were busily constructing a new line of defense almost around the clock. The tension at the border was palpable. The soldiers watched as the Germans brought up more and more units to it.

Meanwhile, as we now know, after the June TASS communiqué - in order to give this deceptive announcement an air of reliability - the Generalissimo had ordered that all the Soviet units that had been moved up to the border to stand down; to remove engines from airplanes and tanks - supposedly for maintenance - and to send all the personnel to training camps not far from the border. Literally several hours before the start of the war, the Kremlin ordered: "Don't respond to provocations!" Such was the "wisdom" of Comrade Stalin that cost the Red Army so dearly. Mark still had a year of service. As soon as he was de-mobilized, he planned to come to see me. We had been close friends since our childhood years. We often met in Kiev or Khar'kov. Mark dreamed of enrolling in the Kiev Polytechnic Institute. Everything turned out differently. The war began and Mark went missing.

I'll allow myself a brief digression here to tell what happened to the rest of my father's extended family in Kiev after the Germans occupied it in September 1941. Berta, my Papa's older sister Leia, their children and grandchildren just barely managed to get out of the city. Uncle Arl, Leia's husband, their daughter and her husband with their three-year-old Vovochka - as well as other relatives - remained in the city. Uncle Arl, an elderly man highly respected by everyone, managed to convince his family circle not to flee Kiev. He had seen the Kaiser's army in 1918. He said: "The Germans are intelligent people, decent and orderly. Everything will be OK." My uncle's relatives were simple, modest, honorable Jewish craftsmen and women. They packed cigarette casings with tobacco; produced or sold general hardware and worked as hairdressers or tailors. Uncle Arl's daughter, Rivka, was an embroidery craftswoman at a sewing factory. They carried out their religious vows earnestly and precisely. They didn't read the newspapers and didn't listen to the radio. Incidentally, had they read the newspapers or listened to the radio, would they have read or heard at least one word about the German army's brutalities against the Jewish population? Wouldn't at least a hint that was addressed to the Jews have reached them: "Leave, save yourselves!" Many Ukrainians, with whom Rivka worked, encouraged her not to believe the rumors about the killing of Jews in Zhitomir, Vinnitsa and Berdichev.

She persuaded herself: "Might there really be some exaggeration in the rumors about the German atrocities?"

As an example of the German brutalities, I'll briefly pass along a story that I heard from a comrade. After the war, he had returned to his native village in Belorussia - where he was born and had spent his childhood years - and learned the following. Several days before the Germans entered the village, the local baker Iankel' had gone around to all the Jewish families and requested flour, poppy seeds and butter from them. He had decided to save the local Jews, for which he intended to treat the Germans to some uncommonly tasty poppy seed buns.

German tanks and motorcycles soon appeared. Iankel' and the most highly esteemed Jews greeted the tankers and motorcyclists on the main street. He presented them with a pile of buns on an enormous platter. The German column halted for a few minutes, and then munching on the tasty buns, the soldiers moved on down the road. There was not even so much as a "Thank you!"

Kicking his heels, Iankel' joyfully shouted: "What a fine fellow I am! I've saved you! Did you see how hungrily the gentlemen tankers devoured my buns?" The Ukrainians who had come out to the main street to meet the conquerors chuckled: "What have the Jews thought up now!"

The next day, an *Einsatzgruppe* unit entered the village. It burned Iankel' and the other Jews to death in the oratory. So many analogous stories have been preserved ... So many!

As became known after the war, only 10 per cent of the Jewish population managed to be evacuated, but in general - during the impetuous German offensive in 1941 - no evacuation of the population from the cities and villages of the Ukraine, Belorussia, Moldavia, the Baltic republics, Leningrad Oblast or other places was ever organized. Primarily, it was the Party and bureaucrats who fled - as well as employees of the NKVD - after first having executed all their prisoners. The story with the Smolensk Party archive, which fell entirely into German hands, is a graphic example.

The fate of Uncle Arl, Rivka, her husband and Vovochka proved to be tragic. In September 1941 they, along with 13 other of my Kiev relatives, were killed at Babi Yar.

The thought never leaves me: Stalin, in that cruel year of 1941, ensured first of all the security of his own power and had no interest in saving his "brothers and sisters" - especially the Jews. He knew about the annihilation of the Jewish population by the Germans. During the war years, on the territory occupied by the *Wehrmacht*, approximately 2.5 million Jews were killed, yet he never showed any intention of saving them.

The Boss more likely rejoiced over such a course of events and supposed that this was a gift from Hitler. "The more, the better," he believed. "A splendid political godsend: all the sinister, bloody work to purge the Soviet Union of Jews was being done by the Nazis". The Western countries, the world community and, of course, the Jewish people themselves would never forgive the Nazis for this. Meanwhile he, Stalin, would seem like a friend and savior of the Jews. Moreover, the General Secretary thought he couldn't ignore the following circumstance: "The annihilation of the Jewish nation would for a long time divert the opinion of the world community away from the Moscow show trials in the 1930s; away from the Gulag and so forth …"

Actually, that is what happened. The victory over Nazi Germany in the Second World War saved the Jewish people from complete extermination. No one rejects the fact that one of the organizers of this victory was Stalin. To be sure, there also exists a different point of view: we won this war not thanks to Stalin, but in spite of him. It reminds us today of the position of the German generals who assert that Germany lost the war thanks to Hitler. The debate on this subject will continue. As more and more documents become de-classified, the latter opinion finds increasing confirmation.

Let's return to my cousin Mark's story. On the third day of fighting, the regiment in which Mark served was crushed. Many of its commanders and soldiers wound up as prisoners, including Mark. On the very first night, when the Soviet prisoners were not yet under adequate guard, Mark and two comrades escaped. The Germans didn't bother searching for them. Why? The German divisions were rapidly marching to the East. They drove tens of thousands of prisoners, like cattle, into specially designated areas; encircled them with barbed wire; set up machine guns on the corners; posted sentries with sub machine guns and made a head-count of the prisoners to report to higher headquarters.

Until the end of 1942, Hitler prohibited the sending of Red Army prisoners to Germany. Just imagine, by this time they numbered more than 3 million.

In October-November 1941, the Germans freed more than 300,000 of their prisoners: Ukrainians, Belorussians and men from the Baltic republics. A small portion of the prisoners was given to rural women as "bachelors" and "husbands". The rest, the majority of them, was sent to linger in prison camps. Primarily, these were Russian soldiers. The bulk of the prisoners, as is now known, perished in the winter of 1941-1942. The Nazis actually wiped out almost the entire regular personnel of the Red Army. I think such a fact must have delighted Stalin. As he must have thought, the Germans themselves had destroyed almost all of the direct witnesses of his own personal ignominy.

In recent years, trying to rehabilitate the "Genius Leader", certain official Russian historians assert that the Supreme Commander had acted that way - that is, he had sacrificed the regular army for the sake of winning time - in order to relocate industrial factories from the central regions of the USSR to the East. This argument itself is blasphemous. However, if we assume that this version is correct, then why did he toss the army that he had been preparing for 20 years to their fates and declare as traitors those soldiers and officers who were taken prisoner?

For almost two months Mark and his comrades made their way to the West; moving to the East, they well understood, they'd never get back to their own side. Once, the refugees bumped into a German constabulary patrol. One of them was killed. Soon the remaining two men reached Polish territory. A wealthy Pole took them in as farm hands. For two years they labored on his farm. He stated that the prisoners were Poles and obtained papers for them. In 1943, German commandants in the Polish General Government distributed an order: "For harboring refugee Russian prisoners and Jews – execution by firing squad". The next morning, having received the menacing circular against his countersignature, the frightened gentleman summoned his two farm hands. He treated them decently; provided them with lard, bread, onions and salt for the road; shod them with decent *choboty* [a type of Ukrainian high boot]; clad them with quilted jackets and bid them farewell.

Now their path lay to the East. They walked in the hope of linking up with partisans. They thought that things had become calmer in the Ukraine. When they reached Ukrainian territory, they didn't know that it was still entirely enmeshed by occupation authorities, just like tentacles, right down to each village. Local police recruited by the Nazis patrolled the roads, while in the villages local elders put in place by the Nazis controlled the lives of the villagers. An elderly forest ranger that they had met didn't cheer up the fellows with his story. They moved at night, guided by the stars. Importantly, the weather was cooperative. Again, it would seem, a stroke of luck ... Somewhere near the Kiev area they encountered a partisan patrol. The situation took shape just like in the Soviet film by Iurii German *Proverka na dorogakh* [*Vetting on the roads*] - a stern interrogation followed by "verification in action". In an exchange of fire with a punitive German expedition, Mark was wounded in the leg while his comrade was killed. The partisans departed and left Mark behind. He was now alone.

Hiding in a deep forest thicket and having bandaged his leg, he spent the entire day there before setting out that night - hobbling along with the support of a thick stick as a cane in what seemed to him to be the direction of Kiev. He wasn't mistaken. After several days, barely still alive with a swollen leg, he approached the village of Kolosenka about 120 kilometers from the Dnepr River. Again, it would seem a stroke of luck – he knew the village. He recognized it immediately. In his childhood he had spent a summer there together with his brother. That evening, Mark crawled through the bushes up to the hut of the Trofims, where they had previously resided, and quietly knocked on the door.

Admitting the wounded man into the semi-darkened anteroom, Trofim illuminated his face with a candle stub he had lit and immediately recognized his summer visitor. Having made the sign of the cross over him he embraced the soldier, helped him enter the living area and calmed him down. His wife, Baba Mavra, fed Mark, gave him some hot herbal tea and then tended to his wound. She washed it, smeared some sort of home concoction over his swollen leg and wrapped it with some clean, warm rags.

Mark spent the next four days hiding in a barn hayloft. On the fifth day, a shaken Trofim climbed up to the hayloft and having given a bow, asked Mark to forgive him. It turned out that Mark could no longer remain with the Trofims. The next day, as the village elder had informed Trofim, Germans would be coming to the village. The elder put up the four of them for the night in his own home. Before sunrise, there was another parting - just like the one in Poland. Trofim supplied

Mark with a bit of lard, a boiled potato and an onion for the road ahead and handed him a jar of Mavra's ointment to treat his leg. Mark slipped away through the darkness. At that point, Mark's trail goes missing.

How did I know this entire story? After the war, when Aunt Berta returned to Kiev, one day Trofim unexpectedly came to see her where she was living in Podol.[7] Was it because just in case he wanted to protect himself from accusations? We couldn't know whether he had betrayed Mark to the Germans or not. Or did he come to tell Berta everything he knew about her son out of genuinely good and honorable intentions? Berta traveled back to the village with him. They rented a britzka [a type of horse-drawn carriage]. Together with Trofim, they investigated all the wartime roads and trails and searched all the forests and fields on foot. They went around the entire district hut by hut - showing everyone they met photographs of Mark both in civilian dress and in his uniform. They searched for any trace of a little mound, even a barely perceptible one, which might indicate a grave. There was nothing …

How many are there like Mark, the so-called "missing persons", lying in unmarked graves even to this day? After the passing of their families and friends, even the memory of them is fading into oblivion forever …

"Is it worth doubting that in the first weeks of the war, millions of Red Army servicemen were killed, wounded or taken prisoner? It is time, at last, to acknowledge at least to ourselves, that it wasn't love for the Motherland or Stalin that emerged victorious in this war, but hatred for the enemy."

Mark Solonin

2

How did Comrade Stalin Deceive his "Brothers and Sisters"? ...

Stalin's speech of 3 July 1941

On the 12th day of the war, the Leader finally addressed his "brothers and sisters" over the radio.[1] After his speech some things had become clearer, some things more murky, but on the whole the overall picture of the start of the war seemed dramatic. Millions of people in the Soviet Union and around the world had been impatiently waiting to hear from Stalin. So far as I recall, the majority received his speech with deep relief and took Stalin's words at first as a program of action in the struggle with the fascist aggressors. However, once the initial thrill wore off they reflected. They began to ask themselves the same questions again and again. For example, why had the border battles been lost? How many years had the people been assured from the highest podiums that "the Soviet border was under lock and key"? Or the following natural questions: Why were the Germans advancing so quickly, while the Red Army was retreating with even greater haste? Why was the Red Army suffering much greater losses than the *Wehrmacht*? Of course, the Soviet people didn't know the full story; they were again relying on rumors. Was the foe really so strong? Where are our guys – "Stalin's falcons" of the air force or the Tank Armadas – about which so many verses had been composed; so many songs had been written and so much had been said?

Good Lord, whom to ask, and who will answer?

On the day of the German invasion - 22 June 1941 - the Red Army had 3.3 million soldiers in the military districts along the western border. It possessed 25,479 tanks - of which 13,718 were in the western districts. Of the 4,906 tanks of recent design and manufacture 2,454 were T-34 and KV tanks, which were nearly invulnerable at that time to German tanks. The Kiev Special Military District alone had 4,300 tanks, which meant that it alone had more tanks than the entire Axis invasion force. It also had 2,000 aircraft, which was half of the *Luftwaffe's* entire complement of aircraft. Nearly half of the Kiev Special Military District's aircraft were contemporary types. The Germans committed 4.3 million troops to Operation Barbarossa, which were one million more than the Soviet side had in the western districts. This was their sole advantage. That's at least what certain historians think today - forgetting that on the main directions of attack, the Germans had concentrated forces that were four to six times larger than the defending Red Army possessed.

There was only one thing left to the Soviet citizens - to believe Stalin's words and the press. It has been taken to be considered that Stalin's speech came at the most difficult hour of the war. However, the Dictator wouldn't have given it if he didn't believe that a suitable moment had arrived for it. By 1 July, 5.35 million men had been mobilized for the Red Army. It was precisely on 3 July - the day of Stalin's speech - that the mobilization was temporarily halted. At approximately 8.5 million soldiers and officers, the Red Army was superior to the *Werhmacht* in numerical strength.

The Dictator constantly concealed from the people his Kremlin life as well as many events of foreign and domestic policy. One of them was the secret protocols to the Molotov-von Ribbentrop Non-Aggression Pact between Germany and the Soviet Union. On their basis, Stalin and Hitler had allocated so-called "spheres of influence" between themselves - after which the dictator immediately set out to seize the new territories that belonged to the Soviet sphere of influence: Eastern Poland, the Baltic countries, the Western Ukraine, Moldavia, Northern Bukovina ...

Stalin skillfully and cleverly released information. He frequently resorted to demagogy and the falsification of facts and figures. In the process, he determined what his subject could know and what it was desirable for them not to know. For example, why should the "brothers and sisters" know that with the signing of this pact, Stalin and Hitler were primarily responsible for causing the Second World War?

In his speech, Stalin justified the conclusion of the Non-Aggression Pact with the Germans, which had supposedly provided the Soviet Union with a delay of one-and-a-half years before the start of the war. From this, everything follows logically and naturally: Hitler treacherously violated the Pact and unexpectedly attacked the Soviet Union. However, even a lazy mind could notice that there were gaps in Stalin's logic.

Hitler's invasion of the Soviet Union really was treacherous, but it is impossible to call it unexpected. In his speech, Stalin acknowledged that 170 enemy divisions had been moved up to the Soviet borders - fully mobilized and standing at full combat readiness. How then can there be any talk of a "surprise"? Meanwhile in the opinion of many historians the pact with Hitler was concluded only with one aim – to bring on the Second World War.

We'll cite several fragments from Stalin's 13 July speech. "In spite of the heroic resistance of the Red Army," said the Leader, "and although the enemy's finest divisions and finest air force units have already been smashed and have met their doom on the field of battle, the enemy continues to push forward - hurling fresh forces into the attack."

"When then would the Red Army stop the foe?" people asked and couldn't answer. Another excerpt from Stalin's speech: "The main forces of the Red Army are coming into action armed with thousands of tanks and airplanes." There's the answer to the people's question! That must mean a turning point would soon come and the aggressors would be hurled from Soviet territory .... In the first days of the war, the "brothers and sisters" sincerely believed the words of the Leader. However, it has long been known how far they were from the truth. In the first 10 days of the war, the Germans seized or destroyed almost 75 per cent of the Red Army's combat equipment including tanks, airplanes, artillery and firearms. Could anyone believe back then that such a fundamentally unimaginable event could happen? How little we knew about what was happening at the front, but how much everyone back then wanted to believe Comrade Stalin.

Stalin also touched upon the causes of the initial defeats in his address to the nation. He pointed to the fact that the entire German army was fully mobilized, but our army was not. Was this the result of something inexplicable? The Leader was being clever. The point is that the German army was brought up to combat readiness, while our army was not. Why? One of the main causes of the Red Army's defeats in the initial period of the war, as Stalin explained, consisted in the aggressor's surprise offensive. In reality, couldn't the Soviet forces have anticipated a surprise attack? What were they doing if not preparing to defend the country? Indeed, why do armed forces exist? An attack without a declaration of war is an elementary practice in modern history. In an analogous case, isn't that just the way the Soviet troops attacked the Japanese in August 1945?

The attack on the USSR really did come as a surprise, but can this surprise be understood? Many people had knowledge of the enemy's intentions from Stalin down to the border military districts. It is known that dissemination of this knowledge was prohibited. The surprise consisted of the fact that the troops were not timely put on combat alert and the command of the armies on the main directions of the attack were stunned by the enemy's enormous superiority. The majority of the district commanders didn't know the plans to defend the State Border from the deployment of the forces to the start of combat operations.

In contemporary literature, a large amount of attention is given to the factor of "surprise" as the main reason for the defeats of the Soviet forces. "As a result of Stalin's faint-heartedness", the Red Army "was dwelling at the moment of the German invasion in a state of complacency". Some historians note the effectiveness of the disinformation, to which fascist diplomacy and propaganda constantly resorted. In the opinion of the German historian J. Dullfer, "the insufficiently full evaluation of the *Wehrmacht's* possible intentions proved to be telling in its initiation and conducting of the Second World War." Against the backdrop of the cruel spy hysteria that was reigning inside the USSR at the time, Hitler succeeded in deceiving Stalin. For example he persuaded the Leader that the German forces, which were preparing to attack the USSR, had been moved in close proximity to the Soviet border only because the English had been subjecting them to attacks from the air in central Germany.

The surprise of 22 June meant not only the loss of the greater portion of the Soviet regular army, but also the loss of enormous materiel, space and time which sharply changed the balance of forces in favor of the enemy. This allowed the *Wehrmacht* to conduct a *blitzkrieg*, upon which Hitler placed his main hope in destroying the Red Army. Certain historians, referring to the invasion's factor of surprise, maintain that this prevented the deployment of the Red Army for a counter-offensive. Subsequently the point of view about the "surprise" reigned supreme in the Soviet historiography. In the Stalinist viewpoint, they accepted his conception of the "objective" and "subjective" causes of the Red Army's defeat. However, given a careful examination, all the "objective" cause are in essence subjective. The USSR was not at all preordained to suffer the terrible defeats in 1941-1942 and the countless losses.

Before the war, Stalin had constantly called upon the army and the people to be ready for any surprise - particularly in his famous speech of 5 May 1941 but in the actual event he slept through the enemy's invasion ...

In the memoirs of G. K. Zhukov, K. K. Rokossovsky, N. N. Voronov, K. S. Moskalenko and L. M. Sandalov there are glimpses of the confusion of Stalin and his circle on the eve of and at the start of the war. It is known that the news of Minsk's capture by the Germans led Stalin to resign his position and to flee to his Kuntsevo dacha for two days. In the difficult situation in front of Moscow, when forward German units at the beginning of October 1941 were just 13-15 kilometers from his dacha there, G. K. Zhukov recalls that Stalin was totally adrift like never before.

It is possible that Stalin's orders, like those in the initial phase of the war and his subsequent famous Orders No. 270 and 227, were borne out of the personal, heavy psychological condition of the Supreme Commander who in them provided the single way out of the difficult situation at the front that had arisen - and not for the first time. But let's return to Stalin's speech of 3 July.

In it Comrade Stalin, addressing his "brothers and sisters", explained how they should behave toward the aggressors. Said Stalin:

> In case of forced retreat of Red Army units ... the enemy must not be left ... a single kilogram of grain or liter of fuel.
>
> The collective farmers must drive off all their cattle and turn over their grain to the safekeeping of State authorities for transportation to the rear. All valuable property, including non-ferrous metals, grain and fuel which cannot be withdrawn, must without fail be destroyed.

The Leader continued:

> In areas occupied by the enemy, guerilla units - mounted and on foot - must be formed; diversionary groups must be organized to combat the enemy troops; to foment guerilla war everywhere; to blow up bridges and roads; damage telephone and telegraph lines and set fire to forests, stores and transports.

> In the occupied regions conditions must be made unbearable for the enemy and all his accomplices. They must be hounded and annihilated at every step and all their measures frustrated.
>
> … We must create a people's militia; rouse all workers for the struggle in order to defend our freedom, our honor and our Motherland with their lives.

It is like an incendiary call cooked up in a hysterical horror. Burn, blow up and poison everything – destroy the entire country.

From Stalin's speech it was not difficult to draw two conclusions. First, the Red Army would have to retreat even further, but how far? Second, it wasn't comprehendible how it might be possible to implement the Leader's directions given the enemy's extremely rapid advance - especially by that part of the population which would fall under enemy occupation. After all, people must live somehow ….

A veteran once shared with me the following story. His father, a communist and chairman of a Jewish collective farm in Belorussia, herded together all the cattle and together with his fellow villagers tried to drive the herd away from the advancing German army - that is, to carry out Comrade Stalin's instruction. Several times the Germans overtook the collective farmers and the herd and repeatedly ordered them to return the cattle. "The herd now belongs to Germany, it is ours!" the German officers told them. However, each time his father managed to shake off the Germans and led the cows, horses, sheep and goats to Kazakhstan. However, this was a successful case. The numerous attempts to destroy the grain and fuel, evacuate the rolling stock and dismantle the plants and factories and send them to the East were not always successful. In some places, people didn't wish to act that way.

As an example, let's look at a hypothetical situation occurring as a result of occupation in one of the villages - let us say in Belorussia or the Ukraine …. Germans enter the village and after consulting with the villagers, appoint an elder. Just try to refuse. Soon a German cavalry unit stops in the village. Immediately, assignments follow: some villagers to wash the underwear; some to remove the manure from the stables; some to work as dish washers or waiters in the officer's Mess; some to dig up potatoes to be shared with the Germans; some to work at the mills; some to work as carpenters or as blacksmiths to make horseshoes for the German horses. Just try to refuse!

A German-language teacher in the village school against her will serves as a translator while three young fellows are appointed as policemen. Can you try to refuse? However, the time will come when the reborn Red Army will return to this village. Then the SMERSH officers[2] will start the process of sorting: "Who is who"? They shoot the schoolteacher and send the elder and policemen into the Gulag - and not only them. They also imprison those women who washed the underwear or the dishes; the grave digger; the peasant who buried the villagers and collective farm members.

Let's take a look at the diaries of Joseph Goebbels, who highly evaluated Stalin's speech as a superb propaganda document and for some time even studied it. Here is what the "greatest falsifier in the history of mankind" wrote in his diary for 3 and 4 July 1941:

> 3 July 1941 … Big noise about Stalin's planned flight from Moscow. … Amann[3] is already busy organizing the establishment of four big newspapers for the occupied area. The *Völkischer Beobachter* in Moscow - now that would be a novelty.
>
> 4 July 1941 … Yesterday: heavy English air raids on North and West Germany. Considerable damage. On the Eastern Front: encirclement at Novgrodok completed. We can expect a huge haul there. One dare not mention the probable figures yet. The advance continues apace in all other sections of the front. … But the Russians are fighting a hard, bitter battle. … Otherwise, however, our casualties so far have been very slight when one considers the scale of the fighting.
>
> The situation on the Central Front is excellent. There the enemy is beginning to wilt. … The Russians have lost a lot of aircraft. They are no longer prepared to launch any night attacks on our eastern cities. For the moment, their main ally is Slavic stubbornness. But one day even that will break.
>
> Early today, Stalin made a speech. A bad conscience talking and shot through with profound pessimism. The speech illustrates the gravity of the situation, calls for the sabotage of our advance and warns against panic-mongers and rumors spread by the enemy ….
>
> Abroad, particularly in the U.S.A. and even in London, they see Moscow's position as very black. They believe that they are seeing the initial stages of one of the greatest wars of annihilation in history….
>
> The Russians' losses in the Bialystok cauldron are enormous. … A disaster for Moscow. … The Reds' resistance seems to be slowly crumbling along the entire front. … Stalin has called on his people to burn the harvests and corn stores. Our response is to declare quite publicly that after her defeat Russia will not be able to expect anything from us and that we shall let her starve. This will probably cool a few hot-heads.[4]

Goebbels concludes his entry for this day with: "News reports come in every half-hour. A crazy, exciting time. In the evening, put the finishing touches on the newsreel. … Then I sit outside on the terrace for half an hour and dream."[5]

Such braggadocio … At the same time, Goebbels was beginning to understand that war in Russia was not a stroll in the park like the easy, victorious battles in Poland and France.

As I have repeatedly noted, a deep anxiety was reigning in Moscow - an inability to understand the causes behind the disasters that had befallen the first echelon of the Red Army - and at times a certain inexplicable fear and despair. At the same time, in those first tragic days of the war, I never heard a single reproach directed at the authorities. It was more like some sort of impersonal, not yet fully conscious rage was growing. The war had caught both the older and the younger generation, probably every person, by surprise. Some people had not yet managed to finish school or graduate from some institute; some people hadn't had time to get married or to travel to say their final goodbyes to their dying mothers. Some people, who had worked for three years without a rest, were finally about to take a vacation while other people hadn't been able to tend to their orchard or vegetable garden in time. The list of unfinished, uncompleted matters could be continued endlessly - war had forced its way into people's lives so unexpectedly.

Often even to this very day, people in the East and in the West - especially young people who have taken an interest in the past war - ask the question: "Did Stalin know in advance about Hitler's decision to attack the Soviet Union?" He knew! Everyone knew!

According to the calculations of historians, over a year to a year-and-a-half before the war (1940-1941), the Soviet leadership received more than 200 warnings from various sources about Nazi Germany's preparation for the war. These sources included the American State Department and the British Government. They included various diplomatic and intelligence channels, the Soviet border troops and anti-fascist circles in Western Europe.

Today it is well-known that the Dictator criminally ignored all the incoming reports and did not come to the necessary political and military conclusions. He didn't secure his "brothers and sisters" and failed to bring the Red Army up to full combat-readiness in time. His own political and military advisers - in the atmosphere of the universal fear and obsequiousness that the Dictator had created in the country and the Red Army - dared not contradict him, held their tongues and submissively agreed with him.

"War," wrote Winston Churchill, "is mainly a catalogue of blunders, but it may be doubted whether any mistake in history has equaled that of which Stalin and the communist chiefs were guilty…."[6]

In connection with Churchill's words, it is not without interest to look at the conduct of the Soviet Ambassador in London, Ivan Maisky. After a conversation in the British Ministry of Foreign Affairs on 13 June 1941 where he was informed about Hitler's pending invasion of the USSR, Maisky nevertheless reported to Moscow: "The entire picture … seems to me to be more than hypothetical … Just as before, I believe a German attack on the Soviet Union to be highly improbable."

Stalin was most of all concerned that the slightest incaution or provocation would deprive him of any chance to postpone the start of the war, which for him was most necessary. Let's compare Stalin's and Churchill's approaches to intelligence reports. Stalin rarely read the source material and more often ignored the intelligence messages - viewing them as disinformation. "He trusted Hitler more than he did himself," the intelligence agents joked. Stalin demanded that his advisors for intelligence (Beria, Merkulov and Golikov) compile summaries on the basis of the source material. Golikov, when preparing the summaries, as a rule split them into two lists. In the first list he would include reports that he believed worthy of attention, while those that he considered disinformation would go into the second list. Stalin, when listening to his assistants' reports, would often rudely cut them off - refusing to accept their most serious arguments about the pending danger.

Winston Churchill, who became Prime Minister in Britain's most difficult days when Germany's enormous air power was poised to pounce upon the country and Hitler was actively preparing for Operation Sea Lion – the *Wehrmacht*'s invasion of the island – believed that intelligence was one of the most important command tools at his disposal in the war with the Nazis. He instructed his advisors to present him with all the original source material. As for whether a report or message would be important or not, this he would decide for himself. Thereby he could, for example, "decipher" the German preparation for an invasion of the USSR. On the basis of one of these reports (dated 6 April 1941) Churchill issued a warning to Stalin through the British Ambassador in Moscow. Stalin refused to receive him. Not until three weeks later did Stalin receive the information from Molotov, which the latter had prepared on the basis of the British Ambassador's message.

On the subject of the information available to the Soviet High Command on Hitler's plans for the invasion of the Soviet Union, the historian V.D. Danilov writes:

> The [Soviet] High Command possessed information regarding the Germans' plans to launch an attack against the Soviet forces north of the Pripiat' Swamps - as well as about the offensive of particularly strong panzer wedges from the area of Warsaw and north of it with the tasks to smash the Russian forces in Belorussia and so forth. Just why had the Soviet General Staff concentrated quite powerful force groupings in the Bialystok and L'vov salients? One needn't be a strategist to answer this question. Even a fleeting glance at the configuration of the Soviet-German border (the lines of the future front) shows the possibility of using the Bialystok and L'vov salients for launching very promising converging attacks here against the Germans. The General Staff couldn't fail to take advantage of this opportunity. However, as was known at the time of the Battle of Cannae (216 B.C.), in certain conditions an enticing salient can turn into a devouring cauldron. The Red Army's troops wound up in just such cauldrons. The triumph of the German command became simultaneously a tragedy for hundreds of thousands of Soviet troops.[7]

The regrouping of German forces with the aim of launching an attack against the USSR began on 2 February 1941. Stalin knew about the assembling German forces. Thanks to his intelligence sources he had information well in advance that Germany was preparing for war. He had even been informed of the approximate date when it would begin. To this day, debates continue about why, when possessing such exhaustive information, he didn't prepare the country to defend against the invasion and failed to reach the single logical decision in this situation - to place the Red Army on a war footing.

Possibly, he was trying to "outplay" Hitler and was confident that he would succeed in doing so. He fully believed in the colossal strength of the Red Army. To this day, most historians assume that Stalin was certain that as long as Hitler hadn't dealt with Britain, he wouldn't dare unleash a war on two fronts.

After the war's conclusion, the French historian Raymond Cartier, who took up the study of the archival materials of the Nuremburg Trials, found documents in them that confirm Stalin's delusion. Ultimately, the stakes he placed on the Axis countries when he approved the Molotov-von Ribbentrop Non-Aggression Pact with Germany - with the simultaneous complete isolation from the countries of democracy - failed. The recollections of his peers about this have been preserved.

I would like to turn the readers' attention to two questions. It's impossible even to imagine how the Second World War would have developed in the future if Hitler had agreed to Stalin's proposal and the Soviet Union had joined the Axis countries.[8] It is an enormous good fortune that this absurdity never took place. In the given case, it is difficult to determine who proved to be wiser: Stalin or Hitler? Now the second question: I think that Stalin was absolutely confident in victory over Hitler and did everything in his strength to delay the start of the war. Meanwhile, he was himself from day to day preparing to pounce upon Nazi Germany. Many facts testify to this view - about which over recent years both Russian and Western historians have related in their books (Viktor Suvorov, Boris Kuznetsov, Joachim Hoffmann, Mark Solonin, V. Danilov, A. Afanas'ev and others).[9]

Until the very last minute, Stalin sought to persuade himself that Hitler wouldn't attack. Even when on 22 June at 5:30 A.M. the German Ambassador in Moscow - Schulenburg -delivered to Molotov a note about Germany's declaration of war against the Soviet Union, the People's Commissar of Foreign Affairs in the most ludicrous, pathetic manner and without any clear basis tried to convince the Ambassador that there was no concentration of Red Army forces on the border and like a child tried to persuade him that any difficulties in relations between the two governments could with goodwill be resolved by diplomatic means.

One of Stalin's most important blunders before the start of the approaching war, which he never once mentioned in any of his speeches, was his decapitation of the Red Army during the purge of the Red Army leadership in 1937-1938. In the Leader's address to the nation, of course he didn't mention a single word about this tragic episode or his crime.

In Hoffmann's opinion, in a complex foreign policy situation the Soviet Union's armed forces were "shaken to the foundation by Stalin's purges." They were a "morbid manifestation, a type of collective insanity." He refutes the lie about the Soviet marshals being simultaneously spies for foreign rivals and exposes Stalin's desire to strengthen his personal power with the help of these murders. One thing is clear: "If there had been no destruction of the military cadres," asserts General A. V. Gorbatov, "we wouldn't have let the Germans reach the Dnepr - much less the Volga." In the opinion of A. M. Vasilevsky: "If there had been no 1937, it is possible that there would have been no war at all in 1941." To a considerable extent, the execution of the majority of the Red Army's commanders meant as a consequence the sharp weakening of the army, which was revealed in the Soviet-Finnish War, and decisively accelerated the invasion of the USSR by Germany and its Allies. "The Finnish War," Vasilevsky recalled, "was a great disgrace for us and gave rise to deeply negative impressions abroad about our army."

Before the war an "ideal" system for controlling the troops had been created and was actively supported in the war's initial phase – "ideal" for destroying our own troops. Not even Hitler himself could conceive a better system for this. Here is how it worked: When the Germans attacked, the commander of a Soviet regiment would report on the situation to division headquarters and wait for an order about what to do next. The division would this report to army headquarters and wait for orders. The army headquarters would pass the report up to front headquarters and from there it would go to the *Stavka* of the Supreme High Command. The *Stavka* would report it to Stalin and only after he had reached a corresponding decision would it devise a plan of actions. This plan would go back down to the fronts, where they would work out their own plans and send them down to the army and so forth. This entire process would take six to 10 days at best.

On the day of the *Wehrmacht*'s invasion of the Soviet Union, Britain's Prime Minister Winston Churchill addressed the House of Commons and delivered his historic speech about supporting Russia in the struggle with Fascism. Stalin never trusted Churchill, but had always had faith in Hitler. He had to change his mind. Stalin attentively read the text of Churchill's speech - as well as all the messages from the British Embassy in Moscow and the intelligence reports from London. He ordered the British Prime Minister's speech to be published in a highly edited form.

In his memoirs *The Second World War*, Winston Churchill cites an interesting episode. In August 1942 he received a letter from Stalin, who wrote: "None of us ever trusted the Germans. For us, the question of life or death has always been connected with them." This is a lie! It is possible to cite numerous public statements of a contradictory nature made by Stalin.

Most surprising was the behavior of the Dictator on the night of 21-22 June 1941. Despite accurate intelligence about the timing of Operation Barbarossa - as well as information from two German deserters obtained several hours before the invasion - Comrade Stalin slept. He didn't bother to mention to his "brothers and sisters" that he had slept through this most treacherous attack.

How Stalin slept through the *Wehrmacht's* invasion of his country

In his book *Vospominaniia i razmyshleniia* [*Reminiscences and Reflections*] - published many years later in an unexpurgated version - G. K. Zhukov described this event:

> At 3:15 A.M. 22 June, an armada of German aircraft began dropping a deluge of bombs on many Soviet cities, major railroad hubs, ports and military airfields. At 3:30 A.M. an artillery barrage began along the length of the entire German-Soviet border. Meanwhile Stalin was sleeping peacefully surrounded by his security guard at his dacha in Kuntsevo. The People's Commissar ordered me to call Stalin. I called. No one came to the telephone. I called repeatedly. Finally I heard the drowsy voice of General Vlasi - the Security Chief.
>
> "Who's speaking?"
>
> "Chief of the General Staff Zhukov. Please connect me with Comrade Stalin. It is urgent."
>
> "What? Now? Comrade Stalin is sleeping."
>
> "Wake him up immediately. The Germans are bombing our cities; war has begun."
>
> Several moments of silence ensued. Finally I heard a dull reply:
>
> "Wait a moment."
>
> Three minutes later Stalin came up to the phone. I reported the situation and requested permission to start retaliatory action. Stalin was silent. I could hear only his heavy breathing.
>
> "Did you understand me?" Again, silence.
>
> I persisted: "Will there be any orders?" Finally, as if he had just woken up, Stalin asked: "Where's the defense commissar?"
>
> "Talking with the Kiev District on the HF [High-Frequency]."
>
> "Come with Timoshenko to the Kremlin. Tell Poskrebyshev to summon all the Politburo members."[10]

According to Zhukov, the Politburo meeting began at 5:45 A.M. and continued for more than three hours. Stalin was pale and sitting at the table with a tobacco-filled pipe in his hand. Zhukov and Timoshenko reported the situation. Stalin asked unexpectedly: "Is this a provocation by the German generals?"

Timoshenko replied: "The Germans are bombing our cities in the Ukraine, in Belorussia and in the Baltic. What sort of provocation is this?"

"If a provocation was necessary, the German generals would bomb their own cities," Stalin said - and having given some thought to the situation for a bit, continued: "Hitler probably doesn't know about this. We must immediately phone the German Embassy."

A curious dialogue, is it not?

Stalin in the first hours of the war

Stalin's behavior in the first hours of the war is incomprehensible, absurd and thoughtless. It plainly testifies to the fact that he believed in Hitler's personal letter to him, which he received shortly before the war. He clutched impotently at the slightest straw, which might be capable of preventing what had already happened. We're not talking about the TASS publication from 14 June 1941.[11] We're speaking first of all about the ludicrous attempts to get in touch with Hitler and about Molotov's effort at Stalin's behest to get an explanation from Ambassador Schulenburg about the rumors that these were not provocations by Hitler's German generals. Stalin simply could not comprehend that what had happened was irreparable.

Let's turn to the memoirs of General Meretskov. In them he talks about the alarming situation which was reigning in the highest circles of the Red Army on the eve of the war. Meretskov recalls: "Already on 21 June, the military leadership was behaving as if the war would begin the next day." On the night of 21 June, Meretskov set off by train to Leningrad. On the eve of his departure from Moscow he had met with the People's Defense Commissar S.K. Timoshenko. Let's read further about what Meretskov says about this meeting:

> My immediate superior, the People's Commissar of Defense - who in recent days had been particularly stressed - summoned me. Then, even though I understood the cause of his nervous condition and even though I had seen with my own eyes what was happening at the western border, I've not forgotten the People's Commissar's atypically shrill and alarming words. Timoshenko said:
>
> "It is possible that war will break out tomorrow! You must assume the role of a representative of the High Command in the Leningrad Military District. You know its forces well and can help the district's leadership if necessary. The main thing is again – do not give in to provocations."
>
> "What is my authority in case of an armed attack?" I asked.
>
> "Restraint, first of all. Be able to distinguish between a real attack and local incidents and don't allow them to grow into a war. But

> be at combat-readiness. In case of an attack, you will know yourself what to do."[12]

It is strange - again this concern about some "provocations" - to which it was forbidden to open fire immediately! If the country had been preparing only for defense, then any conversations about "provocations" would have been senseless. An order should be clear and brief: "Destroy the attacking enemy!" Or, for example, like the order that the commander-in-chief of the Navy Admiral Kuznetsov issued to the three fleets and two flotillas on the evening of 21 June: "Operational Readiness No. 1, immediately!" [Incidentally, Operational Readiness No. 1 was announced after Operational Readiness No. 2, which had been declared on 19 June 1941, but historiographers don't like to remember this.]

Let's examine the three directives sent by the Kremlin to the military districts on the eve of 22 June 1941. Directive No. 1 was drawn up after a three-hour discussion with the military commanders in Stalin's office on 21 June 1941. It warned the troops that an attack by the Germans was possible in the course of 22-23 June. Possibly it would take place alongside provocation. Therefore, standing at full combat-readiness, they were not to give in to any provocations capable of engendering major complications. The coded transmission of this directive to the border districts began after 11:00 P.M. and ended, according to Zhukov, at 0030 on 22 June. It didn't reach the headquarters of the armies, corps and divisions until 0200 or even much later. No one had time to do anything substantial with respect to the directive. Only a limited amount of time remained until the start of Operation Barbarossa. Stalin however, who had calmed down, headed off to his Kuntsevo dacha to go to bed - once again placing his hopes on the decision he had taken.

Directive No. 2 appeared on the morning of 22 June after Stalin had familiarized himself with Hitler's note. Nevertheless, the military commanders convinced him that they were talking not about isolated provocations, but about a genuine war.

In the directive, there was the following language: "With a powerful strike of bombers and fighter aviation, destroy the enemy air force on their bases and smash the main groupings of his ground forces with bombs." The directive demanded: "Take out the ports of Memel and Königsberg with bombs" ... then once again the old motif in the Stalinist formulation: "The ground forces are not to cross the Frontier pending a special order." Idiocy! But who is able to explain this today?

This directive, which was signed by Timoshenko, Zhukov and Malenkov, was sent from Moscow at 7:15 A.M. - that is, more than two-and-a-half hours after the *Wehrmacht* invasion.[13] The directive reached the front between 9:00 and 10:00 A.M. Over the time that had passed since the start of the invasion the German forces, which had easily penetrated the belt of defenses along the Frontier, had moved in three directions: toward Moscow, Kiev and Leningrad. In postwar memoirs, the German generals spoke about the weak security at the Soviet border and about the Red Army's complete lack of readiness to either defend or attack. Who was guilty of this? It wasn't for the "brothers and sisters" to ponder this.

On this same day, Directive No. 3 was released. In it, for the first time a demand appeared: "The forces are to go on the counter-offensive in order to smash the enemy and emerge on his territory, whereby the end of 24 June they are to destroy the enemy's main groupings." At last, Stalin had indulgently allowed the troops to cross the Frontier (which no longer existed) and "to conduct operations without being constrained by the borders." This directive left Moscow around 9:00 P.M. on 22 June. It arrived at the fronts between 10:00 P.M. and midnight. One could easily draw a comparison between all three Directives and the act of firing blanks. It is understandable how they were received at the front. They gave evidence to the fact that neither Stalin, nor his political puppets, nor the military commanders in Moscow, knew of the actual situation at the front. They didn't understand what was happening there, which meant there was no sort of command and control over the troops in the wake of the surprise attack. Tell me, how could Stalin say such to his "brothers and sisters"?

The first day of the war had been lost, and more accurately, lost to the *Wehrmacht*.

The troops in the border districts - not in separate sectors, but in an enormous expanse stretching from the Baltic to the Black Sea - were in these days in a catastrophic situation. In other words, Stalin's absurd, or more accurately criminal, orders became the main reason for the partial de-mobilization of our forces and resulted in them being caught off-guard by the enemy attack.

Meanwhile, what was happening with the fronts (the Northern, Western and Southwestern Fronts) that received the *Wehrmacht*'s main blows? Here are several stories from eyewitnesses and participants in the fighting.

Veterans talk about the Red Army's demoralization and about the absence of any leadership. For example, according to F.Ia. Cheron, who was taken prisoner on 27 June 1941 his anti-tank artillery regiment, which was still in the process of forming up, was positioned 25-30 kilometers away from Bialystok in a little place called Mikhalovo. On 15 June, this unit had approximately 900 men armed with 45 rifles for performing guard duties. For the 50 one-and-a-half-ton trucks that the regiment received a week before the start of the war, only 12 drivers arrived to drive them. The regiment never in fact received their anti-tank guns. F. Ia. Cheron recalls:

> ...At 0400 22 June, in response to an order everyone rushed into the forest and began to hide under bushes and behind trees. Within 30 minutes it became clear that no one was pursuing us. At this point it was announced that the Germans had crossed the border and were moving in our direction. After several hours in the forest, the announcement came to return to our camp. Without any semblance of order, we started plodding back to the unit in groups. Order and discipline were crumbling in front of our very eyes. No one bothered to line us back up into formation. They opened up the baggage warehouse and permitted everyone to take whatever they wanted. It was around 1100. The command

> staff was nowhere to be seen. I still can't imagine where the commanders went. The Red Army men wandered aimlessly and didn't know what to do…

Likely, the senior commanders were frightened by their responsibility and didn't know how to fight using 900 unarmed and untrained soldiers - most of whom still hadn't even held a rifle. The junior officers were unsuccessfully trying to organize the soldiers. The chaos that had arisen turned into a disorganized flight. F.Ia. Cheron writes:

> … Everywhere, people were walking, running, driving, trying to get away from the Germans. Instead of an army, a mob was moving. Somewhere between Baranovichi and Slonim - at a point near where the main roads from Brest and Bialystok merge - a traffic jam had formed in a large forest. Several hundred vehicles, if not thousands, had gathered here. Many of the vehicles already had empty gas tanks. Here for the first time, I spotted the attempt of some colonel to stop the senseless flight. He was standing in the bed of a truck - shouting that this was a disgrace and that we should organize a defense. Likely, he himself was confused because there was nothing with which to defend ourselves. Only a very few men approached the truck where the colonel was standing and listened to him. Most of the people began to walk away, and were looking for somewhere to get away. The preponderance of the soldiers were unarmed … the army no longer existed. There were scattered groups of five, six or more men. The woods and fields of Belorussia were swarming with them. Toward the evening of 24 June, one could already encounter soldiers who had changed into civilian clothing and were without a weapon. Hunger began to tell and all the villages that they encountered along the way became full of men trying to wheedle something to eat from the local population. In the majority of cases, there was nothing but water…

Likely, the demoralized men were not even thinking about imprisonment and had no intention to surrender. However, if a soldier has been abandoned by his commanding officer and has no weapon, how is he to fight?

The situation was analogous on all the sectors of the Soviet-German Front. The Red Army's morale, especially of encircled units, quickly sagged. Many commanders terminated their lives with suicide or deliberately walked into enemy fire seeking death. The concept of military duty and honor - the notions of an army's morale and ethics - disintegrated. One can cite numerous stories about how some commanders began to remove their insignia of rank or to pencil over their surfaces - which had not been faded by the sun - with a black pencil as if fearing the flash of their insignias would attract the attention of enemy snipers; political instructors also hastily disposed of their shoulder patch stars.

Let's introduce another document: "NKVD USSR Report No. 41/303 to the GKO [State Defense Committee]":

> ... On 6 July, the 199th Rifle Division suffered a defeat at Novo-Mikropol' - suffering large losses in men and equipment. ... During the panic that arose in the division's units during the enemy attack, the command was unable to prevent a rout. The division's headquarters command scattered. Division commander Alekseev, deputy political commander Korzhev and the division's chief of staff German abandoned the regiments and together with remnants of the headquarters staff ran away to the rear.
>
> Division commander Colonel Alekseev, deputy political commander Regimental Commissar Korzhev and the division's chief of staff Lieutenant Colonel German have been arrested and committed for trial by a military tribunal...
>
> Deputy People's Commissar for Internal Affairs of the Soviet Union Abakumov

According to data provided by former Politburo member Aleksandr Iakovlev, over the years of the war 954,000 soldiers and officers were executed in the Red Army – almost a million men! If all these executions are considered just, then it happens that Russians are the most villainous and cowardly people in the world because no other army knew such a percentage of those punished for treason or cowardice. The author Mark Solonin talks in detail about what happened in those hot July-August and September days at the front. The Red Army was being crippled under Stalin's directives not only because of their ineptness, but also because so many innocent soldiers and officers were being executed for supposed cowardice.

Timoshenko was appointed as the Head of the *Stavka* - just in case it was necessary to find a scapegoat - although military commanders could not take a single step without the permission of Stalin, a modest member of the *Stavka*. In this same period, until November 1941 Stalin's name was rarely mentioned in the newspapers and his portraits were nowhere visible.

At last Stalin grasped what had happened. He no longer believed in his army, or more accurately, in that army which had in fact surrendered *en mass* to the *Wehrmacht*. This gave birth to Stalin's strange expression: "We have no military prisoners, but we have traitors and betrayers."

Recollections have been preserved about G. K. Zhukov's proposal to Stalin – to launch a preemptive attack against the *Wehrmacht*'s forces that were assembled on the Soviet border. Stalin categorically rejected this proposal. As if mesmerized by a cobra, he kept repeating over and over again: "Don't give in to provocations ..." Where did this word appear in his lexicon? Let's turn to the text of Hitler's personal letter to Stalin of 14 May 1941. Below is a short excerpt from this letter, which "bewitched" Stalin:

> … In order to organize the troops for the invasion [of England] away from the eyes of the English opponent - and in connection with the recent operations in the Balkans - a large number of my troops, about 80 divisions, are located on the borders of the Soviet Union. This possibly gave rise to the rumors now in circulation of a likely military conflict between us.
>
> I assure you, on my honor as a Chief of State, that this is not the case.
>
> From my side, I also react with understanding to the fact that you cannot completely ignore these rumors and have also deployed a sufficient number of your troops on the border.
>
> In this situation I cannot completely exclude the possibility of an accidental outbreak of armed conflict, which given the conditions created by such a concentration of troops might take on very large dimensions - making it difficult if not impossible to determine what caused it in the first place.
>
> I want to be absolutely candid with you.
>
> I fear that one of my generals might deliberately embark on such a conflict in order to save England from its fate and spoil my plans.
>
> It is a question of no more than a month.
>
> By approximately 15-20 June I plan to begin a massive transfer of troops to the West from your borders.
>
> In connection with this, I ask you, as persuasively as possible, not to give in to any provocations that might emanate from those of my generals who might have forgotten their duty. And, it goes without saying, try not to give them any cause. If it becomes impossible to avoid provocation by some of my generals, I ask you to show restraint - to not respond, but to advise me immediately what has happened through the channel known to you…[14]

I'll briefly acquaint the readers with "Hitler's Directive on the Declaration of War against the Soviet Union". For many long years, Stalin and the Soviet leaders after him concealed this document from the "brothers and sisters" and it remained unpublished. Today, it is available to anyone who desires to find out how Hitler explained the attack upon the USSR. In essence, what were Hitler's grievances toward the USSR - for the sake of which the Nazis fell upon Russia? I'll list the main ones:

- Violation of the Non-Aggression Pact's conditions about the partitioning of spheres of influence - primarily this concerned Lithuania, which had been seized by Moscow
- The attempt to occupy Finland
- The enormous concentration of Soviet troops on the western border, where according to German intelligence more than 160 Soviet divisions had assembled
- The seizure of Bessarabia and Northern Bukovina by Soviet forces
- Russia's desire to introduce its troops into Bulgaria
- Russia's attempts to gain a foothold in the Dardanelles
- The Soviet Government's subversive activities in Bulgaria and Romania
- Soviet Russia's active participation in the Yugoslavian conflict and the organization of a coup d'etat in Yugoslavia
- Anti-German actions in the Soviet Union

It seems to me that a letter, written by Hitler to Mussolini on the eve of 22 June 1941 best characterizes his personal views in connection with the decision to attack the Soviet Union. I'll offer one paragraph from it, but it seems to me that it is very important for understanding Hitler's mood at this moment when after a long period of reflections he had decided decisively to break with Stalin. To the present day, historians trying to explain the start of the war also ask the question: "Who outplayed whom: Stalin – Hitler, or Hitler - Stalin?" It is primarily a matter of the timing. Unfortunately, thus far any documents that would cast light on the given historical situation will hardly be de-classified any time soon. Let's return to Hitler's letter to Mussolini:

> ... In conclusion, let me say one more thing, Duce. Since I struggled through to this decision, I again feel spiritually free. The partnership with the Soviet Union - in spite of the complete sincerity of the efforts to bring about a final conciliation - was nevertheless often very irksome to me, for in some way or other it seemed to me to be a break with my whole origin, my concepts and my former obligations. I am happy now to be relieved of these mental agonies...[15]

In the military historical literature there are assertions that the Soviet General Staff supposedly committed a major blunder - having positioned its main reserves of materiel close to the national border. As is known, they came under enemy fire from the very first hours of the war. Within the first two weeks of the war, the Germans overran the territory that contained approximately 200 depots of fuel, ammunition and weapons. The situation became even more aggravated by the fact that when retreating, the Soviet troops had been compelled to destroy a significant amount of materiel.

By the middle of July 1941, of the 170 Soviet divisions that had received the initial attack of the German war machine, 28 had been fully destroyed; 70 divisions had lost more than 50 per cent of their personnel and equipment. Troops of the Western Front suffered especially severe losses. Of the 28 divisions that were completely destroyed on the Soviet-German Frontier, 24 had belonged to this front. The remaining 20 divisions of this front were in a catastrophic situation. They had lost 50 to 90 per cent of their personnel and equipment. During the first three weeks of the war, the Red Army was deprived of an enormous quantity of military equipment and weapons. In the divisions alone (without consideration of combat support reinforcements) losses amounted to approximately 6,500 guns of a caliber of 76mm or greater and more than 3,000 anti-tank guns. In the first three weeks of the war, the Southwestern Front destroyed 1,933 train wagon loads of ammunition and 38,047 metric tons of fuel. No matter how regrettable it is to acknowledge, the positioning of stockpiles of materiel so close to the border was not a simple miscalculation, but was dictated by the need to provide effective support to attacking troops or, to put it more precisely, a planned offensive.

By the end of 1941 the Red Army had lost practically its entire first strategic echelon – the best prepared regular troops. In prisoners alone, as has now been established, it had lost approximately 3.9 million men. By 10 July, the German troops had penetrated into the depth of the country's interior on the main Western direction, 450-600 kilometers, with a pace of advance of 25-35 kilometers per day; on the Northwestern direction, 450-500 kilometers, with a pace of advance of 25-30 kilometers per day and on the Southwestern direction, 300-350 kilometers, with a pace of 16-20 kilometers per day. For sake of comparison, the losses of the *Wehrmacht* over this period comprised approximately 40 per cent of its starting tank strength - of which 20 per cent were combat losses - 900 aircraft and in the Baltic, four minelayers, two torpedo boats and one submarine hunter. The personnel losses of the *Wehrmacht*, according to German data, amounted to approximately 100,000 in killed, wounded and missing. Such losses for the Germans - though they indeed significantly exceeded their losses in the preceding campaigns in Western Europe - were in no way comparable to the losses of Soviet troops.

In connection with all the above, the question arises: What is the cause of the tragedy of 22 June? "Mistakes" and "miscalculations" by the Soviet military-political leadership are normally given among the many factors. However, upon a closer examination, some of these "blunders" turn out to be not at all naïve errors, but are a consequence of fully conceived measures with the aim of preparing a preemptive attack and staging subsequent offensive operations against Germany. The operational dispositions of the troops of the first strategic echelon indeed flowed from this strategic plan. In actuality, they had to start the war with disorganized defensive actions against a powerful, unexpected attack from the enemy. Moreover, the Soviet troops almost everywhere were caught by surprise.[16]

For many years, Russian historiography has been silent about the "war's start". Only in recent years - especially on the eve of the 60th Anniversary of Victory -

did a lot of material dedicated to the tragedy of 1941 appear in the Russian press. However, alas, the history of the start of the war has still not been fully revealed. Primarily this is explained by the fact that many archival documents of the Politburo, the *Stavka*, the General Staff and the KGB and SMERSH remain classified. And just how many documents have been destroyed or falsified?

Unfortunately, in the generals' memoirs, with a few exceptions, the history of 1941 is hardly touched upon. In my own service in the Red Army between 1942 and 1945 I rarely encountered soldiers who had served in the first year of the war. A few officers survived and I talked with them - trying to get a glimpse into their grueling initial combat experience. However, they as a rule avoided this topic of conversation.

In recent times books have appeared in press, worthy of the readers' attention, which explain a lot of what really happened at the start of the war. Among them, particularly valuable are the works of the Russian historian Boris Sokolov and the German historian Joachim Hoffmann. (Boris Sokolov, *Krasnyi kolos. Pochemu pobedala Krasnaia Armiia?* [*Red Colossus: Why did the Red Army Win?* (Moscow: Iauza-EKSMO, 2007); Joachim Hoffmann, *Stalin's War of Extermination: Planning, Realization, Documentation* (Capshaw, AL: Theses and Dissertation Press, 2001)).

It is difficult to assess too highly the publication of a document which has been hidden for many years. Entitled '*Soobrazheniia*' ['*Considerations*'], it contains the plan for the strategic deployment of the Soviet Union's armed forces in case of a war with Germany and its allies. Here's how the well-known progressive Russian historian Iurii Afanas'ev evaluates '*Soobrazheniia*':

> This document - as is said in one of its latest publications - is a manuscript numbering 15 pages on standard typewriter paper, written in black ink by Major General A.M. Vasilevsky. At the bottom of the document is a place for the signatures of the People's Commissar of Defense Marshal of the Soviet Union S.K. Timoshenko and the Chief of the General Staff General of the Army G.K. Zhukov. However, the document has not been signed by them.

According to other publications, this document was presented by G.K. Zhukov for I.V. Stalin's examination. An abridged version of this document was first published in Russia in 1992 by N.V. Kiselev and in full by Iu.A. Gor'kov in 1993. Questions regarding '*Soobrazheniia*' primarily boil down to its date and authorship; who made the corrections to it and whether it was of an active, working nature or whether it was simply one of the numerous draft plans regarding the strategy to pursue in the eventuality of a war with Germany. On the whole the document doesn't raise as many questions as it does pose new problems to researchers. '*Soobrazheniia*' leaves no doubt that approximately from the spring of 1941 the Soviet leadership was shifting from a strategy of defense to broad-scale preparations for a preemptive attack on Germany. Even if one assumes that this was not a working document, because apparently it was signed by no one, then even in that case problems remain: the complete mobilization of troops; their hidden concentration on the western border; the disarming of the fortified districts on the old Frontier; the relocation of military stockpiles to the west and the widespread construction of airfields near the western border. These and many other facts and events of May-June 1941 unfolded in precise correspondence with the instructions contained in '*Soobrazheniia*'.

Foreign and many authoritative Russian historians believe that Stalin, starting from the spring of 1941, had finally resolved upon a preemptive attack against Germany. Moreover, in Russia the most recent publications on the history of the Second World War provide rather convincing substantiation for the notion that the idea of a preemptive attack against Germany was the only real and fully proper one. Some are even more definitive: "A preemptive attack would have saved millions of lives and possibly would have led to the very same political results that came to the devastated, hungry and cold country in 1945 - having lost the flower of the nation; after hoisting the banner of victory over the Reichstag." So there will not be any doubts whatsoever on this account, one final conclusion is offered: "Indeed the fact that such an attack was not launched - that the offensive doctrine which had been thoroughly elaborated in the General Staff of the Red Army and had begun to be implemented in May-June 1941 was not realized - is possibly one of Stalin's main strategic blunders." The results were: the almost complete destruction and imprisonment of two fronts – first the Western front in July 1941 followed by the Southwestern Front in August; the destruction in the summer and autumn of more than 300 of our divisions, which numbered a total of more than 5 million men - lost at a rate of 30-35 divisions each week; the destruction by the enemy of 3,500 aircraft, 6,000 tanks and more than 20,000 guns and mortars in the course of three weeks. Such a colossal catastrophe could occur, obviously, not only because of individual miscalculations - even if they be of the most major sort - nor because of a primitively handled surprise.[17]

The historian, or more accurately the aviation engineer, Mark Solonin exposed the tragic history of 1941 in the deepest manner.[18] He has gone further than the publicist Rezun-Suvorov. Suvorov's *Ledokol* [*Ice Breaker*] gave rise to numerous polemics and criticisms, but the author's position in them occupies a large place. I don't adhere to that point of view, as expressed by Iurii Fel'shtinsky:

> Among the conventionalism and banalities of ideas and the people, whose books you will never distinguish from one another if you tear out the title pages of the volumes they have written, Viktor Suvorov's works *Ledokol* and *Den'-M* stand out. Indeed it is precisely because the author of these books will never convince the large army of professional historians of anything that I am writing – in defense of history, in defense of truth and in defense of the author of such unorthodox books. I am writing with gratitude and with envy, because I myself quite long ago - even before V. Suvorov's articles began to appear in *Russkaia mysl'* [*Russian*

> *thought*] - came to the conclusion that "of course" Stalin himself was intending to attack Hitler. Indeed, only that can explain his conduct in the years 1939-1941. [19]

Mark Solonin spent 15 years and uses almost no archival material, yet he has managed to expose and show realities of 22 June and later on all the main directions of the enemy advance. Viktor Suvorov characterizes Mark Solonin's book *23 iiunia: Den' M* in the following way: "Mark Solonin has accomplished an academic feat; both that which he writes and that which he does are a "gold brick" in the foundation of that history of the war, which will at some time be written."

There's no point in relating the contents of Mark Solonin's book. It is available [in the Russian language] to everyone. So the interested reader can himself seek it out. It is worth the effort!

So what just is this "gold brick"? In 2006, Mark Solonin published an article in the journal *Ogonek*, which laid out the author's main conclusions about the causes of the war's tragic beginning. Here is a condensed version of that article:

> That, which occurred on 22 June 1941 became the start of the largest and, if you will, most disgraceful catastrophe in all of Soviet history. And even though Soviet propaganda sought over the decades to wipe away; to expunge this sense of shame and ignominy – in full accordance with the desire of the people itself! – this subject still nags us at the back of our minds. Soviet propaganda offered the people a very convenient version that was directly contradictory to the truth: a vastly superior adversary fell upon a defenseless country; we were unprepared, one rifle for two soldiers and so on. These absurd assertions have long ago been refuted by the numbers and facts (it was the USSR in 1941 that had absolute superiority over the *Wehrmacht* – not only in personnel strength, but also in equipment). However, they became so embedded in the Russian consciousness that even those who saw the hundreds of thousands of soldiers and officers voluntarily surrendering and the roads at the front choked with abandoned, brand-new equipment, continue to repeat them. This unwillingness to accept the truth about the war is to the present day like some sort of common mental complex ...
>
> But the truth, which is so undesirable to acknowledge, is as follows: a multitude of Soviet people, frightened and impoverished by the Stalinist regime and who had lost their ethical and moral bearings, in 1941 did not want to fight and be killed for THAT regime – for a power that had deprived the individual of all rights and freedoms. This in fact was the most terrible surprise, with which the regime collided in 1941. I am confident that the Red Army's debacle in 1941 happened precisely because the majority

> of the acting army simply refused to fight. Let us say they both didn't know how to fight and didn't want to fight.
>
> Strictly speaking, it is necessary at last to grasp that we didn't have one, but two wars between 1941 and 1945. They were completely different wars. One disgraceful, the other heroic and patriotic, by the efforts of Soviet propaganda merged into one war.
>
> It was simply that the Nazi regime proved to be even crueler than Soviet power. It was Stalin's lot to face just that opponent with which he could be compared - one even more inhumane and infinitely remote from the concepts of humanism and human rights. So therefore the Patriotic War, which began approximately in 1942-1943, was actually won by the people, who, however, were not fighting and dying for the mustachioed man or for world revolution, but for themselves - taking vengeance for comrades who died in German captivity and for their own families who were struggling and dying under the boot-heel of Nazism. Indeed, it was not owing to the regime, but in spite of it, that the Red Army reached Berlin in 1945.[20]

Solonin adds:

> The writer Daniil Granin - speaking on the occasion of Victory Day in 2001 - said that all the objective factors were in favor of the victory of Germany, which, it would seem, could not fail to win, but - it was Russian that won! It was because, they say, we were fighting for our Motherland and for lofty ideals. (These ideals were so virtuous that I cannot recall what Granin called them.)[21]

Mark Solonin's position appears to be more convincing than that of the writer Daniil Granin.

Is Mark Solonin right? Having read his book, I fully share the author's arguments. Only the assertion, expressed by the author in three words, troubles me: In the article, Mark Solonin asserts that the "army didn't fight". That's his response to the question: "What happened in 1941?" I believe that this isn't quite so. In reality, a majority of the army "did not fight" and voluntarily surrendered to the Germans. However, there were more than a few who did fight, who tried to stop the aggressors, if only for a day, for several hours or minutes. In the published memoirs, hundreds of examples have been described of the courage of officers and soldiers who laid down their lives on the battlefields near Bialystok, Vitebsk, Minsk, Belaia Tserkov', Uman', Kiev, Novgorod, Leningrad and in front of Moscow. The struggle of the "Fortress of Brest" has been written into the history of the war in gold letters.

Many of the dying heroes, I am sure, said something like the following: "Comrade Stalin, we so trusted you!"

The Red Army that I joined at the front after finishing military school was a different one that was formed after 22 June 1941.

"The first thing that a new recruit must be taught is that his greatest duty consists in obedience to superiors without consulting with his own conscience."

William Channing, from his biography of Napoleon I

3

How One Must not Fight – "At Any Cost" ...

A soldierly conversation

On the eve of the Victory Day holiday, 6 May 1999 the newspaper *Rzhevskie vesti* published an essay by N. Ladygin and N. Smirnov under the title '*Tak nado voevat'!* *['That's how one must fight!']* I will present a slightly abridged version of it here:

> … For 10 days, from 30 July to 8 August [1942], the 220th Rifle Division under the command of Colonel S.G. Poplavsky - with an attached separate rifle brigade and tank brigade - unsuccessfully assaulted heavily fortified enemy strongpoints: Bel'kovo, Svin'ino and Kharino.
>
> During the attacks on these villages it was necessary to overcome an area of overgrown low ground, which after heavy rains had turned into an almost impassable quagmire. In daily repeated attacks our units suffered enormous losses. The fighting became protracted. Tanks and small rifle elements, having penetrated the enemy's first trench line, lunged toward Bel'kovo but failed to reach it.
>
> On 5 August, a group of soldiers of the 376th Rifle Regiment from the battalion of Captain F.I. Taranets - headed by Political Instructor S.I. Vyzhimov - broke into the outskirts of Bel'kovo with an impetuous attack and destroyed six enemy earth-and-timber bunkers. With machine-gun and mortar fire, the Nazis cut off this group from the main forces. All 18 men were killed.

On 9 August, division commander Colonel Stanislav Giliarovich Poplavsky personally led the attack. Later, now General of the Army, Poplavsky recalled the following episode from this day:

I was summoned to the telephone by front commander I.S. Konev, who was at the command post of the 30th Army.

"Why aren't you using the attached tank brigade?" he asked.

"Almost all the tanks are stuck in the swamps," I replied.

"So tow them out yourself and lead them into the attack and bring the infantry up after them."

Only four tanks managed to be ready for the next attack. Following the commander's order in a literal sense, Poplavsky took a seat in the lead tank - having first given an order to the commander of the 673rd Rifle Regiment Lieutenant Colonel Maksimov to move out after them and to seize Bel'kovo with a sudden advance. At this point, the two other rifle regiments were then supposed to go on the attack.

The tanks had no possibility to maneuver in the conditions of the swampy terrain, but the lead tank with Poplavsky - skillfully handled by the tank commander I. Vorontsov - reached the northwestern outskirts of Bel'kovo. The remaining three tanks were still moving across no-man's land.

At this time the Germans separated our infantry from the tanks with a dense curtain of artillery and mortar fire, and Poplavsky issued an order over the radio to the tank crews to stop and fire. However, when pivoting, one track of Vorontsov's tank fell into a deep trench. The machine firmly settled on the ground with the bottom of its hull. Poplavsky reported this over the radio to Maksimov, but the latter had been wounded and was unresponsive. Small groups of Nazi soldiers began making their way toward the tank. Opening the hatch, the tankers hurled grenades at the enemy.

Possibly, the enemy decided to attempt to take the crew alive. The tank company commander, who was also in this tank, volunteered to try and get help but he was killed while on his way back to friendly lines. The three remaining tank crew members and Poplavsky repeatedly fought off the attacking Nazis until darkness fell. All of them by now had been wounded. Just in case, they exchanged addresses and agreed that if anyone survived he would write the deceased men's families.

> Unknown to them, earlier in the day the commander of the 653rd Rifle Regiment, I.A. Kurchin ordered his chief of staff, G.V. Skovorodkin to organize an assault group and personally lead the effort to liberate the tank crew. Skovorodkin's group had managed to prevent the enemy soldiers from approaching the tank with its fire and throughout the afternoon had kept them at a safe distance from it.
>
> With the arrival of darkness, a battalion of the 673rd Rifle Regiment under the command of Major N.I. Glukhov reached the tank and together with Skovorodkin's group successfully extracted the crew and Poplavsky back to the division's lines. Glukhov gave Poplavsky the Western Front commander Konev's order immediately to report from the observation post of the neighboring brigade. A half-hour later, Poplavsky arrived at the observation post and began to report, but after just a few phrases the connection was broken. Then the chief of staff of the 30th Army, General G.I. Khetagurov, reassuring Poplavsky, told him: "Reassume command of your division."

On 12 August at 1100, the 653rd and 673rd Rifle Regiments broke into Bel'kovo. Between 12 August and 21 August, with savage fighting the division closed upon Rzhev and seized the village of Opoki and the airbase where it captured 15 enemy aircraft in good working order.[1] The losses of our units were high. For example, the 653rd Rifle Regiment in the latter half of August had only around 300 men left and in the fighting for the airbase, its commander I.A. Kurchin, was killed. An article was published in the divisional newspaper *Za Rodinu* [*For the Motherland*] entitled 'Bit' vraga, kak tankist Vorontsov' ['Defeat the foe, like tanker Vorontsov'], which described how in the battle for one strongly fortified enemy position, tanker Ivan Vorontsov charged the enemy-held village in a tank and destroyed the Nazis. But the tank became immobilized when its right track fell into a German trench. The enemy rejoiced! However, Vorontsov in unequal combat kept firing for 12 hours and killed 18 Nazis; destroyed three dug-outs and shot down three Germans at point-blank range who were charging the tank…

Having read this essay, I recalled a little episode that took place in the convalescent battalion where I spent more than a month after being wounded in 1942 near Rzhev.[2] While looking through the army newspaper, I spotted an article entitled: 'Tak nado voevat'' ['That's how one must fight']. Toward evening, during a cigarette break, a typical soldier's conversation started. It turned out that other soldiers had noticed the article as well. Curiously, this newspaper came to us from a different army: convalescing soldiers from the 220th Rifle Division had brought it. I was with the 215th Rifle Division before winding up in the medical sanitation battalion and then in the convalescent battalion.

How did the conversation go?

First soldier: "The authors really messed up when they entitled that article."

Second soldier: "And you, Ivan, what would you have called it?"

First soldier: "To be accurate, I would have called it 'That's how one must not fight!'"

Third soldier: "Oh, a wise guy!"

It seems that with that exclamation, the conversation ended. Yes, to be honest, everyone was more interested in the news that doctors from the medical sanitation battalion were scheduled to arrive the next day in order to identify those healthy enough to return to the frontlines.

Before falling asleep that night, I thought: "Was the first soldier right?" What sort of good sense prompted the division commander to climb into a tank? Did he really believe that the machine would get as far as Bel'kovo through the impassable muck? Did he really imagine that his courageous act alone, which was not without serious risk, would inspire the soldiers and they would show boldness and resolve?"

I quickly forgot about our unfinished arguments over that event. The Rzhev newspaper reminded me of it almost 60 years later. Having passed through many battles and having drunk from their bitter cup, I decided to return to that soldiers' dialog in the convalescent battalion and voice my support for the first soldier who had disagreed with the title of that article.

The reading of generals' memoirs; of books by local Rzhev authors and familiarity with the materials in the Tver' Consolidated State Museum and Rzhev Regional History Museum allows one to present a picture of the famous July-August offensive in 1942 - the so-called First Rzhev-Sychevka Operation. In Russia's official historiography, right up to the present day, there have been no serious appraisals of it. Military historians strive to avoid this unpleasant fact in the history of the Great Patriotic War.[3]

The commanders that headed this operation (I.S. Konev and G.K. Zhukov) restrict their discussion of it in their memoirs to a few meager lines. By the way, are there many known cases where commanders discuss their own defeats? In the historical essay *Boevoi put' 31-i armii* [*The Combat Path of the 31st Army*], in which the 220th Rifle Division fought, there are only panegyrics. I'm not even talking about the academic volume *Istoriia vtoroi mirovoi voiny 1941-1945* [*History of the Second World War 1941-1945*]. In the pages of this 19-volume edition one can read about the victories of the Red Army, but as for its defeats, the authors evidently decided to leave the discussion of them to future generations.

One tormenting question to which I tried to find an answer consisted in trying to find out whether any effort was made to delay the launch of the offensive. Recent raging and endless downpours, over a short time, had turned the entire zone of combat operations into an impassable quagmire. It is understandable that only Konev and Zhukov might have been able to obtain the *Stavka*'s permission to postpone the operation. They didn't do this. To be sure, the Western Front went on the offensive only several days after the Kalinin Front, but this doesn't change the essence of the question.

Certain Western military historians who write about the Eastern Front and who have touched upon the fighting for the Rzhev-Viaz'ma salient are unable to understand why the Russian commanders acted so senselessly when they decided not to wait for more suitable weather conditions in the area of the planned offensive. After all, by choosing not to wait they for all practical purposes deprived the attacking troops of the support of tanks and aircraft - and in part of artillery as well. However, these historians fail to consider two fundamentally important circumstances: the Soviet totalitarian system - which was inseparable from the Red Army - and the nature of the Russian soldier who'd become accustomed to blind obedience. As for the Russian military historians and the generals who fought around Rzhev, in their books and memoirs they have proved to be terribly "forgetful" or simply "liars".

And just how can one comprehend Georgii Konstantinovich Zhukov, who in November-December 1942 undertook another offensive at Rzhev (Operation Mars) in even more unsuitable conditions (snow, snow storms, freezing temperatures and icy roads)?

A word about the Russian soldier

So, the fatal decision had been taken ... Five armies, the air force, tank brigades and artillery regiments were put into motion. Let's think a bit about this. Starting the offensive, on what were the new "Alekandr Nevskys", "Suvorovs" and "Kutuzovs" placing their hopes?

Why did I name our generals in this way? It is known that in contemporary Russia, just as yesterday, remembrance of the War of 1812 is widely cultivated. It is not a coincidence that in Moscow the famous Cathedral of Christ the Savior has been practically raised anew, which in its own time had been built at the people's expense in honor of Russia's victory over Napoleon.[4] In 2007, in Moscow it was proposed to begin preparations to celebrate the 200th Anniversary since the start of the Patriotic War of 1812. There is still one more reason why I've mentioned the great Russian commanders of the past. Many of the generals who fought at Rzhev were decorated for their contributions with Orders that bore the names of Nevsky, Suvorov and Kutuzov.

Stalin introduced these Orders in the war years. Were there sufficient justifications to honor the contemporary commanders with them?

On what were the commanders hoping when they started the operation?

On God? Only in one case: if He would put an end to the mess in nature, which was under His control. If such had happened, it would have been sufficient cause to toss down a cup of vodka. But the miracle didn't happen! Filled with vanity, immeasurable hubris and self-confidence after the defeat of the Nazis in front of Moscow, they seriously overestimated their own capabilities to attack and underestimated the enemy's capabilities to defend.

I, for example, was surprised by the following fact. When the commander of the Western Front G.K. Zhukov was informed that Colonel General Walter Model, the new commander of the German Ninth Army, was now defending the Rzhev-Viaz'ma salient, he flippantly and jokingly responded about the change in German command that had occurred: "Model, so what? We'll beat Model" – that's what Zhukov himself wrote in his memoirs. Just the opposite happened! Walter Model, directing the defense of the Rzhev-Viaz'ma salient, demonstrated superb command qualities. There was a reason why Hitler called him "the Lion of Defense".

Did the Soviet commanders really think that aircraft - lacking radios and the latest navigation instruments in the poor flying conditions (and in the presence of the powerful *Luftwaffe* and their anti-aircraft units) - would win the sky above the battlefields, which meant they would be able to provide air cover for the attackers? This didn't happen!

Perhaps the tanks would be able to overcome the road less terrain between their jumping-off positions and the German defenses and would destroy enemy firing points and assist the infantry assault by providing cover to the attacking troops with their strong armor? This didn't happen!

In 1942, no matter how much the Soviet press bragged about the quality of domestic weapons - extolling them for propagandistic purposes - this was far from the truth. We, the soldiers, knew the truth, but also knowing that a military tribunal awaited anyone caught praising German equipment, we kept silent. Our famed PPSh sub machine gun - with its drum magazine that was very inconvenient to reload - was inferior to the German MP-40 Shmeisser in every respect. The cumbersome 19th-century Mosin rifle with its long bayonet was inferior to the German Karabiner 98k. The aged, water-cooled Maxim caused machine gunners a lot of trouble, especially in summertime - and with its textile ammunition belt in foul weather. Former machine gunners recall the Degtiarev light machine gun for its inordinate weight for a weapon of this type. When the rapid-firing, compact MG-42 machine gun first began equipping the German Infantry, our attacking battalions hardly stood any chance of surviving under its fire (a rate of up to 1,000 rounds per minute). Such a machine gun deployed in an advantageous position could wipe out an entire battalion in a matter of minutes.

As always, the army commanders and commissars were very confident in the high sense of duty and patriotism in the officers and soldiers. Were the results as expected?

The main hope, which the command didn't advertise, rested on the Russian soldier; on his endurance and capability to withstand any physical and psychological burdens. This in fact did show itself, but its effect proved not to be so great.

Days without sleep; without decent food; without creature comforts; weeks without washing; lice-ridden; constantly exposed to the cold or the frost, the rains or snow; making endless – from Moscow to Berlin – marches and shifts in position on their own feet, at times 40 to 50 kilometers a day or night; years deprived of a woman's caress; wretchedly clad; experiencing the constant pressure from above from commanders and commissars; the perpetual fear of the Special Department personnel – tell me, the soldier of what other army could withstand all of that?

The soldier at Bel'kovo didn't let down the command. He uncomplainingly went on the attack, up to his knees in water. He fell dead on the damp, cold ground and no one ever gave him a proper burial - neither at the time or later. The soldier, going on the attack, for all intents and purposes remained one-on-one with the adversary and knew that he would receive no help: not from God; not from commanders and not from their own aircraft, tanks and artillery.

Trying to understand and make sense of this abnormal life occurrence, which by its plot one could easily compare with the famous painting by the artist Karl Briullov, '*The Last Day of Pompeii*', I had the following thought: Both there, in the raging scene of the painting, and here, on the battlefield, people's hearts were filled with despair and complete resignation. I would call the fighting at Bel'kovo sheer madness, bordering on a crime. I think that in the days of the fighting for Rzhev, Soviet generals were primarily deceiving themselves and others. For this, no great capabilities were required.

In all democratic countries, a date has been established by law after which the government must de-classify its secret documents. In Russia, the statute of limitations on documents from the Great Patriotic War expired long ago, but much archival material remains inaccessible even to this day. One of the reasons for this is the presence of "blank spots" in the history of the war - unsuccessful battles which were swept under the rug by the regime and ignored by historiography. So far, they either have not been fully revealed or we know little about them.

The battles for Bel'kovo

I will discuss one of them, which became publicly known only quite recently: the fighting of the 220th Rifle Division for three villages - Bel'kovo, Svin'ino and Kharino - which were located 6-7 kilometers north of Rzhev. They comprised one of the enemy's heavily fortified sectors on the path to the city.

The division had been prepared in the best possible manner for the upcoming battle. It numbered 14,000 soldiers and officers. It possessed in addition an attached tank brigade (numbering approximately 50 tanks); a separate artillery regiment; a special brigade of cadets and several battalions of rocket launchers. Power! It outnumbered the defending Germans by eight to nine times in men; 50 times in tanks; and four to six times in artillery. The division had rich combat experience. It had passed through the fires of 1941 - defending Vitebsk and Sychevka - and it had driven the foe from the gates of Moscow. Colonel Stanislav Giliarovich Poplavsky, a professional soldier of the Red Army, was commanding the division. In 1941 he'd been a major and regiment commander. He had distinguished himself in the battles of January 1942 west of Rzhev - in the famous Monchalovsky woods.

The question boils down to one: Did the "Aleksandr Nevskys", "Suvorovs" and "Kutuzovs" capably handle the human and combat superiority over the Germans on the battlefield? In other words, did they display command prowess?

On the very first day of the offensive - already at dawn - rain began to fall, which then turned into a deluge. An interesting question: Where were the meteorologists? Quickly the ground turned into a black, muddy mess and became practically impassable. The water in the rivers, lakes and streams went out of their banks and spread - flooding everything around. To be honest, it should be noted that our ground attack aircraft managed to conduct one sortie and made one attempt to plaster the German trenches.

Separate recollections of veterans - participants in the fighting for Bel'kovo - have been preserved. They disclose the full picture of the battle "with no sheltering umbrellas". Here is what they relate: The sappers' attempts to construct so-called plank roads were unsuccessful. Under the heavy weight of the tanks and guns, the planks sank deeply into the totally saturated ground. The entire area became flooded. Men, guns and horses became stuck in the mud. It was necessary to drag horses and guns from the morass by hand using ropes. The infantry virtually was left without the support of tanks and artillery.

Such has been the way in war: there is nowhere for the infantry to go in inclement weather. At Bel'kovo for almost all the days of the battle, the soldiers lived and fought in the rain; fought to stay dry in the rain; slept in the rain and, in the morning if they were successful, lit small campfires and warmed themselves up a bit around them. There were no buildings left at all in the area - which saw fighting day and night - where it might have been possible to take shelter from the daily deluges for a little while.

I'll offer a brief chronicle of the combat operations:

The first day – 30 July

Two regiments attack. There is no success. The losses of the attackers are high. The battlefield is blanketed with the first corpses.

The second day – 31 July

No matter how many soldiers damned the sky for the rainy weather - or begged for the exchange of "wrath for mercy" - it remained indifferent to their appeals. The division commander threw all three rifle regiments into the fighting. Exhausted, tormented by the mud, the artillerymen sought to keep up with the infantry with their 45mm and 76mm guns - deploying them for direct fire. Despite the hurricane of artillery, mortar and machine-gun fire the soldiers forced their way toward the eastern part of Bel'kovo, seized some outlying huts and cleared them of German sub machine gunners. However, heavy fire from undamaged earth-and-timber emplacements within the village forced them to retreat. Over the second day of fighting, the division's casualties amounted to 340 killed and 714 wounded.

The third day – 1 August

5:00 A.M. – three regiments (the 653rd, 376th and 673rd Rifle) attack Bel'kovo. It is an impressive sight – nine battalions, 27 companies … no success.

5:50 A.M. – the Germans open strong artillery fire and go on the counter-attack against the positions of the 653rd Rifle Regiment with two companies of infantry and a cavalry squadron. The counter-attack is driven back and soldiers of the 653rd (commanded by Lieutenant Colonel I.A. Kurchin) take possession of the south-eastern outskirts of the village.

7:00 A.M. – the 376th Rifle Regiment attacked the northwestern outskirts of Bel'kovo while the 673rd charged the northern outskirts. Both attacks are thrown back by the enemy.

11:30 A.M. – a battalion of German infantry under the cover of artillery fire again tries to break through the positions of the 653rd Rifle Regiment, but falls back without achieving its goal.

3:00 P.M. – after a 15-minute artillery barrage against the enemy's positions (there were not enough shells for a longer preparation), the 376th and 673rd Rifle Regiments again advance on Bel'kovo, but are pinned down after just 100 meters. They are unable to overcome the enemy fire. Still more corpses cover the battlefield. The procession of the wounded - dragging themselves along the washed-out roads toward the medical sanitation battalion - becomes ever longer. That night, replacements arrive in the division - 486 privates. Half of them are poorly-trained fresh conscripts.

The fourth day – 3 August

At dawn after a short artillery preparation and a heavy salvo from two battalions of rocket launchers - which for some reason targeted Svin'ino - a human wave launches a fresh assault against Bel'kovo and after it, another and another …

At 2:00 P.M., the order comes to fall back. A powerful barrage from rocket launchers is proposed. At 3:20 P.M., a salvo from four rocket battalions howls and the fiery projectiles streak toward Bel'kovo to no purpose. The eastern part of the village is worked over by the fire, not the northern part as planned. A lot of the shells fall short. Immediately after the salvo the division commander, without assessing its effectiveness, once again hurls all three regiments against Bel'kovo - this time accompanied by eight tanks.

Only one of the T-34s overcame the deep stream in front of the village and broke into Bel'kovo - Lieutenant Grigorii Pavlovich Eshtokin's. The divisional newspaper wrote about this feat. The remaining tanks got stuck in the swampy muck and simply became immobile targets for the German artillery.

6:00 P.M. – despite strong resistance, soldiers struggle forward to the northern outskirts of Bel'kovo and break into Svin'ino. It seems that now the enemy - unable to withstand the onslaught of the attackers - will falter and retreat. The division commander is confident of success. However, at this decisive moment, Junkers appear from the direction of Rzhev. Bomb strikes and bursts of machine-gun fire rain down upon the infantry from above - forcing it to fall back and to scatter across the field.

"Where are our fighters?" the soldiers ask with plenty of accompanying curses. They slither and crawl back to the water-filled slit trenches - pressing themselves into the muddy ground; gripping their helmets with both hands. Tears of bitterness sting their eyes. Enormous eruptions of ruddy-brown earth hurl torn-apart bodies across the field; heads, arms and legs are flying around overhead. When will the bombing cease? After the first wave of German bombers, a second appears. The hellish process repeats.

Colonel Poplavsky called the army commander and asked: "Why isn't our air force operating?" The latter in a fit of temper answered him: "The front commander is at my observation post; just ask him!" The division commander sensed an insidious chuckle in the army commander's voice. "Fine," the division commander resolved. "We'll get by without the airplanes." It didn't turn out that way.

That night, the results of the fighting over the previous four days were summed up. The division lost, as the count established: 817 men killed and 3,083 wounded. Despite the replacements, the regiments are down to just 100-150 men each.

If the last reserves of hope run out, what happens? Even aware of the well-known Order No. 227 [5] and what awaited a soldier for fleeing the battlefield without orders, nevertheless many soldiers - using any pretext - sought to leave it citing total exhaustion; the dismal weather; bloody diarrhea; a general malaise or any sort of ailment. Soldiers searched for other ways to avoid near certain death: helping wounded men off the battlefield; stopping to give assistance to signalers or even by simply hiding wherever and however they could.

In the 220th Rifle Division, a blocking detachment of 100 men with machine guns was deployed 1.5-2 kilometers behind the frontline. In addition, groups of sub machine gunners were organized in every regiment in order to assist the blocking detachments.[6]

In the first days after their appearance, searches were conducted for those who had fled the battlefield. They were seeking to return them to the fighting at gunpoint. Later they judged such "cowards" and "panic-mongers", sent them into the penal companies or shot them.

It is known according to very incomplete data for the 30th Army that between 31 July and 8 August 1942 - that is to say, over the first 10 days of the offensive - 547 men fled the frontline (some even leaving behind their weapon). Of this total, 386 were soldiers of the 220nd Rifle Division. A shameful blot upon the army's honor! The command sought to conceal it. If you extrapolate these numbers on the scale of the entire Western Front, then it isn't difficult to determine that thousands of men ran away.

Once again, attacks and more attacks … With short intervals they follow one after the other. This went on until 12 August 1942 - the 14th day of the offensive. Early on the troops nicknamed the field of battle that stretched from the jumping-off positions to Bel'kovo (500-600 meters) the "Valley of Death".[7]

Muddy, unshaven, unwashed, half-famished with frayed nerves and a totally frazzled psyche - with no longer any faith in "God or the Devil" - people had turned into semi-wild creatures. What had happened to simple speech and sincerely good human feelings? Soldiers beseeched their commanders: "Give us just one little night, one little hour to relax." Their appeals went unheeded.

Ask the soldier, who by some miracle survived at Bel'kovo, what remained in his soul after just one day - 3 August - when in the course of the day groups of 15 Stukas dove upon the division 20 times. The next day, as some sort of "gift" to the infantry (at least that's how the soldiers appraised it) our airplanes appeared in the sky overhead for 15 minutes between 9:30 A.M. and 9:45 A.M. All at once they proceeded to bomb our own men. Fortunately, only one horse was wounded.

How often both then and later - in the cruelest situations of the war - it was our youth that helped us, the officers and soldiers to continue to live; to fight; to suppress the fear within us and to keep faith in eventual victory! In these battles, as I found out later, young fellows turned into old men. Men's hair often turned gray; they lost their courage; their self-confidence; their inner strength and sometimes even their minds.

The endless, bloody attacks with no hope of success, which time and again dispelled all illusions, in just a short time turned both the young and the old into mechanical implementers of someone else's will and made them obedient servants of the war. Did all this come from fear? No, they forgot about fear; it was replaced by a complete indifference to their own selves, to life and to their comrades. I can say this because I was there.

In the most desperate moments of the battle for Bel'kovo, soldiers rarely cried. What reason was there for crying? They'd long ago become numb to suffering. At the same time a sense of helplessness grew in people; its roots grew ever more deeply in the soul. There were few who hoped to emerge from the slaughter at Bel'kovo alive.

At night, a vast glow brightly illuminated the "Valley of Death" - all around, villages were burning. There were mountains of corpses, both ours and German. It has long been known that civilized savagery is the worst of all forms of savagery. However, that which was happening at Bel'kovo, Svin'ino and Kharino cannot be defined by any measure or standard by the word "savagery". It was mindless murder without any sense of responsibility for human fate; without shame or any concept of guilt.

Each and every day in those hellish two weeks - according to information in headquarters' operational summaries and dispatches from the Political Departments - the division lost 100-150 men killed and 600-700 wounded. I believe these numbers are understated.

What stood out from these dry operational summaries and political reports? First of all a great deal of lying and ornate - like painted Easter eggs - embellishments about "mass heroism"; about "individual exploits" (primarily of communists and Komsomol members); about the flood of petitions "from the combatants" to be accepted into the ranks of the Communist Party. For example, evidence like the following was given: at the height of the most furious fighting between 3 and 10 August, more than 200 petitions to join the Communist Party were turned in at the front. Perhaps at the beginning this in fact happened and these men were made Communist Party members - and then, you terminate them ...

During the fighting for Bel'kovo, a wry joke circulated among the men about a Ukrainian soldier who before a battle had written a request to join the Party: "If they kill me I request that you consider me a communist, but if they do not, then don't."

A typical example of the type of material in the political dispatches is the bogus story in the divisional newspaper about the heroic tanker I. Vorontsov, which was quite far from the truth. Later in the war, I often happened to see how the political workers put together these reports. There were so many lies in them! Tell me, what sort of "flood" of petitions can be written when the soldier is driven again and again toward German machine guns? He simply could not in those days and nights deliberate over anything, comprehend anything or sense something other than his own helplessness and, obviously, justifiable pity for himself. It is in this, and not the political reports, that the truth is found.

Throughout the war, either in front of Rzhev or Berlin, none of the desk-bound warriors in the headquarters or those in the political organs ever once said or shouted at full voice the very most important thing: "An attack without first suppressing all of the enemy's primary means of fire is impermissible!" Meanwhile, unfortunately, this demand was not implemented in a single one of the operations of the Red Army's Kalinin and Western Fronts (I, II 1942; I 1943) against the Rzhev-Viaz'ma salient. From this come the colossal losses and defeats - as well as one of the reasons for the successful German defense. All of us, from the generals down to the soldiers in the ranks, were woefully ignorant of how to fight at the time!

Just take a look at all of the memoirs of marshals, generals and commanders of all ranks that came out in the 1960s and 1970s – hundreds of books. In any particular one of them you will find the author's complaints that there was no success in suppressing all of the enemy's means of fire.

Despite all of the aforementioned difficulties, on 12 August 1942 toward evening, two regiments of the 220nd Rifle Division drove the Germans out of Bel'kovo, Svin'ino and Kharino. They were able to do this after Major General P.G. Chanchibadze's 2nd Guards Rifle Division was thrown into the fighting in order to crack this tough nut in the German defenses (in the summer of 1942, this division had been shifted from the Rzhev area and sent to Stalingrad).[8]

After each battle the ranks of the regiments, battalions and companies became ever thinner. When the results of the fighting were tabulated, this was the result: there were 40 men left in the 376th Rifle Regiment; 48 men left in the 653rd Rifle Regiment and 64 men left in the 673rd Rifle Regiment. The total: 152 soldiers and officers left in the three rifle regiments of the 220nd Rifle Division. At the start of the offensive they had numbered a total of almost 8,000 men.[9]

Perhaps it was at Bel'kovo that the ominous expression "expendable soldier" originated. How did it come about? Who thought it up? Possibly it came by analogy with such expressions as "disposable syringe" and "expendable suit" to prepare the deceased for burial. The essence of the matter is not the search for such analogies, but the fact that the soldier - who wound up on the frontlines around Rzhev - immediately felt himself to be expendable.

Perhaps what I have narrated to the reader seems like a delirious fantasy. In order to bring additional confirmation to what I have written, I will cite a short excerpt from a German intelligence "Informational Bulletin" from January 1942. Here is what it says:

> ... The Russian attacks are conducted, as a rule, strictly and always according to plan - in large human masses, several times without any changes. The attacking infantry in compact groups leave their positions and from a great distance rush into the attack with the cry: "Urah!" Officers and commissars follow behind and shoot at anyone who is lagging. Thanks to their superiority in numbers, this method has allowed them to obtain many major successes...

Here is what a German officer wrote to his family about the attacks of the Red Army in August 1941 near Kiev:

> ... We opened fire at a range of 600 meters and entire squads in the first wave of attackers fell to the ground... Solitary survivors apathetically kept advancing. It was cruel, unbelievable, inhumane. Not one of our soldiers would have kept moving forward. The second wave also suffered casualties, but closed ranks over the bodies of their comrades who had fallen in the first wave. Then, at a signal, the lines of men began running. As they approached, a discordant, rolling "Ura-a-a!" carried to us.... The first three waves were destroyed by our fire. The onrush of the fourth wave was slower; the men were plowing through a carpet of corpses... I will not hide the fact that they frightened us... If the Soviets can allow themselves to lose so many people - trying to liquidate even insignificant results of our offensive - then just how often and in what number will they be attacking if the objective is actually important?...

Poet-lyricists in the war years came up with highly patriotic verses, while composers wrote fine music for them. Soldiers sang these songs with pleasure, although they knew that many of them were remote from the harsh frontline realities. Take, for example: "A bullet fears the brave man; a bayonet will never catch the bold" or "No bombing frightens us; it is too soon for us to kick the bucket – we still have a lot to do back home" and so on and so forth. War is harsh and doesn't always happen like the songs that are sung.

Ancient wise men said: "Blind is he that does not see and does not want to see." I met so many zealous stripe hounds among the commanders and commissars in the war years that had lost that valuable human quality "to see", which means also to sympathize. When we officers talked about this subject, almost everyone - as a rule - came to the same conclusions. "Who would permit disobedience or the refusal to carry out an order in a frontline situation?" Is the result all gloom and doom? Not at all. History has preserved from the war years quite a few cases and names of commanders and commissars who refused to drive soldiers, like cannon fodder, toward German machine guns or to advance tanks under enemy bombs or the fire of anti-tank guns. Alas, in the battles for Rzhev I never heard about comparable case.

The verdict on the commanders

How should the behavior of the 220th Rifle division's commander at Bel'kovo be assessed? Was he really a soulless careerist - or perhaps he shouldn't have taken the order of the Western Front commander so literally? Did Poplavsky really not understand that both the lead tank and the tanks following it would get stuck? Is it possible that the colonel lost his head; didn't find the best solution or even still worse, quailed in front of higher command? How many men and how much equipment did the division commander expend - and yet Bel'kovo remained untaken? He knew he wouldn't have to answer for these (and perhaps for even greater) losses. "We won't haggle over the cost!" Do you remember those words from a popular wartime song? But here the failure to carry out an order "at any cost" must carry a strict response.

Stanislav Giliarovich [Poplavsky] understood that the greatest courage and highest ardor - such that can't even be imagined - will never replace combat skills and capable direction of the battle. Therefore he could hardly have hoped that his fearless, but in my opinion reckless act, would be crowned with success since effectively for a certain time while isolated in his tank he had lost all command and control over his division. In his act, as it were, obviously two impetuses came together: a desire to carry out the order of the front commander at any cost and at the same time, as it seemed to him, he viewed his actions as something important, purposeful and heroic. Is it so?

A few words about the Western Front commander: When Colonel General Konev asked the division commander: "Why aren't you using your attached tank brigade?" This sounds, excuse me, naïve. It is like asking a first grader, for example: "What place does the letter 'A' occupy in the Russian alphabet?" What was his demand: "Tow out the tanks!" worth? Sheer hypocrisy! How? With tractors - of which there were none? With their bare hands under enemy fire? Ivan Stepanovich [Konev] knew no worse than the soldier the real situation at the front. Meanwhile, his demand threatened an entire tank brigade with destruction. That, in fact, is what happened. We know though that the lead tank in which the division commander was located - which was directed by the best tanker - became stuck and the latter was compelled to request urgently that a party be sent to rescue them!

How though did Konev assess the division commander's "exploit"? It is possible that he thought the following about the commander of the 220nd Rifle Division: "Fool. He took my words literally and he wasn't able to find a different solution. If he got a scare, that's fine. 'Failure teaches success' - that's what he'd been taught back in the First World War. It's only bad that sitting in the tank, the Colonel lost control over his division."

But why did Konev demand the impossible from the division commander? Obviously, Ivan Stepanovich wanted to send a victorious report to the Supreme Commander as soon as possible, but he was unable to do so. He also knew the *Stavka* wouldn't be asking him about the losses of men and equipment, but he would have to answer for the failure of the offensive and the non-fulfillment of the *Stavka*'s directives.

Let's take a brief look at the 35th Tank Brigade, which was attached to the 220th Rifle Division. Over the first nine days of fighting, the Brigade lost 16 tanks. That figure doesn't include any of the British Maltida tanks obtained through Lend-Lease. Understanding the difficulties of employing tanks in a swampy area with no roads, the brigade commander Lieutenant Colonel Burlyga expressed his opinion to Poplavsky, saying: "A tank is not a wild beast. You can't force it to move through swampy terrain with a prod." Seemingly, the division commander agreed with this sensible argument, but on the next day everything suddenly changed. Stanislav Giliarovich [Poplavsky] demanded from the brigade commander the best tank and his most experienced driver. Poplavsky would take a place in the lead machine and ordered that three more tanks follow him into the battle.

Approximately seven or eight months after the fighting at Bel'kovo, I happened to meet Lieutenant Colonel Skovorodkin - who at the time was now commanding the 653rd Rifle Regiment. I reminded him of the Bel'kovo saga - in particular the episode to rescue the division commander. A more gentle and level-headed man you won't find. Sighing heavily, he replied: "I remember it all clearly, but we lost a lot of guys. All night long the Germans, sending up flares, laid mortar fire on us from every direction. The fighting to reach the division commander lasted hours. Stanislav Giliarovich was lucky. He got away with a light wound, but gained a lot of fame and soon thereafter his general's epaulets as well."

Having buried some of their dead and having collected their wounded, the Germans - licking their wounds like an injured animal - abandoned the villages and fell back to a new line of defense. Just who had been our adversary there? According to prisoner interrogations it was I.R. [Infantry regiment] 481 of the 256th Infantry Division commanded by Major General Danhauser, which had been defending this fortified sector. To assist the regiment, a reserve infantry battalion composed primarily of new recruits had been transferred to Bel'kovo. It was first introduced into the heavy fighting on 30 July. The German defense numbered approximately 1,200 soldiers and officers armed with mortars, machine guns and sub machine guns. The *Luftwaffe* and artillery gave them support.

So suddenly, there was silence. It settled upon the men unexpectedly. It was difficult to become adjusted to it since no one could imagine a time when it might arrive. How to grasp that you had survived - and to recall that you were a human! When this finally happened, then there was a strong desire to rid your bodies of the lice; to wash up; to smell soap; to put on clean underwear; to shave; to obtain new boots, trousers and combat tunic. The old trousers and tunics were tattered and stank so badly that it was utterly impossible to wear them any longer. Finally, it was time to throw away the filthy, stinking, plastered-together foot bindings. The soldiers asked: "To hell with it, was all that really possible?"

The command did everything possible to satisfy the soldiers' wants. How many of them remained, the heroes? Even in the final action on 12 August 1942 24 soldiers were killed and 97 were wounded. Those who remained alive were decorated and a few of the dead received posthumous decorations. For this occasion the commanders addressed us respectably; allowed us to sleep in tents rather than out in the rain; washed us; fed us; dressed us in new uniforms and sent us to the rear for re-formation. So nevertheless, no matter what difficulties life brings it is beautiful!

In conclusion I consider it fitting to include here a letter by Nikolai Grigor'evich Volkov, a former resident of Rzhev, which appeared in the *Rzhevskie vesti* newspaper. In its contents, focus and pathos it supports my judgments that Bel'kovo was an example of how one must not fight! Judge for yourselves! I'll cite this letter with a few small abridgements:

For Victory Day (6 May 1999). The editorial board of the newspaper *Rzhevskie vesti* has received a letter from Odessa Oblast from a former native of the Rzhev region who was born in the village of Murav'evo, Nikolai Grigor'evich Volkov, in which he addresses I.Z. Ladygin and N.I. Smirnov - the authors of the book *Na Rzhevskom rubezhe* [*On the Rzhev line*]:

> Esteemed Igor' Zinov'evich and Nikolai Ivanovich, greetings! Last summer while I was on vacation I visited my brother, who lives in the village of Murav'evo near Rzhev. He gave me your book about Rzhev and the Battle of Rzhev, which are both dear to my heart. Thank you for your splendid book - for remembering those who gave their lives for our city, for our land, for all of us.
>
> Back then I was 10 years old and I recall much that happened in the village after it was occupied by the Germans - though perhaps with a dollop of childhood imagination. I haven't lived in my native area since 1943 since I wound up in an orphanage.
>
> You read books about the Great Patriotic War, become familiar with its documents - which were kept concealed from us for many years - and you think: "Just when will we learn to love and take care of our soldier? To show concern for him like the great commanders Suvorov and Kutuzov once did?" Some historians present the correlations of those killed in many battles as 10:1 not in our favor. How is it possible to avoid asserting that they drove the soldier to an unjustified and unavoidable death, but then later they wrote articles about his feats and heroism? So many lies and misrepresentations have been written on this subject; so much window-dressing has been put up. Indeed the writer Afas'ev was right when he said that we poured out our blood and overwhelmed the adversaries with our corpses because we didn't know how to fight; we fought with numbers - not sparing the soldier. You are also completely correct when you write that often there were not battles at Rzhev, but senseless slaughters and the extermination of our soldiers, and you offer clear examples. Why

Leliushenko, the commander of the 30th Army, dedicated only 23 lines to the fighting at Rzhev is not difficult to answer.[10] He himself was guilty of a lot, but feared for his fate and was afraid to acknowledge the losses - just like many other military commanders. From the conversations of veterans who fought under his command, I repeatedly heard that he was cruel and indifferent to his soldiers.

Reading in your book the article "Cherez ognennyi koridor" ["Through the fiery corridor"], the question arises why S.G. Poplavsky - who left more than 3,000 soldiers of his 185th Rifle Division dead around the village of Tolstikovo, for which the division had been fighting - didn't say a word about this in his skimpy memoirs as if it was nothing. I think that these unavailing sacrifices are on his conscience, and thus he didn't mention them.[11]

The [winter 1941-1942] operation was plainly not prepared. You write that the attacks of our army's units most often were conducted without the support of tanks, aircraft and artillery in extremely difficult conditions: deep snow, temperatures down to -30° C. [-22° F.] and with no possibility to get warm and dry out the uniform. The delivery of ammunition, food and medications from depots located dozens of kilometers to the north failed to meet the needs of the army and so forth. All that has been written is true. This was one of the reasons why the attempt to take Rzhev between 17 and 20 January 1942 failed. How was it possible for famished Red Army soldiers who'd been exhausted in the preceding fighting - and were equipped only with a rifle, sugar and a red banner - to liberate the city, which had been converted by the Germans into an impenetrable fortress crammed with large amounts of troops and equipment? This is nothing less than a plain crime! After all, for an entire year after this they were bogged down in front of the walls of the city and continued to carpet the Rzhev land with the bodies of our soldiers. Are there really just a few such criminal actions perpetrated against the simple soldier by the short-sighted, untalented military commanders? After all, war is war – and war writes off everything.[12] The outcome is the main thing and victors are never judged.

I still want to relate what happened near Tolstikovo and on the field next to it. Attacking units of the 185th Rifle Division had taken the village of Tolstikovo, in which a German food warehouse containing schnapps and baked items was located. One can say that the Germans yielded it without fighting - calculating that the haggard, hungry Russians would jump at the chance to eat and drink; after all, it was 30° below 0 C. [-22 F.]. The German plan worked perfectly.

The Germans called up a large tank assault group, which rolled through our village the entire night. In the village of Murav'evo itself, mortars were positioned around the buildings - the yards of which looked out upon Moscow - Riga railroad (and beyond it Khebtovskoe Field and Tolstikovo) and they were conducting intensive fire on our attacking troops. The mortars with their crews were concealed behind by a wall of snow, which stood about the height of a man. There were two mortars positioned next to our house. Having fired a few rounds, the Germans would enter our home to warm up and then go back outside to fire more rounds. Hot ham and pea soup, bread and hot cocoa were brought up to them in their fighting positions. The Germans had deployed machine guns among the bushes along the railroad bed, which were cutting down our onrushing attacking soldiers, while the tanks blanketed the entire field with high-explosive shells. The fighting went on almost the entire day. It became quiet by evening. The German tanks returned to Rzhev - again rolling through our village on the way back.

The German hospital in the village was full of wounded men who'd been brought in that evening and night from in front of Tolstikovo. On the next day, the Germans collected their dead and buried them in their new cemetery behind the village. They finished off all of our wounded as they were gathering their own. The Germans removed the warm clothing from the bodies of our dead: fur caps, short fur coats, felt boots and gloves. The snow covered the bodies of our fallen with a white shroud until April 1942.

In the spring, the Germans forced the citizens of Murav'evo and Tolstikovo to bury the corpses. Bomb and shell craters served as their graves. I walked the field with my father (he was killed later in the autumn of 1942) and saw the terrible scene of the results of the battle. The still not fully decomposed bodies of soldiers were lying in various poses and the majority of them had been completely stripped of their clothing. Many were without both feet. Instead of rifles, the majority of them had fence posts lying next to them. At my age at the time, I didn't understand much of what I was seeing that day. It turns out that our own compatriot-looters from our village and neighboring villages had cut off the corpses' feet and removed their underclothing. They'd been coming to this field, digging up the bodies from under the snow and removing their underwear; with an axe they would chop off the boots from any body that still had them on their feet because the Germans hadn't been able to remove them as the boots were frozen to the legs. They would take them home, steam the boots out in banias, toss aside the feet and then either wear the felt boots or exchange them - together with the washed underwear that had been removed from the corpses - for salt, potatoes or bread in distant villages.

For a long time, I doubted my conclusions on this subject. Adults who hadn't witnessed all this told me that this was only the "fantasies" of a 10-year-old child, but then one day I visited my older sister, who lives in Moscow Oblast. She is 87 years old, but still sprightly for her age - and her memory, thank God, is still clear. She lived through the entire German occupation of the village together with her son and two little daughters. Later, the two girls died from starvation. In a conversation with me on the subject of the war, the occupation and the events of those days in our area she recognized my "fantasies" as the pure truth. "The fence posts lying next to the soldiers were there because at the moment of the attack they were drunk," she said. "They'd forgotten where there rifles were, but they had to go on the attack." She also explained why the bodies were naked. "Once," she said to me, "an acquaintance and I also decided to stoop to doing similar business. We left the village and asked each other: 'Listen, where are we going, and will we really be stripping someone?' So they turned back. She still can't forgive herself for this. Wiping away the bitter old tears of a widow, she said: "After all, my own Peten'ka was also lying dead somewhere and I can't imagine someone stripping him naked." In fact, she still doesn't know about the fate of her husband Petr Ravnov, who supposedly went missing in action.

Esteemed Igor' Zinov'evich and Nikolai Ivanovich, likely, having read your book many people are writing to you - and especially those who in some way are connected with those events. It is impossible to read through this book and forget it. It should be read cover to cover in tears - despite the fact that a lot of time has passed since then.

Sincerely, a working pensioner and 67-year-old mechanic with the Il'ichevskii Marine Trade Port, Nikolai Grigor'evich Volkov.

An afterword

Two worlds - two systems. In the United States army, just as in the British army, officers were obligated to give consideration to minimizing their casualties - otherwise they inevitably would have been removed from their posts and would have faced a hearing.

In the Red Army, the most terrible crime was the failure to carry out an obviously impossible and at times even criminal order of a superior commander. Refusal to obey an order could be met with immediate execution or something which was almost the same - consignment into a penal battalion. One's own commander was more frightening than the enemy. It was precisely because of this, in von Mellenthin's evaluation, that:

> ... The junior officers - and many among the middle command group - were still clumsy and unable to take decisions; because of draconian discipline they were afraid of shouldering responsibility. Purely rigid training squeezed the lower commanders into the vice of manuals and regulations and robbed them of the initiative and originality which are vital to a good tactician. Among the rank and file the gregarious instinct is so strong that an individual fighter is always submerged in the "crowd". Russian soldiers and junior commanders realized instinctively that if left on their own they were lost - and in this herd instinct, one can trace the roots of panic as well as deeds of extraordinary heroism and self-sacrifice...[13]

The rigidity of the Red Army Command Staff's operational and strategic thinking was more than compensated by the senseless, murderous frontal attacks. Marshal Bagramian expressed this eloquently: "It was necessary to rely above all on the resilient spiritual strength of our people; on the fact that for them there are no tasks which cannot be fulfilled." That is in fact why, they say, the troops were given plainly unrealistic orders with surprising persistence.

In Western armies, soldiers and officers might refuse to carry out an order to go on the attack across a minefield and this might have led to a hearing and the replacement of the commander. Soviet soldiers, on the contrary, knew well that to complain about higher command was a ruinous business. What is the significance of a rank and file soldier in an army where marshals struck generals in the face; generals, colonels and division commanders were shot without trial in front of the assembled formation? "Mr. Nice Guy" Konev preferred to instruct his subordinates with a thick stick. Recalls Colonel General G.F. Baiduk, who commanded an aviation division in the Kalinin Front: "... we were summoned to the front's Military Council. We arrived. Out of the huts steps Matvei Zakharov - the chief of staff and future Marshal of the Soviet Union - wiping blood from his nose: 'He punched me, the swine!'"

"Once upon a time an old woman had a little gray goat
That's so, that's so – a little gray goat
The old woman so loved the little gray goat
That's so, that's so – so loved the little gray goat
Gray wolves pounced upon the little gray goat
That's so, that's so – the gray wolves
Left to the old woman – the hooves and horns
That's so, that's so!"

A Russian childhood ditty

4

Stalin's Favorite Animal – a Little Goat! ...

Personal frontline sketches

The appearance of the play *The Front*

In his memoirs, Marshal I.S. Konev relates a very interesting story that happened to him. The Marshal writes:

... Once in the summer of 1942, Stalin suddenly phones me at the front and asks:

"Can you come?"

"I can."

"Then come right away."

At the time I was with the Kalinin Front. I grabbed an airplane and flew to Moscow. I present myself to Stalin. Zhukov was with him and - I can't recall - someone else from our circle. Stalin asks me:

"Have you read Korneichuk's play *The Front* in *Pravda*?"

"I've read it, Comrade Stalin."

"What's your opinion of it?"

"It's very bad, Comrade Stalin."

I felt like I hadn't hit the right note, but I'd already begun to speak and I said more. I opined that it was improper and harmful to ridicule a front commander. If a commander is bad it was in his power to remove him, but when a front commander is defamed and mocked in a production that has been printed in *Pravda*, this no longer has limited significance; we're no longer talking about one commander, but casting a shadow on all of them. Stalin angrily cut me off:

"You don't understand anything. This is a political matter - a political need. In this play there is a struggle underway with the outmoded; the elderly; with those who are dragging us backward. This is a fine play that has correctly posed the question."

I said that in my opinion there were a lot of falsehoods in the play. In particular, when Ognev himself - who has been appointed to replace the front commander - delivers the order about the commander's removal and his own appointment; I remarked that this, from the point of view of any military man, is totally inappropriate and does not happen. Here I let slip a statement that I wasn't defending Gorlov; that I was more from among those people who implicate Ognev, but I didn't like any of this in the play. Here Stalin completely let me have it:

"The hell you're Ognev! You're not Ognev, you're too proud of yourself. You've overreached and you're too proud. You military men, you know everything, while we civilians understand nothing. We understand better than you what is necessary and what isn't."

He returned to this point several times more - that I was too proud and fluffing my own feathers - and he heatedly kept insisting on the correctness and usefulness of Korneichuk's play. Then he addressed Zhukov:

"And you, what's your opinion of Korneichuk's play?"

Zhukov was luckier than me. It turned out that he hadn't yet read this play, so the entire blow in the given case fell upon me.

> However - and this was characteristic of Stalin - later he gave a direction to all members of Front Military Councils to question commanders and all the top generals regarding their opinion of Korneichuk's play. Indeed this was done. In particular, Bulganin spoke with the Western Front's commander of artillery General Kamera. That commander told him: "I don't know what I would do with the writer who wrote this play. It is a mediocre play and I would fix him for such a play." Well this, of course, went into a report.
>
> On my next trip to Moscow, Stalin asks me what kind of man this Kamera was. I had to spend a long time convincing him that he was an outstanding, highly-capable front artillery commander with considerable achievements in the past - and in this manner sought to defend Kamera. This I managed to do, but if things had gone a bit differently his response about Korneichuk's play might have cost him dearly…

There are three personalities in the story I've just cited: the Supreme Commander, the playwright Aleksandr Korneichuk and the commander of the Western Front, I.S. Konev. Before assessing the actions of our heroes it is probably useful to discuss the events that led to the appearance of this play, its contents and the reaction to it from several circles of society.

The play *The Front* appeared in the country's public arena at one of the most critical phases of the war. On 28 June 1942 a 2 million-strong German army launched a new summer campaign. The two Soviet Fronts opposing it - unable to withstand the powerful assault - collapsed. The German command had selected the timing of the offensive successfully: shortly before, Soviet forces had suffered two major defeats in the Crimea and at Khar'kov.

Just as in 1941, the Supreme Commander erred once again in determining the enemy's choice of the strategic direction for the offensive. Stalin was firmly convinced that Hitler would launch an offensive in the center of the Soviet-German Front and try to capture Moscow. Therefore at his direction the *Stavka* had concentrated the Red Army's main reserves on this sector of the front.

Positioned in front of Rzhev at that time we soldiers acutely suffered the loss of the Crimea, the unimaginably cruel assault on Sebastopol', the Khar'kov disaster and the lunge of the Nazi panzer armies across the Don steppes toward Stalingrad. Imagine, in just 20 days the German forces advanced 600 kilometers, reached the Volga River and were at the gates of Stalingrad!

To be sure, many details of those dramatic events reached us with delays, in fragments or we weren't aware of them at all. The "soldiers' telegraph" was tipping us off about something. All the same, we were deeply worried. We needed no prompting to understand that a grave threat was hanging above the country.

In order to get out of the desperate situation in which the Red Army found itself, Stalin in 1942 and at the beginning of 1943 implemented three major political and organizational acts. On 28 July 1942 he issued Order No. 227 - the "No step back!" order. He eliminated the institution of the commissars in the Red Army, which had existed off and on since 1918. At every level of the Red Army he introduced unity of command and established a unified system of ranks (28 October 1942). Finally, he introduced officers' ranks and shoulder boards.

Against the backdrop of what was happening, which people in Russia and the West were intently following, an event took place in Moscow... seemingly nothing extraordinary - a normal literary event. But it generated enormous public resonance in the country, the Red Army and abroad. In the pages of *Pravda* - the newspaper of the Communist Party's Central Committee - in four editions between 24 and 27 August 1942 Aleksandr Korneichuk's play *The Front* was published in its entirety to the surprise of everyone.

Immediately the question arose: "Why, suddenly, has the Party's main newspaper given such a "great honor" to this play?" Everyone understood that the play's publication in the pages of *Pravda* would be unthinkable without the prompting of the Generalissimo. But there was a lot that happened afterward - not all of it explicable.

The unimaginable happened. The Party's organs drew broad masses of the population, the press, the radio and the army into a routine discussion of the play. Selected excerpts were read from stages. The best theaters performed the play on their stages. Among them were the three leading theaters in Moscow: the MKhAT [Moscow Art Theater], the Malyi Academic Theater and the Central Theater of the Red Army. Famous actors played the key roles in the play.

I have overlooked foreign responses to the play and what was said about it. Among them, particularly interesting and original were two review essays: 'Around the front' and 'On the Public Front' published in the journal *Sotsialisticheskii vestnik*. Their author was the literary critic Vera Aleksandrova. There was more truth in them than in the Soviet press, but the main thing is that they expressed valid reasoning about the "who" and "what" that stood behind this play.[1]

To what is this play devoted?

I will briefly familiarize the reader with the contents of Aleksandr Korneichuk's play, *The Front*. At the center of the play are two characters: a front commander (Ivan Gorlov) and an army commander (Ognev). Gorlov is a hero of the Russian Civil War who learned to fight not in an academy, but in combat. However, in reality, as the dramatist writes, this man in the Red Army embodies the "past"; the "outdated"; narrow-mindedness; ignorance and old military methods that no longer correspond to the contemporary principles of conducting a war. The main qualities of a commander, in his opinion, are personal bravery and daring. He has surrounded himself with military chiefs and comrades from the Civil War.

Set opposite to him is the talented, young commander Major General Ognev. Gorlov doesn't hide his attitudes toward Ognev: "He began to fight as a colonel. Within three months he was a major general, and now the commander of an army. A dizzying rise! But a man of little strength. Well, now he's started to plot."

Ognev doesn't hide his own opinions of Gorlov. When the latter issues an order on how to escape from encirclement and praises the "audacity" of the plan, Ognev immediately parries him: "You speak of audacity. There is no audacity in this order. There is no sense in it either; everything is approached with 'Urah!'; with 'perhaps', as if the enemy were a fool or sleeping ..."

It is not the army or dedication to the rank and file soldiers that is keeping Gorlov in his high post, but the apparatus of power. "Correspondents" of the central press like Khripun support him. On the matter of one of these parasites, who flatter Ivan Gorlov, his own brother Miron exclaims: "Lord Almighty, when will there come an end in our country to fools, ignoramuses, sycophants, ninnies and scoundrels?" Breaking himself off, he adds up the consequences: "It is too late for reasoning. It is necessary to beat these self-centered ignoramuses; beat them bloody, beat them into a pulp and replace them as quickly as possible with new, young, talented people. Otherwise, it might be the ruin of our great cause." That, if you will, is the play's main idea.

The play's conclusion is known to the viewers already from its opening scene. An order comes from Moscow about removing Ivan Gorlov from the post of front commander and about appointing Major General Ognev to replace him.

The play - which criticizes empty verbiage, departmentalism, conceit, the unwillingness to grasp the significance of war's new strategy and tactics - seemed to many Soviet generals, especially veterans of the Russian Civil War (whom I.V. Stalin hadn't yet knocked off), to shake the very foundations of the Red Army. The play seemingly "explained" to everyone "who was guilty" and "what needed to be done" in order to conquer the adversary.

The author of the play was searching for scapegoats - the generation of Red Army commanders who had made their mark in the Russian Civil War and who since had rested on their laurels and become windbags and "fancy pompadours".

When the play was published, the "highest permission" came down to allow freedom of expression - of course, within the confines of the play's contents. "To an outsider," wrote Vera Aleksandrova, "who is unfamiliar with the details of Soviet life, the play might seem to be an earthquake that shook any and all foundations of life. However, people should know that in Soviet society nothing is done without permission from above ..." and later offers this conclusion:

> ...In the days when the fate of Stalingrad and the entire country was being decided, it was necessary to give the army and society at least the appearance of freedom to speak out about events ... Even the boldest criticism, permitted from above, is less dangerous than most timid and tongue-tied criticism of "whisperers" from below...

At the front, the play prompted a varied reaction. It bewildered the not-indifferent and caused them to ponder the commonly indifferent. Many were at a loss - not knowing how they should act in the future. This particularly applied to the political workers. The writer Pavlenko wrote honestly about this discomfiture and confusion in the pages of the journal *Oktiabr'* in 1943. Coincidentally, one day when *Pravda* had begun to print the play, he was at the front in the Political Department of one of the divisions. Pavlenko writes:

> ... The chief of the Political Department, raising his head from the pages of the newspaper, confusedly said: "Some sort of scandalous story ... Have you read it?" and offered me the paper. I began with the forward, but the chief of the Political Department, noticing this, hastily added: "No, no, take a look at the play ..."
> ...

There were a lot of confused people. Among some Soviet citizens, a fear arose that it signaled a new purge in the Red Army. Letters and reviews of the play in the press testify to this. The play's author proved to be not among the confused. In his opinion, the play was engendering the courage to struggle against everyone who had outlived their usefulness. He wrote: "It teaches: he who doesn't struggle against the old has himself become aged and become ueseless to his own time. The play forces the reader - and even more the viewer - to think about the fact that the fate of Russia is in his hands; that these self-same hands might save or destroy it." All the official Soviet criticism was on pretty much the same level.

The writer was dissembling. Who was responsible for the military blunders? He knew. As far as I can recall, during the entire Stalinist era, this was the first and last time that so-called "free criticism" was permitted to Soviet people.

How the front received the play

The echo of the "storm in a glass of water" - as we now understand today 60 years later - even reached as far down as our division. Somewhere around the beginning of 1943, the officers and political workers at the regimental level were gathered in order to get their opinion of Korneichuk's play.

The division commander opened the meeting. It would have been interesting to learn his own opinion of the play and what sort of hero he was. We didn't get the chance. General Poplavsky gave the word to Borisov - his Deputy for Political Affairs.

"The play was printed in the *Pravda* newspaper," Borisov said simply and honestly, "and if so, then naturally it reflects the opinion of the Party's Central Committee." Then he continued:

> ... But this doesn't mean that we frontline-communists have no right to our own opinion and have no freedom of expression.

> That is in fact the point of this meeting. The Main Political Directorate wants to know the opinion of the frontline men about the play. You shouldn't be concerned about any rebukes or service complications. We're talking about the fate of the country. The sooner we overcome the shortcomings in the Red Army, which is what the play addresses, the sooner we will defeat the enemy!...

Battalion Commissar Kirill Akimovich Koshman set the tone of the talk:

> ...It isn't a play, but some sort of misunderstanding. Take a look at our front commanders and army commanders. Almost all of them participated in the Civil War. They didn't finish any academy, but who of us will cast the first stone at them? What do they have in common with the Gorlov types? Nothing! I don't see any sort of conflict...[2]

Regiment commander Colonel Razumovsky asked to speak:

> ... Here is what I would like to ask the comrade playwright. It's what, Gorlov's fault that everyone ran away from the border in 1941 in their drawers? General Pavlov was like one of the Ognevs; he fought in Spain and was a Hero of the Soviet Union. But he couldn't hold the front. For this he had to pay. Would Major General Ognev have saved the situation back then? I doubt it. At the same time, the play compels one to ponder those who have outlived their usefulness to the army. We are in need of new field regulations, the restructuring of the entire system of communications and a more active study of combat experience...

The division's chief of engineering made an emotional statement. The gray-haired Colonel-Engineer said:

> ... Let's take a look at ourselves through the eyes of the play's heroes and give a thought about this. In 1941 I was serving on the old national border. We were dismantling the fortified districts and building new ones. I'll give an example. If the commander of the Brest garrison on the first day of the war had assumed all the responsibility, the enemy wouldn't have been able to cross the Bug River. The Red Army had major forces on this sector of the Western border at the start of the war. The regular troops were well-trained. Really even now are there not similar military commanders among us?...

Someone hurled the reply: "Give us an example!" The Colonel didn't get rattled. He calmly replied: "You yourselves know." The division chief of staff, without any hesitation, rudely dumped on the play: "What does Comrade Korneichuk take us for? The play is harmful. This is an open attempt to drive a wedge between the different generations of commanders."

The assembled officers clamored - offering opinions and interrupting those trying to speak. The division commander attempted to restore order. The 30-year-old Lieutenant Colonel Tolia Kochergin, the commander of the artillery regiment, expressed himself even more harshly:

> ... The GLAVPUR [Main Political Directorate] wants to know our opinion ... I'll ask, Comrade GLAVPUR members, the way the Ukrainians do: Isn't this play just sheer hooey? Where did the comrade playwright see these Gorlovs, these cavalrymen? They were purged from the army even before the war. Someone from higher up has decided to dump all of their own sins onto the heroes of the Civil War...

I overheard the head of the division's Special Department, who was sitting not far from me, whisper: "What is that scum saying? Throw him into the slammer? Not just yet, but we'll remember."

I glanced over at Leonid Fedorovich Borisov and felt sorry for him. He was flustered. He likely hadn't expected such a stormy reaction against the play, which was also - as he believed - a demonstration against the will of the Party's Central Committee as well. He offered to wind up the discussion: "Seemingly all is clear ..." The whirlwind of emotions around the play and the discussion of it had gripped everyone - and the people present didn't cool down quickly.

Why didn't the front accept Korneichuk's play? I thought about this and came to the following conclusion. The matter is not that we were hacked off. All sorts of Korneichuks had been defaming us - the men at the front - and more than once. Obviously, many, having read the play, saw the recently raised curtain as some sort of "free thinking" from which they had long ago grown unaccustomed. However, no one - from the generals down to the lowest ranking officer - refrained from seeing something behind this play or to speak out openly about it.

Unfortunately, few of us then understood that the playwright was only serving as the Party's instrument. He wrote this agitprop [a contraction of agitation and propaganda] play and Stalin elevated it to an almost unattainable height.

Why? Stalin knew full well: it was now the second year of the war and the army, the people and the world community were increasingly raising the questions: "How could the catastrophe of 1941 have occurred? How can it be explained? Who was guilty for this enormous tragedy in Russian history?" Let's assume that Stalin explained what had happened by the unexpectedness of the invasion. In 1942 however, there could no longer be any complete surprise. But again, the Red Army was suffering disaster - and what a disaster!

With Stalin, as was the case with Hitler, political considerations always trumped military ones. The play *The Front* was designed to explain to the millions of alarmed citizens: Comrade Stalin, the Generalissimo, wasn't guilty for the new catastrophes; it was the army commanders like Gorlov that were responsible ....

It is known that Stalin to his dying day never acknowledged his own guilt either for the shameful defeats or for the innumerable human losses - which to the present day still remain not completely known - which means essentially, his responsibility for the death of several generations of Soviet people. In any democratic country, for similar crimes the perpetrator is punished to the full extent of the law.

A few words about Marshal Konev ... with a soldier's directness he had expressed to Stalin what he thought of the play. Could Ivan Stepanovich tell Iosif Vissarionovich that the game the latter had contrived was a dishonorable one? Of course not!

How was the play received in the Red Army's summits? Let's take a look at the memoirs of General Shtemenko:

> ... It [the play] appeared unexpectedly in the pages of *Pravda* and shook the Red Army's entire officer corps. And although in the General Staff our every minute at that time was accounted for, even the busiest members read the play. With all our heart we were on the side of the young Ognev and spoke out against Gorlov ...
>
> Yet within the General Staff and outside it - even among the most meritorious military leaders - there were those who perceived the play *The Front* as a unique diversion against the Red Army. The *Stavka* received several telegrams requesting that the publication of the play in *Pravda* be halted and to ban the performance of it in theaters as something extremely harmful.
>
> We, the young men on the General Staff, if it is possible to say such about people in the middle ranks of leadership - who are still not senior in age - took *The Front* as an expression of Party policy; as its call to increase the level of our military art and leadership methods over the troops...[3]

How the Moscow intelligentsia reacted to the play

How did the intellectual circle in Moscow react to the play and what did the actors themselves think of it? The well-known author Vsevolod Ivanov talks about this in his book *Dnevniki i pis'ma: Moskovskie tetrad* [*Diaries and letters: The Moscow notebooks*].

In 1942, the writer returned to Moscow from evacuation and began writing his impressions about what was happening in the capital; about interesting people and the cultural life of the city, which continued even in the war years. Here are several of his entries:

> ... In the evening (7 November, Saturday 1942) we were at the MKhAT to see the play *The Front.* Three theaters are staging the play simultaneously - to be more accurate, all the available theaters in Moscow. They say that it is going better in the Malyi than in the MKhAT, but I don't believe this; it [the play] is very bad indeed. People were split into the old and the young just like horses - and the drama did not justify the talent of the young. Knowledge of matters at the front isn't helpful, but it hinders the playwright; he speaks about an offensive in such detail that you won't understand what they're arguing about. The play is similar to the multitude of "manufactured" plays, which we saw in a sequence. The audience glitters with Orders...

In this diary entry, the writer also recalls the words of Boris Pasternak: "If it was possible to win a battle by means of a play, I would go see it every day. However, since this is impossible, then why put it on?" - A very accurate and sensible description.

A sketch from Ivanov:

> ... The vestibule of the hotel is empty. The humorist Lench is taking the elevator up with us. He also went to see *The Front*, but at the Theater of Drama.
>
> "Well?"
>
> "Boring - and plainly so boring that he couldn't sort out the attributes."...

One more excerpt from Vsevolod Ivanov's recollections:

> ... On 20 November an article about *The Front* was printed in *Pravda*, which argues that the Artistic and the Malyi Academic Theater is nothing in comparison with the Dramatic. That is to say that Livanov[4] wound up in just the same situation as Gorlov. The power-driven situation with the command staff has been transferred into the realm of art. Livanov rushed around, raked the remnants of his hair, shouted that he'd been killed and drove away from the theater.
>
> I was given to understand that this was not a play, but they were performing *The Front* as a directive!...

Further Vsevolod Ivanov writes:

> ... You sometimes think that knowledge lags behind appointments. *The Front's* falsehood is not that such events don't happen; that people don't want to learn, but that there is no time to study; no one to learn from - and most importantly, time is short. We shorten it

> - we want to convert a century into five years - yet time, the cursed thing, was standing still there in the way only it is able to do so...

It is also interesting to read the writer's story about his discussion of the play with generals in the Central Theater of the Red Army: "It began when a general with a face like a lampshade said: 'Does Comrade Korneichuk know that they're putting on *The Front* in Berlin? In a word, they were grumbling and groaning like only they can.'"

When at the end of the 20th Century they partially opened in Russia the armored safes holding the "top secret materials" for a short while, history brought out its sentence upon Stalin and his "cunning, disingenuous game" around the play *The Front.* Who today remembers the play? Who knows it?

It turns out that in contemporary Russia there are people (and they are not small in numbers) who consider Stalin more holy than the Pope and they remember and know the play *The Front.* In 2003 the Moscow publisher Eskmo-Algoritm released the 10-volume *Staliniana* on the 50th Anniversary of I.V. Stalin's death. In one book from this series, under the title *Polkovodets Stalin* [*Commander Stalin*], there is a discussion of Aleksandr Korneichuk's play. Let's get acquainted with the text:

> ... I.V. Stalin always showed exceeding concern over the development of literature, science and art. Here are several of the more characteristic facts. In 1942 A. Korneichuk wrote the play *The Front.* It focused upon attitudes toward the conducting of the Patriotic War ... I.V. Stalin immediately understood the value of the play and recommended it for publication in the newspaper *Pravda* ... It gave rise to diverse reactions - including sharply negative ones. In I.V. Stalin's personal archive, a correspondence concerning this play has been preserved. On 28 August 1942 the commander of the Northwestern Front, S.K. Timoshenko, sent I.V. Stalin a telegram in which he observed: "The play by Comrade Korneichuk, which has been published in the press, merits special attention. This play will inflict harm upon us for centuries to come; it must be revoked. Bring the author to responsibility and investigate those guilty in connection with it."

On this same day, I.V. Stalin answered S.K. Timoshenko with the following telegram:

> Northwestern Front
>
> To Marshal Timoshenko
>
> I received your telegram about Korneichuk's play *The Front.* You are incorrect in your assessment of the play. The play will have enormous educational significance for the Red Army and its com-

> mand staff; the play correctly notes the Red Army's shortcomings and it would be incorrect to close our eyes to these deficiencies. It takes courage to acknowledge shortcomings and to take measures to liquidate them. This is the only path to improving and perfecting the Red Army.
>
> I. Stalin

> Stalin sent the playwright a copy of S.K. Timoshenko's telegram and his own response to it. He advised: "… the playwright should improve his work and make it more relevant." (We'll note, not more artistic, but more relevant!)
>
> The play *The Front* in those years played with great success in many theaters across the country. Stalin proposed to make a film based on the play. The directors S.D. Vasil'ev and G.N. Vasil'ev (well-known Soviet directors who had created the 1934 film *Chapaev*) were assigned to this task. The film was shown in movie theaters and clubs. Everywhere heated debates went on - which did much to contribute to the correct understanding of the essence of the character of the Great Patriotic War - and to conducting it with contemporary methods…

I will only ask: "What relationship to the subject of Stalin's role in the development of literature, science and art in the war years does the story in *Polkovodets Stalin* have?" It occupies almost 14 pages in the book. However, it was likely the authors' opinion that it offers an explanation for the appearance of the play *The Front*. That's the crafty move they conceived.

It is hardly possible that a playwright under Stalin would have taken up the writing of such an edgy political play, which touches upon the authority of the high brass and officer corps, without authorization from above. In that I am certain!

In his telegrammed response to S.K. Timoshenko, Stalin distinctly revealed his view about the future conduct of the war without the Gorlovs. Pushkin called Catherine the Great a "Tartuffe in a petticoat" for her double dealing.[5] Stalin's hypocrisy and cunning in the production of the play *The Front* are boundless! Catherine the Great's hypocrisy fades into insignificance compared to Stalin's.

Iosif Vissarionovich knew also about the staging of Korneichuk's play in Berlin. It was Goebbel's idea: "Here, look comrades, at what a collapse the Red Army has reached!" In Russia, the best theaters put on the play. It was a directive!

Using his unlimited power - resorting to craftiness and cunning - Stalin sought to duck responsibility for the mistakes he had made. This includes Stalin's famous speech of 3 July 1941 and the execution of the Western Front's entire command, which was headed by General Pavlov. This also includes his effort to shift the burden of responsibility for the defeats at Viaz'ma and in front of Moscow to the military commanders. This is also the famous Stalin Orders No. 270 and 227. How many heads of upstanding citizens rolled and how many more would have to roll for the sake of one man? How false and demagogic did I.V. Stalin's postwar speech sound at a reception in the Kremlin in honor of Red Army commanders on 24 May 1945? Here is part of its text:

> ... Our government made quite a few mistakes; moments of a desperate situation in 1941-1942 when our army was retreating - abandoning native villages and cities. Any other people might have told the government: "You have not justified our expectations. Be gone with you; we'll put in place a different government, which will make peace with Germany and secure our tranquility." But the Russian people didn't do this, since they believed in the correctness of our government's policy and sacrificed themselves in order to ensure Germany's destruction. Indeed, this trust of the Russian people in the Soviet Government was that decisive strength, which secured the historic victory of mankind's foe - over Fascism...

Good Lord, how much hypocrisy, demagogy and open dissembling are in this address ...

Stalin and Hitler had much in common. Similar to the "Great Soviet Commander", the "German Genius" also loved to place the blame for his own blunders and failures on other shoulders - most of all on his own generals. It is known that Hitler accused the OKH Chief Field Marshal Walter von Brauchitsch for *blitzkreig's* failure in the battle of Moscow and made him and other generals the scapegoats. Together with von Brauchitsch, Hitler sent 34 generals into retirement ...

A brief note on the Red Army's Command Staff

After the conclusion of the Russian Civil War, the Red Army was reduced to a tenth of its former size. Among the remaining command staff, approximately 30 per cent were former officers of the Imperial Russian army. Many of them occupied the highest posts in the Red Army.

Between the end of the 1920s and the end of the 1930s, 47,000 commanders were discharged from the RKKA [Workers' and Peasants' Red Army]. The majority of them were officers who had received their command ranks during the First World War. Those who by some miracle avoided Stalin's repressions actively participated in the Great Patriotic War: Boris Shaposhnikov, Aleksei Antonov, Aleksandr Vasilevsky, Leonid Govorov, Ivan Petrov, Fedor Tolbukhin and many other excellent commanders. Essentially, all the front commanders - as well as 40 army commanders - began their military service in the First World War.

After the whirlwind of violence that swept through command ranks of the Red Army in 1937-1938 - as well as the Navy - there was a shortage of commanders (as expressed in percentages): 1938 - 34.0; 1939 - 32.0 and 1941 - 19.0. If for example we convert the 19 per cent shortfall in 1941 into real numbers, then this is equivalent to 80,000 commanders.

At the start of the war, the Red Army not only suffered a shortage of commanders. Much of the command staff lacked the necessary professional education. This is apparent from the following figures: only 7 per cent had a higher education; 60 per cent had a middle education; 25 per cent had an accelerated middle education and 8 per cent had no general or professional education at all.

The aforementioned lamentable figures are the result of Stalin's purges - during which more than 40,000 commanders were repressed, most of which belonged to the higher command staff. In addition, more than 6,000 commanders were discharged from the army between 1936 and 1938. Naturally, a massive reshuffling of the command staff resulted in the Red Army. Over nine months of the year 1938, 58,000 commanders were promoted to a higher rank and 40,000 were transferred to a new position.

The year 1939 became special for the Red Army. More than 246,600 commanders, which amounted to 69 per cent of the entire command staff, were occupying new posts. As a result of the unthinkable cadre leapfrogging, at the moment of the war's start more than half of the command staff were in posts that they'd been occupying for less than three months. Many armies, corps and divisions were being led by commanders who'd been in that position for less than six months.

The annual graduation of commanders from the military schools in the pre-war primarily lagged behind the growth of special types of forces. For example, the personnel strength in the armored forces grew 5.9 times between 1938 and 1941 while the graduation of commanders from higher military schools for the armored forces increased by only 1.9 times.

Striving to keep pace with the Red Army's technical re-equipping, between July 1939 and December 1940 47 new military schools were opened in the country. But by the start of the war, not a single one of them had managed to graduate a class. Altogether in 1941, there were 234 military schools of various types in the Soviet Union.

In addition to the opening of new military schools, in the years between 1937 and 1940 a broad network of special courses for the training of platoon commanders was organized in the army itself. Over a short period of time, they generated 448,300 junior lieutenants - often through an accelerated course of training. They only acquired the necessary experience through combat itself.

Trying to overcome the crisis in the number of military cadres - especially in the middle ranks - even in the pre-war years the cadets' period of training was reduced from three to one-and-a-half years, which naturally adversely affected the quality of the training. Very soon after the start of the war, the period of training for the cadets in the military schools was further reduced to just six months. Often, in difficult periods of the war, the schools sent cadets to the front after only three to four months of training. In such cases, they didn't acquire their ranks as junior lieutenants until after the first battles. To the present day, the fate of many of these military schools and their pupils is still not fully known.

Despite the measures taken for preparing the army's command staff, by the start of the first year of the war there was a shortfall of 160,000 officers in the active units. It was urgently necessary to call up reservists. Unfortunately, there is no accurate data on the number of commanders from the reserve that re-joined the army.

From the first days of the war, the Generalissimo - seeing that the events at the front were not developing according to his will - began to search for scapegoats so as to deflect the people's wrath over the major failures of the Red Army away from himself and thereby save his own reputation. In 1941, for the slaughter of that goat, he put six Soviet generals of the Western Front - who had been unable to keep the front from collapsing - to death by execution.

Who knew in June 1941 that the Germans had assembled four times more mobile forces on the western direction for the offensive? The central direction was to be their primary axis of advance. The "Great Strategist" had believed otherwise and it was at his direction that the Red Army had concentrated its armor in the south.

There was a new enormous failure in 1942. Once again it was at the fault of the "Great Commander", who thought Moscow would be the German objective for the summer campaign rather than the oilfields in the Caucuses. As a result of the fresh disasters, the play *The Front* appeared. It established the new scapegoats - many of which were his old cronies from the Civil War days that he had placed in command. Indeed, the drama itself and all of the unimaginable clamor around it were designed to divert the people's attention away from any of the Leader's own mistakes. But still some Muscovites astutely called the play a well-conceived lightning rod.

Many of the Dictator's acts in the war years constitute evidence that the falsehoods, cynicism, blame-shifting and his rapid and cunning identification of scapegoats can all be explained by the confidence in his own impunity. Who might become his next favorite little goat never particularly troubled the Dictator. In his sophisticated and insidious policy, morality, public opinion, station and rank or past merits played no role whatsoever.

It is known that when he considered it useful, Stalin even sold out his main government assistant for the course of decades (Comrade Molotov) for a half a copper - dumping blame on him for the Non-Aggression Pact with Germany.

The following text offers a story about another potential little goat. This event occurred during the battle for Moscow on 21 October 1941. On this day Stalin called the Editor of the *Krasnaia zvezda* newspaper, Daniel Ortenburg, and gave him an instruction to publish the State Committee of Defense's new decree about assigning General of the Army G. K. Zhukov responsibility for the defense of Moscow and making him the commander of the Western Front.

Stalin simultaneously asked that a large photograph of the general be published in the newspaper. This had never been done previously.

What does all this mean? Comrade Stalin had decided to present to the people of the Soviet Union, the enemy and the entire world the man upon whose shoulders rested the ultimate responsibility for the defense of Moscow. However, in case of a possible defeat, public attention would immediately be focused upon Zhukov, which would allow Stalin "honorably" to create a new little goat to take the blame.

Zhukov knew quite well the habits of his Kremlin patron and expected nothing good from him. The Dictator had resorted to similar tricks many times already.

"In war, any notion of humanity is a pernicious delusion - an absurdity."

Carl von Clausewitz,
Prussian general and 19th century military theoretician

5

The Clash of Two Dictators ...

There is an old, wise Ukrainian saying: "When masters struggle, it's the people that suffer." It is plain that the entire war, from beginning to end, was a cruel and uncompromising struggle between two dictators - Stalin and Hitler. However, the many months of fighting for the city of Rzhev had not only a particular strategic significance to them, but also symbolized their ambitious interests.

The First Dictator

No matter how badly the situation at the front was in 1942, Stalin never lost sight of Rzhev. He could not reconcile himself with the thought that the staging area at Rzhev and Viaz'ma remained in German hands.

After the powerful physical and emotional shocks of 1941 - having barely caught his breath and just having restored his former self-confidence - Stalin with every passing day was becoming bolder and more demanding.

This was no longer that bewildered person who in G.K. Zhukov's memoirs, in the critical days of the fighting for the capital, asked the general in an anxious voice: "Are you sure we'll be able to hold Moscow? It hurts me to ask you this ...." This was no longer that hysterical Stalin who in 1941, having phoned I.S. Konev at the front, tried to convince the general - speaking about himself in the third person: "Comrade Stalin is not a traitor; Comrade Stalin is not a betrayer; Comrade Stalin is an honorable person. Comrade Stalin will do everything that is in his strength to turn around the situation that has arisen."[1]

The German defeat in front of Moscow gave him new strength, elated him and inspired hope in his heart that in the end he'd get the best of Hitler - even soon, perhaps. Despite the initial military successes in the winter of 1941-1942, despite his bellicose mood, certain personal feelings nevertheless continued to trouble Stalin. He was totally unable to switch them off; to forget his torments and perhaps even the humiliation that he had experienced in front of the very same Zhukov and Konev when he, to be sure not for long, lost his strong-willed, iron foundation as leader of the world proletariat. For the first time in his life, an unimaginable fear had swept over him when the forward German detachments had closed to within 17-20 kilometers of Moscow.

Stalin sought to forget those dismal days and hard, sleepless nights. He was deeply convinced of the need to seize Rzhev as soon as possible - at any cost - and to drive the Germans a bit further from Moscow! He assumed, and not without reason, that as long as the Rzhev-Viaz'ma staging area remained in enemy hands this essentially would give Hitler a serious chance to have another go at Moscow again. Knowing Stalin's ferocious stubbornness, no one in the *Stavka* dared to try to convince him otherwise or even to cast the slightest shadow of a doubt over the reasonableness of his fears.

In his memoirs, G.K. Zhukov writes:

> … The Supreme Commander assumed that in the summer of 1942 the Germans would be capable of waging major offensive operations simultaneously in two strategic directions - most likely the Moscow and the southern. … Of the two sectors in which Stalin expected strategic offensive operations, he was most concerned about the Moscow sector where the Germans had assembled 70 divisions. He believed that Hitler would not hurl his forces to seize the Caucasus and the south of the country without having taken Moscow first…

The Marshal's memoirs are exceptionally important. They suggest several additional subjects for pondering. During the offensive in the south in 1942, the Führer didn't allow his headquarters to touch the Central Front. Even when von Paulus's Sixth Army wound up encircled in Stalingrad, Hitler's position didn't change.

In his memoirs, General S.M. Shtemenko offers numerous recollections of how the fate of Moscow agitated Stalin and how he forced the General Staff officers constantly to monitor the activities of the German Army Group Center. The Supreme Commander examined any reports from the *Stavka* and the General Staff from the point of view of the threat to Moscow.

During the fighting for Stalingrad and even the Battle of Kursk, Stalin never excluded that in the final analysis the Germans' main goal was Moscow as long as the Rzhev salient existed. When Hitler three times postponed Operation Citadel - his planned 1943 summer offensive at Kursk - each time Stalin became nervous. He was assuming that the German command, possibly, had changed its strategic plans and would be sending its armies once again toward Moscow.

Stalin is not the only one guilty in the incorrect determination of the main strategic axis of the enemy offensive in the summer campaign of 1942; the General Staff also erred. Hitler signed the top secret Directive No. 41 under the code name "Blue" on 4 April 1942. It spelled out the German command's strategic plan for the 1942 summer campaign on the Eastern Front. The main task amounted to the destruction of the enemy west of the Don River and the seizure of the oil fields in the Caucasus - and only then would Stalingrad become an objective.

Soviet intelligence obtained timely information about Hitler's plans even before he signed Directive No. 41 (see Vladimir Lott's article 'Sekretnyi front General'nogo shtaba' ['Secret front of the General Staff'], which is available in Russian on the Internet). However, neither Stalin nor the General Staff managed to make use of this valuable information. As a result, just as it had in 1941 in front of Moscow, the Red Army's position became critical in the area of Stalingrad in 1942. This can be explained primarily by the position of the Generalissimo. As has already been noted Stalin continued to cling to the idea that the *Wehrmacht*'s main objective remained the seizure of Moscow, but this time by outflanking it from the south. Having guessed incorrectly and striving to prevent a complete collapse in the south, the *Stavka* urgently sent enormous reinforcements there. In just two-and-a-half months, between 17 July and 30 September 1942 50 rifle and cavalry divisions and 33 brigades - including 24 tank brigades - were dispatched to the Stalingrad area according to data from M. A. Gareev (as cited in his book about Zhukov).

There was a reason for Stalin's maniacal concern about Moscow. In 2002, the two-volume *Stalingradskaia bitva* [*Battle of Stalingrad*] was published in Moscow on the 60th Anniversary of the battle. It cast light upon many events connected with the situation on the Central Front in 1942 and 1943.

Noteworthy is the transcript of the interrogation of General Field Marshal Wilhelm Keitel on 17 June 1945 (as found on pages 542-546 in the second volume). Under questioning, the Field Marshal stated: "The 1943 plan foresaw in the case of particular success (at the Kursk bulge) the possibility of an advance to the northeast in order to cut the railroads leading to Moscow from the south."

The conviction of some Russian historians that the Germans weakened the center of the front by transferring divisions to the Stalingrad area in 1942 is a concocted one. Another document from this volume: 'From the transcript of the conversation with General Field Marshal von Paulus - 8 June 1948' (found on pages 554-558 of the second volume) convincingly supports this conclusion:

> Question: What explains the fact that the German command in the course of the summer and autumn of 1942 kept large forces on the Moscow axis?
>
> Answer: At this time the German command was expecting a Russian offensive from Moscow, which might come as a counterweight to the German offensive in the south. In connection with this, a commensurate grouping was created on the Moscow axis. The German grouping built up here simultaneously threatened Moscow so the Russian command couldn't maneuver reserves to the south since it might give the impression of the possibility of a German offensive at any moment - though there were no plans for one.

And further:

> It was planned that in 1942 the lines of the Don River and the Caucasus should be occupied and in 1943 an offensive toward Moscow should begin. If the mission to seize Stalingrad had been carried out in 1942, then anyway an offensive toward Moscow would have been possible only in 1943 …

Wishing to demonstrate his "genius of command" (and Stalin fully believed he had this after crushing the German *blitzkrieg* in 1941), he confidently assumed the responsibility of Supreme Commander - just like Hitler had done previously. The dimensions and tragedy of the many months of fighting in front of Rzhev; the tiny successes and the colossal defeats… all of this, as history has shown - in both the large and the small to a significant degree - depended upon the Dictator's will. I don't doubt that if there had not been Stalin's constant and crude interference in the Rzhev battles, possibly the successes would have been greater and less blood would have been spilled.

During one of his meetings with historians after the war, G.K. Zhukov talked about how primitive Stalin's thinking was as a commander:

> … He demanded that we attack! He said: "If we have no results today, then tomorrow there will be - yet you will be pinning down the adversary and at this time the result will be on different sectors." Of course this is childish reasoning! There were a lot of sacrifices, a great expenditure of materiel, but no general strategic result whatsoever…

Historian D. Volkogonov offers another conclusion about the Supreme Commander:

> … Stalin long ago became accustomed to manipulating the lives of millions of people. "They were the masses, and he - the Leader." He was convinced that this is the way it always was in history and how it always would be. Having familiarized myself with hundreds of operational documents, dictated or signed by Stalin over the four years of the war, it seems that I never encountered a single one where he might have set as the task the sparing of human lives - not to throw them into unprepared attacks; to show concern about the preservation of our citizens…

Stalin and Hitler directly oversaw the fighting at Rzhev. When making any decision about combat operations, Stalin (as well as Hitler) as a rule ignored any circumstances at the front: the troops; their condition; their equipping; the availability of supplies; the weather or the difficulty of the terrain. He, like Hitler, took little interest in the adversary, his armaments and tactical and operational possibilities. He never knew the distinctions between one area of combat operations and another

- or the details of their real conditions in which the troops were obliged to carry out his orders.

At the same time Stalin, being the Supreme Commander just like Hitler, constantly meddled in the decision-making of his military commanders right up to and including the Berlin operation. As G.K. Zhukov writes in his *Vospominaniia i razmyshleniia*, "... his professional knowledge was inadequate not only at the start of the war, but also right up to its very end." In the Rzhev epopee, this interference acquired an inconceivable and oppressive, illogical and often petty character. Taking the final decision about operations, Stalin established precise deadlines for their preparation and execution. Often this led to overriding the military commanders. Without directions from the Generalissimo - which were often done in the name of the *Stavka*, but with his signature - no front commanders, army commanders or often even division commanders could show any sort of independence in any operation.

In effect, commanders were deprived of operational initiative – the ability to act in correspondence with local circumstances. The British military historian Kenneth Macksey wrote: "The lack of initiative of officers and generals under the 'eye of the State' had a literally catastrophic influence on the combat qualities of Soviet troops in offensive operations." The opinion of the Germans is interesting. They believed for example that having fallen into encirclement, Soviet commanders and soldiers operated superbly if they had lost communications with the High Command. As soon as communications were re-established, they could immediately detect a notable loss of initiative.

Often, that which Stalin would declare in his public addresses, *Stavka* directives and in orders, letters and telegrams diverged from reality. Naturally, this placed the commanders in an awkward position and gave rise to bewilderment, aggravation, a sense of insult and bitter disillusionment among the soldiers. In such cases, normally the commissars sought to make adjustments to the unexpected situations. For example, so many times throughout 1942 and 1943 we heard the Supreme Commander promise to destroy the foe and to end the war, but it, the damned thing, dragged on. In 1942 Stalin asserted that the German army was taking its last breath, yet the Red Army in the same year of 1942 suffered cruel defeats at the hands of this "expiring" foe at Rzhev; lost the Crimea; fell into great misfortune near Khar'kov; yielded Voronezh and Rostov-on-Don and allowed the Germans to conquer enormous expanses of territory in the south.

At Rzhev, a strong opponent under the leadership of the talented General Walter Model - who was determined to hold the salient - opposed the Soviet forces. After the winter retreat from Moscow, the Ninth Army organized a powerful defense on the lines it occupied around the three-sided salient. It fought bitterly for each clump of soil as if it was its native land. Often, the Soviet frontline men after a battle would ask each other: "For the sake of what are the Fritzes fighting so stubbornly and bravely?"

A short aside: At Rzhev the commanders and we, the soldiers, learned to attack while the Germans gained the combat experience of an active, positional defense.

Certain historians and writers, for example V.V. Beshanov, are indignant at the Soviet generals' declaration that in 1942 they were still learning how to fight. He even published a book - entitling it: *God 1942 – Uchebnyi* [*1942 – The Training Year*] (published in Minsk by the Kharvest Press in 2002).

I'll linger for a moment on several of the author's arguments. Here is what Beshanov writes:

> ... generals everywhere - especially beaten ones - often complain about the command, mistakes of subordinates, the lack of strength, or about the unfavorable weather conditions. Soviet marshals also widely use these arguments. However, in addition they conceived a truly unique justification for their failures: it turns out that in 1942 they still didn't know how to fight. All of them - leaders of fronts, commanders of armies, chiefs of staff - with a childlike frankness report that they were still only studying, familiarizing themselves with the enemy and acquiring experience...

I think that the author in his impassioned anger is mistaken by failing to consider several serious circumstances that should not be waved aside. Beshanov doesn't like the generals' statements. I don't either. However, I understand them while he doesn't even want to try to understand them. For example, is it really possible to forget the massive repressions, organized by Stalin in the pre-war years, when all the higher cadres of the Red Army were executed? The bloody killing of them continued both in 1941 and in 1942 .... Finally, in 1941 after 22 June practically the entire regular army perished - including many generals and lower-ranking commanders. In 1942, it was necessary to select not the best of the best, but the best of the worst. It should be considered also that the Red Army joined battle with the strongest army in the world, which was equipped with up-to-date weapons; had experienced generals; abundant combat experience; a superior organization of command, control and communications and professional soldiers.

What sort of childlike naiveté can there be here?

Speaking about how they were learning to fight, the commanders aren't dissembling. They'd been entrusted with the command of million-man armies, thousands of guns, new rocket equipment and hundreds of tanks and airplanes. They were learning to lead large masses of troops. It was necessary to train them, arm them, timely bring them into battle and coordinate different types of forces. However, to command troops without contemporary means of communication; without professionally-trained regiment, battalion and company commanders and expertly trained soldiers - under the "Sovereign's eye" .... Here our generals proved to be not very capable students. From this follows the endless defeats at Rzhev, the enormous losses and the constant fear of the wrath of High Command for each failure - and all this despite a huge superiority in numbers of men and equipment. Yes! They were learning to fight, but the cost of this study for everyone - from the Supreme Commander down to the platoon commander - proved to be inconceivably heavy. Who can calculate what it cost?

However, no matter how astonishing, the frontline soldiers - godlessly cursing the commanders up and down for their ignorance and calling everything that happened on the battlefields the "Rzhev Academy" - still believed when going into battle that their commanders eventually would learn to fight no worse than the Germans. "May it be even on our bones …" World history is full of examples when the vanquished learned from the victors. Peter the Great didn't consider it shameful for himself to learn from the strongest army in the world at that time, the Swedish army of Charles XII. German generals prior to the war in the East assiduously studied the tragic experience of the campaign of Napoleon's *Grand Armée* in Russia.

Stalin kept close tabs on his generals and clearly saw their blunders. Repeatedly, rising into a fury, he would exclaim: "Just when will they learn to fight?!" At the same time he stubbornly forced them to achieve success "at any cost". He believed that a time would come when they would learn to win and begin to fight not with numbers, but with skill. Under the Generalissimo's harsh tutelage, they strove to defeat the foe not with skill, but with their massive superiority in numbers and preponderance in combat equipment. Generals became so accustomed to simple methods of command over their obedient soldiers that many of them made no effort to learn new methods before the war's conclusion.

Dmitrii Volkogonov cites a noteworthy conversation between Stalin and A.I. Antonov, the Chief of the General Staff's Operations Department. Here is a small fragment from it:

> … "Comrade Antonov," asked the Supreme Commander, "have you ever pondered why many of our offensive operations in 1942 weren't completed? Look, the Rzhev-Viaz'ma Operation of two fronts… [Stalin proceeds to list other "uncompleted" operations] How do you explain these failures?"
>
> "We operated routinely and unimaginatively," replied Antonov. "We hadn't learned to break through a defense simultaneously on several sectors and made poor use of the tank formations for developing the success … "
>
> Stalin interrupted Antonov and concluded: "The main thing consists in the fact that having learned to defend, we didn't know then - and even now not much better - how to attack well. … Putting it briefly, we still hadn't learned to fight."[2] …

Incidentally, the phrase "uncompleted operation" instead of "failure" or "defeat" belongs to Stalin. The generals took such a fancy to it that in their reports up the ladder, they introduced it into constant circulation with an easy conscience.

During the prolonged fighting for Rzhev, and on other fronts as well, the *Stavka* worked out so-called "directives" and sent them to the fronts. Their contents determined the strategic and operational-tactical assignments of each operation and designated the deadlines for its preparation and its start date. Over the years of the war the *Stavka* forwarded several thousand such directives. A collected volume of them has been published in Moscow, which allows us to review this colossal work of the *Stavka* and the General Staff. I want to present eight directives, issued between January 1942 and February 1943. They are all associated with Rzhev …

The *Stavka* Directive from 7 January 1942

Signed by Stalin, it directed the Kalinin Front:

> … to implement an offensive west of Rzhev in the general direction of Sychevka with two armies consisting of 14-15 rifle divisions and the 11th Cavalry Corps. Destroy the German forces and together with the Western Front, encircle and destroy the enemy's Rzhev-Gzhatsk-Viaz'ma grouping…

Fulfillment of the 7 January 1942 Directive

The Kalinin Front on 8 January 1942 launched the so-called Rzhev-Viaz'ma Operation. It continued until approximately 20 April 1942. In the course of 120 days of combat, three armies (the 22nd, 29th and 39th) as well as the 11th Cavalry Corps wound up encircled. Here's how A.M. Vasilevsky, the Chief of the Red Army General Staff, describes this operation: "… several times Soviet corps and entire armies ruptured the German defenses and passed into the enemy rear. But behind them the passage closed again - as a result of which those who penetrated into the enemy rear fell into encirclement."

The isolated commanders and soldiers fought courageously. In July 1942 the German radio transmitted an announcement: "West of Rzhev, a 100,000-strong enemy grouping was encircled and smashed." The Germans conducted the conclusive operation to wipe out the remaining Soviet pockets under the codename "Seydlitz" between 2 and 12 June 1942. The Soviet press didn't refute the German announcement, but also didn't mention it. This tragedy was later ignored by Soviet historians, while the commanders and generals in their memoirs said nothing intelligible about it. When the Stalingrad tragedy occurred to the German Sixth Army and 105,000 of von Paulus's generals, officers and soldiers surrendered, in Germany a three-day period of mourning was declared. Bells rang for them in all the churches.

Gradually, individual episodes of the annihilation of a 100,000-strong Soviet grouping west of Rzhev became known. A few veterans who survived the ordeal shared some information about it. The most important thing which the "de-classification" of the Rzhev-Viaz'ma Operation was making clear was the active role played in it by the Generalissimo. I'll present one case, but there are many more. In the middle of February 1942 the headquarters of the encircled 29th Army received a query from Stalin: "What do you need to hold out for 48 more hours?" The commander of the 29th Army, V.I. Shevtsov, replied that with air support they could hold out for two more days. The 29th Army's Military Council circulated a directive among the troops:

> … Comrade Stalin knows about our situation. I.V. Stalin asked: "Can we hold on?" They will drop rations and ammunition from transport aircraft. As you see, the Supreme Commander of the Red Army - Comrade Stalin himself - considers the area we are defending to be very important and is taking measures to give assistance to us…

The soldiers, inspired by the promise of Stalin's speedy assistance, fought to the limits of human endurance against the Germans. However, Stalin, much less the front commanders, couldn't help the encircled men. Even the air bridge, organized by the *Stavka*, never got underway. As one of the men who managed to make his way out of the encirclement recalls: "It was absolute hell." For example, he related how on one of these days 15 German bombers bombed the village of Brekhovo, where badly wounded men were lying in all the cottages and buildings. After just 15 minutes, only ashes remained of the village and men.

Airplanes were sent to evacuate unit banners out of the pocket. Units that managed to break out of the encirclement brought out 1,000 wounded men with them. Many senior commanders and commissars committed suicide. Certain historians condemn the decision of the *Stavka* and G.K. Zhukov to leave three armies and a cavalry corps in the German rear without adequate support and regard the decision an example of adventurism. Colonel M.M. Efremov, the son of the 33rd Army commander Mikhail Grigor'evich Efremov, who shot himself in encirclement, offers convincing documentation regarding this.

Incidentally, was it possible at all back then in January-February 1942, to speak of any serious support? The attacking troops didn't have enough arms and ammunition. The Western Front's entire air force numbered less than 100 aircraft. In those days, as the last remnants of Soviet soldiers were pouring out their blood and perishing in the Chertolino woods west of Rzhev, the *Sovinformburo* reported: "On the Western Front, fighting of local significance is going on ..."

Curiously, why did the Rzhev-Viaz'ma Operation - the only one of the four conducted around Rzhev - wind up in the historiography of the war as a strategic operation?

The *Stavka* Directive from 11 January 1942

Soon after the Rzhev-Viaz'ma Operation began, I.S. Konev received a directive from the *Stavka*. It related:

> … The commander of the Kalinin Front in the course of 11 January and no later than 12 January in any case is to seize Rzhev.

> The *Stavka* recommends for this goal to use the available artillery, mortar and aviation forces in the given region and to smash all of Rzhev - not sparing the city of serious devastation. Confirm receipt and report upon the fulfillment. I.V. Stalin...

Fulfillment of the Directive

Rzhev was not taken - not on 11 January or 12 January. However, pursuant to the order of the Supreme Commander, Soviet artillery and aircraft demolished the city, which the Germans hadn't done after they had captured the city. One can imagine the psychological condition of the Rzhev citizens as bombs and shells from the Soviet side rained down on their heads.

In his memoirs *Vospominaniia i razmyshleniia*, G.K. Zhukov gives the following explanation of the causes why the Rzhev-Viaz'ma Operation of the Western and Kalinin Fronts in 1942 "wasn't completed": "Viewing the events of 1942 critically, I can say now that we misjudged the situation in the Viaz'ma area. We had overrated the potential of our troops and underrated the enemy. He proved to be a harder nut to crack than we believed ..."[3] Is it possible to agree with such an explanation?

The *Stavka* Directive from 20 March 1942

"The *Stavka* demands to continue the fulfillment of the previously assigned tasks. Liberate Rzhev no later than 5 April..."

The Directive's fulfillment

In those difficult spring days, G.K. Zhukov and I.S. Konev requested the *Stavka* to halt the fruitless and senseless self-destruction of the armies. Stalin didn't even want to hear about a cancellation of the directive. The Supreme Commander demanded: "Attack more energetically!" The Dictator knew what he was doing. He was training the generals to fight "at any cost" and to be indifferent to the casualty figures. In exchange for the obedience that they demonstrated, he pardoned their failures and praised their bloody successes. The Soviet press colorfully described the victories and gushed over the growing military skill of the Red Army. Stalin nurtured hard, strong attitudes among his generals - freeing them from any moral qualms - and trained them like children to be personally devoted to him and to believe in his infallibility. They would learn that if they valued his trust in them and followed his orders unquestioningly, they would become marshals. "If they didn't pass 'Stalin's school' - the Leader loved to speak about himself in the third person - "let them take the blame. Then remove them! No one is irreplaceable!"

"It is necessary for us," wrote the Supreme Commander, addressing Zhukov and Konev, "at the beginning of summer to destroy the Rzhev-Viaz'ma grouping where the German forces are holding a major staging area and have large forces ..." This message became a most important order for the commanders in the Western and Reserve Fronts. The armies began to prepare for summer battles.

The *Stavka* Directive from 16 July 1942 (the First Rzhev-Sychevka Operation)

This Directive ordered: "...at any cost, take Rzhev no later than 1-2 August 1942. Four armies, as well as two air armies, should be committed to the offensive..."

Stalin demanded: "Clear the enemy from the territory to the north of the Volga River in the area of Rzhev - as well as the territory to the east of the Vazuza River in the Zubtsov, Karamazino and Pogoreloe Gorodishche area. Seize the cities Rzhev and Zubtsov, reach and strongly dig-in on the Volga and Vazuza Rivers..."

Fulfillment of the Directive

On 30 July 1942 350,000 soldiers and officers of the Kalinin and Western Fronts went on the offensive. By the end of the offensive, more than 1 million men had been thrown into the fighting. According to the official version, the offensive continued until 23 August - that is, for 53 days. Really, it dragged on until the beginning of October. For example, the 215th Rifle Division, in which I served, entered the battle between 24 and 26 August. At the cost of colossal losses over only two months of fighting (August-September), in which six armies participated, more than 20 districts of the city of Rzhev were seized - as well as the towns of Zubtsov, Pogoreloe Gorodishche and more than 100 villages. The Germans were driven from the left bank of the Volga River. However, Rzhev and Sychevka still remained in enemy hands. Over the course of the offensive, 158,819 men were lost.

Here's how G.K. Zhukov evaluates the summer offensive in his memoirs: "According to the *Stavka*'s plan, the westward thrust our forces undertook in the summer and autumn of 1942 against the Nazi Army Group Center was to disorient the enemy; to make the German command think that it was precisely at this point, and nowhere else, that we were preparing for a major winter campaign."[4] The undertaken operation did nothing to confuse the German Ninth Army. I'll speak about the winter operation, which actually took place, a bit later.

Here's "limited offensive operations" for you! More than a million Red Army soldiers and officers took part in them. In the area of Pogoreloe Gorodishche, between 7 and 10 August, a tank engagement occurred that drew in more than 1,500 tanks from both sides - more armored vehicles that took part in the famous tank battle at Prokhorovka during the Battle of Kursk. As a result of the summer offensive, our forces in several locations pierced the enemy's defenses. Only 6 kilometers remained to reach Rzhev! Stalin exulted! What's 6 kilometers? The exuberance of the Supreme Commander quickly evaporated. It would take more than seven more months of bloody battles to overcome these 6 kilometers.

On 14 July 1942 the *Sovinformburo* announced: "The Germans are losing thousands and thousands of men daily on the Soviet-German Front. And this, regardless of the temporary successes of the German forces, is gradually eroding the Nazi war machine and preparing the basis for its defeat in this war." Many years later I was told that supposedly it was Stalin who dictated the text of this announcement. It was supposed to repudiate Berlin's victorious announcement about the final destruction of the remnants of encircled Soviet troops west of Rzhev. The *Sovetskaia voennaia entsiklopediia* [*Soviet Military Encyclopedia*], which came out in 1960 (18 years later), characterized the past operation in a completely different light - now in the context of the events in the south:

> ... The main goal of the operation (Rzhev-Sychevka, 30 July to 23 August 1942) consisted in pinning down the enemy strength on the Western direction; deprive him of the possibility of transferring divisions from Army Group Center (commanded by General Field Marshal H. von Kluge) to the south - where the German Nazi forces had launched their main attack in the summer campaign of 1942 - and to compel the regrouping of part of their strategic reserves to the central sector of the front...

In this fashion, the 1942 First Rzhev-Sychevka Operation effectively lost any independent significance. Has the official assessment of the summer operation, which has receded into the background in the historiography of the Great Patriotic War since the Encyclopedia came out, changed at all? Unfortunately, no.

No matter how the history of the war has been retouched in the postwar period, since the summer of 1942 life has connected us, the soldiers who fought near Rzhev, with Stalingrad. Commanders and commissars were constantly calling upon us: "Strike the enemy harder! That's how we will better help Stalingrad - where the fate of the country is being decided." Soon the name of the Hero-City became a symbol of courage and tenacity. The Germans called Rzhev the "Stalingrad of the North", while the commanders directing the battle called us "Stalingraders".

S. A. Gerasimova, a research scholar on the staff of the Tver' State Consolidated Museum, has conducted research on the Rzhev-Sychevka Operation.[5] Relying upon documents, she has proven that the official date given for the end of the operation - 23 August 1942 - as given by the *Soviet Military Encyclopedia* and other sources does not correspond to reality. German scholars place the conclusion of the Soviet summer operation to seize Rzhev as the middle of October.[6]

Only on the 58th day after the launching of the operation did there appear the first official *Sovinformburo* report about how it was going - in a semi-truthful fashion: "Fifteen days ago, the troops of the Western and Kalinin Fronts on the Rzhev and Gzhatsk-Viaz'ma directions went on the offensive with part of their forces ..." In her study, S.A. Gerasimova presents evidence of the enormous casualties - using the example of the 30th Army, to which the 215th Rifle Division belonged. During the summer fighting for Rzhev, the 215th Rifle Division - which started the battle with 14,000 soldiers and officers - lost 7-8,000 primarily young, blossoming lives. Among them perished many of my fellow cadets of the Tiumen' Combat-infantry School.[7]

The *Stavka* Directive from 29 August 1942

This Directive stated:

> In the aims of the most rapid destruction of the enemy's Rzhev grouping, the seizure of the city of Rzhev and to facilitate control of the troops, the 29th Army is made subordinate to the Kalinin Front's 30th Army.

Fulfillment of the Directive

Reading the combat dispatches of the 30th Army's command from the end of August through September, approximately one and the same phrase is encountered over and over again: "The 30th Army is continuing to develop the success in seizing Rzhev." However, it didn't take possession of Rzhev in either August or September.

The *Stavka* Directive from 10 October 1942

This Directive established a concrete task:

> Encircle and destroy the German Ninth Army. Seize Rzhev and the cities Sychevka, Belyi and Velikie Luki.

The offensive was designated to begin on 23 October… In order to carry out the assigned tasks, the *Stavka* allotted to the two fronts (the Kalinin and Western): 1.89 million soldiers and commanders, 24,000 guns and mortars, 3,300 tanks and 1,100 aircraft. Enormous strength! Army Group Center at that time numbered 72 divisions: 1,680,000 soldiers and officers and 3,500 tanks.

Fulfillment of the Directive

The start date for the offensive was postponed several times either due to the fact that preparations hadn't been completed or because of poor weather conditions. The Second Rzhev-Sychevka Operation began on 25 November 1942 under the codename "Mars" and concluded on 20 December. The directive was not carried out. Of the cities designated in it only Velikie Liuki was taken - and at that only in January 1943.

In the opinion of the American historian David Glantz, this was Marshal Zhukov's greatest defeat.[8] The total losses of the Kalinin and Western Fronts amounted to 500,000 men and 800 tanks (on 26 August 1942 G.K. Zhukov had been appointed Deputy Supreme Commander. He handed over his Western Front to I.S. Konev. Lieutenant General M.A. Purkaev took command of the Kalinin Front).

The *Stavka* Directive from 8 December 1942

This Directive specified:

> The Kalinin and Western Fronts are to destroy the German grouping in the Rzhev-Sychevka-Olenino area by 1 January 1943.

The Directive was signed by both I.V. Stalin and G.K. Zhukov.

Fulfillment of the Directive

The Directive was not carried out. Rzhev and Sychevka were not taken.

The *Stavka* Directive from 6 February 1943

> To the commanders of the Western Front, V.D. Sokolovsky, and the Kalinin Front, M.A. Purkaev: on conducting a new Rzhev-Viaz'ma offensive operation. The main forces of Army Group Center should be encircled and destroyed and seize Rzhev. Commit four armies of the Kalinin Front and eight armies of the Western Front to the offensive. It is ordered by 1 March - no later - to take Rzhev.

Fulfillment of the Directive

Army Group Center in fact could not be destroyed. At 1800 hours 2 March 1943 the Germans voluntarily abandoned the city of Rzhev. The main forces of the withdrawing Ninth Army managed to gain separation from the attackers.

In March 1943, only after the Germans abandoned their defensive positions, Soviet forces entered Gzhatsk (5 March), Sychevka (8 March) and Viaz'ma (12 March). Different terminology was present in the *Sovinformburo* announcements: not "entered", but "seized", "drove out", etc.

Incidentally, the reader might be interested to know how the Germans themselves called their withdrawal from Rzhev. Here is what Major General Horst Grossman, commander of the German 6th Infantry Division, said in his book:

> In the report of the Ninth Army about the abandonment of Rzhev, there was the following: 'On the evening of 2 March 1943 the last German rearguards, under no enemy pressure, left the already long abandoned city...'[9]

In contrast with this, a Russian military report from 3 March 1943 stated: "Several days ago our forces began a decisive offensive toward Rzhev. Today, after prolonged fighting, they took the city."

The entire battle for Rzhev is evidence of Stalin's cruelty and lack of military talent. His military chiefs were unlucky at the Rzhev salient: G.K. Zhukov, I.S. Konev and D.D. Leliushenko. Factually speaking, right until the very end they failed to carry out a single one of the *Stavka* directives. Often, certain historians and writers - striving to whitewash the commanders' failures - attribute their defeats to a shortage of personnel and equipment; point to the weather conditions and so on. All these are fairy tales. G.K. Zhukov asserts in his memoirs - referring to the summer Rzhev-Sychevka Operation - that if he had at his disposal just one or two more armies he might not have only defeated the enemy in the Rzhev area, but the entire German Rzhev-Viaz'ma grouping.[10] Why were one or two more armies necessary to him when he already had at his disposal nearly 1 million troops?

The armies of Zhukov and Konev had an enormous superiority in numbers of both troops and equipment over the enemy. The Germans assert that the Russians in the summer of 1942 had a two or three-fold superiority in numbers, but on designated breakthrough sectors this advantage grew to six or eight times the German numbers. According to the data of N. Belov and T. Mikhailov, the superiority of the 30th Army over the enemy - for example, in the summer fighting of 1942 - could be placed at 10 to 20 times the number of troops and 20 to 30 times the amount of armor.[11]

The Second Dictator

Beginning the discussion of the "Second Dictator", Hitler, first of all I'll acquaint the reader with a document that became known quite recently. It casts more light on this repulsive personality.

What sort of man was Adolf Hitler? Who was this Nazi beast who carried away during the Second World War the lives of 50 million people? Prior to leaving the White House, President Bill Clinton declassified previously secret documents, which provide a psychological portrait of the war criminal Adolf Hitler. They carry the code number 0695930/18.05.2000 and became a document of world history. These completely secret papers of the CIA number 68 pages. The date 3 December 1942 is stamped upon them. The "Documents about Hitler", perhaps, are not a sensation for historians, but they contain a psychological profile of the dictator that is of general interest. Professor Guido Knopp offers comments, supplements and where necessary makes corrections to the text.

After 1945 of course, there could not have been any talk about Hitler's "excellent physical endurance". Hitler's physical condition prior to the years 1939-1940 was relatively stable - therefore it is unsurprising that this time coincided with the period of his successes. However, as a purely subjective hypochondriac, Hitler was firmly convinced that he would die at an early age. He was afraid that his time was slipping away. In 1939 on the occasion of his 50th birthday, he said: "It was better for me to begin the war at 50 rather than 55 or 60." On another occasion he expressed the opinion that subsequent generations would not have been able to do this. Only he could start a war. He connected the fate of entire peoples with his apprehensions about his own life. In the summer of 1939, he was most of all troubled by the possibility that "at the last moment some sort of swine would offer him a compromise proposal." His closest comrade-in-arms Hermann Göring turned out to be one of these swine when he timidly admonished: "It is time to stop this *va banque*." To this Hitler replied: "It is the only call I ever make."[12]

It is indicative that starting in 1942, the condition of his health greatly deteriorated. Already in the summer of 1941, he had been diagnosed with progressive arteriosclerosis. During the war, his personal doctor Theodor Morell prescribed a total of 90 different medications for Hitler - starting with strong sedatives and ending with amphetamines - in order to counter his chronic fatigue. Even the 28 different pills that he took each day could not keep in check the physical collapse of his organism. Moreover, he took "Dr. Kester's pills" against flatulence in connection with his complaints about his digestive tract, as well as other medicines which contained strychnine and opiates.

This didn't influence Hitler's dreams about living space and extermination of the Jews - they were from the very beginning a product of the obsessive ideas of a madman who too many followed for too long and too obediently.

Without the Führer's authorization not a single army, single division, single regiment, single battalion, single company or single soldier had the right to abandon an occupied position. "The German soldier has no right to retreat from wherever his foot has stepped!" Hitler hammered this iron rule into his generals and soldiers. Hitler, trying to prevent the full collapse of the Ninth Army as it was retreating from Moscow, and recalling the dramatic story of Napoleon's *Grand Armée* had issued an order at the beginning of 1942: "The Ninth Army takes not a single step back! Hold the line of defense reached on 3 January 1942!" In the summer of 1942, the soldiers of the Ninth Army had to give a special oath not to abandon their defensive positions. The Führer repeatedly, as the commander-in-chief of the *Wehrmacht*, demanded that Rzhev be held at any cost. Often he called this city, as well as Smolensk, the "Eastern Gates" to Moscow.

Comparing the deeds of the two dictators during the war, it isn't difficult to note that their actions were based on certain identical behavioral stimuli: an underestimation of each other and a constant willingness to play *va banque*; of course, at the expense of their soldiers. However, there also existed a serious difference between them. Stalin came to understand better than Hitler about how far he should go and where it wasn't worth taking a risk. To be sure, the Generalissimo still occasionally had lapses.

Hitler highly regarded the *Wehrmacht* and often repeated with pride: "With my soldiers, I can do anything I want." At the same time the "Second Dictator", like Stalin himself, was always indifferent to frontline sacrifices. He strove to make his generals conduct themselves just as pitilessly as he did. General Guderian told an interesting story on this subject. When he attempted to move Hitler to pity over the heavy casualties in his Panzer Group, he heard from the Führer in response: "Do you think, general, that it was easier for Frederick the Great's grenadiers to die?" The death of the Sixth Army is a striking example of Hitler's complete indifference to his soldiers and officers - as if he would never have to acknowledge his guilt before them.

Field Marshal Erich von Manstein, who knew Hitler well, relates:

> ... although Hitler was always harping on his "soldierly" outlook and loved to recall that he had acquired his military experience as a front-line soldier, his character had as little in common with the thoughts

> and emotions of soldiers as had his party with the Prussian virtues which it was so fond of invoking ... I still never had the feeling that his heart belonged to the fighting troops. Losses, as far as he was concerned, were merely figures which reduced fighting power. They are unlikely to have seriously disturbed him as a human being...[13]

The losses of the German army in the fighting for Rzhev (1942-1943), as declared in Germany, amounted to somewhere between 300,000 to 450,000 men; Russian casualties according to the same source numbered around 1 million.[14]

Hitler knew that the *Werhmacht* had limited human resources - much fewer than Stalin had. However, neither Hitler or the prognosticators of his General Staff, when starting the war in the East, had any full notion of how large the Russian reserves were - and most importantly, that Stalin would be able to place approximately twice as many men under arms than could Germany. This was one of the serious miscalculations of the German command in the war with Russia. Hitler didn't know either that from the beginning of the war in many areas of the Soviet Union threatened by German occupation, the youth still under draft age were evacuated to the east as a future reserve of the army.

The command of Army Group Center expended during the summer (1942) and winter (1943) campaigns its main combat strength - especially by the end of Operation Mars. After the destruction of von Paulus's Sixth Army at Stalingrad, the German command finally convinced Hitler of the need to abandon the Rzhev-Viaz'ma salient. On 3 February 1943 Hitler finally authorized the staged withdrawal of the Ninth Army and units of the Fourth Panzer Army from Rzhev to a line that defended Smolensk. After careful preparations, in March 1943 Model withdrew 20 divisions out from under the nose of 10 Soviet armies to a previously prepared new line of defense.

Military historians still continue to debate the numbers of Red Army soldiers and officers who fell in battle at Rzhev and Viaz'ma. The total losses in only the four operations that I have discussed amounted to a gigantic figure - 1,324,823 soldiers and officers (according to official Soviet/Russian data). This figure is greater than the casualties sustained separately in the battles of Moscow, Leningrad, Stalingrad, Kursk and Berlin.[15]

An even more terrible casualty figure was divulged from the podium at an academic research conference in 1999 that was dedicated to the Battle of Rzhev - around 2 million. Marshal V.G. Kulikov (who as a captain fought near Rzhev as a tanker) has placed the number of killed, wounded and missing in action as 2.5 million ....[16] Whether or not these estimates are close to the real figures, they are sufficiently horrifying. In the fraternal graves of 1942 on Rzhev land lie the remains of troops from more than 140 rifle divisions, 50 separate rifle brigades and 50 tank brigades.

Give a thought to how many people were killed at Rzhev, Viaz'ma, Sychevka, Belyi, Polunino and Bel'kovo! "We've never anywhere seen a greater number of such, and never will!" That's what veterans who by some miracle survived this inhumane slaughter, in which more than 3 million men and women participated, have subsequently said when recalling the fighting around the Rzhev-Viaz'ma salient.

Combat on the Rzhev and Viaz'ma lines lasted for 502 days. In the opinion of certain Russian and Western historians, this battle was the most savage and bloody of the war. Each patch of native soil won back from the enemy here cost approximately 10,000 human lives. Such enormous losses, obviously, have never been known before in any other single battle in the history of mankind!

This great tragedy consisted not only of the unparalleled sacrifices, but also the fact that the offensive fighting brought no success. The failures led to the veil of silence and distortions in official historiography about the Rzhev tragedy. Death and the inconceivable human suffering were not rewarded with the joy of combat successes, but rather gave rise to bitter despair and an unbearable grievance among those who survived. Official historiography is silent about the psychological wounds.

That's the way the bloody struggle between two dictators over the Rzhev-Viaz'ma staging area concluded - about which the writer Vasilii Kozhanuk accurately wrote:

> ... The mutually consuming Rzhev battle, like a fight between two buffaloes, confirmed both the wretchedness of both the Berlin and Kremlin leaders and revealed their essences as geniuses of destruction. One from afar listened with delight to an explosion in Rzhev;[17] the other, a half-year after the end of the battle, wished to see the cratered landscape of the very same Rzhev and to feel an enthralling tingle from the sight of the destructive power of his beloved God of War - the artillery. It is not coincidental therefore, that with an escort of many thousands, he [Stalin] visited the ruins of Rzhev on 5 August 1943...

It cannot be better said! (Well, except for the fact that Stalin didn't actually visit Rzhev; he surveyed it from the higher left bank of the Volga River through binoculars.)

All the same, Stalin believed that even after the German retreat from Rzhev, Viaz'ma and Gzhatsk, a mortal threat to Moscow remained. On Russian land, which the German soldier possessed, there existed one more salient: the Orel-Kursk bulge. A new battle lay ahead!

A short postscript - based on material from the Russian website '*Pobeda-60*' ['*Victory-60*']

It was called "the key to Moscow" and "the key to Berlin". The soldiers curtly and harshly called it "the Rzhev meat grinder"; 1.3 million casualties on one side, 500,000 on the other. So far there is still no accurate count of the dead at Rzhev. Of the 25,000 residents of the city before the war, only 250 remained in it after the battle.

Entire armies were consumed in the battle for the Rzhev salient. From the numbers involved and the length of the fighting, there was no other such massive and bloody operation in the entire history of the Great Patriotic War. So far, historians still cannot establish an accurate number of the fallen.

Before the 60th Victory Anniversary, a diorama entitled: *'The fighting for Rzhev, 24 September 1942'* was unveiled in Rzhev. Frequently, the still-surviving veterans of those events are invited to conduct tours to the battlefield and diorama. You can overhear fragments of their presentations. A former private who survived the fighting by some miracle: "It was the 24 September 1942. Soviet troops went on the attack and captured several city districts, but the operation was doomed to failure." Another veteran recalls: "Our commanders were shouting: 'Only forward!' We were cannon fodder - attacking without cover. It was extremely painful. After all, your friends are getting killed around you, yet I could do nothing to help them."

During the Soviet era, the city of Rzhev never became a Hero-City - an honorific title bestowed upon other cities like Smolensk, Leningrad, Stalingrad and Moscow. However, historical justice has partially been served. In 2007, the city of Rzhev was awarded the title "City of Military Honor".

"In war, truth is the first casualty."

Arthur Ponsonby

6

Stalin's Myths and the soldiers' telegraph

The origin of the soldiers' telegraph

Early on the morning of 30 July 1942 the thunder of artillery shook the air. We could hear the rumble of the barrage for a long time - even though our division was in the second echelon. Just consider, at the nearest we were about 30 kilometers behind the frontlines. On that day, none of us knew what this meant. Toward evening, good news reached us: the front had gone over to a grand offensive. Several days after the Kalinin Front, its neighbor, the Western Front, moved out on the attack.

Optimism in those days gripped all of us - from the division commander down to the last soldier. You could hear triumphant notes in the words of the commanders and commissars. "This time Rzhev will be taken!" the frontline press pealed. But soon, sad rumors reached us: the battle had turned into a cruel defeat and rivers of blood. Discussions immediately started up among the soldiers: "It is clear that they'll soon call for us too, since they haven't done so yet."

The frontline press and the command - the commanders and commissars - were silent, as if nothing had happened anywhere. The soldiers exchanged whispers: "How can it be, it isn't understandable, when they hurled so many men and so much equipment against the enemy? The dead blanketed the ground, but they took about 30 villages - or more accurately former villages - and only advanced several kilometers. So nothing was accomplished." The sad news filled the soldiers' hearts with a burning pain.

How did the truth in such a succinct form become known to us about the latest battle for Rzhev? The so-called "soldiers' telegraph" helped this happen. It isn't known when this first appeared at the front. It goes without saying that it arose not in response to an order from the command. In May 1942, when I reached the Kalinin Front, it was already in existence (in his memoirs, N.S. Khrushchev mentions "the soldiers' telegraph" and "by the soldiers' radio").

In the Red Army, the "soldiers' telegraph" did a yeoman's job over the entire Patriotic War. Who it really was who had the surprising idea of circulating current news by mouth and who it was that implemented it - the frontline men at the time gave little thought to this; a war was going on.

Now 60 years after the end of the war, thinking about the past, we can't pass over such an unusual phenomenon. How in fact the "soldiers' telegraph" did arise, or more accurately, why it arose and how it became such an irreplaceable source of information for the soldier against the command's will, I will now relate.

Throughout the entire war, especially in the first two years, a soldier hardly had any idea about what was going on outside the trenches or what was waiting for him the next day: bad, good or whatever. It wasn't for him to know. It was just like the English poet W.H. Auden aptly wrote: "The rabbit is happy in the morning because it isn't given to it to know what the hunter was thinking when he awoke."

It was often the case that a soldier had no interest in the news. Then he would say: "Bugger it all!" This would happen, for example, during an offensive or a retreat; a difficult march of many kilometers or when in encirclement; while hospitalized and so forth. All the same, for whatever reason it was impossible to get by at the front without news. Without any newspapers, the soldiers fed upon rumors and it was boring and difficult to get by without newspapers. There were no radios. Primarily, we read newspapers - or newspapers were read to us: primarily the central newspapers *Pravda* and *Krasnaia zvezda* or the frontline press. Each army, just as did each division, had its own newspaper.

The journalist and propagandist Il'ia Ehrenburg wrote: "In days of war, a newspaper is like air itself. People open a newspaper before they open a letter from a close friend; a newspaper first and only then a letter addressed to you personally. Because your fate depends upon whatever is in the newspaper."[1]

Newspapers often reached the trenches sporadically or arrived late. That's when, characteristically, the "soldiers' telegraph" would help out.

Together with the newspaper, the command at the front took its bearings from the commissar's "living word". Despite the enormous size of the political staff, its rhetoric often wasn't effective. There was a greater amount of falsehoods in it than there was in the press; it lacked warmth and spirit and without those qualities, the rhetoric paled in comparison and didn't touch the soldier's heart. The word of the "soldiers' telegraph" proved to be close to the soldiers' milieu if only because there was nothing false in its messages.

Often commissars when holding a discussion with the troops told them bald-faced lies. In so doing they often operated according to orders from above: "One should act so as to raise the spirit of the soldiers. A soldier, who has lost faith in success, withdraws into himself and feels deceived, which doesn't strengthen [his] willpower in the struggle with the foe."

What did impress the men? A statement like: "Yes, on our front there have been minor successes and a lot of casualties; however, on other fronts the Red Army is attacking successfully and routing the Germans." This deception knocked down the soldier's apathy for a while, instilled hope and raised spirits. There were occasions when soldiers protested against a lie; for example, when they were being assured of the strength and power of Soviet aviation - of the superiorities of our pilots and aircraft. "How can that be so," the soldiers argued, "what sort of superiority can there be, when hardly a single day goes by when the sky is not as black as the inside of a kiln with Germans?" Based upon my own observations, I can say that the Germans ruled the skies until the end of 1943.

German propaganda, as prisoners related, was also busy with analogous gimcrackery. One such striking example was the first bombing of Moscow.

Here is a summary transmitted by the *Sovinformburo*:

> … At 2210 on the evening of 22 June 1941 200 German aircraft attempted to conduct a massive attack on Moscow, but it failed. The anti-aircraft defenses around the capital didn't allow the bulk of the enemy aircraft to pass. Only solitary bombers penetrated. In the city, several buildings were left in flames, which were quickly put out...

Here is what German radio reported about the very same event: "Fires were raging in Moscow all night long, and in the morning Muscovites saw the ruins of the Kremlin - through which some people were wandering in search of something." In the next radio message, the German listeners heard: "The central electrical station has been completely destroyed. The movement of city traffic has come to a halt; the population is fleeing from a shattered, smoking city." Neither the *Sovinformburo* report nor the German radio reports were accurate. I'm an eyewitness!

Once among a circle of like-thinkers, Joseph Goebbels let slip a phrase about a lie. As he put it, the more absurd and flagrant the lie the easier it was for people to believe it. Later he spun a lot of such fibs, which were often completely contradictory in essence. However, in the USSR (and now in Russia as well), for some reason this utterance of Goebbels has acquired simply phenomenal notoriety. Perhaps this is because Soviet propaganda lied so absurdly and flagrantly.

In the zone of the front, German pilots scattered thousands of leaflets bearing approximately the same tales about the destruction of Moscow. Soldiers and officers - especially the ones from Moscow - were naturally alarmed. The commissars had to refute the false German propaganda.

Incidentally, as I now understand, lying has been part of warfare since the beginning of time. I'll allow myself a short digression. People who've seen the famous film *Aleksandr Nevsky* by Sergei Eisenstein possibly recall how nimbly the Russian troops dealt with the Livonian knights on the frozen Lake Chudskoe in 1242 - almost 700 years ago. In the film, they entomb hundreds of them beneath the ice.

After the Patriotic War, listening to the lecture of one historian, I learned the following: In the ancient Novgorod chronicle it is written that 400 knights were killed and 50 captured in this momentous battle for Russia. In reality, a total of 40 knights were killed and 6 captured. We'll note that it was obviously unknown to the Novgorod chroniclers that the Livonian Order had no more than 200 knights …

Let's return to the days of the war …

The warring sides, striving to increase the combat spirit of the soldiers, employed various psychological artifices in their propaganda practice (from the most elevated down to the lowest and filthiest). Manipulating the minds and emotions of people, they put into operation such tested propaganda concepts as love for the Motherland, patriotism and adherence to duty. They had no aversion to the most extreme distortion of accurate information - hiding or understating their own losses and exaggerating enemy losses. The commissars, like the press itself, sought primarily to inform the fighters only about victories. With joy they cited instances of enemy defeats.

I still recall the satisfaction with which they told us about how on 30 May 1942 a thousand British aircraft had devastated the city of Cologne with bombs. The commissar said: "Now the Germans themselves are experiencing the suffering which they are bringing to our own people." One of the Red Army men honestly asked: "What about the children?" The commissar dispassionately replied: "Why pity them? The Nazis show no mercy to our women and children."

Soviet propaganda preached self-sacrifice to the utmost. Red Army soldiers were constantly called upon to destroy the enemy at the cost of their own lives. This was the source of the myths about the 28 Panfilov heroes led by Political Instructor Vasilii Klochkov, the five Sebastopol' sailors led by Political Instructor Nikolai Fil'chenkov, and Private Aleksandr Matrosov.

All three examples had nothing in common with reality. There were not 28 of Panfilov's men at the Dubosekovo crossroads, but 140. After the battle, indeed there were approximately 28 survivors, but there were around 110 men who'd been killed or taken prisoner. They knocked out 5-7 panzers - not the 20 as claimed in the newspapers - and did nothing to delay the enemy's advance. The truth was revealed in 1948 when one of the 28 heroes was sentenced for his subsequent service in the German police. The initial impulse was to send the commander and commissar in front of a military tribunal for allowing a breakthrough on the sector of Klochkov's company, but only after a clamor was raised in the press around the fighting at Dubosekovo did they have second thoughts about putting them on trial.

There could also not have been the exploit of Political Instructor Fil'chenkov's five sailors, who supposedly on 7 November 1941 in the fighting for Sebastopol' tossed grenade bundles under German tanks and destroyed 10 or 15 of the armored monsters. This legend is refuted by a single fact. The German-Romanian Eleventh Army that attacked Sebastopol' in November 1941 did not have a single tank.

Let's take a look at the war's start. For example, the *Sovinformburo*'s report about the results of the first clashes said:

> … Cut off by our forces from their bases and infantry - and under the uninterrupted fire of our aviation - the enemy's motorized and mechanized units wound up in an extremely difficult position.

> Over seven days of fighting they have lost 2,500 tanks and approximately 1,500 airplanes, and more than 30,000 prisoners. The offensive spirit of the German army has been broken…

In other words, over one week two-thirds of the German invasion forces' armor and almost half of their air force had been knocked out. In actual fact, the antagonist by the end of June 1941, as is known, already occupied Minsk; had reached the Western Dvina and was continuing to advance at just the same heady pace into the interior of Soviet territory. Who was the Soviet leadership trying to deceive with such primitive lies and why? After all, it was obvious that all the same the truth would soon be known. However, of course in the meantime the effect of the "released sparrow" that could now "not be caught" remained.

Here are several examples from the Soviet press in the first years of the war. Two essays by the writer Boris Polevoi were printed in *Pravda*. In the first, under the title '*Pod mertvym Rzhevom*' ['*Above lifeless Rzhev*'] he colorfully described the "heroic" defense of the city before it was seized by the Germans. "When on that October night," writes the author, "the bands of Nazi barbarians forced their way into Rzhev, the city desperately resisted for a long time … partisans defended every street." All of this is nonsense. The Germans entered Rzhev freely; no one offered them any resistance. It occurred in the daytime of 14 October 1941 - not at night. There were no partisans there or anywhere around. In the second essay, the author savors the conversion of the city into a cemetery under a hail of Soviet bombs and shells - this act of villainy was executed in response to an order from Stalin.

When after the war Boris Polevoi arrived in Rzhev and met with city residents, he recanted in front of them: "As it is said, brothers, those were the times." This story has a continuation. The army newspaper *Vpered na vraga* in the issue dated 11 September 1942 published an article entitled 'Baianist iz Rzheva' ['The accordionist from Rzhev'] that repeated every single word of Boris Polevoi's "legends". The explanation is one and the same - the desire to ignite the flame of hatred toward the enemy in the soldiers' hearts.

It is impossible not to mention the history of the famous tank battle at Prokhorovka, where P.A. Rotmistrov's tankers, it would seem, gained a glorious victory over superior enemy forces! The reader can judge the degree of this "superiority" if he compares the numerical strength of the 5th Guards Tank Army - 850 tanks and self-propelled guns - and of General Hausser's II S.S. Panzer Corps that was opposing it: 273 tanks and assault guns - including eight captured T-34s. I think it is also possible to draw an unmistaken conclusion about which side was victorious by comparing their respective losses at Prokhorovka. The German panzer corps lost 5 panzers irrevocably and another 54 tanks and assault guns were damaged. Rotmistrov's tank army, in contrast, had irrecoverable losses of 334 tanks and self-propelled guns and approximately another 400 were damaged. Immediately after the battle, Stalin thought to punish Rotmistrov harshly for his bungling handling of the now wrecked tank army, but later the Supreme Commander decided that for propaganda purposes it would be better to treat the defeat at Prokhorovka as a victory (so he didn't send Rotmistrov in front of a tribunal). At the time, we knew nothing about the details of this mythical victory by the Soviet tankers. The "soldiers' telegraph" gave us sketchy - though accurate - information, but did so quite surreptitiously.

From the first days of the war, Soviet artists also did everything they could to fan the flames of hatred toward the enemy. In 1986, a unique exhibition called "Graphic Artists of the War" took place in Moscow. Its producers went through private collections and dug up the most interesting copies of propaganda posters, popular prints and series of caricatures publications from the war years. One of the popular prints depicts Ivan Smoliarchuk, a former Siberian hunter who had served under Chapaev during the Russian Civil War, ensnaring German tanks in the anti-tank pits that he had constructed. Another print shows Sergeant Major Petr Nikidimov with an axe in his hand, who has crawled up to a German tank that is blocking the advance of the infantry with its machine-gun fire, clambered onto it and with a blow from his axe he has bent the machine-gun barrel. It seems that the subject of the print is reminiscent of Aleksandr Matrosov's historic deed: that's how "victory" was won. You can believe it if you want, or not believe it. Thank God, these fairy tales didn't wind up in the hands of the men at the front. But in the rear, many people believed them - or to put it more accurately, wanted to believe them.

Let's return again to the facts. In May 1942 near Khar'kov, several Soviet armies (the 6th, 9th and General Bodkin's Operational Group) fell into encirclement and were wiped out. A Berlin communiqué announced the capture of 240,000 men. As was its tradition, the *Sovinformburo* worked to refute this report. Incidentally, this isn't even the most interesting thing about it - it is rather that official Russian historiography about the past even today continues to dispute the data of the former opponent with maniacal stubbornness.

It continues, even though in his memoirs, N.S. Khrushchev - who was one of the primary guilty parties of that crushing defeat - confirmed what really happened. He acknowledges that together with S.K. Timoshenko, he drove the armies right into the middle of a trap. It is clear why no one else shows any inclination to take the blame for similar sins. But let's give Nikitia Sergeevich credit; he found within himself the courage to write the truth. A glance in his memoirs shows this:

> ... As I flew toward Moscow I could clearly see the tragic aspect of my own predicament. I put myself in the hands of fate. I was ready for anything - including arrest.
>
> At first Stalin didn't give any sign of whether he was furious with me or sympathetic toward me. ... His face was a mask of inscrutability. Then he said:
>
> "The Germans have announced that they have captured more than 200,000 of our solders. Are they lying?"

> "No, Comrade Stalin, they're not lying. That figure sounds about right. We had approximately that number of troops - perhaps a few more. We must suppose that some were killed and the rest taken prisoner."[2] …

For the capable use of even a relatively simple weapon, a professional and thoughtful approach is absolutely necessary. But such an accurate and double-edged instrument like information requires twice as much intellectual handling. However, the Soviet Union's system of promotions for the leading cadres in 1941-1945 proved to be traditionally ineffective - and not only on the propaganda front. Therefore victory had to be attained in the typical Russian style - with a vast expenditure of the country's enormous material resources and completely unjustified enormous losses in personnel.

Lies especially held sway in the information about the constantly changing axes of combat in 1941 and 1942 and about the cities that had been abandoned by the Red Army. Here, the "soldiers' telegraph" often helped clarify the situation; not always, but frequently and accurately!

All of the primary Soviet information organs (TASS, the radio, newspapers and the *Sovinformburo*) sought to depict the most insignificant victories in rosy colors and to conceal from the army and the people even the smallest defeats. Statistics on the losses of personnel and equipment turned into a continuous juggling of numbers. In war, as a rule, any side understates its own casualties and exaggerates the enemy's losses, but in the Soviet media this took on a truly fantastic nature. Such a falsification of the history of a war has never been known.

Here are a couple of examples: In the leading article of the *Krasnaia zvezda* newspaper for 1 July 1941 there are the following lines: "The truth consists in the fact that the Nazi '*blitzkrieg*' is suffering a debacle … The fact is that over the first eight days, the Nazi army has received major damage." On 3 July 1941 I.V. Stalin's famous address to the people over the radio took place. The Leader informed the people and the whole world that "… the enemy's finest divisions and finest air force units have already been smashed and have met their doom on the battlefields …"

On 6 July 1941 Franz Halder, the Chief of the German Army's General Staff, entered into his diary of combat operations the German casualties in the East up to 3 July 1941: 41,807 (1.64 percent of 2.5 million) including 8,904 killed (542 officers and 8,363 non-commissioned officers and privates).[3]

The Generalissimo repeatedly presented examples of how to treat statistical data and how to create myths. For example, the figures that he gave in his address of 6 November 1941 - which were spun out of thin air - are far from reality. The Dictator went on to claim that Germany was already becoming exhausted; that "hunger and impoverishment" were stalking it: "Just a few months more, another half-year, perhaps a year… Nazi Germany should collapse under the weight of its crimes." But Germany, as we know, didn't collapse right up until the final capitulation.

So often the Dictator represented the desirable as the actual, and tried with "little sweet lies" to support the national spirit. The Dictator's biggest blow to the truth was concealing the losses of the Red Army and the civilian population in the Great Patriotic War. Having publicly announced 7 million as the number of dead from the war, Stalin set into stone a false number for the USSR's losses right up until his death almost seven years later. This untouchable myth deprived the country's historians of the right to research such an important question and the real losses became a riddle for foreign historians. Yet the explanation, as always, was one and the same: "Why trouble the people?"

Over the years, the Soviet press became so tied up in knots with its lies that at times it could not itself distinguish the truth from the half-truth and the lie. Censorship - both the Party's and the military's - was rife and constantly gripped editors, writers, journalists and military historians by the throat. If you tried to enter just one politically awkward phrase into the information arena, it would be your end! David Iosifovich Ortenburg, the chief editor of *Krasnaia zvezda*, wrote in detail about these editorial torments. In his books *Krasnaia zvezda v 1941* ['*Red Star*' *in 1941*] and *Krasnaia zvezda v 1942* ['*Red Star*' *in 1942*] he talks with melancholy about how difficult the publishing of each daily edition was for him and his colleagues.

Even in our day, in the Internet era, it is not a simple matter to find complete and accurate information about the failures of the Red Army in the Great Patriotic War such as those at Rzhev, Smolensk, Viaz'ma, Khar'kov, Kiev, in the Baltic republics, in the Crimea and the long torments of Leningrad. In the war years though, the "soldiers' telegraph" somehow brought news to us about these and many other dramatic events.

Who will do, for example, the following experiment? Who will try to count up the losses of the German army on the Eastern Front according to the *Sovinformburo* communiqués published over the entire 1,418 days of the Great Patriotic War? I guarantee that this total will have a place on the pages of the Guinness Book of Records! It is likely not coincidental, therefore, that today in Russia the newspapers from the war years are classified.

According to data from the Soviet General Staff and the *Sovinformburo*, from the start of the war until March 1942 the *Wehrmacht*'s losses amounted to 6.5 million men. This figure is approximately just as many men as Germany lost on all the fronts of the Second World War. In reality, from the start of the war until 1 March 1942 the Germans actually lost 6 times fewer men on the Eastern Front - 1,005,600 men.[4] In contrast, one should especially note the comparable figure for the Red Army for 1942 alone - the year of the Red Army's greatest losses in the Great Patriotic War. According to the study '*Grif sekretnosti snia*' ['*The seal of secrecy has been lifted*'] it amounts to 3,258,216 men.[5] Dmitrii Volkogonov estimates their number to be one-and-a-half times greater. Certain contemporary historians believe that even his estimates are too low. According to German statistics, the German army in 1942 lost 519,000 men - that is, approximately 6.5 times fewer.

The losses in the war until now are not precisely known and even to this day various data are given. They are constantly being checked and adjusted. So far, the enormous number of "missing in action" has not been ascertained. For example, annually searchers in two Russian oblasts - Smolensk and Tver' - are finding approximately 5,000 additional remains of Soviet soldiers and giving them a proper burial. According to recent data, on Russian land approximately 5 million Red Army soldiers and officers lie in unmarked graves.

When, for example, at the front the commissar in a discussion with the troops cited the figures for German losses - based upon the speeches and orders of the Supreme Commander - or referring to reports in the domestic press, could they really believe him? The soldier had his own statistics; the real ones. He met with them on any day at the front.

Marching ever further from Moscow to the west in 1943 and 1944, the soldier saw dozens of our corpses lying on the fields of former battles for each German corpse. As the Soviet troops advanced, this correlation changed only gradually. It was that way until the end of the war, because as is known, the Soviet generals fought not with skill, but with numbers! Incidentally, searchers, who are discovering unmarked graves from the war years, confirm the same correlation.

According to my own observations and calculations, the Soviet daily combat summaries normally exaggerated German casualties by two or three times or even more. Here the "soldiers' telegraph" often sought to correct them.

The frontline press

What sort of indoctrination did the soldier get from the army's newspaper? Little more than glorification of the Supreme Commander; "the Stalinist way was the path to victory". There were constant hymns to the Communist Party and to Soviet patriotism and heroism; exposure of the cruelty of the Nazi occupiers and their "New Order", which, in the opinion of the commissars, ignited hatred for the foe. Such, if you will, was the main content of the frontline gazettes. The material was usually conveyed under bold headings: **"Act like …!", "Follow the example of …!", "We'll do our duty!", "Follow experience!"** The latter was an aggregation of examples from frontline experience. There was no sort of critical analysis of combat situations or actions - only triumphant reports! Soldiers, looking through the latest edition of the army newspaper, liked to joke: "Wham, Bam, Urah! We've smashed the foe!"

In the 220th Rifle Division, in which I served from October 1942 to July 1944, the gazette *Za Rodinu* was published. Its four columns didn't have room for much. Nevertheless, the journalists contrived to squeeze the maximum amount of various types of information into this small space. The newspaper offered lively commentary on regimental life and sought to highlight the exploits of commanders, commissars and the rank and file Red Army men - of course, primarily those of Party members and Komsomol members. The editors willingly offered the pages for frontline creativity - finding space for poems, feuilleton and sketches (especially those with patriotic themes). It is an understandable matter that no commander or soldier could ever find in it an answer to such questions as: "Why is it impossible for us to reach Rzhev?" or "Why do all the offensives end in defeats and why are the losses so great?" These questions often came up in the soldiers' conversations. They asked them of the commissars as well, but even after their responses, many couldn't understand what was happening at the front.

The minds of the editors of the frontline newspapers, right up until the summer of 1944, were preoccupied with the subject of a Second Front - naturally at the indication from higher ups. We didn't know what was happening up above us; what diplomatic struggles were unfolding between Stalin and the Allies over the subject of opening a Second Front. We often learned about the Second Front from the Germans - of course with a well-known amount of deception. True, in 1942 Stalin in his holiday October speech tried to explain the causes of the Red Army's defeats by the absence of a Second Front. In 1943 the Germans wrote leaflets about the disagreements between Stalin and Churchill, which they scattered on the fields where the frontlines ran. At the beginning of 1944, they were assuring us that the Allies had deceived us and that there would be no Second Front. They expressed it directly in the following: "The Allies have tricked Stalin."

Just how did the commanders and we the soldiers react to the fact that the Allies were slow in invading Europe? Gradually, incomprehension of what was occurring emerged and even a certain amount of distrust toward the Allies. A simple and understandable thought pierced everyone: Delaying the opening of a Second Front was prolonging the war - and this meant more losses. The Red Army was pouring out its blood while they, the Allies, were sharing promises, tinned meat and army boots. The frontline press and the commissars constantly stirred up such moods like only they could. Here's an example from the army newspaper. A conversation between two soldiers is occurring. One asks: "How can a Second Front be opened more quickly?" The other answers: "American boots, I suppose, will help us get to it more quickly."

Who of the frontline men knew at the time about the enormous dimensions of the Allies' military supplies to the USSR? Without Lend-Lease, the Red Army would hardly have been capable of fighting for very long.

However, eventually American tanks, aircraft and their famous Studebaker trucks and Willys jeeps appeared at the front. The soldiers cheered up. The day of the Allied landing in Normandy - 6 June 1944 - became a holiday for the frontline soldiers. I'll cite a few jokes that circulated among the soldiers back then which reflect the newly buoyant moods. They admiringly nicknamed the Studebaker ("Studer", as the soldiers referred to it) - a reliable frontline vehicle that fundamentally improved the movement of Soviet infantry and artillery - the "Breezy Fellow". When American Bell P-39 Airacobra fighters appeared overhead, the soldiers would tightly roll their hands into a fist and, looking up into the sky, joyfully shout: "Fellows, give the Germans some stronger venom!" Once, one of the soldiers, while looking at the American airplanes in the sky, remarked that our top pilots were flying them. This was the truth. For example, the famous Soviet ace Aleksandr Pokryshkin - who scored 59 official victories personally in the war - flew the P-39 Airacobra off and on from 1942 until the end of the war.

The Red Army loses its guise

Gradually, changes began to take place in the Red Army which no one had previously anticipated - and at first the sense of them wasn't clear. The terms "*Krasnoarmeets*" ["Red Army man"] and "*boets*" ["fighter"] were replaced with the words "*soldat*" ["soldier"] and "*riadovoi*" ["private"]; simultaneously the words "*offitser*" ["officer"] and "*offitserskii sostav*" ["officer staff"] appeared; links with the pre-Revolutionary army and Russia's military traditions began to be established.

Suvorov, Kutuzov, Brusilov, Ushakov, Nakhimov and other army and navy commanders were mentioned more frequently. The terms "Red Army" and "Red Navy", which were introduced in the years of the Revolution and Civil War, gradually began to disappear - giving way to "Soviet army" and "Soviet navy". Then the astonishing Decree of the Presidium of the USSR Supreme Soviet that introduced the epaulette to the country's armed forces appeared. In the winter of 1943, the epaulette began to adorn the uniforms of the soldiers. These changes were significant - as if a new stage of the war was starting together with them. Sure, some soldiers were saying then: "What's the difference between one and the other - commander or officer?" Some puckishly asked: "Perhaps, fellows, now the officers will start to cuss less and command better than the previous commanders?"

In those years it was possible to hear not only from the soldiers, but from the officers as well, that life after the war would change for the better - and often the soldiers connected this with the hope that the collective farms would be abolished. Despite the strict military censorship of letters, information reached the front about how life was going on in the village. And if, as Soviet propaganda asserts, we could not have withstood the adversary's onslaught without the collective farms, then with just the same confidence we can consider that no other system of land tenure could have victimized the peasants to the extent that collectivization did. In the war years the rural community became a typical shabby village with its squalor and the high-handedness of the local bosses, which with difficulty could be justified by the wartime hardships.

We were issued new uniforms with the shoulder boards. We looked at each other with amazement: epaulettes on the shoulders ... we had seen such previously only at the theater or on movie screens. We quickly became accustomed to them and had a sense of pride.

A special service of the "soldiers' telegraph" consisted of informing the soldier about the character, capabilities and professional qualities of their commanders. What sort of commander was he? A "*palochnik*" - one who beats subordinates with a walking stick? A "*mordoboishchik*" - one who readily punches the faces of his subordinates? An inveterate swearer? One quick to send men in front of a firing squad? Or a commander who could carry several of these labels simultaneously? A "deaf man" or a fatherly commander? A "cold fish" or the kindest soul? A swashbuckler or scaredy-cat? It was important to know: was the commander capable? Did he use his brains? According to which principle did he relate to higher command? Did he seek wriggle room in orders? Was he a hard-driver? Did he extemporize? Often, the superior commanders looked for these same characteristics in the responses they received.. Legends circulated about Kalinin Front commander I.S. Konev's walking stick. Many subordinate commanders experienced a blow from it. The commander of the 4th Ukrainian Front, Eremenko, was widely recognized as a commander who quickly resorted to his fists to enforce his orders. The general often referred to permission from the Generalissimo to justify his ugly behavior and acts.

Under Stalin, the value of human life fell to a level never before seen in the history of Russia. In other States that participated in the Second World War, heroes who destroyed a multitude of enemy soldiers, tanks, airplanes and ships were mythologized - but by no means at the cost of their own lives. The Japanese kamikazes would be the only exception. In this respect Stalin and his generals fully embraced the samurai tradition, according to which the main thing for a warrior was to die heroically in battle - not to preserve his own life - in order to continue to kill the enemy.

If tankers managed to save themselves - or to escape from knocked-out and burning tanks and make their way back unharmed to friendly lines under enemy fire - then SMERSH agents accused them of a crime: "Come now, you abandoned your tank!" Or, for example, when artillery fire opened without authorization from higher command, such an incident was viewed and treated as a crime even if there was a need for this.

In the Soviet system humans were cogs in a machine - and it seemed that there was so many of them, one or more million of them could be sacrificed without any problem. Eremenko once said about Zhukov: "It must be said that Zhukov's operational art amounted to a superiority in force by 5 to 6 times - otherwise he wouldn't undertake the task; he didn't know how to fight without numbers and built his career upon blood." These words are applicable to almost any Soviet commander, beginning with the Generalissimo.

From where did the "soldiers' telegraph" obtain its information? What paths, unknown to anyone, did it follow in order to reach the mass of soldiers? I will tell about one such case in which I directly participated.

One day, the regiment in which I was serving was suddenly raised on an alert and within a couple of hours already the entire division was making a rapid march to the nearest railroad station. We marched all night - not knowing where we were going or why. What, had the Nazi beast made another lunge for Moscow? Here someone recalled the commissar's recent words: "A mortal danger is hanging over the country: the German is keen to reach the Volga." The "soldiers' telegraph" put a stop to all the various rumors: "The division is being sent urgently to Stalingrad!"

Overnight we marched approximately 30 kilometers. Without any explanation, the division was halted and directed into some woods. The short rest barely enlivened us after the difficult march. Then we turned around and moved out behind the departing equipment and rear units, which prior to our stop had been bringing up the rear of the column. The "soldiers' telegraph" promptly tapped out a fresh message: "Stalin has found out about us and has ordered not a single soldier to be taken from Rzhev!" So I never wound up at Stalingrad. It is known that in 1942, approximately 50 divisions were sent to the Stalingrad area - including several from the Western Front. For some reason they didn't touch our division, which was still in the process of forming.

Approximately three or four months later, when we were now occupying the former German trenches on the left bank of the Volga (November-December 1942 and January-February 1943), the "soldiers' telegraph" delivered two new reports. The first was about the victory at Stalingrad. Now we were announcing this major defeat of the German army to the German soldiers. At the same time, it became known that a new offensive on our front at Rzhev had been started. It continued from 25 November until 20 December and ended in a terrible defeat. Neither the central media nor the frontline press uttered a single word about it.

The soldiers thought highly of their "telegraph". The commissars and Special Department officers sought to block all possible conduits through which we were receiving the unofficial information! They tried to impress the soldier of its harm and unreliability. They declared the information that was being spread through the "soldiers' telegraph" to be enemy propaganda. They tried to convince us that the "soldiers' telegraph" was diverting the frontline men from their combat tasks and instilling confusion in the minds of the troops. Nothing helped; all of their efforts proved to be fruitless! We could no longer imagine life at the front without the "soldiers' telegraph".

I don't recall a single time in the years of the war - whether at my combat-infantry School, where I trained for four months, or later at the front - when any of the commanders or commissars talked to us soldiers about the Germans; about their professionalism; about their habits at the front; about their weapons. It is known that our adversary were highly trained troops furnished with the latest equipment. The German soldiers from their youth had constantly been around new technology - radios, telephones and electrical devices … Seventy per cent of our infantry, if not more, consisted of peasants in soldiers' boots. The railroad that took them to the front was for many of them the first that they had seen.

Despite the fears of the commissars and Special Department, the "soldiers' telegraph" played a substantial role in the struggle against enemy propaganda. Information is a tenacious thing. It can exist for a long time and travel around the world and often it is used on behalf of the truth. When the German army invaded the Soviet Union, the *Wehrmacht* soldiers and officers saw the poverty of Russian life and the hard living conditions. One of the first Nazi propaganda productions was a 60-page brochure: *The Soviet Union through the Eyes of German Soldiers: Letters from the East.*

The letters were carefully selected to strengthen National-Socialist awareness in the army - stressing the importance of the German army's offensive against Soviet Russia with the aim of liberating the people from Bolshevism. If it had only been so!

For the 60th Victory Anniversary, the book *Ia eto videl* [*This I saw*] was published in Paris. It consisted of carefully chosen letters from veterans which had been sent to the *Izvestiia* newspaper - of course after perestroika had started in the country - a bit more than 40 years after the war. The writer Svetlana Aleksevich comments on all 300 selected letters:

> ... These weren't heroes, but everyday people - or, as they call themselves, "frontline proletariat". Their stories are simple and guileless ... and because of this they are even more chilling ... All the letters are soldiers' letters, coming from the pen of former privates to colonels. Here's a line from one of them: "Soldiers win wars, and generals too, if they are good soldiers..."...

Here is an excerpt from one of the letters, written by V. Ivantsov from Miner-al'nye Vody:

> ... We had enough of everything, including humor. Once I wrote in a combat dispatch that the battery had wiped out 10 men and scattered approximately a platoon. The regiment's chief of staff summons me: "That's too little! Write that you've destroyed up to a platoon and scattered up to a company ..." Later these falsifications were amended. Experience came with blood, with unimaginable casualties. We had just moved into positions next to a neighboring state farm. The battalion commander and two sappers left in two ZIS trucks in order to select an observation post in a building there. Suddenly, the division commander is beckoning me and ordering me to open fire on the state farm: "Germans are there - I've just received the intelligence." I felt dizzy and my hands were shaking, while he was brandishing a pistol in front of my nose. Well, in fact I added up to 600 meters to the estimated range to the state farm - calculating that my shells would impact beyond the target. How-ever, the map proved to be inaccurate. The fire blanketed the state farm. I ran howling with tears in my eyes. The assistant regiment commander in some sort of wild rage furiously swore at the colonel. They say that this type came to a sticky end."...

Incidentally, did the "soldiers' telegraph" tell lies? It did happen that mistakes were made in haste. However, in distinction from the press it never caused umbrage or disillusionment, but on the contrary made life in the frontlines less onerous.

Often the "soldiers' telegraph" quickly spread jokes, anecdotes and funny stories through the trenches. A lot of time the laughter, or at times even the guffaws, made the command uncomfortable. No matter how hard the enemies of the "soldiers' telegraph" tried, they were not able to stifle it.

A dramatic episode in the history of the "soldiers' telegraph" in the Rzhev region was the news of the Germans' withdrawal from Rzhev. It is known that the frontline and army commanders often developed cold feet under the gaze of the Supreme Commander. In this case they dawdled in entering the city, fearing new complications, even though many reports were coming in from the reconnaissance scouts that the Germans were gone.

The memoirs have been preserved, for example, of the commander of one of the 220th Rifle Division's regiments (Lieutenant Colonel Skovorodkin) - as well as of the writer Elena Rzhevskaia and even of the scouts themselves; they all confirm what I've said about the command's apprehensions and reluctance to move into the city. As a consequence, the Germans were able to pull out of the city quietly and to steal a march on our units. Quite an embarrassing fact! On 2 March 1942 German units were retreating from Rzhev. For three days after, the city was empty of German forces. Army and divisional intelligence missed the enemy's sudden disappearance - even though the "soldiers' telegraph" delivered this exceptional news to certain commanders, albeit perhaps a bit late.

If Zhukov and Konev had promptly put the troops in motion and had taken Rzhev on the heels of the retreating enemy, how many human lives would have been saved? The operational situation on the entire front would have changed for the worse for the adversary.

"There is no greater shamelessness than to pass off as the truth an assertion, the falseness of which is patently known."

Kabuk

7
The Petty Storyteller

The "armchair commander"

On 2 March 1943 German units after a 15-month defense abandoned Rzhev. On the next day, small reconnaissance detachments of the Western and Kalinin Fronts cautiously probed the city.

As soon as Winston Churchill learned about this event, he immediately sent Stalin an open letter: "Accept my warmest congratulations on the occasion of Rzhev's liberation. From our conversation in August, I know the great significance that you attach to the liberation of this point."

Stalin replied: "Although we've recently had several successes at the front, it is precisely now that exceptional exertion of force and particular vigilance with respect to probable new enemy actions is required of the Soviet troops and Soviet command. In connection with this, I'm forced **more often than usual to drive out to the troops, to one or another of the sectors at the front**...."

One can imagine how the British Prime Minister had fun, having received Stalin's response to his congratulatory letter. He was perfectly aware that Stalin never "drove out" to any troops. A petty storyteller!

Stalin's message to Roosevelt on 8 August 1943 is also interesting. "Only now," the Supreme Commander writes in it, "upon returning from the front can I answer your latest letter of 16 July. I don't doubt that you keep our military situation under consideration and will understand the delay with the response. I more often have to spend time personally on various sectors of the front, and subordinate all else to the interests of the front."

Still one more interesting document .... Roosevelt and Churchill in a joint message to I.V. Stalin on 19 August 1943 properly assessed, in Stalin's view, the Generalissimo's personal leadership at the front: "We fully understand," they wrote, "the strong reasons which lead you to remain on battlefronts, where your presence has been so fruitful for victory."

Now the Generalissimo could be fully satisfied: who would be able to rebuke him for being a "desk strategist", who knew the front only from newsreels and from the stories of generals of the General Staff or the army-level commands. What sort of trip to the front was the Supreme Commander mentioning in his letters to Roosevelt and Churchill?

For the sake of history

Knowing that Hitler until 1944 constantly visited the Eastern Front, Stalin decided to make an appearance as the Supreme Commander and, as Dmitrii Volkogonov suggests, "for the sake of history" to drive out to the front after all. That's how the Generalissmo referred to his trip. In actual fact he drove not to the front, but to a place somewhat removed from the front where it would be quieter. The trip took place 158 days after the liberation of Rzhev on 1-5 August 1943. Stalin selected two destinations for his trip: Gzhatsk and Rzhev. He decided to see the liberated cities in person - they had caused him so much trouble and inner agitation.

He had other motivations for selecting them as well. It was precisely Churchill who reminded him of them. Secondly (and this obviously was the most important for this event), by his personal visit to Rzhev Stalin was seeking to emphasize his own role in the liberation of the Rzhev-Viaz'ma salient! At first the Supreme Commander visited Gzhatsk where he met with the commander of the Western Front, V.D. Sokolovsky, and a member of the Military Council, N.A. Bulganin; then near Rzhev there occurred his meeting with the new commander of the Kalinin Front, A.I. Eremenko.

Many apologetic, humorous and sad stories have been written about this trip. Soviet sappers had long ago rebuilt the bridge across the Volga at Rzhev, which had been blown up on Hitler's orders during the withdrawal of the German units - and both the city and all the roads leading into it had been fully swept of mines. However, the Supreme Commander decided to stop in the village of Khoroshevo, which stands about 5 kilometers outside of Rzhev.

Comrade Stalin's entire trip, as always, was accompanied with large and small subterfuges and secrets. In the given case they were simply fantastic! Of all things, Lavrentii Pavlovich [Beria] found out about it only a day before Stalin's journey. An entire army blocked all the highways and roads for 100 kilometers around - from Moscow to Gzhatsk and Rzhev. At one of Moscow's suburban airfields, a squadron of fighter planes with ace pilots stood by at combat readiness.

The train consisted of two dilapidated boxcars, which were pulled by an old steam engine; several platform cars carrying firewood had been attached to them (for deception purposes). Today these boxcars are on display as historical relics in Stalin's homeland in the city of Gori. The Generalissimo himself with his entourage and security was located in a salon wagon, which had been disguised to resemble the rest of the train's composition.

The cottage in Khoroshevo where Stalin stayed is now a museum dedicated to him and his visit. It became known as well as the place where Stalin issued an instruction to prepare an order for the first artillery salute in honor of the liberation of Orel and Belgorod.

He didn't head out to visit the troops in order to meet with officers and soldiers in the frontlines. After spending the night in the village of Khoroshevo, he returned to Moscow by automobile - together with Beria - under extra security.

I'll cite one more document. It dates to the eve of the 1943 Teheran conference. It is a letter from Molotov on 22 November 1943 addressed to the US *charges d'affaires* in the USSR. In it, the People's Commissar of Foreign Affairs reports: "At present Marshal Stalin is at the front, but I have a report from him that he will be at the designated place no later than 28-29 December. I ask you to inform Mr. President of this ...." What a crock!

One interesting detail, which cannot but be mentioned, can be found in Boris Solov'ev's and Vladimir Sukhodeev's book *Polkovodets Stalin*, which came out in 2003 as part of the *Stalinia* collection released on the 50th anniversary of Stalin's death. The authors write:

> ... In the difficult days of Moscow's defense, Stalin traveled to the front in order to familiarize himself with the situation of affairs on the spot. A.T. Rybin, his alleged accompanying bodyguard, says in his *Zapiski: Stalin na fronte* [*Notes: Stalin at the front*]:
>
> > ... In 1941-1942 Stalin rode out to the frontline sectors - to the Mozhaisk, Zvenigorod and Solnechnogorsk defensive lines. On the Volokolamsk axis he toured a hospital; he visited Rokossovsky's 16th Army, where he inspected the work of BM-13 rocket launchers [Katiushas] and spent time in Panfilov's 316th Rifle Division. Within three days after the 7 November 1941 parade on Red Square, Stalin rode out on the Volokolamsk highway to one of the divisions that had arrived from Siberia and inspected its combat readiness. In 1942 the Supreme Commander rode out beyond the Lama River to an airbase where new aircraft were being tested. On 2-3 August 1943 Stalin visited General Sokolovsky and Military Council Member N. Bulganin of the Western Front and spent 4-5 August with General A. Eremenko of the Kalinin Front...
>
> Sometimes on this subject other authors exclaim: "He seldom traveled, and what is even worse, they say he was afraid." They either pretend to ignore or spitefully omit the fact that the Supreme Commander couldn't travel to the front more often; it would have been impossible for him to oversee the general direction of the war. And that is the most important thing.

Then why did Hitler travel to the front between 1941 and 1944? It is known that over three-plus years of the war, Hitler showed up in Uman', Zaporozh'e, Smolensk and Vitebsk. He visited Borisov, Poltava, Belaia Tserkov' and Nikopol'. Field headquarters of the Führer were located in Vinnitsa and Belaia Tserkov'. In the first year of the war in the East, Hitler visited individual armies, corps, divisions and even regiments - and dropped by hospitals and proving grounds.

Bodyguard A.T. Rybin's stories about Stalin's travels in 1941 are suspect. I haven't found evidence of them in any sources for 1941. If indeed Stalin's trips back then had actually taken place, one can imagine how the Soviet press would have written about them later. Vasilevsky, Shtemenko, Zhukov and Rokossovsky say nothing about them in their memoirs. But here is a correct assessment of Rybin's writings:

> In the 1960s, the interview and brochures of the now deceased A.T. Rybin - who for a short time at the beginning of the 1930s served in Stalin's security escort - received broad circulation. Practically everything that concerns a description of Stalin's life "in close-up" was compiled by him from the words of officers who served in Stalin's personal security escort, but the commentary and conclusions of Rybin himself are all too often striking for their ignorance and failure to grasp that what he has written can easily be used by interested parties hostile to Stalin and Socialism. Yet together with Rybin's interview in the journal *Sotsiologicheskie issledovaniia* [*Sociological research*], in the newspapers *Sovetskaia Rossia, Patriot* and even *Moskovskii Komsomolets* they had a wide circulation ...[1]

Here is what D. Volkogonov wrote in his book *I.V. Stalin – Triumf i tragediia*: "After the failed trip to the front in October 1941, when Stalin only reached the Volokolamsk highway and saw the flashes of the front that was approaching Moscow just 10-15 kilometers from the place his cavalcade had reached, Stalin never made another trip to the front." I've already talked about the so-called trip "to the front" in 1943.

Naturally, the question arises: Had the authors of *Polkovodets Stalin* ever read Volkogonov's book, which was based upon declassified documents, and not conjecture? I'll simply say here that the "notes" in Rybin's *Zapiski* are simply bunk ...

I'll also remind the reader of the memoirs of one of Comrade Stalin's closest companions, Anastas Mikoian. He knew that Stalin never was at the front even a single time and does not mention any visit by Stalin to the front in his memoirs![2]

During the war and in the initial years after it, Soviet artists created an entire gallery of artwork based upon the theme of "Stalin at the front" - approximately a dozen paintings. In the postwar years, prints of them decorated the garrison officers' clubs, barracks and headquarters' offices.

One large canvas from this collection has been preserved. On it, the artist depicted Stalin standing on the high northern bank of the Volga River looking through binoculars at the ruins of the former city of Rzhev, which had been devastated at his personal order during the fighting for it. Standing next to him in the scene are A.I. Eremenko and L.P. Beria. In due time, the figure of L.P. Beria had to be painted over. Today, a commemorative plaque marks the "historic" home in the village of Khoroshevo where Iosif Vissarionivich stayed during his "trip to the front"; often, individual citizens of Rzhev bring flowers to it ....

On his trip to America that never took place

Three times during the war years, President Roosevelt proposed to Stalin a meeting with him in any territory of his choosing. Stalin thanked Roosevelt, but each time courteously declined to meet with him - pointing to the difficult situation at the front or the necessity of his presence in Moscow or at the front. Roosevelt invited Stalin to visit America - promising to send his most powerful battleship for him. In his return letters, Stalin expressed doubts about a possible trip: would the American people extend a warm welcome to him?

The American President, when making the invitation to the "Chief Communist of the Planet", understood that in reality, many conservative citizens would protest the arrival of the Red Leader on blessed American soil. But Roosevelt pledged to Stalin that he would do everything possible to ensure that Americans would greet him courteously - first of all as the United States' main ally in the struggle against Nazi Germany.

How sweeping the naiveté of the American President was toward "Uncle Joe" - as he called Stalin - is evident from the following example. Roosevelt, as is known, didn't allow his assistants to criticize the Soviet Leader or permit them to make any critical comments about him. Roosevelt never had to experience disappointment with "Uncle Joe", who replied with ingratitude toward America for the assistance it had rendered to the enormous Soviet Russia in the cruel struggle with the German army. The great American President didn't live to see the collapse of the Allied coalition, in which he so believed, before the Cold War, which Stalin contrived in order to serve his own political interests. Certain Russian historians reproach Stalin for not availing himself of Roosevelt's warm feelings for him and for having never met separately with him, which might have allowed a wedge to be driven between the United States and Great Britain - thereby isolating Churchill in the resolution of the many important global political problems of the time.

President Truman also invited Stalin to visit the United States - offering to send the battleship *Missouri* for him if he would agree. Stalin demurred, saying he wanted to appear in the U.S.A. as an ally in the war, but that he would be viewed wrongly - just as Truman himself would be wrongly perceived in Russia. Truman replied that he would do everything in his strength to correct this perception at home; Stalin gave him an "exceptionally sincere" smile and said he would do the same in Russia. Stalin formally accepted the invitation, but having returned to Moscow from the Potsdam conference he didn't confirm his agreement. In March 1946 after

Churchill's speech in Fulton, Missouri in Truman's presence that warned that an "Iron Curtain" had fallen across the continent "from Stettin in the Baltic to Trieste in the Adriatic", Truman extended another invitation to Stalin. He offered Stalin the opportunity to present a speech in Fulton, but received a brusque rejection.[3]

The Soviet press didn't say a single word about any of this. However, it quite adeptly and smoothly falsified Churchill's speech while simultaneously smearing President Truman. In the opinion of certain historians, a trip by Stalin to the United States would have undoubtedly been a political sensation and might have played a significant role in Soviet-American relations and in raising the prestige of the USSR and of the Generalissimo himself.

Those historians who express this opinion are mistaken. The "Kremlin Wonder" never gave a thought about sincere relations with the Allies. The only thing that mattered to him was defeating Hitler with their assistance. Stalin sought to deceive the Allies by any means and to exact from them, at a minimum, advantages for his own imperial ambitions. All three international conferences conducted during the Second World War - Teheran, Yalta and Potsdam - testify to this. The Yalta conference is particularly noteworthy in this respect. On that conference's 60th Anniversary, President George Bush - as well as certain American historians and media sources - recognized the many decisions taken at Yalta as a serious mistake by President Roosevelt.

Moscow in fact violated almost all of the agreements reached at Yalta. Roosevelt and Churchill didn't stipulate conditions that might have ensured the fulfillment of the terms. They took "Uncle Joe" at his word. Particularly enlightening in this respect is the meeting between Harry Truman and V.M. Molotov that took place during the latter's trip to the United States on the occasion of the San Francisco conference that drafted the Charter of the United Nations. En route, Molotov visited the American President in Washington D.C.

Here's what Nikolai Zlobin has to say about this meeting:

> ... Truman told the Soviet guest that the U.S.A. was prepared to carry out all the concluded agreements, but also sharply expressed his suspicion that the USSR was violating them one after another. The U.S. President spoke particularly harshly on the subjects of Soviet policies in Poland and with respect to the U.N. The U.S.A. would do everything necessary for the creation of the U.N., the President said, but if the USSR didn't want to do this then "it could go to hell." Molotov was shocked. "I have never been talked to like that in my life" he declared. Truman retorted: "Observe the agreements and we won't have to talk to you like that."[4]...

A bit later in his memoirs, Truman would write:

> ... I have no faith in any totalitarian State - be it Russia, Germany, Spain, Argentina or Japan. They are all based on the false

> premise that a lie is justified; that old, worn-out Jesuitical formula that the end justifies the means and that it is necessary to support the authority of government. I don't agree, and I don't believe that this formula will help mankind in implementing its hopes...

"'Honest Communism', as it is described in the Book of Acts, will work. The 'Russian godless crooked system' will not work."[5] What an apt characterization!

One can see the despicable, personal fingerprints of the Dictator and his constant cunning in one example from the Yalta conference. I'll call attention to one half-forgotten but distinctive episode from those long-ago times. In May 1944, when the Red Army drove the Germans out of the Crimea, as the first order of business the entire Crimean Tatar population was deported at the Dictator's order and the Artek Pioneer Camp was reestablished - after which, a famous Soviet intelligence operation took place under the codename "Zlatoust".

Operation Zlatoust

In the concluding days of the Yalta conference, Roosevelt and Churchill received a warm invitation from the Young Pioneers to visit their Artek Camp. Clementine Churchill, the wife of the British Prime Minister; Kerr, the British Ambassador in Moscow; and Averell Harriman, the American Ambassador, accepted the invitation. The Young Pioneers and Soviet intelligence officers dressed as Pioneer leaders festively greeted them.

The campers received generous gifts. Clementine Churchill brought them 15 tents with a 40-person capacity and handed them a check for 5,000 pounds sterling. Pioneers who came to the Artek Camp continued to stay in these tents until 1960 when grandiose seaside housing was erected in their place. Ambassador Harriman handed the children a check for $10,000.

The notes and correspondence of the camp's long-time director, Vladimir Tikhonovich Chistov, have been preserved. Here is what he wrote about this espionage operation, which entered into the history of Soviet intelligence as one of its most successful feats:

Writes Chistov: "We didn't suspect at the time that the Artek Pioneers would become participants in an intelligence operation ..."

The events proceeded in the following fashion: the guests were shown the newly renovated camp and then attended a concert at the camp where the children together sang the American national anthem. When the concert ended, the Artek Pioneers ceremoniously carried in an American bald eagle - crafted from precious types of wood (mahogany and ebony, European black alder, Persian ironwood, coquito palm etc.) - and presented it to the American Ambassador.

"What a beauty!" Harriman exclaimed with delight. "But what will I do with it?" Stalin's personal translator, Berezhkov, who'd been sent with Ambassador Harriman to Artek, immediately gave him a piece of advice: "Hang it in your office. The English will die from envy."

The "Eagle" - with a hidden microphone inside it - hung in the Embassy office of the American Ambassador for eight years. Over this time the ambassadorship was changed four times, but the skillfully crafted "wire" inside the eagle daily supplied the Kremlin with secret information. The microphone was fed by a special microwave device set up in a building next to the Embassy.

"Uncle Joe" personally directed the operation. The secret microphone was eventually discovered by accident - and for a long time the Americans were silent about this embarrassing story.

In 1960, when an American U-2 spy plane was shot down over the Soviet Union, the Soviet Government accused the United States of espionage activity and persistently demanded that the U.N. condemn it. In response, at the next meeting of the U.N. General Assembly, the American representative demonstrated the "Eagle Spy" in front of the U.N. delegates. Ever since, the wooden eagle has been preserved in the CIA Museum in Langley.

One more thing should be said. The Chekists[6] had thoroughly probed the character of Averell Harriman - his tastes, interests and hobbies - so it was no mere chance that the eagle, crafted from precious types of wood, was given to the American Ambassador...

Conclusion

I would like to acquaint the reader with Winston Churchill's telegram to I.V. Stalin, sent to him from London after the Yalta conference:

> Received 18 February 1945
>
> A message from Mr. Churchill to Marshal Stalin
>
> On behalf of HM Government I send you grateful thanks for all the hospitality and friendship extended to the British delegation at the Crimea conference. We were deeply impressed by the feats of organisation [sic] and of improvisation which enabled the conference to meet in such agreeable and imposing surroundings - and we all take back with us most happy recollections. To this I must add a personal expression of my own thanks and gratitude. No previous meeting has shown so clearly the results which can be achieved when the three heads of government meet together with the full intention to face difficulties and solve them. You yourself said that co-operation would be less easy when the unifying bond of the fight against a common enemy had been removed. I am resolved, as I am sure the President and you are resolved, that the friendship and co-operation so firmly established shall not fade when victory has been won. I pray that you may long be spared to preside over the destinies of your country which has shown

> its full greatness under your leadership, and I send you my best wishes and heartfelt thanks.
>
> 17 February 1945

Stalin courteously thanked the Prime Minister. Then, oh how he must have chuckled while gently giving a twirl to his mustache, as he thought of Operation Zlatoust. So how true the saying: "He who laughs last, laughs best."

"Magnanimity is proper for the conqueror."

Koz'ma Prutkov[1]

8

How "Uncle Joe" Outplayed the American President and British Prime Minister[2]

This event occurred during the famous Yalta conference in the Crimea between 4 and 11 February 1945. Little time remained until the Allies' final victory over Nazi Germany. The "Big Three", at Roosevelt's initiative, decided to gather to take up and discuss documents about the postwar arrangement of Europe and first of all, Germany.

On the eve of the forthcoming meeting, Soviet intelligence presented Stalin with a copy of a telegram that had been sent by Churchill to Roosevelt. In it, the British Prime Minister examined the question of how best "to outplay" Marshal Stalin at the upcoming conference. In actual fact, in the negotiations everything went to the contrary. Stalin proved to be not only a fantastically hospitable host, but also better prepared for the negotiations than his guests; at the highest theatrical level he adeptly "outperformed" his guests. This he succeeded in doing despite the fact that before the flight to Yalta, the American President and British Prime Minister secretly met in Malta. There they sought to consider the possibilities of harmonizing their points of view with Moscow.

At the conference, for the most part Roosevelt was concerned with three problems: the United Nations; the Soviet entry into the war with Japan; and the postwar order in Europe. On all these points, Roosevelt received Stalin's full support.

At Yalta, Roosevelt hoped to strengthen friendly relations with Stalin. In his foreign policy activities, the American President assigned the primary role to so-called "personal diplomacy". He came to believe in the idea that he could personally influence the Soviet ruler even after the war. As was said back then, he could "tame" him; soften the regime in Russia; obtain the Kremlin's greater tolerance of the Orthodox Church; lead Stalin to reject many ideological dogmas that were confusing mankind; and to conduct economic reforms for the benefit of the country. Calculating in this manner, Roosevelt assumed that he had already obtained the first concrete results along this path: The Patriarchy had been newly restored in Soviet Russia; in 1942 the institution of the commissars had been abolished in the Red Army; in 1943 the Communist International had been dissolved; and Soviet propaganda had dropped a lot of preposterous Bolshevik dogma and was employing something more like nationalist-patriotic slogans.

Even without Roosevelt, Stalin already long understood that only the regeneration of the people's nationalist-patriotic spirit would help him overcome Hitler. He had to occupy himself with uniting the Slavic peoples as well as to create the Jewish Anti-Fascist Committee and to organize a Muslim Union headed by a mufti.

Harry Hopkins, Roosevelt's closest friend and special advisor - and his mover and shaker in personal diplomacy - once declared that Stalin would have been pleasantly surprised had he known how far the American President was ready to go to meet the interests of the Soviet Union. Hopkins himself believed that it was only possible to deal with Stalin within the framework of the anti-fascist alliance. In his turn, Stalin considered Harry Hopkins: "the first American with whom he felt close." This man rendered an enormous influence on both Roosevelt and Stalin - trying to bring together the two men's respective positions.

Roosevelt assumed that despite the ideological differences between the United States and Soviet Russia, it was possible to reach agreements with "Uncle Joe". Beginning in 1942, he sought personal meetings with Stalin, but the latter declined them under various pretexts. Historians believe that this was a serious political miscalculation of the Soviet Leader.

At Yalta, Roosevelt promised to offer Stalin $4.5 billion at the war's conclusion - a colossal sum for those times - on advantageous credit terms for the reconstruction of the devastated country. On his part, Stalin offered to the Americans to organize major concessions for favorable commercial terms in the Soviet Union. This never happened. Just 55 days after the Yalta conference, Roosevelt passed away. In a telegram to Stalin at the time, Harry Hopkins wrote: "Russia has lost its best friend in America."[3]

On the first day of mourning, Stalin received the American Ambassador Averell Harriman in the Kremlin and told him: "Roosevelt has died, but his work should carry on." Curiously, Stalin at the conclusion of the discussion advised Harriman to disinter Roosevelt's body: "Did his opponents make off with the President, or did they poison him?"[4]

In their book *The Cold War*, Jeremy Isaacs and Taylor Downing write: "The Yalta conference represented the high-watermark of Allied wartime cooperation." However, at the same time they add: "But Yalta was also the beginning of the postwar world; the divisions between East and West became apparent." Was that the way it really was? I think that at the time, Roosevelt didn't believe so.

Much has been written about Yalta. If you will, even more than has been written about the Teheran and Potsdam conferences. Obviously, this is because the Yalta conference reached momentous decisions that determined the development of world events for the next 50 years. The conference approved the basic principles of the work of the United Nations.

It seems to me that Churchill wrote about Yalta more fully and better than anyone else. He paid great attention to the subject in his historic memoirs *The Second World War*, which received a Nobel Prize in 1953.[5]

I'll mention another author who wrote about Yalta, who today is little-known. However, it is not only useful to get acquainted with his book, but also amusing. It is the *Zapiski* [Notes] of the culinary specialist William Pokhlebkin, who recreated in detail "that grandiose Stalinist staging of the event that accompanied the conference."

Aleksandr Gennes's marvelous article[6] about Pokhlebkin's book states:

... Palatial residences for 350 people were prepared for the conference. Two airfields and two independent electrical power stations were constructed; water and sewer lines were built - as well as laundries and a bomb shelter with a reinforced concrete roof that was 5 meters thick...

However, the main thing - literally a ceremonial activity - took place at the dinner table. The description of this culinary spectacle is striking for its titanic scale.

Pokhlebkin writes: "Stalin played the decisive role even in these purely gastronomic spheres; he kept a sharp lookout to ensure that the table was organized in way that would stun the other parties with its assortment, quality and a menu like one never seen before in the Soviet Union - and in the end 'crush the adversary by culinary means.'"

Over 18 days, all the preparations were made to conduct such banquets as haven't been seen since the time of the Bourbon monarchs. Beria speaks about this in an entry of a report to Stalin:

... On location, reserves of meats and game; gastronomical, grocery, fruit and confectioner items; and types of drinks have been created. The local catch of fresh fish has been organized. Special bakeries have been set up and three independent kitchens equipped with refrigerators have been created at the locations of the three delegations - the Lividia, Iusupov and Vorontsov palaces; 3,250 cubic meters of dry wood have been brought in from Russia for the bakeries and kitchens...

Under the word "meats" - as Pokhlebkin decodes - Beria meant: "lamb, cattle, piglets, fattened calves, turkeys, geese, hens, ducks and rabbits."

The table settings required enormous efforts:

For it, 3,000 knives, 3,000 spoons and 3,000 forks (as well as 10,000 dishes of various sizes); 4,000 saucers and cups and 6,000 tables, goblets and wine glasses were needed. All this had to be acquired in a country in which 35 million males had been mobilized for the army - of which by this time approximately 10-12 million had already been lost - and in a country where for five years already there had not been a single table setting. Moreover, over all these years millions of such breakable, fragile objects had already been destroyed in the chaos of the war and evacuation.

For their contributions to staging the Yalta conference - the results of which (in Pokhlebkin's opinion) were greatly determined by the endless series of banquets - the authorities decorated an entire army of servants with Orders and medals. Altogether 1,021 men and women were awarded Orders and medals. Almost a third of the awards - 294 - went directly to the kitchen staff, table service and other personnel.

Reading these nearly tediously detailed descriptions, the reader cannot avoid the impression of barbaric, blasphemous luxury. It seems that Stalin was trying to intimidate his Allies, who had become his rivals, with his readiness to ask further sacrifices from his people in order to put on an extravagant display at a time when much of his country lay devastated by nearly four years of war. After all, in the Russian language, the words "engorgement" and "sacrifice" share the same root and a common origin.

For a long time already in the West, many politicians and journalists have been criticizing the Yalta agreements in the press. Moreover, they stress that Roosevelt arrived at the conference already fatally ill, so he was unable to take a detailed look at important documents and didn't even read some of them - fully relying instead on his assistants.

But who are the judges?

Criticism of the Yalta creators is primarily focused upon four issues. First, critics assume that the price that Stalin obtained for Russia's entrance into the war with Japan was excessive. Stalin demanded in return for the Red Army's participation in the war with Japan a guarantee of Mongolia's independence; the return to the USSR of the southern portion of Sakhalin and Port Arthur, which Japan had seized from Russia after the latter's defeat in 1905; internationalization of the port of Dairen and the Kurile Islands; the recognition of the USSR's western borders as of 22 June 1941; and the occupation of Manchuria. In exchange for all these demands, Stalin promised to enter the war with Japan within three months following the conclusion of combat operations in Europe.

A curious fact: the list of concessions seemed insufficient to Stalin and he later tried to seize another portion of Japan (the island of Hokkaido) by force; however, General MacArthur, the commander-in-chief of the U.S. army forces in the Far East, blocked the Red Army's access to Hokkaido and also rejected any Russian claims for a role in the occupational regime in Japan. Even today, no peace agreement has been concluded between Russia and Japan. The reason is Russia's unwillingness to return the Kurile Islands to Japan.

The atomic bomb still wasn't ready when Roosevelt went to Yalta. The Japanese army still numbered 6 million men and was continuing to offer stubborn resistance. So Roosevelt still considered Soviet participation in the war with Japan necessary.

General MacArthur promised Roosevelt that he would compel Japan to capitulate through aerial bombing. By this time, the American strategic bombing fleet already wielded enormous power. However, the experience in Europe was suggesting that the war could not be won without ground troops. Truman, as is known, tried to avoid an agreement with Russia about its entrance in the war with Japan, but he obtained nothing from this idea.[7]

The second issue, perhaps, was the most troubling: this was the implementation of the "Declaration on the Political Independence of Eastern European Nations". Indeed, this was primarily the concern of the Western Allies over the future of Poland. Subsequent events after Yalta demonstrated that the document approved by the "Big Three" was nothing more than a stack of papers to Stalin. His subsequent aggressive actions prompted even greater alarm in the United States and Great Britain. It was a time when Molotov said: "We had to consolidate what we had won." Even Stalin, in his own words, "was full of resolve not to miss this historic opportunity and not to 'blow it', as the West had often done in preceding wars with Russia."[8]

Historians at times express the thought that "Yalta in effect betrayed the Eastern European countries" and handed them over to the Kremlin's authority. Soviet rule over the region, as we know, continued for more than 40 years. The question is: "Could Stalin's refusal to comply with the Yalta agreements have been avoided?" The Allies attempted to use economic leverage against the USSR. In September 1945 they ceased Lend-Lease assistance to the Soviet Union, but this was awkward and unsuccessful; they also refused Moscow's request for credit and so forth. However, Stalin continued to establish a pro-Soviet regime in one country after another. There was only one way to attempt to block Stalin's aggressive intentions - war with the Soviet Union. Yet it was impossible to consider such a step seriously in the political climate that had developed at the end of the Second World War.

How was it possible to trust Stalin with respect to such a serious and fundamental question that touched the fate of millions of people? Historians raise this question. I offer only one example.

Churchill, speaking before the House of Commons about the Yalta conference, said:

> ..."Most solemn declarations have been made by Stalin and the Soviet Union that the sovereign independence of Poland is to be maintained, and this decision is now joined in both by Great Britain and the United States."[9]...

It is known that the British Prime Minister repeatedly said that Stalin always fulfilled everything that he had promised to Churchill. It turns out that even Churchill in the given case was again relying upon Stalin's word.

As a commentary on the words of the British Prime Minister, I'll cite one episode from diplomatic history. It was 1942. The outcome of the Second World War was still far from clear. A friendship and mutual assistance agreement between Great Britain and the Soviet Union had still not been concluded. Eden in Moscow - and then Churchill and Eden in London (now during Molotov's trip there) - refused to sign an agreement due to a categorical Soviet demand that its national boundaries as of 22 June 1941 be recognized. With alarm, Molotov and the Soviet Ambassador to Great Britain, Maisky, reported to Stalin: "Without the cited article, the agreement is just a piece of paper." Such was their surprise when Stalin in response gave them the order to sign the agreement right away. "As for the borders," Stalin said, "we will achieve them by force."

That is exactly how Stalin behaved after Yalta. Already just two weeks after the Yalta conference, at the end of February 1945, Romania's Government was toppled at Stalin's order and with the assistance of Soviet tanks. Petr Groza, who'd been brought in from Moscow, was appointed the new Head of State. Young King Mikhail, who had been awarded the Order of Victory by Moscow, soon was compelled to leave Romania and flee to Switzerland.

In December 1945, when I received my discharge papers from the Red Army and was traveling to Moscow, I spent three days in Bucharest. By that time, the entire country had been reorganized on the Soviet model; every trace of the King had been wiped away.

Chekists from Moscow brought in the legendary anti-fascist hero Georgi Dimitrov to Bulgaria and made him Premier. Stalin permitted free democratic elections in Hungary, Czechoslovakia and Poland. However, their results for Stalin were lamentable. So in the future he refused to take any risks. In the final analysis, communists seized power in all of these countries. I still have personal impressions of the "elections" in Hungary, which I will share with the reader.

In the autumn of 1945, when I was serving in Hungary, one day the division commander took me along to a meeting in Budapest. Commanders of all the Red Army units stationed in Hungary had gathered there, and here is why. At that time, a so-called "Control Commission" was operating in the capital. The Commission included representatives of all four victorious countries: the USSR, the U.S.A., Great Britain and France. K.E. Voroshilov represented the Soviet Union. The first postwar elections for Parliament were taking place. Understandably, as far as we could we assisted the communists. The not ignoble Matyas Rakosi addressed the meeting. As he spoke, the assembled generals almost fell into a trance. His message was essentially: "Don't bother us. We can manage by ourselves. It is better for you to bring order to your troops." The generals then heard a whole list of highly unpleasant examples.

K.E. Voroshilov spoke up: "The Control Commission has been overwhelmed with the complaints of Hungarian citizens against the Red Army. Our adversaries and the bourgeois press are eagerly taking advantage of them. I request you urgently draw the appropriate conclusions. If you do not, we will!"

On the road from Budapest back to the division, I asked the general: "What did Voroshilov's word 'we' mean?" He burst out laughing and simply replied: "The old fellow is joking … there's nothing in hell he can make us do."

On the eve of Election Day, the communists organized a demonstration and paraded down the streets of the city where our unit was stationed, with posters. I watched as people hurled pots of dishwater down on the heads of the marchers from the roofs of buildings, while young people on the sidewalks hissed and booed at the demonstrators. The elections were held. The communists received 26 per cent of the country's vote. The Independent Smallholders Party won the election. Soon thereafter I received my discharge and traveled to my parents' home in Moscow. When I was heading back home, I read in the central newspaper *Pravda* that the Communist Party, headed by Matyas Rakosi, had won the election. There you have it!

The third issue at the Yalta conference was connected with reparations. The Western Allies were astonished - having learned that Stalin was renouncing any gold. Playing the role of a totally modest (in the Western concept) gentleman, Stalin put forward his plan of reparations - according to which each of the countries would collect reparations from that part of Germany that it was occupying. Churchill and Roosevelt agreed. It turned out in reality that "Uncle Joe" had "outmaneuvered" his partners. There ensued the literal plundering of Soviet-occupied Germany and its citizens - as described in detail by Gavriil Popov.[10]

Finally, the most sensitive issue: it concerned displaced people and Russian prisoners of war. Even on this point, Churchill and Roosevelt "lost" to Stalin.

This decision was reached on the last day of the conference - 11 February 1945 at the Livadai Palace - where all the plenary sessions normally took place out of deference to Roosevelt's health, and where the "Big Three" gathered for the last time. It is also where the English-Soviet plan "Agreement on Russian prisoners of war" was confirmed.

The discussion of this Agreement was perhaps the sole case at Yalta that demanded effort from Stalin and caused him clear troubles. Let's pay attention to Stalin's words; to his style of speech; to his unusual behavior; when for the first time in his life he wasn't issuing orders; wasn't insisting; wasn't demanding, but literally entreating or even something more like imploring. Oh, what was the great actor seeking? He was hoping that the Allies would return to the USSR its former Soviet citizens who'd been driven from their lands by the aggressors and forced into slave labor in Germany - as well as the Russian prisoners of war - as soon as possible. Stalin promised that all these people would find a solid defense of their rights; that they'd be immediately separated from the German prisoners of war and receive care and proper treatment. These were Soviet citizens! They would be adequately fed and rendered necessary medical assistance.

The American President entrusted one of his assistants, General Fred M. Dean, to sign the Agreement on behalf of the United States. Roosevelt himself didn't even read the document - upon which the fate of millions of people depended.

At first glance, the text of the draft Agreement - which had been previously agreed upon by Russian generals and British diplomats in Moscow prior to Yalta - didn't raise any objections. Certainly, a few insignificant changes - more of a stylistic nature - had to be made to the document.

Only one question arose: who should be considered "Soviet citizens"? They agreed that all of the former Soviet citizens as of 17 September 1939 should be considered Soviet citizens. As it turned out, even Stalin recognized that residents of the Baltic republics, Western Ukraine, Moldavia, Northern Bukovina - as well as people who were part of the first wave of emigration from the USSR after the Revolution and the Civil War (especially those White Guard Troops who served in

Hitler's *Wehrmacht*) - would not be considered Russian prisoners of war.

Stalin understood that a certain portion of the displaced people and Russian prisoners of war did not wish to return to the Soviet Union. Thus, he was extremely interested in the adoption of strict conditions that would guarantee their return. He did everything possible so that the fewest number of witnesses to the "Soviet Paradise" would remain in the West as possible.

The Western Allies couldn't understand why people located in German prison camps might strive to avoid a return to their homeland. Stalin indeed reckoned with this circumstance and obtained from the creators of the Yalta agreements strict wording about compulsory repatriation, which had to be conducted independently of the desires of the displaced people and the prisoners of war - and which in fact contradicted the democratic principles of Great Britain and the United States (as well as international law).

It seemed to the American President and the British Prime Minister that this issue was the simplest of the entire complex of problems that they discussed at Yalta. In practice it turned out to be much more complicated than they had supposed. Repatriation generated an entire thicket of contradictions of the political, judicial and moral order and gave rise to a storm of protests on the part of social activists, churches, judges and diplomats.

The Western Allies were forced to use the army and military police in order to force people to return to their homelands against their will. This, in turn, resulted in enormous confusion and a large number of Russians - emigrants, who'd left Russia after the 1917 Revolution - wound up among the repatriates. In total, the Western Allies handed over approximately 2 million Russian prisoners of war back to Moscow.

Just what was guiding the Western Allies, on their way to meet Stalin, to take such fateful decisions? First of all there was the fate of their own prisoners of war, who'd fallen into the hands of the advancing Red Army as it overran German prisoner of war camps. There were approximately 232,000 American and British citizens in the camps that had been liberated by the Red Army.[11] Secondly, they had to consider that Stalin had promised to enter the war with Japan. Thirdly, before the end of the war and immediately after its conclusion, the problem of betrayal became an exceptionally acute one. This concept applied primarily to Russian prisoners who had voluntarily served in the German army and to those that the Germans called *kiwis*. Among them in the Allied camps were members of Russian combat units that had served in the *Wehrmacht*, Cossack units - as well as members of Vlasov's Russian Liberation Army. All of them had surrendered to the Allies in German uniforms.

Well, tell me for example, how should a *kiwi* driver - who delivered shells to the frontlines - be regarded? Take another example: a Russian volunteer who helped German armorers load bombs onto German aircraft?

Very often, the Americans and British - not to mention the Red Army - believed all the Russian military prisoners were Vlasovites, which is incorrect. In total there were approximately 120,000 men in Vlasov's Russian Liberation Army, which is approximately 5 per cent of the total number of Russian prisoners of war.

By the end of the war the number of Russian, Ukrainian, Belorussian and other volunteers from the Soviet Union comprised approximately 20 per cent of the total number of personnel in the *Wehrmacht*'s divisions. Russian, Ukrainian, Belorussian and other volunteers - especially from the Baltic republics - also served in the S.S.

Another astonishing example: there were more than 50,000 Russian volunteers serving in von Paulus's Sixth Army at Stalingrad. They fought fanatically in encirclement - and obviously those that remained alive after the surrender of the entire army were summarily shot.

When speaking about the military units of former Soviet volunteers, I can't fail to mention the following: In the estimate of the German historian I. Hoffman, over the entire period of the war the German army had 90 *Ost* battalions - of which 26 were from Turkestan (20,500 men); 15 were from Azerbaidzhan (36,600 men); 13 were Georgian (19,000); 12 were Armenian (7,000); and 9 were from the Northern Caucasus (15,000). There were also eight battalions of Crimean Tatars (10,000); seven battalions of Volga Tatars; and other peoples from the Volga and Ural regions (12,500). In 1942, in the zone of Army Group A's operations, a Kalmyk Cavalry Corps (5,000 men) was formed.[12]

Alongside the combat units in the *Wehrmacht*, there were 11 cadre battalions which served as the basis for forming march replacements - as well as 15 supply, construction and transportation battalions and 202 separate companies: 111 Turkestanian; 30 Georgian; 22 Armenian; 21 Azeri; 15 Tatar and three North Caucasus. Some of these companies were used to staff the 162nd (Turkic) Infantry Division. Thus, military formations comprised of Turkic and Caucasian nationalities numbered almost 150,000 men. A majority of them wound up as prisoners of war.

The American and British commands didn't view these prisoners of war through rose-tinted glasses - although when first taken prisoner, they were promised that they would not be turned over to Soviet authorities. In their turn the prisoners of war believed the Western Allies, who in their promises referred to the honor of the British Imperial Crown or American democratic institutions.

During the Second World War, the Allied troops landing in Normandy encountered numerous German combat units comprised of Russians. Russian volunteers served in Rommel's Afrika Korps and left behind bitter memories among the Italian people when they were committed against Italian partisan units. They also fought against Tito's army in Yugoslavia.

Often in the West the question is asked: "Didn't Roosevelt and Churchill understand what was awaiting the prisoners of war and the displaced people, who didn't wish to return to the Motherland, once they were handed over to Soviet authorities?" I believe basically that they did understand![13]

The Western Allies sought to avoid responsibility for the Russians - who wound up in their zones of occupation - and to avoid thinking about their difficulties, living arrangements, sustenance and other matters connected with them. In their own countries, they had their own returning veterans whom they were obliged first of all to care for.

As a result of the indifferent attitude of the Western Allies and world public opinion, the repatriation process turned into so-called "extraditions", which is normally applied to criminals. Arbitrary treatment often reigned and blood was spilled.

In the West, a multitude of books have been written about these shameful "extraditions" and hundreds of personal testimonies have been collected. In the Soviet Union, this subject was taboo for many long years.

According to the latest data, in the course of the Great Patriotic War 4,059,000 Soviet soldiers and commanders wound up as prisoners of war - of which 2 million perished in imprisonment, 1.83 million returned to the Motherland and the remainder managed to avoid repatriation - becoming part of the Russian diaspora in the West.[14]

Already after the campaign against Finland in 1940, practically every Soviet soldier who returned from captivity was condemned in a judicial or extra-judicial manner. This approach existed unchanged through all the years of the Great Patriotic War and decades after it. Whether the soldier had escaped captivity, emerged from encirclement or had turned up on liberated territory, he received 10 years of imprisonment without exception. All these "former service personnel of the Red Army"- as these people were called in official documents because they'd "been exposed to the influence of German ideology" - had to pass through "political vetting" while in confinement. Those who while in German prison had held senior positions in the barracks or who had served as doctors, nurses, translators or cooks were regarded as "agents of German intelligence organs". Meanwhile, those who'd been liberated by British or American troops were suspected of having "connections with British or American intelligence". For the rest of their lives, these people were deprived of the benefits that other war veterans enjoyed. There were no legal documents whatsoever which would have permitted an objective re-examination of their fates. Only on 24 January 1995 did a decree appear - signed by the Russian Federation's President - "On the re-establishment of the legal rights of Russian citizens"; the former Soviet military prisoners and civilians who'd been repatriated during the Great Patriotic War and in the postwar period.

To this day there are no precise statistics on the "former Soviet citizens". How many of them were brought back to Soviet Russia in prisoner railcars and steamship jails and what was their fate? It was particularly tragic for the former members of Vlasov's Russian Liberation Army. I'll cite one paragraph of an interview with Vladimir Bashev:

> ... The Russians, who fell into the hands of the Western Allies, were treated very dishonorably. They were promised that they wouldn't be given back to the Soviets, but according to the Yalta agreement each one who'd been a citizen of the USSR on 1 September 1939 was subject to repatriation. Anyone who on 22 June 1941 had been wearing a Red Army uniform was moreover supposed to be returned - into the hands of SMERSH. They

> indeed had a very sad fate. Most of the repatriated officers were immediately shot. Soldiers were sent into the Gulag. The British and Americans - especially the British - betrayed them...[15]

I will discuss the woeful fate of Russian prisoners of war in a subsequent chapter.

"God can't change the past; historians can."

Samuel Butler

9
The Meeting at the Elbe

The Echo of the Elbe

That is the name of a monument that has been erected in the German town of Torgau in honor of the link-up between American troops and Russian troops on 25 April 1945.[1] In the last springtime days of the war, photographs that captured this historic meeting flew around the world. American Lieutenant Bill Robertson and Soviet Lieutenant Aleksandr Silvashko are shown standing on the supports of the bridge across the Elbe that the Germans had demolished the day before - extending their hands to each other in a friendly handshake.

A half-century later Bill Robertson - speaking on behalf of the veterans of the 273rd Regiment of the First Army's 69th Division at a commemorative ceremony in Washington D.C. - said:

> ... This was the culmination after lengthy waiting and worries. We cheered and celebrated. A feeling of triumph seized all of us. We offered toasts. We clapped each other on the back. We embraced. We exchanged souvenirs. We understood that our meeting was significant and meant the end of the Nazi *Wehrmacht*. We were happy that we had survived to see victory and felt that we wouldn't have to wait long for peace...

Of the approximately 150-200 American officers and soldiers who appeared on the eastern bank of the Elbe after Lieutenant Robertson, 35 were able to attend the ceremony in Washington D.C.

To the Soviet soldiers and officers who had passed through the long years of the war, it seemed on those unforgettable spring days that a long-awaited hour had finally arrived. The American and Soviet armies met roughly 75 miles to the south of Berlin - thereby splitting remaining German territory in two and closing the gap between the Eastern and Western Fronts. One of the American newspapers from that time wrote about the event:

> ... The link-up - which Washington, Moscow and London announced simultaneously - occurred on the afternoon of 25 April in Torgau on the Elbe River. The Russian soldiers could be described best of all as just like the Americans: a feeling of irrepressible happiness swept over all of them; a grand new world was opening...

Just by chance, Lieutenant Robertson wound up on that day on the bank of the river opposite a Russian unit. His patrol was conducting a search for wounded American soldiers. Aleksandr Silvashko, having noticed the American flag, took it as an enemy ploy and the Russian soldiers opened fire. However, the alarming situation quickly dissipated. The famous photo of "Ryan and Ivan" appeared in the world press.

The American former corporal Joe Polovsky requested that he be buried in Torgau - which was indeed done in 1983. Before his death, he said that the soldiers of both countries gave an oath on the Elbe: not to allow a new war. As he recalled: "All of us simple soldiers - both American and Russian soldiers - were national heroes when we met." The American veteran Roland Hay recalled of these days: "We were just happy."

In honor of the 50th Anniversary of the "Meeting at the Elbe", an exhibition was unveiled in Torgau's town hall where the organizers also displayed the famous photo of Robertson and Silvashko. The former Lieutenant Silvashko attended the opening ceremony. At the time, he was 83 years old. He spoke without embellishment about how the meeting between the Russians and Americans had taken place 50 years before.

Why not drink up to such a joyous event? So they drank with a vengeance! Colonel-in-retirement Stepan Stankov recalls: "There were two or three barrels of vodka sitting on our bank of the river. We quickly emptied them. The Americans liked our 'frontline drink', but the Russians didn't care for whisky." General Omar Bradley even issued a curious order. Officers being sent to meet with the Russians were mandatorily ordered to eat 50 grams of butter prior to breakfast in order to hold up against the onslaught of their amicability. Did it help?

How did the Soviet press note the "Meeting at the Elbe"? Here's a lengthy excerpt from the *Krasnaia zvezda* newspaper for 28 April 1945:

> ... Approaching the Elbe, our soldiers and officers knew that here in Saxony the first meeting with troops of our Western Allies would take place. The first to make contact with units of the American Twelfth Army Group were our radio operators. Conversation between our radiomen and the Allies' radiomen were occurring at a moment when the forward units of the 1st Ukrainian Front were already less than 30 kilometers from our comrades-in-arms. "We'll soon meet with you," our signalmen transmitted.

The forward units of our Allies had people among their radiomen who knew the Russian language. They supported radio communications with our radio operators - while transmitting greetings to them from their own soldiers and officers - and reported that in all of their units, they were waiting with excitement to link-up with the Red Army.

Where would the encounter take place? Who first would shake the hand of an ally?

The long-awaited event took place under the following circumstances: A battalion of our Guardsmen were approaching the river. A castle from the Middle Ages - surrounded by a high, thick wall with turrets - towered above its left bank. Captain Dolgy's battalion took this German strongpoint by storm. At this time, several armored cars under a red, white and blue flag were approaching the castle from the west. Soldiers in camouflaged uniforms and round helmets hopped out of the vehicles. We could hear shouts: "Moscow!"; "Chita!"; "Victory!" An astonishing coincidence seemed to be a happy omen to all the witnesses. The American battalion commander happened to share the same last name as the Soviet commander and even turned out to be related to him. As far as we could understand from his tale, his ancestors had left Russia for the Pacific Coast at some time in search of a better life. Each of the kinsmen that had met unexpectedly knew nothing about the existence of the other, but now the combat brotherhood against Nazism had linked them even more closely than blood ties. They tightly embraced - and this moment was forever captured in a photograph.

Link-up occurred at two points in the area of the town of Torgau. Henceforth this small Saxon city, with its ancient Town Hall which stands on the banks of the Elbe and is known for Martin Luther and the Seven Year's War, will enter history. Soviet and Allied officers visited each other. The combat banners of the Soviet regiments fluttered in the spring breeze. Soviet and foreign photo correspondents took hundreds of photographs to capture the historic moment. A particular cadre enjoyed particular success among the Western reporters that had rushed to the place of meeting: Russians who were distributing little souvenirs to their Allies such as various insignia, little stars, etc.

Guards Major General Petrov hosted a reception in his division for the American brigadier general and his retinue. At the reception both commanders exchanged welcome speeches. In his speech,

> the American general declared: "I'm experiencing the happiest days of my life. I am proud and happy that my division was lucky to be the first to meet with units of the heroic Red Army on German territory. Two brotherly Allied armies have come together. This meeting will accelerate the final defeat of Germany's armed forces."
>
> In his return speech, Guards Major General Petrov replied: "The long-awaited and joyous day has arrived. Two great armies have met on German territory. The heroic Red Army has traveled a long path of intense struggle and glorious victories. The meeting of two Allied armies is a major historic event in the struggle with Nazi Germany. Let this meeting serve as the guarantee of the rapid and final defeat of Hitler's army and the establishment of an enduring peace."
>
> The "Meeting at the Elbe" will remain forever in the memory of all who in these days are located on German territory - far from the Motherland, fighting for peace and happiness for all mankind…

After the end of the Second World War - after Potsdam and the occupation of conquered Nazi Germany - for a long time the Cold War cast a pall over the once friendly relations of the Allies in the war years. In 1949, at the height of the "chill", a new film by Grigorii Aleksandrov appeared on Soviet screens entitled: *Vstrecha na El'be* [*Meeting at the Elbe*]. It had nothing to do whatsoever with the real events. On the contrary, it had a direct relationship with the Cold War.

Three former frontline soldiers - I and my friends Isaak Sokol'sky and Tolia Konopel'kin - went to the Coliseum movie theater in the Chistye Prudy neighborhood of Moscow to see our favorite actors and actresses: Liubov' Orlova, Faina Ranevskaia and Aleksandr Kadochnikov. Our "reunion" with them proved to be lamentable! When the lights came back on in the hall, we went outside and were silent for a long time. Tolia broke the silence with a single word: "Shameful!"

The plot was primitive and the characters were caricatures. An American spy (played by Orlova) seduces a Soviet officer (played by Kadochnikov). The Americans in the film are depicted as spies, anti-Soviets, speculators and forgers … but the Soviet press praised this cheap piece of propaganda to the heavens. Very quickly the film gained cult status in Russia. However, in our soldiers' hearts Tolia's single-word review remained as the proper one.

Ending this story of the "Meeting at the Elbe" I'll introduce a little-known fact about one more "disgrace" - an inter-office memorandum written by A.V. Khrulev, General of the Army and the Supreme Commander's deputy in charge of the Red Army rear services on behalf of Beria, Malenkov and Voznesensky. The cited text speaks for itself:

> ... The appearance of our Red Army soldier and officer sharply contrasts with the appearance of the soldiers and officers of the Allied armies, whose cotton uniform preserves its original color for a long time. The unflattering sight of our faded uniforms particularly stands out in the zones of contact between our troops and Allied troops...

Conclusions followed quickly. They urgently began to remove manufacturing lines for the production of colored textiles from Germany to the USSR. But they didn't stop with this: socializing between the Soviet soldiers and their Allies was curtailed. To be honest, the faded Red Army soldiers' tunics were not at all the sole reason for this.

I'll cite one more bit of text - a "special message" as they were called back then - written by an Agent "Fisherman":

> ... Summoned for a discussion about the final stage of the war and about the meeting with the Allied soldiers, Subject "Perch" acknowledged the praiseworthiness of foreign military equipment - going so far as to confirm the superiority of some of its types over their Soviet counterparts. In particular, he asserted that our forces acutely lacked the armored personnel carriers like those that equipped the German-fascist aggressors - as well as the American and British armies. To my statement that: "Our infantry was the queen of the battlefield", Subject "Perch" said word for word: "A queen perhaps, only her slippers are quite painful in the mud - a pain in the neck!" which was a jibe over the well-known expression of Comrade Stalin himself. He recalled with pleasure the "Meeting at the Elbe" with his relative - an officer of the White Far Eastern army - but asserted that this meeting took place "purely by happenstance" - without any preliminary agreement - and as he assures, there were no further contacts.
>
> Agent Fisherman

The "Meeting at the Elbe" - and not only it alone - gave rise to many malicious and vile "special messages" like this one.

On the eve of the 60th Victory Anniversary, film director Marina Drozdova created a new documentary film: *Vstrecha na Elbe* [*Meeting at the Elbe*]. The film was shown on Russian television at 11:00 P.M. on 9 May 2005.

Many veterans of those years - soldiers of the Second World War - didn't live to see the 60th Anniversary. Lieutenant Robertson died in 1999. Lieutenant Silvashko passed away a little later. However, the grateful remembrance of the first "Meeting at the Elbe" between Russian and American soldiers lives on!

The Supreme Commander intently kept a wary eye on the "Meeting at the Elbe" with the American troops. "How will the Red Army officers and soldiers conduct themselves in contacts with them? Will there be fraternization or friction?" Stalin read the daily summaries of the political organizations and SMERSH - as well as about the events happening at the Elbe. The meetings with the American troops were occurring in a festive atmosphere. Here's what happened when General Rusakov, commander of the 58th Rifle Division, met with General Reinhardt, the commander of the American 69th Infantry Division: toasts, speeches, gifts and cheers. Katkov, the chief of the 5th Guards Army's Political Department, reported:

> ... at this meeting, the Americans sought to get their hands on stars, epaulettes and buttons as souvenirs. The general added that: "the Soviet soldiers were surprised by the fact that it was difficult to distinguish a general from a private among the Americans. They all wore the same uniform. What a difference with us: a general stands out from a distance"...

Stalin privately was in agreement with the Soviet soldiers. He after all loved his marshal's uniform and now never parted from it - often lingering in front of a mirror for a minute or two. "The Americans with their rotten democracy don't understand: a society must have a hierarchy. In dress it is immediately visible to all ...." Katkov added: "Incidentally, the writer Konstantin Simonov was at the meeting." The Supreme Commander likely noted to himself: "He doesn't write badly about the war. Now they're fraternizing, but how much effort it took to get the cooperation going!"

In those days, the Supreme Commander's attention wasn't only focused on the "Meeting at the Elbe"; the army remained his bigger concern. According to information from the *Stavka*, there had already been lamentable combats between Soviet and American airplanes resulting in dead and wounded.

In the last days of April and the beginning of May, Antonov daily reported to Stalin about our units' encounters with the Allies. For the Supreme Commander, this was that aspect of the war which he (and not only he!) had linked with prolonged waiting, hopes, disappointments, renewed hopes and – finally - military cooperation. A whole bundle of dispatches lay on Stalin's desk: from the headquarters of the 58th Guards Rifle Division; the headquarters of the 1st Belorussian Front; from the commander of the 61st Army; the commander of the 2nd Belorussian Front; chiefs of the Political Departments of the 5th Guards and 13th Armies; the headquarters of the 3rd Ukrainian Front; the Political Directorate of the 2nd Belorussian Front; and other headquarters and political organs.

Stalin had especially requested these dispatches. He wanted to get a sense of the immediate mood of the generalship, the officers and the rank and file; he wanted to find out about the behavior of the Western Allies in order to calibrate his future course in relations with them. After all, the war was ending only in the West. The leaders of the "Big Three" - who had extended a hand to each other in Teheran, at Yalta (and would soon do so in Potsdam) - had at the same time taken several major steps toward securing a long-awaited peace. In the spring of 1945, it seemed that the alliance of the former rivals would be firm and long-lasting. Given all of Stalin's orthodoxies, for the sake of the anti-fascist coalition he had sacrificed the Communist International; pushed ideological postulates far to the side; and closed his eyes to Churchill's anti-Soviet hostility and that of the Western democracies as a whole. At the most critical moments and turning points, pragmatic thoughts were always first and foremost in Stalin's mind. Normally the Supreme Commander read only General Staff summaries, messages from the fronts and reports by the *Stavka* representatives. But now, in the days of the approaching triumph, he was looking through a lot of reports of a completely different nature.

Vasilii Askallov, a Cossack, had served in Budenny's army in the Russian Civil War. He'd been arrested in 1937 for showing "disrespect to DOSAAF [the Voluntary Society for Cooperation with the Army, Air Force and Navy]." According to a denunciation of an eyewitness, he had tossed a DOSAAF stamp that he had purchased into an urn. He was lucky: several months later, he was released. Rumors went around that Semen Mikhailovich Budenny himself had interceded on his behalf.

They allowed him to rejoin the army. He entered the Great Patriotic War as a colonel. He commanded the 173rd Guards Rifle Division at Stalingrad. He made it all the way to Berlin - finishing the war as a major general and with the title Hero of the Soviet Union. He participated in the meeting on the Elbe with the Allies. SMERSH received word from an informant that the general "had been smiling broadly at the Americans." The report traveled up the chain to Abakumov [the head of SMERSH] and then to the Supreme Commander. Comrade Stalin pronounced: "An investigation is necessary."

Hero of the Soviet Union and Major General Vasilii Askalenov Askallov was arrested. Then they "investigated" him so thoroughly that the Cossack was left half-dead both physically and morally before they released him. They brought him home on a stretcher, but a couple of weeks later he died ....

On 23 April 1945 the *Stavka* of the Supreme High Command issued Directive No. 11075, which laid out instructions to the troops on how to act during encounters with ex-compatriots. In accordance with it Marshal Zhukov prepared and distributed an order to the troops which precisely specified how to act, what to say, what to keep silent and to take no initiative in organizing meetings (but to report everything up the chain of command) and: "to provide no information to anyone about our plans and the combat tasks of our forces."[2]

The most important thing for Stalin in those historic days was to take care that the Allied armies didn't cross into the Soviet zone of occupation as established at the Yalta conference - the boundary of which was marked by the Elbe River. To mark their respective locations, Soviet troops were supposed to fire red signal flares while the Americans were supposed to use green ones. Everything went wrong....

In Lavrenov's and Popov's book *Krakh Reikha* [*Downfall of the Reich*] the authors explain in detail that in those April days during the encounter at the Elbe, "what was really happening" depended on the respective perspectives from the West and the East.[3]

In the present day, the concerns of the Soviet command and its assessments of the conduct of Allied troops seem amusing and foolish; the Soviet generals and officers back then viewed each question asked by the Americans as almost a wicked ploy - as attempts to uncover some sort of deep and dark secrets of the Red Army. All of this the authors of the book cited above lay out in detail.

One example is how suspiciously the Soviet command viewed the energetic behavior of an American female journalist of the *St. Louis Post-Dispatch* newspaper with the last name of Irwin. She made an attempt to leave the regiment that received the Americans, but she was turned back and then returned to the western bank of the river. The American journalist had conducted an interview with a nurse from the 58th Guards Rifle Division's medical sanitation battalion, Senior Sergeant Liza Parnikovaia. In one of the political reports, the nurse informs in detail that the American journalist had asked a lot of questions - and having slung a sub machine gun around her neck, she took photographs of the esteemed nurse. Parnikovaia demonstrated vigilance even to the question: "What unit were you in when you arrived to meet with the Americans?" She replied evasively: "I came from a medical school." ... Incidentally, the American army didn't conceal the identity of their combat units (army, corps, division) from the Germans. They believed that it was best not to make a secret of this because the Germans would know anyway what unit they were facing. In the Soviet army, as we know, from the beginning of the war to the end soldiers were told not to reveal their combat unit. But regardless, the Germans had precise information on the identity of the Red Army units opposite them.

The encounters at the Elbe between the Allies continued until 17 May 1945. It has been described in detail in many newspapers and journals - and films have been made about it in both the West and the East. They concluded with a meeting between I.S. Konev, the commander of the 1st Ukrainian Front, and Omar Bradley, the commander of the American Twelfth Army Group. In his postwar memoirs General Bradley wrote a lot about these meetings, which, unfortunately, I.S. Konev didn't do in his own memoirs.

Very soon on the banks of the Elbe River, where just recently American and Russian soldiers had been meeting, other encounters were taking place - about which the Soviet press kept silent - and for many years afterward, no one could even guess what might have happened here.

It turns out that there was a rather large prison in Torgau, which had housed criminals during the Nazi regime. Having inspected it, SMERSH officers who had arrived at the Elbe declared that it was fully suitable to receive the "Returnees".

On almost a daily basis, they met barges arriving from the American zone. The barges were carrying displaced Soviet citizens. SMERSH members courteously greeted the Americans, but their conduct instantly changed as soon as the barges shoved off from the shore and headed back to the opposite bank. A senior officer would appear and shout in a menacing voice: "Hey, you traitors, get your bags and form into a line!" Soldiers with hellish dogs, ready to pounce upon the people in a flash and tear them to pieces, would materialize.

The men and women, who were stunned and agitated after such an unexpected reception of them by the first Soviet people they'd seen, would go limp and obediently begin to form a column. They were encircled by sub machine gunners who without any extra words escorted them to the prison in Torgau.

One wing of the prison was holding Vlasovites, members of Vlasov's RLA - or other Russians who had served the German military - who'd been sentenced to be shot. There are stories that through a window of that wing, the condemned men would shout: "We died for the Motherland, but not for Stalin!" A colonel who wound up in a hospital - having learned that his female doctor was from the political branch of the Red Army - told her: "Obviously, they're going to shoot me soon, but our hatred is for the Bolsheviks…"

"There is nothing more frightening in life than the absolute impossibility to change that which you have already done."

Golsuorsi

10

The Political and Military Fervor Surrounding the Taking of Berlin

Is Valentin Falin correct?

Valentin Falin, who holds a Ph.D. in History and is a rabid anti-Westerner who has served as a Party functionary and diplomat, categorically asserts: "Without the storming of Berlin, a Third World War would have been in store for Russia." He laid out his views in a series of dubious assertions in an article with that statement as its title.[1]

At first Falin attempts to answer the question: "Was the slaughter - almost 120,000 Soviet soldiers and officers killed or mortally wounded [sic] - worth the taking of Berlin under Soviet control and raising the Victory Banner above the Reichstag?" True, a story likely conceived by a Russian historian has circulated that supposedly the Germans proposed to surrender Berlin to the Western Allies without resistance. However, the *Wehrmacht*'s behavior on the Western Front until the last days of the war gives no support to this assertion.

Giving his answer to the question, Falin believes that the capture of Berlin by the Red Army - despite the high casualties - was not a gamble as some Western historians treat it, but a deeply considered political, military and psychological step calculated to prevent a new war, but now one against the Western Allies. The main idea of a step like this one, in Stalin's opinion, consisted in demonstrating the Red Army's enormous power by storming the Reich's capital and seizing it by force. In this way, he hoped to impress the Western Allies with a display of Red Army invincibility. Was this so? Let me say a few preliminary words before I give my answer.

Winston Churchill turned with the question of whether or not Berlin should be seized ahead of the advancing Red Army not to the President of the United States Franklin D. Roosevelt, but to the Supreme Commander of the Allied Expeditionary Force in Europe Dwight Eisenhower. The British Prime Minister argued that the war was coming to an end and political problems were coming to the forefront. Thus, first of all, it was necessary for the Western Allies to capture Berlin before the Russians did. He pointed out that American troops would reach the Elbe River prior to the Soviet divisions and therefore might quickly be able to cover the remaining distance to Berlin from the river.

Eisenhower replied to Churchill that he had no intention of taking Berlin because it was of no military value. In addition, the demarcation line that had already been agreed upon with the Russians would still run 150 kilometers to the west of Berlin regardless of where the Allied forces were standing at the final moment of the war. Finally, Eisenhower told Churchill that they had already calculated the probable losses if the Allied troops pushed on to Berlin and captured it - and they would amount to no less than 100,000 men for the sake of some uncertain political advantage. On this the conversation stopped.

As for Stalin's position - "Take Berlin at whatever the cost" - this is well-known. When his military commanders reported their conclusions to the Supreme Commander and gave their estimates that the capture of Berlin - which had been converted by the Germans into a fortress-city - would entail heavy casualties, Stalin without pausing to reflect replied: "We don't need a cheap victory!" So all the lads in pants with trouser stripes, forward!

In order to fulfill Stalin's order, the Red Army lost not the 120,000 as Falin asserts, but 300,000 if not more. Who was counting? Zhukov? Konev? Hardly...

I have read about the "Berlin operation" in the memoirs of Marshal Konev, the commander of the 1st Ukrainian Front, several times. There is not even a word or half-word in it about the human losses of his armies! To be sure, the Marshal reports the loss of 800 tanks and the wounding of one of his subordinate military commanders. S. Ia. Lavrenov and I.M. Popov have written in detail about the casualties of the 1st Belorussian Front.[2] They place the number of dead in the 1st Belorussian Front alone at 140,000 - as well as the loss of more than 2,500 tanks and self-propelled guns.

Did the Western Allies have an opportunity to seize Berlin before the Soviet forces reached it? Leaders of the Western countries - as well as Eisenhower and Montgomery - believed that they did! In particular, Roosevelt believed that: "We should get Berlin and let the Soviets claim the territory to the East."[3] Prime Minister Churchill and Field Marshal Montgomery designated Berlin as the main objective. In that case, why did they yield Germany's capital to the Red Army?

Now let's turn to the "facts" - as set forth by Falin:

The First Assertion: According to Falin, by March 1945 German resistance on the Western Front had entirely ceased. Dwight Eisenhower, the Supreme Commander of the Allies in Europe, believed otherwise. He expressed his views of the events that were unfolding back then on the Western Front in his memoirs.[4] As Eisenhower details, in March 1945 the Allied armies were forcing the Rhine River and bloody fighting was still continuing for the Ruhr basin. By 1 April, Allied troops had fully encircled the Ruhr and powerful Allied force groupings were now advancing through the territory of Germany itself. The Germans had almost fully lost the Ruhr, the Saar and Silesia. The remnants of industry, which had been scattered across the entire central region of Germany, could no longer support the army - though it was continuing to fight. According to Eisenhower, the German communications system had been so thoroughly destroyed by American strategic bombing that "no Nazi senior commander could ever be sure that his orders would reach the troops for whom they were intended." For all practical purposes, the forcing of the Rhine and the subsequent encirclement and surrender of the Germans' 325,000-man Ruhr grouping at the end of March 1945 put an end to the *Wehrmacht*'s organized resistance in the West.

On 31 March, Eisenhower - having described the hopelessness of their situation - appealed to the German troops and people to cease their resistance. "But," Eisenhower writes further, "the hold of Hitler on his associates was still so strong and was so effectively applied elsewhere through the medium of the Gestapo and S.S. that the country continued to fight."

The German troops in the West were inspired by the thought that they were in effect guarding the rear of the *Wehrmacht* forces in the East. If they ceased to resist, the Eastern Front in turn would collapse. With the aim of preventing the armies from retreating in battles against the Allies, Hitler organized so-called "flying special tribunals" headed by the Nazi fanatic General Hübner. This general received the right to execute soldiers and officers for cowardice or refusing to carry out the Führer's orders. Many officers and soldiers were killed this way.

The Second Assertion: Falin reproaches the Allies for accepting the separate capitulation of the Germans in Reims. Representatives of the German command had been making contacts with Allied commanders - seeking to draw out the negotiations and trying to convince the Allied High Command to agree to a German surrender only on the Western Front. However, such proposals had been categorically rejected. An Act of Unconditional Surrender on all the fronts was signed in Reims on 7 May 1945 at 0241. According to it, combat operations were to cease at midnight, 8 May 1945. Russian and French representatives also signed the Act. The story of the signing of the Instrument of Unconditional Surrender in Reims deserves particular attention - especially because of the participation in this procedure of a Soviet representative, General Susloparov.

Falin discusses the act of signing the Germans' surrender in Reims almost in terms of a detective story. Here is what he writes:

> ... it required enormous efforts from us to compel Truman to agree to a confirmation of the surrender in Berlin. With the participation of the Soviet Union and the Allies, there was agreement

> to make 9 May the sole "Victory Day". Incidentally, there was another put-up job that occurred in Reims. The Yalta conference had confirmed the text of an agreement about Germany's unconditional surrender. Roosevelt, Churchill and Stalin all validated it with their signatures. However, the Americans acted as if they'd forgotten about the existence of this document, which incidentally was lying in the safe of Eisenhower's chief of staff, Smith. A circle around Eisenhower led by Smith put together a new document, which had been purged of Yalta's stipulations that were undesirable to the Allies. Moreover, this document was signed by General Smith on behalf of the Allies while the Soviet Union wasn't even mentioned - as if it had not taken part in the war. That's the type of show that played out in Reims. The document of the surrender in Reims was transmitted to the Germans even before it was received in Moscow…

The story of the signing of the surrender document in Reims and all of Comrade Falin's insinuations merits more detailed commentary.

The document regarding Germany's military capitulation was signed by representatives of the *Oberkommando der Wehrmacht* [OKW - or the Supreme Command of the German armed forces] in Reims and in Berlin-Karlshorst where the headquarters of the Allied Expeditionary Force (General Eisenhower) and the Red Army (Marshal Zhukov) were respectively located. However, neither in Reims nor in Berlin-Karlshorst were the German representatives presented with the European Advisory Committee's document concerning Germany's unconditional surrender because at this moment, the question about whether the Germans should sign the initial version - which had been approved by representatives of all four powers in London, or the later version that had been re-examined by the "Big Three" in Yalta - had still not been conclusively resolved. With this question unresolved, Eisenhower was forced to create a completely new document of surrender on the basis of directives concerning local, partial surrenders and submit it for the signatures of the OKW representatives.

The unconditional total surrender of Germany came into effect on 5 June 1945. Since at this time the government of the German Reich and the leaders of the OKW were now in Allied military prison camps, the unconditional military and full State-Political surrender of Germany was announced by the four victorious powers in the form of a declaration from the European Control Commission [ECC]: the "Declaration Regarding the Defeat of Germany and the Assumption of Supreme Power with Respect to Germany by the Governments of the United States of America, the Union of Soviet Socialist Republics, the United Kingdom and the Provisional Government of the French Republic." In addition, the ECC issued terms that concerned the occupation zones and the control mechanism in Germany. A comparison of the European Advisory Committee's surrender document with the European Control Commission's declaration shows that all of the articles of the former document without exception were transferred to the latter document without substantial changes. When accusing Eisenhower and the Allies of attempting to pull a fast one, Valentin Falin revealed his complete ignorance of the question that he was examining regarding the unconditional surrender document.

G.K. Zhukov recalls in his memoirs that Stalin gave an order to him and said: "We reached an understanding with the Allies that the Surrender Act signed in Reims should be considered a preliminary protocol of surrender. Tomorrow, representatives of the German High Command and representatives of the Supreme Command of the Allied forces will arrive in Berlin. You are appointed representative of the Supreme Command of the Soviet forces."[5]

But in the West, the war was already considered over with the signing of the Reims surrender document. On this basis, the USA and England proposed that on 8 May the Heads of State of the three powers should announce the victory over Germany. The Soviet Government couldn't agree with this for the reason that combat on the Soviet-German Front was still continuing. Now let's turn to the German, Soviet, British and American documents.

Stalin tried to convince Harry Truman and Winston Churchill to consider 9 May as Victory Day in Europe - not 8 May - but nothing came of this idea. I'll submit a message from Stalin on this subject and the replies to it from the American President and British Prime Minister:

PERSONAL AND SECRET MESSAGE

FROM MARSHAL J.V. STALIN

TO THE PRIME MINISTER, MR. W. CHURCHILL

I have received your message from 7 May regarding the announcement of Germany's surrender.

The Supreme Command of the Red Army is not sure that the order of the German High Command on unconditional surrender will be executed by the German armies on the Eastern Front. We fear, therefore, that if the government of the USSR announces today the surrender of Germany we may find ourselves in an awkward position and mislead the Soviet public. It should be borne in mind that the German resistance on the Eastern Front is not slackening but, judging by intercepted radio messages, a considerable grouping of German troops have explicitly declared their intention to continue the resistance and to disobey Dörnitz's surrender order.

For this reason the command of the Soviet troops would like to wait until the German surrender takes effect and to postpone the government's announcement of the surrender until 9 May, at 7:00 P.M. Moscow time.

7 May 1945

Prime Minister Churchill's reply:

7 May 1945

PERSONAL AND MOST SECRET MESSAGE FROM MR. CHURCHILL TO MARSHAL STALIN

I have just received your message and have also seen the letter from General Antonov to General Eisenhower suggesting that the announcement of the German surrender should be postponed till 9 May 1945. It will not be possible for me to put off my announcement for 24 hours as you suggest. Moreover Parliament will require to be informed of the signature at Reims yesterday and of the formal ratification arranged to take place in Berlin today. I have spoken with General Eisenhower on the telephone and he assures me of his intention to cooperate to the full with all forces against the fanatical groups of the enemy who may disobey the orders they have received from their own government and High Command. This would of course apply to all British and United States forces under General Eisenhower's command. I shall make it clear in my announcement that there is still resistance in some places. This is not surprising considering the immense length of the front and disorganized condition of the German Government. I believe that President Truman is making his announcement at 09:00 A.M. American Time today and I hope that you will be able with the necessary reservations to make yours arranged.

8 May 1945

On 8 May, President H. Truman sent a letter to the Soviet Ambassador in the United States, A. Gromyko, with the following contents: "I request that you inform Marshal Stalin that his message to me was received in the White House today at 1:00 A.M. However, when the message reached me, its preparation had taken so long that it proved impossible to examine the question of postponing my announcement of Germany's surrender."

Finally, the story regarding the signing of the Act of Germany's Surrender in Reims by General Susloparov, the Chief of the Soviet Mission with the Supreme Command of Allied forces, should be briefly told. It is not without interest.

On the evening of 6 May, Dwight Eisenhower's adjutant flew into Paris to see General Susloparov. He handed the chief of the Soviet Mission an invitation from the Supreme Commander to come immediately to his headquarters. Eisenhower received I.A. Susloparov. Smiling, he informed him that Hitler's General Jodl had arrived with a proposal to surrender to the Anglo-American forces but to continue to fight against the USSR.

A little later Susloparov was again invited to see Eisenhower, who informed the Soviet representative that after the Allies' demand for total surrender the Germans agreed to sign the corresponding Act. Eisenhower requested Susloparov to report the text of the surrender document to Moscow, to obtain its approval and to sign it on behalf of the Soviet Union. The signing, in his words, was scheduled for 0204 7 May 1945 in the premises of the Supreme Headquarters' Operations Department.

The draft of the document that Susloparov received spoke of the unconditional surrender of all ground, sea and air forces located under German control at the given moment. The German command was obliged to issue an order to cease combat at 0000 hours, 1 minute (Moscow Time) on 9 May. All German troops were to remain in the positions that they were occupying. It was forbidden to disable weapons and other means of armed struggle. The execution of all the orders of the Supreme Commander of the Allied Expeditionary Forces and the Soviet Supreme High Command was guaranteed.

Several hours passed before Susloparov's telegram reached its addressee. In Reims it was past midnight and the time for signing the surrender had arrived. However, instructions from Moscow still hadn't arrived. The situation had arisen where an Act of Germany's Surrender could be signed only between Germany, England and the United States - which would give the Germans the opportunity to continue combat operations on the Eastern Front.

The position of the chief of the Soviet Military Mission was extremely difficult. Everything now depended upon him. Should he sign the Act on behalf of the USSR or refuse?

Ivan Susloparov understood full well that in the event of some negligence on his part, the Germans' maneuver to surrender only to the Western Allies might result in the greatest misfortune. He read and re-read the text of the surrender document and didn't find any concealed, evil design in it. Meanwhile, in front of the general's eyes were images of the war which was carrying away a multitude of human lives with each passing minute. The chief of the Soviet Military Mission made the courageous decision to sign the document.

Incidentally, Susloparov insisted on adding a special note to the document - according to which the ceremony of signing the Act of Surrender must be repeated again if any one of the Allied Governments requested it. Dwight Eisenhower and the representatives of the other powers at his headquarters agreed with Susloparov's note. At 2:41 A.M. in a hall where film and photo cameramen of the Supreme Commander of the American and British forces were busily recording every moment, the protocol of Germany's unconditional surrender on every front was signed ...

Susloparov immediately sent his report on this historic event to Moscow, but a return wire was already en route from there: "Don't sign any documents!" The announcement of the 7 May surrender was banned in the Soviet Union. The general's name disappeared from military-historical literature and he worked quietly in the Military-Diplomatic Academy for many years. He passed away on 16 December 1974 in Moscow where he was buried in the Vvedensky Cemetery. I will add: General Susloparov acted at Reims with no evident concern about his own personal fate.[6]

As noted, Major General I.A. Susloparov, the Head of the Soviet Military Mission with Allies' Supreme Headquarters, went ahead and signed the Reims protocol on behalf of the USSR even without Stalin's approval. It seems that he'd been unable to contact Stalin in time. I personally have doubts about this. A major general would never have signed any document of such significance without Moscow's approval. Moreover, Eisenhower had already informed Moscow about this pending event, which Susloparov mentioned in his message. Likely, Stalin feigned showing dissatisfaction with Susloparov, but then called Vyshinsky [Stalin's favorite prosecutor] in Berlin and informed him that he didn't have any grievance against the general. In September 1945 General Susloparov returned to Moscow where he received a promotion and was given a rather important post as Chief of the Red Army's Higher Intelligence courses. In 1950, he received another promotion and was appointed to a similar post at the Military-Diplomatic Academy. It follows, in addition to all else, that most likely General Susloparov was a high-ranking Soviet intelligence officer at Eisenhower's headquarters. It should be remembered that many prominent military figures after the war were either discharged from the service or received appointment to much lower posts. So Susloparov wasn't punished at all for signing the Act of Surrender in Reims; rather, he was rewarded. Stalin had required a pretext in order to refuse to acknowledge the Act - which had been signed in Eisenhower's headquarters -as the final one. He very much wanted for this event to take place in vanquished Berlin and to have Soviet Marshal G.K. Zhukov be the Soviet representative to sign the document of unconditional surrender.

The Soviet Leader proposed to postpone the announcement of Nazi Germany's surrender to 7:00 P.M. Moscow time on 9 May 1945. On the evening of 7 May, when in the Western capitals crowds of people were already celebrating the not-yet-declared official victory, a celebratory concert was taking place in Moscow. It was anticipated that the official announcement of Victory in Europe would occur there. The step was taken to invite the American and British ambassadors in Moscow, G. Kennan and F. Roberts, to the concert. However it turned out that the concert was not dedicated to Victory in Europe, but instead to the 40th anniversary of Popov's invention of the radio. A half-century later, F. Roberts wrote about these events: "In the middle of the evening, G. Kennan and I walked up to Vyshinsky and told him: 'We don't have anything against your Mr. Marconi, but you have a more serious reason for celebrating.' With that we left the concert hall ...."

The Western Allies were more accommodating than Stalin. Therefore without any particular persuasion, they had politely attended the concert at the Soviet side's request.

The Third Assertion: Falin accuses the Western Allies of refusing to participate in the parade to mark the victory over Nazi Germany - seeing in this the first signs of a split. Here's how Eisenhower explains his conduct:

> … the Allies had been invited to the signing ceremony [in Berlin], but I personally believed that it was improper for me to go there. Germans had already appeared in the headquarters of the Western Allies in order to sign the Act of Unconditional Surrender. So I believed that the ratification in Berlin should be the Soviets' business. Therefore I appointed my deputy, Chief Marshal of the Royal Air Force Tedder, to represent me at the ceremony…

(Incidentally, Stalin gave Eisenhower a documentary film of the 9 May German signing of the Act of Unconditional Surrender in Berlin and the Victory Parade.)

The Fourth Assertion: Falin maintains that the Western Allies made no attempt to take Berlin because they supposedly lacked the forces for such an operation. However, Eisenhower declared in his memoirs that on the day of surrender - 7 May 1945 - he had 3 million men under his command and 61 American divisions. This was more than sufficient to take Berlin. Moreover, back in March 1945 Allied troops had already closed to within striking range of Berlin. We haven't even mentioned the enormous airlift capabilities of the Western Allies, which was capable at that time of delivering thousands of soldiers and officers to any sector of German territory within a matter of several hours.

The Fifth Assertion: Falin claims that even before the end of the war, the Allies in Europe had already begun to prepare for an attack against the USSR. However, General Eisenhower in his book says that even a month before the German signing of the Act of Unconditional Surrender in Reims, the Allied High Command began preparing to transfer troops to the Pacific Theater of Operations and to discharge others and return them to America. On 18 June 1945 Dwight Eisenhower resigned his authority as Supreme Commander of Allied forces. He remained only as the commander of American troops in Europe.

The Sixth Assertion: Falin accuses the Allies of the premeditated bombing of Dresden and the Czech Skoda factories - knowing that the territory where they were located would soon be transferring to the Red Army's control. However, the bombing of Dresden was agreed upon with the Red Army command. To be sure, some historians write that the Allies conducted it in order to demonstrate their own strength![7] As concerns the Skoda factories, they were bombed just like any other enterprises on German territory - or the countries it was still occupying - that continued to supply weapons or munitions to the *Wehrmacht*. Falin's examples are far-fetched - contrived only so that he can accuse the Allies of something.

Falin's **Seventh Assertion** concerns supposed political "games" surrounding the capture of Berlin. Eisenhower writes: "A natural objective beyond the Ruhr was Berlin. It was politically and psychologically important as the symbol of remaining

German power. I decided, however, that it was not the logical or the most desirable objective for the forces of the Western Allies."[8]

Further, Eisenhower writes:

> ... When we stood on the Rhine in the last week of March we were 300 miles from Berlin, with the obstacle of the Elbe still 200 miles to our front. The Russian forces were firmly established on the Oder with a bridgehead on its western bank only 30 miles from Berlin... But if we should plan for a power crossing of the Elbe, with the single purpose of attempting to invest Berlin, two things would happen. The first of these was that in all probability the Russian forces would be around the city long before we could reach there. The second was that to sustain a strong force at such a distance from our major bases along the Rhine would have meant the practical immobilization of units along the remainder of the front... It was desirable to thrust our spearheads rapidly across Germany to a junction with the Red forces - thus to divide the country and effectually prevent any possibility of German forces acting as a unit...[9]

The Eighth Assertion: As concerns Falin's discussion of the archival materials disclosed in England regarding Operation Unthinkable - a British plan to attack the Soviet Union - none of this has any connection to the intensity of emotions surrounding the taking of Berlin. So it of course requires a separate discussion. Incidentally the very name of the operation, "Unthinkable", this was indeed Stalin's full violation of the Yalta agreements and the obligations he had accepted when he signed them. He went on to establish a totalitarian regime in six countries of Eastern Europe and in the Baltic countries. "Unthinkable" is his flagrant betrayal of the Allies regarding free elections in Eastern Europe. "Unthinkable" is his subjugation of Poland, for the sake of which Great Britain and France had entered into a war with Hitler.[10]

It is indisputable that Stalin viewed the taking of Berlin also on a purely emotional level as a "gift to himself"; as the crowning of his glory as a military commander; as the fulfillment by his people of his order "to kill the beast in its lair and to raise the Soviet flag above the Reichstag." As the Generalissimo he could toss aside any plan presented to him - and with regards to what the Berlin operation would cost, this question - as always - didn't trouble him.

Incidentally, let's turn to the well-known British historian Max Hastings. Well after the war he published a series of articles about Winston Churchill in the *Daily Mail* newspaper. In one article from this series, entitled: 'Operation Unthinkable: How Churchill wanted to recruit defeated Nazi troops and drive Russia out of Eastern Europe',[11] Hastings wrote:

> ... When Churchill learned in the spring of 1945 that the Americans were going to halt their advance on Berlin from the west and leave Hitler's capital to the Red Army of the Soviet Union, he was furious. ... Keep on going eastward was Churchill's advice to the Allied armies until the Russians showed some willingness to keep their side of the bargain about the future shape of Europe... Meanwhile, Stalin was in a paranoid mood - fearful that the West was planning to make its own deal with the Germans, cut him out and possibly even turn on him. He was deeply suspicious of what Churchill was up to... But Churchill wasn't up to anything because the Americans wouldn't let him. They showed no interest in diplomatic brinkmanship with the Kremlin...

Hastings goes on to note that back in 1941 Churchill had assumed that the United States and the British Empire would emerge from the war as the most powerful bloc in world history, but by 1945 the Soviet Union was much stronger - and Great Britain much weaker - than Churchill had anticipated. Once the war ended, Churchill was also tormented by the fate of Poland.

Hastings writes: "Within days of Germany's surrender, Churchill had astounded his chiefs of staff by inquiring whether Anglo-American forces might launch an offensive to drive back the Soviets" - adding that he wanted to secure "a square deal for Poland".

His chiefs of staff were told to assume that they "would be able to count on the use of German manpower and what remains of German industrial capacity". In other words, the beaten Germans would be mobilized on the West's side. There was even a target date for such an assault - July 1 1945...

Hastings writes that the Foreign Office and the commander-in-chief of the British army, Sir Alan Brooke, were horrified by Churchill's belligerence. Nevertheless, under the conditions of strict secrecy the British army High Command faithfully set to examining scenarios for military action against the Soviet Union. "Needless to say," Hastings observes, "Stalin learned very quickly what was going on in the British camp." However, for the broader public, Churchill's request remained a State secret until the relevant papers were released by the National Archive in 1998.

The planners' report to Churchill was not optimistic about the prospects of a war with Russia. It pointed out that the Red Army could resort to the same tactics it had used to defeat the Germans by withdrawing into the endless expanses of Soviet territory. The generals calculated that 47 divisions would be required for the offensive - of which 14 would need to be armored divisions. Another 40 divisions would have to be held in reserve for defensive purposes or occupation tasks. Even so, the Russians would have twice as many tanks and troops. It concluded that any war with the USSR would be protracted and costly. As for the participation of the defeated German army in any such offensive, the report noted the planners' doubts that German soldiers who had experienced the fighting on the Eastern Front would be eager to resume it.

In his diary, Brooke called Churchill's idea "of course fantastic and the chances of success quite impossible. There is no doubt that from now onwards Russia is all-powerful in Europe." In the written opinion of the chiefs of staff that accompanied the submitted draft plan to Churchill, there was no hope of defeating the Russians without "a large proportion of the vast resources of the United States."

In response to the draft plan and the note, Churchill requested that the chiefs of staff analyze how Great Britain could defend its coastline if the Red Army continued its advance right up to the English Channel. Given the Soviet Union's limited naval strength, the planners concluded that the Red Army would resort to an intensive rocket bombardment - the defenses against which would require the massive force of 230 fighter squadrons and 300 bomber squadrons.

Hastings writes: "A few days later, the "Unthinkable" file was closed: A cable had arrived from President Truman which made it clear that there was not the slightest possibility that the Americans would lead an attempt to drive the Russians from Poland by force, or even threaten Moscow that they might do so." Yet the author adds that in his certainty regarding the malevolence of Soviet intentions in Eastern Europe, Churchill was ahead of his time. In August 1946 - sufficiently apprehensive of a conflict with the Russians - the U.S. chiefs of staff began planning for one, while in London the "Unthinkable" file was retrieved and dusted off. Hastings concludes: "Though at no time was it ever deemed politically acceptable or militarily practicable to attempt to free Eastern Europe by force of arms, military preparations for a conflict with the Soviet Union became a staple of the Cold War."

Churchill offered Montgomery cut-and-dried support in the attempt to take Berlin, but against the will of the American President and Eisenhower, the British could do nothing. On 28 March 1945 - at his own initiative and even without informing his British colleagues - Eisenhower had informed Stalin directly by wire about his plans and stated that he had no intention of taking Berlin. This prompted a furious reaction in London, but relief in Moscow. In reply Stalin deceptively wrote that he fully shared the opinion of the American commander that Berlin no longer had any strategic military significance - and that he himself was in no hurry to capture it.

Stalin did hurry. On 16 April, at Stalin's order Marshal Zhukov launched the final assault on Berlin - even though he admitted that he was not ready for it.

Now a little more detail on what was happening in the camp of the Allies during this time. General Eisenhower had communicated his plan to Stalin - believing that this was fully within the scope of his authority to do so. However, it soon turned out that Churchill was unhappy with the actions of the Allied Supreme Commander-in-Chief and seriously objected to the telegrams. Eisenhower writes in his memoirs:

> ... He disagreed with the plan and held that, because the campaign was now approaching its end, troop maneuvers had ac-

> quired a political significance that demanded the intervention of political leaders in the development of broad operational plans... He was greatly disappointed and disturbed because my plan did not first throw Montgomery forward with all the strength I could give him from the American forces in the desperate attempt to capture Berlin before the Russians could do so. He sent his views to Washington...[12]

General Eisenhower devotes almost five pages of his memoirs to Churchill's complaint to Washington. In the end, the American Chief of the General Staff, General Marshall, supported the Supreme Commander of the Allied Expeditionary Force.

How did Stalin react to the plan he had received from Eisenhower? In a personal and top secret telegram, Stalin informed Eisenhower that the plan he had proposed "to split the German forces by linking up Soviet forces with your forces fully agrees with the plan of the Soviet High Command." Stalin was in agreement with the general that the place where the Red Army should link up with Allied forces should be the Erfurt-Leipzig-Dresden area, and presumed that the main attack by Soviet forces should be launched in this direction. Stalin wrote: "Berlin has lost its former strategic significance and thus the Soviet High Command is thinking to send secondary forces in the direction of Berlin." Approving the American plan of creating a second, additional ring of encirclement by linking Soviet and Allied forces in the Vienna-Linz-Regensburg area, the head of the Soviet Government designated "approximately the second half of May" for the launching of the main Soviet attack.

How did the real events surrounding the taking of Berlin unfold? Striving to beat the Allies to the German capital, Stalin decided to mislead them about the Red Army's genuine intentions and sent them - as is obvious from Stalin's reply to Eisenhower - false information about the directions of the main attack by the 1st Belorussian and 1st Ukrainian Fronts, as well as about when the offensive would begin. On the night of 1 April 1945 Stalin signed together with Antonov the directive about preparing the Berlin operation and designated 16 April as its launch date - even though the 2nd Belorussian Front wouldn't have time to be ready for the offensive by that date.

There is no doubt that the receipt of Eisenhower's telegram about the intentions of the Western Allied forces had a substantial influence on Stalin's decision to conduct the final offensive toward Berlin. Characterizing the accomplished fact, it is impossible not to agree with Churchill's opinion about the political mistake General Eisenhower had committed. In contrast with the time that Stalin had given to Eisenhower, the Soviet offensive against the German capital was organized a month earlier. The implementation of the grand Berlin operation began on 16 April 1945 just as the *Stavka* had planned. By 19 April, troops of the 1st Belorussian and 1st Ukrainian Fronts had broken through the German defensive line along the Oder and Neisse Rivers and set about the process of encircling the main forces of the *Wehrmacht*'s Berlin grouping. On 25 April 1945 Soviet forces reached the area northwest of Potsdam and closed the ring of encirclement around the entire grouping of German Nazi forces in Berlin. On this same day, Marshal Konev's troops linked up with troops of the American First Army that were advancing from Leipzig near the town of Torgau on the Elbe River.

There is one more consideration that shouldn't be neglected. Was it necessary to storm Berlin's defenses after the city had been encircled by the forces of two fronts? Was it necessary to send troops into the city where each street and every building would have to be taken through bitter fighting? Naturally, this is a separate topic - about which Falin remains silent.

At the end of March 1945, the Allies were crossing the Rhine and compelling the surrender of German forces in the Ruhr. A direct road to Berlin was opening in front of the Allies. On 11 April 1945 an armored division in General Simpson's Ninth Army reached the Elbe River at Magdeburg. On the following day, the division seized a bridgehead on the opposite bank of the river by sending three battalions across it and began work on a pontoon bridge. However, the Germans prevented the construction of the bridge and liquidated the 2nd Armored Division's bridgehead with a sharp counterattack. Just a few kilometers downstream, the 83rd Infantry Division had also reached the Elbe at Barby and began sending units across over a rapidly constructed bridge. On the night of the 14th, men of the 83rd Infantry Division and the 2nd Armored Division were moving over the bridge at Barby. Only 80 kilometers separated the Americans from Berlin; at a similar pace of advance they could be in the German capital within 48 hours.

On this same day, the commander of the American 12th Army Group, Omar Bradley, ordered General Simpson to halt his forces.

"Where in the hell did you get this?" Simpson demanded.

"From Ike," Bradley simply replied.

The Allied successes caused even greater alarm in Stalin. He had not been expecting such an impetuous advance on their part after taking the Ruhr. So already on 1 April, he had adopted the firm decision to hasten with the entry into Berlin.

Stalin wasn't only lying to the Supreme Commander of Allied forces, but also to his own commanders - Konev and Zhukov - and to their officers and soldiers. Here is what I. S. Konev says in his own memoirs:

> … On 1 April 1945 the commander of the 1st Belorussian Front, Marshal Zhukov, and I were summoned to Moscow to the *Stavka* of the Supreme High Command. Stalin received us, as was typical, in the Kremlin. Members of the State Defense Committee were present; the Chief of the General Staff, A. I. Antonov, and the Chief of the Main Operations Department, S. M. Shtemenko.
>
> We'd barely had time to greet each other when Stalin raised the question:

> "Do you know how the situation is developing?"
>
> Zhukov and I replied that we knew the situation as far as the intelligence that we each had at the front. Stalin turned to Shtemenko and told him:
>
> "Read them the telegram."
>
> Here is what Shtemenko read aloud: "England: the English command is preparing an operation to seize Berlin - giving the assignment to take it before the Soviet army. The main grouping is being organized under the command of Field Marshal Montgomery…" The telegram ended with the fact that according to all available intelligence, the plan for taking Berlin ahead of the Soviet army was being viewed in the Allied headquarters as fully realistic and the preparations for carrying it out were proceeding at full speed.
>
> Stalin addressed Zhukov and me:
>
> "So, just who will be taking Berlin - we or the Allies?"
>
> As it happened, I was the first who had to answer the question and I replied:
>
> "We will be taking Berlin and we'll take it before the Allies."
>
> Zhukov answered second. He reported that the troops were ready to take Berlin…

The Supreme Commander warned that Berlin had to be seized as soon as possible - thus the time available to prepare the operation was extremely limited. At the conclusion of the "show" that the Supreme Commander had organized, the plans that had been worked out in the General Staff designated 16 April 1945 as the start date. They had calculated how many gun barrels would be deployed per kilometer of front; which armies would be launching the main assault; the composition of the combat groupings; the necessity of additional reserves assigned by the *Stavka* to the fronts; the logistical requirements of the operation … all this was determined by Konev and Zhukov together with the General Staff in a matter of days - only, as always, they didn't bother to calculate the estimated casualties.

So readers, what did you think of the performance arranged by Stalin? And all of this took place after Eisenhower's message to Stalin, which we'll note was on 28 March and after Stalin's deceptive reply.

Veterans who took part in the fighting for Berlin have told me that they were constantly being hurried: "Faster, faster, forward! Otherwise the Allies will overtake us!"

What Montgomery said

Now let's get acquainted with the memoirs of Sir Bernard Montgomery, who was one of the major commanders of the Second World War. Of course, in the given case we are interested in his perspective on the events connected with the fall of Berlin.

In September 1944 - more precisely on 4 September 1944 - in a letter to Eisenhower Montgomery holds forth on the prospects of future battles with the enemy: "I consider we have now reached a stage where one really powerful and full-blooded thrust towards Berlin is likely to get there and thus end the German war."[13] This initiated an exchange of views between the Supreme Commander of the Allied Expeditionary Forces and Montgomery regarding Berlin as an objective. On 15 September 1944 Eisenhower wrote the following in a message to Montgomery:

> ... Clearly, Berlin is the main prize ... There is no doubt whatsoever in my mind that we should concentrate all our energies and resources on a rapid thrust to Berlin.
>
> Our strategy, however, will have to be coordinated with that of the Russians - so we must also consider alternative objectives... Simply stated, it is my desire to move on Berlin by the most direct and expeditious route with combined U.S. - British forces supported by other available forces moving through key centers and occupying strategic areas on the flanks - all in one coordinated, concerted operation. It is not possible at this stage to indicate the timing of these thrusts or their strengths...[14]

In response to Eisenhower, on 18 September 1944 Montgomery wrote in part: "In brief, I consider that as time is so very important we have got to decide what is necessary to go to Berlin and finish the war; the remainder must play a secondary role."[15] Two days later, Eisenhower replied:

> ... Generally speaking I find myself so completely in agreement with your letter of 18 September that I cannot believe there is any great difference in our concepts... Specifically I agree with you in the following: My choice of routes for making the all-out offensive into Germany is from the Ruhr to Berlin... There is one point however, on which we do not agree, if I interpret your ideas correctly. As I read your letter you imply that all the divisions that we have - except those of the 21st Army Group and approximately nine of the 12th Army Group - can stop in place where they are [emphasis in original] and that we can strip all these additional divisions from their transport and everything else to support one single knife-like drive toward Berlin. This may not be exactly what you mean, but it is certainly not possible...[16]

From the exchange of letters it is apparent that in the final analysis, the Supreme Commander of the Allied Expeditionary Forces didn't support Montgomery's strategic concept and the opportunity was lost: at this time, the Soviet army was still over 100 kilometers from Berlin. By March 1945, Berlin had turned into a meaningless point in Eisenhower's strategy.

Montgomery writes:

> ... Once over the Rhine I began to discuss future operational plans with Eisenhower. We had several meetings. I had always put Berlin as a priority objective; it was a political centre [sic] and if we could beat the Russians to it things would be much easier for us in the postwar period. It will be remembered that in his letter to me dated 15 September 1944 Eisenhower had agreed with me about the great importance of the German capital and had said: "Clearly, Berlin is the main prize. There is no doubt whatsoever, in my mind, that we should concentrate all our energies and resources on a rapid thrust to Berlin."[17]...

Summing up his bitter recollections, the English commander writes: "The Americans could not understand that it was of little avail to win the war strategically if we lost it politically; because of this curious viewpoint we have suffered accordingly from VE Day onwards - and are still suffering."[18] Montgomery makes clear that he believes that the possibility to secure a political balance in Europe by seizing key political centers like Vienna, Prague and Berlin before the Russians was wasted. In conclusion, Montgomery writes:

> ... If the higher direction of the war had been handled properly by the political leaders of the West - and suitable instructions given to Supreme Commanders - we could have grabbed all three before the Russians...[19]

This is Montgomery's explanation for how the Russians were able to take Vienna, Prague and Berlin.

In the postwar years, the press in the United States and England asserted that their troops might have captured Berlin, but never made this their objective. Thus, the American Ambassador in Moscow, General W. B. Smith - who during the war had been Eisenhower's chief of staff and had signed the Germans' capitulation in Reims on 23 August 1948 during the Berlin crisis - declared in a discussion with Stalin that the Allies could have hurled 2-3 million soldiers toward Berlin and the German capital would have been taken by them. Smith observed that the Allies had been naïve in those years, or the "Big Three" had trusted each other more.

The Head of the Soviet State replied that after the German forces had begun moving toward Bavaria that he had considered Berlin to be of secondary importance, just like the Allies. Incredibly, he went on to say that on this basis, *only*

Marshal Zhukov's 1st Belorussian Front had been directed toward Berlin but its offensive had bogged down. Moreover, according to Stalin, an entire German army was moving to outflank Zhukov's forces from the southwest. Stalin declared: "We therefore had to give a fresh order to Konev: to remove two tank armies from the southwestern direction and to send them to the Potsdam area in order to pocket this German army which was trying to cut off Zhukov's forces - encircle it - and to facilitate Zhukov's advance to Berlin. Rokossovsky was told to pivot his left flank to the southwest in order to create link-up with Konev and Zhukov west of Berlin. This plan was successful and Berlin was encircled." Stalin noted that all this was done on the fly and that he didn't report to Eisenhower during the operation, but later informed him about it. "The German army," Stalin stressed, "that wanted to encircle Zhukov was captured. About a third of its troops were killed. Thus, Berlin from an insignificant point turned into an important point. Here there was no deceit." For crying out loud!

Smith diplomatically agreed that there had been no deception and that even at that time the Allies well understood this, but he continued to insist that "the Allies might have nevertheless moved large forces against Berlin and occupied it."

Stalin observed that he knew that Churchill had been pressing to take Berlin before the Russians arrived there, but that Eisenhower hadn't agreed with this - fearing to wind up in a difficult situation since he had little force available for this: "If you look at things objectively, then Berlin was in our zone of occupation. Morally we should have taken it; we were obliged to do this. In the second place, our Allies back then had a small force facing Hitler - only 70-80 divisions. It would have been difficult for them both to occupy their zones and to take Berlin, but we had 280 divisions and we could implement such an operation as the capture of Berlin."

At a conference in London in 1944 that discussed the boundaries of the spheres of influence, which included representatives from all of the Allies, it had been agreed that in case of practicality in achieving military goals the agreeing parties could ignore the agreed upon boundaries. This did in fact happen.

There is one more comment from Falin that should be discussed. There is an explanation for Churchill's failure to implement Operation Unthinkable. Firstly, there was the position of the American military commanders on the matter. Secondly, there was the Berlin operation itself. Thirdly, Churchill lost the elections and was no longer Prime Minister. Finally, Britain's own military commanders opposed the plan because they were convinced that the Soviet Union was too strong. I will repeat again: Operation Unthinkable was only a plan in the event that the Red Army continued its advance to the Atlantic!

The American Ambassador to the Soviet Union responded in the following way to Stalin's statement that the United States didn't have enough divisions in Europe to seize Berlin: "One must consider the fact that an American division was twice as large as a Soviet division, and at the time the [Western] Allies had 6,000 heavy bombers and 7,000 other aircraft. The Allies were able then to carry out any task with respect to the German army." Stalin doubted this and said: "Hardly ..."[20]

In the words of Zhukov, from his numerous postwar discussions with generals of the Allied armies, it was revealed that:

> … the question about taking Berlin was finally dropped from consideration only after the Red Army had launched its powerful attack against the German army on the Oder and Neisse Rivers and had reached the Oder just 100 kilometers from Berlin.

> After the war and my demobilization from the army, as a Reserve Officer I was summoned to military meetings for about the next 10 years. As a rule, they didn't last long. At maneuvers, the officers who led them would name imperialistic America as the USSR's main adversary…

11
The Last Five Days of the War

Czechoslovakia, May 1945: the *Sovinformburo* announces:[1]

7 May 1945

... Following a lengthy siege, forces of the 1st Ukrainian Front today fully seized the city and fortress of Breslau. In the middle of February, Soviet units conducted a swift outflanking maneuver and encircled Breslau. The Germans had prepared for a lengthy defense of the city. They barricaded the streets and converted sections of them into anti-tank ditches. Every stone building was converted into a pillbox with a large number of firing positions. In a number of places the Hitlerites - in order to slow the advance of the Soviet troops - blew up buildings in order to fill the streets with rubble...

8 May 1945

... Troops of the 1st Ukrainian Front today seized the city of Dresden. Two days ago our reconnaissance units had attacked the Germans northwest of Dresden and had driven them from their fortified positions. Then the main Soviet forces entered the fighting... Developing an impetuous offensive between the Elbe and the Mulde Rivers, our mobile formations and infantry cut the Chemnitz-Dresden highway...

9 May 1945

... Troops of the 1st Ukrainian Front - as a result of a rapid night maneuver by tank formations and infantry - broke enemy resistance and on 9 May at 0400 liberated the capital city Prague of our ally Czechoslovakia from the fascist aggressors. The German troops under the command of Field Marshal Schörner - in violation of the Act of Surrender - refused to stand in place and lay down their weapons. In view of this, forces of the 1st Ukrainian Front attacked Field Marshal Schörner's forces and continuing to advance, occupied many Czech cities on the territory of Czechoslovakia.

Seeing the threat of encirclement by our forces, one of Field Marshal Schörner's groups began to surrender without order. Over 9 and 10 May, forces of the 1st Ukrainian Front took more than 35,000 German officers and soldiers as prisoners.

A different group under Field Marshal Schörner also violated the terms of surrender and began to retreat to the west; forces of the 4th Ukrainian Front, pursuing the enemy, took many cities on the territory of Czechoslovakia. On 9 and 10 May, forces of this front took more than 20,000 German soldiers and officers as prisoners.

The German forces under the command of Colonel General Wehler - facing the forces of the 2nd Ukrainian Front - also violated the act of capitulation and refused to stand in place and lay down their weapons. In view of this, forces of the front attacked Colonel General Wehler's forces, and advancing, seized the city of Budowicze on the territory of Czechoslovakia. Over 9 and 10 May, troops of the front took 8,000 German soldiers and officers as prisoners of war.

Forces of the 3rd Ukrainian Front on Austrian territory linked up with English [sic] troops west of the city of Graz. Over 9 and 10 May, forces of the front accepted the disorderly surrender of more than 23,000 German soldiers and officers from Colonel General Wehler's forces - including four generals.

I would like to go into a bit more detail about the situation in Prague before its "liberation" by the Red Army - in particular regarding the Prague uprising. This noble and yet tragic episode again illustrates Stalin's coldly calculating nature and brutality.

On 4 May 1945 General Eisenhower made an appeal to the Red Army's Chief of the General Staff, Antonov. Considering that the American Third Army - under the command of General Patton - was at the time within 40 kilometers of Prague, he proposed that the Americans take the city. However, he received a refusal. Antonov pointed to the previously concluded terms of the Yalta treaty and also informed the commander of the Allied forces in Europe that the Red Army was already closing in on Prague. This claim wasn't true.

In the first days of May there was a popular uprising against the occupiers in Prague. Streets of the city were barricaded. Thousands of residents joined the fighting.[2] The former Union of Military Servicemen prepared the uprising and actively took part in it, but it was directed by the quickly-organized Czech National Council - headed by a Prague University Professor, A. Prazhak. Official Soviet sources strive in every possible way to diminish the role of the Czech National Council in organizing the uprising. Likely this is chiefly because the Council entered into active contact with the commander of the Russian Liberation Army, General Vlasov.

In the early hours of 5 May, the rebellion scored successes: they seized the radio station, the post office, the telegraph center, train stations and the bridges over the Vltava River. The German garrison - which consisted primarily of reserve units - initially showed confusion, but soon it began to put up resistance. Schörner ordered that the uprising in Prague be suppressed. German troops advanced on Prague from various directions: the bulk of S.S. Panzer Division *Das Reich* from the north; the S.S. Panzer Division *Totenkopf* from the east; and a regiment of *Das Reich* from the south. Naturally, by themselves the rebels would have been unable to withstand such major German units. Anticipating this possible course of events, back on 2 May representatives of the Czech National Council and some of the uprising's commanders met with the commander of the Russian Liberation Army's 1st Division, Major General Sergei Kuz'mich Buniachenko, in the city of Kozoedy.

On 5 May at 1233, the signal for beginning the uprising went out over the radio. The day before, Buniachenko reached the decision to enter into an agreement with the Czech delegation and to act against both Fascism and Bolshevism by liberating Prague from the Nazis before the Red Army arrived. In this spirit, leaflets were composed and scattered. The German command was informed about the defection through a signals officer:

> The division chief of staff, Colonel Nikolaev, considers it obligatory to inform Major Schweninger openly that the division command - on the threshold of the collapse of the Third Reich - in order to save the personnel from inevitable reprisal in the event they are captured by Soviet troops, sees no other option than to honor the request of the Czech national circles for assistance in the hope of receiving asylum from the newly recreated Czech Government.

This was soon followed by an open appeal by the commander of the Russian Liberation Army, General A.A. Vlasov:

> Czech and Russian Brothers!
>
> In its death throes, the dying system of National-Socialist Germany is trying to suppress the liberation movement of the Czech people for its independence.
>
> A rebellion in Prague has been raised against the stranglers of freedom and freedom-loving peoples - against National-Socialist Germany.
>
> We, the Russian soldiers - who are fighting for the freedom of our Motherland Russia against its further enslavement by Bolshevism - cannot stand apart from the struggle of such a freedom-loving people.
>
> I have issued an order to the Committee of the Liberation of Russian Peoples to support the uprising of the Czech people.
>
> The moment has arrived when mankind must free itself from National-Socialist Germany. I am calling all faithful sons of the Czech and Russian people to a joint struggle. We will not be alone in this struggle since we are raising a struggle for independence - for freedom.

> The Nazi clique has led to the death of millions of people and has brought forth no less injustice and slavery than Bolshevism has brought to Motherland Russia. All hail freedom! Long live the unity in the struggle against the enemies of mankind - National-Socialist Germany and Bolshevism!
>
> The commander-in-chief of the armed forces
> Committee for the Liberation of the Peoples of Russia
> Lieutenant General A. Vlasov

5 May 1945

Buniachenko believed that the actions of his division to save the uprising citizens and Prague from destruction would foster a beneficial relationship with the Western Allies. These hopes proved to be illusory. Eisenhower looked upon the national liberation movement in Czechoslovakia negatively. In addition, as is known, he acknowledged the Red Army would be Prague's liberator.

The RLA 1st Division - displaying steadfastness and courage - fought desperately; it wiped out German units and seized an airfield while in the process destroying 50 German aircraft - as well as approximately 100 German armored vehicles. The Czech population greeted the Vlasovites joyously as liberators. Even in the worst years of the Stalin and Brezhnev periods, Prague citizens continued to believe that they were liberated not by Soviet forces but by Vlasov's troops - and that they had saved the city from destruction. Many of its areas, buildings and bridges had been mined by the Germans. Though there are no precise numbers, the RLA 1st Division lost somewhere between 300 and 700 men in the fighting to liberate Prague from its occupiers.

The Czechs highly esteem the memory of their liberators. After the so-called "Velvet Revolution" the residents of Prague erected a large cross bearing a crown of thorns over their fraternal graves in the Russian section of the Ol'shansky Cemetery.

On 7 May - the most critical day of the uprising - its leaders appealed to the Red Army over the radio for assistance. They asked it to send tanks and aircraft. The Red Army sent them neither tanks nor aircraft, but it could have done so.

On the evening of 7 May, the Vlasovites - after the fighting with the Germans - no longer had the slightest doubts that Soviet troops would occupy the city. At 0300 8 May, General Buniachenko issued the order for the RLA 1st Division to withdraw from Prague.[3]

During the combat operations of the anti-communists against the occupiers in Prague, the Americans unexpectedly shifted its demarcation line further to the west from Prague. As a result of the altered deployment, the Vlasov Division - having abandoned Prague - reached the Americans' new frontline with difficulty. The Americans refused to take them in, which led to the imprisonment of more than 20,000 soldiers and officers of the division by units of the Red Army and the arrest of all the top commanders of Vlasov's Russian Liberation Army.

Two events occurred on 6 and 8 May - unexpectedly for Prague's citizens and for Moscow - which led to a fundamental change in the situation in the city: on 6 May, Army Group Center initiated a general retreat from Czechoslovakia and on 8 May German forces in Prague abandoned the city. According to terms of the agreement with the leaders of the uprising, as the Germans withdrew from the city they left behind all of their heavy weaponry: tanks, artillery, mortars, self-propelled guns etc. Soviet propaganda, speaking about the German departure from Prague, thundered: "What sort of capitulation is this?" ... as if the Soviet propagandists couldn't understand that at this moment the most important thing for the Prague citizenry was to rid themselves of the occupiers and to spare the city of further destruction.

Thus the terms of the German armed forces' capitulation agreement - which was signed by the Chairman of the Czech National Council, Professor Prazhak, and his deputy the communist Smirkovsky on 8 May at 1600 - fully corresponded to the interests of Prague and its residents. It is impossible to consider this document shameful for the Czech side. Incidentally, examples of agreements on the unhindered withdrawal of enemy garrisons can be found in preceding wars as well. For example, in 1813 the victorious Russian and Prussian forces gave honorable terms to the French garrisons - allowing them to withdraw from them *even without surrendering their weapons.*

Only those for whom considerations of prestige are more valuable than the fate of an ancient city and its residents - and for whom it was important to finish off the surrendering foe (and from this squeeze political capital) - could call this act of capitulation "shameful". But for the Soviet Union, which gained the honor as the liberator of Prague, there was nothing left to do than to repudiate the agreement that allowed the German troops to retreat unhindered from Prague to the west before the arrival of Red Army units. On 9 May at 0440, tanks of the 1st Ukrainian Front entered Prague. Major General Ziberov, whose forward detachment at dawn broke through to the city center and seized the bridges across the Vltava River, didn't meet any "organized resistance" and by 1000 the final nests of resistance by die-hard Germans were wiped out. Doctor Stepanek-Shtemer justifiably remarks that: "Prague ... factually had already been liberated from German forces on the morning of 8 May; Soviet tanks entered an already liberated Prague."

The assertion that Prague was liberated by forces of the Red Army is dictated exclusively by notions of a political-propagandistic nature and this argument is maintained only in order to obscure the historic role of the RLA 1st Division in the Prague events of 6-8 May 1945 and to discredit the Czech National Council's agreement with the German commander on 8 May. In this connection it is interesting to take a look at how Soviet authors assessed the role of the Russian Liberation Army in those instances when they neglected the ban on mentioning it. In the newspaper *Krasnaia zvezda*, the authors Goncharenko and Shnaider simply misrepresent the historic facts by asserting that Hitler "rushed to put down an uprising by the traitor Vlasov's army." The commander of the 1st Ukrainian Front, Marshal Konev, only briefly mentions capturing Vlasov and "General Buniachenko's division" to the southeast of Prague, but says nothing about the fighting in the Czechoslovak capital that preceded this. According to General of the Army Leliushenko, the commander of the 4th Guards Tank Army, "Vlasov's band" was completely destroyed at Chemnitz (!). General of the Army Shtemenko, postwar Chief of the Soviet Army's General Staff, although he does resort to insulting labels - speaking about "derelicts" and "cutthroats ready for anything" - nevertheless writes that: "some Vlasovites entered Prague … when the time was ripe there for a decisive uprising against the German occupiers" and that "some Vlasovite groups joined the fighting at their own initiative - even though the Czech National Council supposedly didn't have any interest in their offer of assistance." Of course, all the documents connected with these events fundamentally undermine the version about the liberating role of the Red Army. Indeed, the attitude of the Soviet representatives toward the members of the RLA - and even toward the members of the Czech National Council after the Red Army occupied Prague - points to the fact that they understood this from the very start.

Soon after entering the city, General Rybalko arrived at a session of the Czech National Council in order to clarify some questions that were extremely important to the USSR: "to learn about the thinking behind the uprising; its course; the participation of the so-called Vlasov's army in it; and the capitulation of the Germans." Judging from the general's reaction, the reports he had received hadn't satisfied him. He announced point-blank that all the Vlasovites would be shot. In response to the "energetic and heartfelt requests" of the Chairman Professor Prazhak and other members of the Council to spare these men who had fought for Prague, General Rybalko made a "magnanimous gesture" and declared that not all of them would be shot.

Hundreds of RLA soldiers were killed in the fighting for Prague and many more were wounded. The wounded were allocated to separate wards in the Prague hospitals - the entries to which at first bore signs stating: "The heroic liberators of Prague". Very soon after the Red Army entered the city, SMERSH organs began to register the wounded. What happened next is told by Doctor Stepanek-Shtemer, who subsequently emigrated to Israel:

> … I had an acquaintance, a fellow native of Moravia - E.P. Ostrava - a young woman who by some miracle survived Auschwitz, Dachau and Theresienstadt. In the initial days after the end of the war she was working in Motol - a suburb of Prague. (There was a large camp for German prisoners next to the hospital there; I often went there to interrogate the prisoners.) E.P. told me that there were approximately 200 wounded Vlasovites in the hospital in Motol. One day, Soviet soldiers equipped with sub machine guns entered the hospital. They forced all the doctors and nurses to leave the building, entered the wards where the severely wounded Vlasovites were lying and soon long bursts of sub ma-

> chine gun fire rang out ... All of the wounded Vlasovites were shot directly in their hospital beds...

The very same fate awaited other wounded RLA soldiers lying in the other hospitals. S. Ausky - on the basis of reliable sources - reports that more than 600 RLA members were executed in and around Prague.

The same thing befell the Vlasov soldiers who remained in the city after Buniachenko's division left the city and fought side by side with the Czech rebels until the very end. All were executed on the very first day that Red Army units entered Prague - 9 May 1945.[4]

Questions without Answers

First Question: To the present day, official Russian historians continue to believe that the uprising in Prague - in a country where more than 120 partisan units were operating - to be one of the most irresponsible cases of adventurism in the history of the Second World War. Was it really?

Second Question: In essence, Buniachenko's division was the only real force that saved the Prague uprising from being crushed and the city itself from being destroyed. Having defeated the Germans, it was what forced the Germans to abandon Prague quickly. The Red Army didn't enter the city until 9 May 1945 - five days after the start of the Prague uprising. If Vlasov's men hadn't supported the uprising, the Germans would have violently suppressed it in a matter of 24 hours and any of the participants left alive would have been hung from lamp posts. A natural question arises: why didn't the Russians or the Americans support the uprising?

Third Question: The Czech National Council and the uprising's leaders played a shameful and treacherous role with respect to Buniachenko's 1st Division! Having used its assistance, the Council declined any further collaboration with the Vlasovites and effectively forced them to flee the city. This was done under the pressure from the Czech communists on the Council.[5] However, this didn't even spare them from repression under the new regime and the Communist Party, which took control of the country in 1948.

Members of the Czech National Council - who had concluded the agreement with Major General Buniachenko and later the one with General Toussaint, the German military commander in Prague (thereby depriving the Red Army of the laurels as the saviors of the city) - were all subsequently persecuted. All of the members of the Council who signed the protocol on 8 May 1945 suffered: Professor Prazhak was dismissed from his position at the University; the representative of the Social Democrats, Dr. Kotlry, also lost his job; General Kuttellwascher was sentenced to 20 years of imprisonment; and a staff officer, Captain Nekhansky, was executed. The Deputy Chairman of the Czech National Council, Communist Party representative Smirkovsky, received a life sentence. Among the accusations against him was the charge that he had summoned Vlasov's regiments into the city, which doesn't correspond with reality. Even in 1949 there were echoes of the events of those days in May 1945: Valerian Zorin, the Soviet Ambassador in Prague, declared at a meeting where the former Head of the Czech National Council, Otakar Machotka, was present that those Czechs who had entered into negotiations with the Russians and Germans and who had signed the agreement with General Toussaint about the unhindered withdrawal of German troops from Prague "had lost honor."

Fourth Question: Stalin behaved toward the nationalist uprising in Prague exactly as he did toward the Warsaw uprising in 1944. Likely, he was most interested in standing by and watching as the Germans crushed it - just as he had back in 1944 when he stopped the Red Army outside Warsaw. He couldn't forgive the Czech National Council and the uprising's leaders for establishing contacts with the Vlasovites and the Germans.

The Poles in 1944 fought for more than two months. Warsaw, set ablaze by the S.S. troops, burned for 63 days as the Germans were systematically wiping out the population of the city. More than 200,000 people were killed. All this time, Soviet forces stood by on the opposite bank of the Vistula River and observed the slaughter. They not only watched as the Nazis were killing Warsaw's citizens. The Russians also prevented the Americans and British from rendering assistance to the Poles. Stalin didn't want the Poles, whom he called a "criminal band", to liberate Warsaw. Therefore he banned Allied aircraft loaded with weapons destined for the uprising to land on Red Army airfields. For Stalin, it was better that the Nazis drown the uprising in blood.

If you will, the Western Allies behaved even worse toward the Prague uprising than they had toward the Warsaw uprising. In the latter case they at least made an attempt to help, but the Russians blocked it. In Czechoslovakia, they showed a complete indifference to the Czech nationalists. The Supreme Commander of the Allied forces in Europe effectively allowed the Red Army to seize all of Czechoslovakia. Why?

Fifth Question: The Red Army suffered 140,000 casualties in the combat operations in Czechoslovakia; on the day Soviet tanks entered Prague - 9 May - the Soviet press reported that more than 1,000 men had been killed or wounded! What was the source of these casualties? After all, the Germans had retreated from the city overnight between 7 and 8 May. Meanwhile, Army Group Center had abandoned Czechoslovakia on 6 May.

Sixth Question: Undoubtedly, the Americans made two blunders when they failed to aid the uprising. Using it as a precedent, they could have occupied Prague completely! They restricted themselves to sending two officers into Prague on 7 May, who informed the uprising's leaders about Germany's unconditional surrender and recommended that they halt the uprising - even though Germans were still in the city. At the time both Prague citizens and, in part, the Vlasovites were still involved in fighting with them.

The correspondence between Winston Churchill and Harry Truman in those days is known. The British Prime Minister asked the American President to intervene in the events that were taking place and to compel Eisenhower to take Prague. Truman declined to do this - declaring that he would not interfere in the actions of the Supreme Commander of the Allied forces. Obviously, Truman at that time still hoped for a continuation of the alliance with Stalin.

The French philosopher Montesquieu once said: "Everyone is obliged, if necessary, to give their lives for the Motherland - but no one is obligated to lie in the name of the Motherland." Apt words, though not for the Stalinist tyranny. Soviet propaganda adopted any lie in order to smear and hush up the role of the Russian Liberation Army in the liberation of Prague. In all Soviet and Russian (official) publications right up to the Great Soviet Encyclopedia, the members of this anti-communist movement are viewed as apostates and traitors of the Motherland.[6]

Then, finally, whatever retorts and arguments Major General Buniachenko's decision has since provoked it has become a part of history because out of the chronology of events of those days it follows incontestably that the main credit - if not the entire credit - in the liberation of Prague belongs precisely to the RLA's 1st Division. That is an established historic fact.[7] The version of Soviet historiography - according to which troops of Marshal Konev's 1st Ukrainian Front liberated Prague - simply cannot withstand academic scrutiny.

When President Benes flew into liberated Prague from London, he joyfully received Soviet officers in the Prague Old Town Square and decorated them with his country's medals. My rifle division didn't take part in the direct fighting for Prague. Nevertheless, the Soviet Government awarded all of us - officers and soldiers alike - with the medal "For the Liberation of Prague" that it had established. Altogether, approximately 350,000 people were awarded this medal - of which approximately 40,000 went to Prague citizens.

I will express the seditious idea that the soldiers and officers of Buniachenko's 1st Division deserved this medal most of all. However, it is known that the RLA's main commanders - including the commander of the RLA 1st Division - were hung in Moscow in 1946 in the Butyrka Prison. All the lower officers were shot - and some of the soldiers were shot - while the majority of them were sent into the Gulag. The medal "For the Liberation of Prague" was conceived and established in order to buttress the supposedly historic role of the Red Army in the liberation of Prague.

With this I wanted to end my discussion of what took place on the final days of the war. However, I recently read the Russian translation of a book by the German historian Joachim Hoffmann, *Stalin's War of Extermination 1941-1945: Planning, Realization and Documentation*, in which he gives a story about the 331st Rifle Division in which I served and its commander Major General Berestov. Practically speaking, the German historian's book is an historical indictment against Stalin, the Red Army and its commanders not for their role in the start of the Second World War but also in its concluding stage on German territory. The author, relying on German documents as well as the testimony of prisoners of war and those people who became refugees in 1945, accuses all Soviet commanders of being war criminals - responsible for the immoral conduct of their subordinate officers and soldiers in East Prussia.

I was an eyewitness and participant in the fighting on the shores of the Baltic and also subsequently spent three months in Lower Silesia as part of the Red Army's occupation forces. Thus I can speak to the events that happened back then. Naturally I cannot vouch for the conduct of all the formations and elements of the 3rd Belorussian Front, but I know more than Hoffman about what happened in my rifle division and how its officers and soldiers treated the civilian population.

It is true that the Red Army, having entered German territory, took full revenge against both the *Wehrmacht* and the civilian population for the totally monstrous crimes perpetrated on Russian, Belorussian and Ukrainian lands. Thus, Red Army soldiers made no distinction between the Nazis and the civilian population. There was widespread raping, looting, executions and isolated cases of murder (as well as cruel mass deportations) but nevertheless I have doubts about what Joachim Hoffman reports - more particularly about what he relates regarding the conduct of personnel of the 331st Rifle Division. I will cite several fragments from his book that I have selected.

The author writes that in Landsberg, Soviet soldiers of the 331st Rifle Division confined hundreds of the stunned residents in cellars, including women and children, before setting fire to the buildings and shooting the panicked people who sought to escape the flames. Many, according to Hoffman, were burned alive.

Hoffman states that in a village on the Landsberg-Heilsberg road, Soviet soldiers of the same rifle division held 37 women and girls - who were locked in a cellar - for six days and nights. Many of them were chained together and raped several times a day with the participation of Soviet officers. Because of their desperate cries, according to Hoffman, two of these Soviet officers cut out the tongues of two of the women "with a curved knife" in front of the eyes of everyone. Two of the women, their hands placed one atop the other, were staked to the ground by a bayonet that had been driven through the palms of their hands. German tankers, in the end, managed to free only some of the unfortunate women; Hoffman states that 20 of the women died from the outrages inflicted upon them. The author goes on to say that at the village of Hanshagen near Preussisch-Eylau (today known as Bagrationovosk, Russia), Red Army soldiers of the 331st Rifle Division shot two mothers who were trying to prevent the rape of their daughters - as well as a father whose daughter was dragged out of the family kitchen and raped by a Soviet officer. In addition, a married couple - schoolteachers with three children - was murdered as well as an unidentified young female refugee; an innkeeper; and a farmer whose 21-year-old daughter was also raped. In the village of Petershagen near Eylau, members of this same rifle division murdered two men and a 16-year-old boy named Richard von Hoffman - having first subjected the women and girls to cruel rapes.

The facts cited by the German historian Joachim Hoffman were dug out by him from the archive of Section Foreign Armies East of the German General Staff, which was led in the war years by Major General Richard Gehlen. Primarily, these are written notes of German army officers based on witness testimonies. It is known that witness testimony is not always truthful or accurate and sometimes it distorts what actually happened. I've already acknowledged the many illegal crimes - including those that were perpetrated in our division as well. However, the notion that that the tongues, noses and breasts of German civilians were cut off; that civilians were beheaded or had their stomachs sliced open; that feet and hands were chopped off; that they were smothered or had God knows what carved into their breasts; that children were hurled into bonfires; infants were murdered; eyes were cut out; that people nailed to planks or ripped apart by tanks... excuse me, these are all just typical examples of propagandistic rhetoric. Both Germans and the Red Army were busy with generating and spreading accusations like these.

Yet here's what I read about the commander of the 331st Rifle Division, Major General Berestov, in Hoffmann's book:

> ... Major General Berestov - the commander of the 331st Rifle Division - on 2 February 1945 in Petershaten near Preussisch-Eylau - together with one of the officers accompanying him - raped the daughter of a peasant that he had forced to wait upon him as well as a Polish girl; moreover, he carries / bears responsibility for the numerous war crimes committed by his division around Preussisch-Eylau and at Landsberg - only a small fraction of which are known...

Once again, Hoffmann's evidence for this has been obtained from German documents of Major General Gehlen's archive.

The author repeats his charges about things that supposedly happened in Lower Silesia. I was in the town of Friedeberg, Lower Silesia for approximately three months after the war and I met with a lot of Germans. I can say that they didn't feel any great fondness for us, their conquerors. However, nearly all of them acknowledged the humane treatment that the 331st Rifle Division and the division commander gave to the civilian population.

Hoffmann also speaks about the historic significance of the Prague operation. The author asserts that that genuine contribution of the Vlasovites to the Prague uprising should be viewed independently of their previous allegiance to the Germans and the success of Buniachenko's own plan. Entering the struggle at a critical moment, the RLA 1st division, with the exception of only a few pockets of German resistance, managed to seize the entire western portion of Prague and a broad swath on the eastern bank of the Vltava River as far as Strasnice. The RLA Division lacked sufficient strength to occupy the entire city, but having split the city into two pieces the Russians interfered with the link-up of German reserves approaching from the north and the south.

S. Ausky correctly notes that if not for the RLA 1st Division, the Germans would have been able to occupy Prague's western districts on 6 May and to crush the uprising entirely on 7 May. Even the unexpected cessation of combat operations on the night of 7 May and the withdrawal of RLA units from the city had positive consequences - indirectly contributing to the agreement between the Czech National Council and General Toussaint regarding the unhindered withdrawal of German troops. Soviet historiography's version of the events, according to which Prague was liberated by Marshal Konev's 1st Ukrainian Front, is just a legend.

"Everything, from strategy to tactics, was marked by Stalin's inhumanity."

K. Simonov

12

For Many, Victory Didn't Mean Liberation

As I described in my memoirs *Through the Maelstrom: A Red Army Soldier's War on the Eastern Front* (University Press of Kansas, 2009), VE Day - 8 May 1945 - found my division, the 331st Rifle Division, and me in the Czech Sudeten. After the heavy fighting in East Prussia, the division was in bad need of rest and refitting, but it was sent to the Sudetenland in Czechoslovakia where we anticipated taking part in the liquidation of the final German resistance from Schörner's Army Group Center - on paper, at least, it was still a powerful grouping. However, the army group had begun retreating to the west before our arrival in Czechoslovakia so our battered division was assigned to a quiet sector where we were positioned when VE Day arrived.

The 331st Rifle Division spent only a month in the Sudeten before it moved to Germany's Lower Silesia - or more precisely to the German town of Friedeberg, where I spent the first 90 days after the war's conclusion. Very soon, the division was disbanded there.

Back in the 1970s, I read General Gorbatov's memoirs in the journal *Novyi Mir* [*New World*]. From them I learned about the fate of the 1st Ukrainian Front. With Nazi Germany vanquished, three of the front's five armies were sent to the East where they were to take part in the final destruction of Japan. The other two were disbanded - including our 31st Army. Many of the older officers and soldiers returned to the Soviet Union where they were demobilized, while the younger officers and personnel remained in the army. I and many other officers were given a choice to drive to Vienna to join the Reserve of the Central Group of Forces or to move to a new post in Hungary. I chose the second option.

According to the agreement of the Soviet Government with the Allies at the Yalta conference and at Potsdam, Lower Silesia - where we were located - was to be transferred to Poland. Stalin issued an unpublicized order: before turning it over to Poland, German territory was to be "stripped bare", which in fact was done.

Engineer units arrived and specialist fitters and assemblers, electricians and mechanics were brought to Lower Silesia. They closed the railroad in Lower Silesia to troop movements. Entire factories - as well as furniture collections, iron, boarding, textiles, bricks (even sand), cement, nails, animals, grain, books ... all were shipped out by railroad. Meanwhile, five officers - including me - who had opted to go to Hungary, were assigned to an artillery brigade. It was to be relocated to Hungary, but got stuck in Lower Silesia and had to wait until the completion of the movement of "foreign goods" in the form of repatriations to devastated Russia.

It became known that pursuant to Stalin's order, so-called filtration camps were set up in order to vet liberated "guest workers" - former Soviet citizens who'd been forcibly moved by the occupiers to work in Germany - as well as Russian military prisoners who'd been held in camps that were now in American or British hands. All those people, who during the Second World War had been forced by the Nazis to leave their native lands, received the shortened title "D.P." (Displaced Persons) as defined by the League of Nations.

People - who'd gone through severe trials, forcible separation from those near and dear to them and who'd endured much suffering in the Nazi State - couldn't imagine in those first joyful postwar days that Comrade Stalin had already distributed among the punitive organs a secret quota for millions of new "*Zeks*"[1] for the Gulag - a force of free labor for the regime. It was ordered by any means to extract all the displaced Soviet citizens living in the Allies' camps and deliver them back to Russia.

In those days, as I recall, from dawn until dusk Studebaker trucks were passing us on the roads. Above the driver's cabin, all the vehicles had a firmly attached plywood sign bearing the bold, large letters of the words: "*Rodina-mat' tebia zhdet!*" ["*Mother Russia is waiting for you!*"]. The trucks all followed the same routes: toward the American and British occupation zones of Germany and then back to filtration camps in the Soviet zone.

I often stood by the side of the road and watched the flow of vehicles. They were always empty as they moved in one direction, but always full of men and women as they returned. The people aboard - not realizing what awaited many of them - joyously greeted us, the officers and soldiers of the Red Army. We returned their greetings and wished them happiness! Now it is known that happiness didn't smile on all of them; the "Returnees" as they became to be known.

First I'll cite a few facts and figures from official statistics. By the autumn of 1944, there were approximately 7.5 million foreign workers in Germany. All of them had been brought forcibly to Germany from occupied countries. They'd been sent to industrial plants, factories, farms, coal mines, hospitals and construction teams. In every country occupied by the *Wehrmacht*, the Germans searched out healthy men, women and adolescents and by force sent them into slave labor in the Third Reich. The operation to carry out these barbaric actions carried the codename "Hay Harvest". Wherever this impressment met resistance, the Germans would burn the villages to the ground while the residents were carried away in trucks. Of the millions of slaves - as was established at the Nuremburg Trials in 1946 - barely

200,000 had agreed voluntarily to work in Germany. As the General Plenipotentiary for labor deployment in Nazi Germany, Fritz Sauckel oversaw the process of securing forced labor for the Third Reich.[2]

By the end of the war, there were more than 5 million former Soviet citizens in Germany and in the other European countries occupied by the Germans. This number included those military prisoners who were still alive and those workers and peasants enslaved by the Nazis to work for them, but it also included thousands of people - entire families - who had opted to leave with the Germans when they retreated as well as a significant number of emigrants who had wanted no life under a communist regime.

Women comprised 2.5 million of this total number of displaced people. They worked primarily in agriculture. Of course, their living conditions were somewhat better, but they were still harsh.

Here are some of the terms under which the forced laborers worked and lived. They could not make any complaints whatsoever. They were not allowed to visit churches or cultural sites. Sexual relationships were strictly prohibited - punishable by execution. Forced laborers had no right to use the railroad or public transportation. Employers were allowed to use corporal punishments. As a rule, they housed their workers in a variety of utility buildings and subsidiary premises unsuitable for normal living. They paid them miserable wages.

With the intention of organizing the rapid repatriation of former Soviet citizens, back in October 1944 a special agency had been created within the USSR Council of People's Commissars called the Department of the Plenipotentiary of the Council of People's Commissars for Repatriation Matters. It was headed by the former Chief of the Soviet Main Intelligence Directorate, General F.I. Golikov. According to the statistics of Golikov's department, by March 1946 a total number of 5,352,963 Soviet citizens had been repatriated back to the USSR - including 1,825,774 former military servicemen. This figure also includes displaced people within the Soviet Union.

The Fate of the Returnees

Three months before the end of the war, on 18 January 1945 a secret directive went out to all the fronts' Military Councils - as well as to the commanders of the western military districts. It was signed by the Red Army's Chief of the Rear Services, General Khrulev, and by General Golikov. For all practical purposes this directive sealed the fate of hundreds of thousands of displaced persons and military prisoners who were located in Germany and in other countries.

All of the people in the filtration groups were checked to see if they belonged to one of three different categories:

1st Category: military prisoners and those close to them

2nd Category: ordinary policemen, village elders and other citizens caught in traitorous activities

3rd Category: draft-age citizens found living in enemy territory

I'll cite several of the points from the first section of the directive:

1. Non-commissioned officers and soldiers were to be sent to collecting transit points of the operating fronts. After being investigated, those men who didn't raise any suspicions were to be sent to reserve units of the armies and the fronts.
2. People serving in the German army and in special German construction formations; men serving in Vlasov's army, and police and other people who raised suspicion were immediately to be sent to special NKVD camps.
3. Officers who'd been prisoners of war were also to be sent to special camps of the NKVD.

Subsidiary sections of the 1st Category concerned citizens who had ended up on German territory either voluntarily or by force. Thus, by this directive, Soviet officers who'd become German prisoners were automatically treated as equivalent to Vlasovites [formally, men serving in Vlasov's Russian Liberation Army but widely used to describe any former Red Army members serving with the *Wehrmacht*] and men who'd served as policemen for the Germans - with all the entailing consequences for them. Further directives amended and supplemented this, but its essence remained unchanged and military officials followed it unswervingly.

We'll note two circumstances connected with this directive. First, this menacing document appeared prior to the Yalta conference in strictly secret form, but Stalin didn't mention it to the Allies. He understood that had he done so, it would have been difficult to foresee the response of the Americans and the British and might have jeopardized their signing of the "Agreement on the Return of Prisoners of War". The directive had a nefarious impact on the forced exile of entire peoples from their native lands, which was undertaken by Stalin in 1944-1945. Hundreds of thousands of people were liquidated, evicted from their native lands or sent into the Gulag. Remember, this was done after a victorious war! Meanwhile all these bloody, unjust and illegal acts were done secretly without any mercy. Finally, this directive became a guide for all the KGB organs - from top to bottom - on how to exert control over the country's entire civilian population.

A whole laundry list of menacing questions faced those people who'd lived under German occupation: How did they dare live without Soviet power? How did they dare plow and seed? How did they dare feed the nanny goat and lay in stockpiles for winter? How did they dare share the same air with those who were fighting Soviet power? Who gave lard to the Germans; who fed the Nazi aggressors? Who brought the icons down from the garrets; repaired the churches; sewed robes for the clergy and spread the word of God? Who served on the municipal councils; groveled before the occupiers; and defended the Nazi scum? Thus, starting in 1943 many Russians, Ukrainians and people of other Soviet nationalities headed westward together with the retreating Germans without waiting for the return of their "own" authorities.

German occupation organs didn't collect official statistics on refugees. It is known, as an example, that in the period between 25 January and 20 February 1943 alone - during the German withdrawal from the Kuban and the North Caucasus - 312,000 people (including the elderly, women and children) were evacuated. Hundreds of representatives of the technical and humanitarian intelligentsia left the occupied territories together with their families as the Germans retreated.

In the years 1944-1947, the Western Allies forcibly handed back to the USSR more than 2.2 million Soviet citizens who'd been serving in the *Wehrmacht*'s Eastern volunteer formations (this number includes the family members of the soldiers and the refugees that had accumulated around one or another of the volunteer units). Upon their arrival back in the Soviet Union 20 per cent of them were shot or sentenced to 25 years in the Gulag, which in essence was equivalent to a death sentence; another 15-20 per cent were sentenced to 5-10 years in the camps; 10 per cent were exiled to remote areas of Siberia for a period of no less than six years; 15 per cent were sentenced to forced labor in the Donbas, Kuzbas and other regions that had been destroyed by the Germans (they were allowed to return home only after completing their sentenced term of labor); and only 15-20 per cent were allowed to return to their home areas. As is obvious, these figures do not add up to 100 per cent. Likely, the remaining 15-20 per cent consisted of people who managed to conceal themselves back in Soviet society, who died in route or who managed to escape.[3]

These figures also do not give a picture of the sort of fate that awaited each of the categories of the Eastern volunteers. It should be acknowledged that the Soviet justice system treated the soldiers and officers of the Russian Liberation Army the most severely.

According to information from N. Krasov - the great nephew of an ataman - the officers surrounding General Vlasov and his staff officers were immediately separated from the rest, while the rest of the Vlasovites were immediately transported to a special camp at Kemerovo where competent Soviet organs began to sift through them to identify all the officers - all the way down to battery commanders and platoon commanders. Particular attention was paid to those officers who'd received German propaganda training in Dabendorf. The majority of them were sentenced to be shot by tribunals of the Eastern Siberian Military District while the remaining received sentences of time in Gulag labor camps - most often 25 years (primarily at Kolyma, in Vorkuta and in Dzhezkazgan). Something similar awaited the soldiers and officers of the Cossack and other formations that had served in the *Wehrmacht.* With the passage of time, by 1946 the Soviet organs stopped distinguishing between the different category of "Eastern" volunteers, and in all the official and unofficial documents they began to be referred to as "Vlasovites".

Of the civilian repatriates, 578,616 were sent to various branches of industry (coal, construction, etc.) to serve in labor battalions. However, very quickly these battalions were disbanded. However, their members were re-assigned to specific enterprises and to a place of residence. Workers who fled were pursued. Nevertheless, the number of those fleeing was indeed high. People were striving to return to their homelands.

Years and years passed before the Soviet Government granted legal rights to those displaced persons and former prisoners of war who remained alive. The first historical act of justice was established in 1956 - that is, almost 11 full years after the war's conclusion. I'm talking about the decree by the CPSU Central Committee and Council of Ministers: "On eliminating the consequences of the crude violation of legal rights with respect to former prisoners of war and members of their families." However, it would take almost 40 years before this law was actually put into effect. Here one cannot forget the deed of Boris Yeltsin, who issued a decree: "On the restoration of the legal rights to Russian citizens - former Soviet prisoners of war and civilians - repatriated in the Great Patriotic War."

A significant number of displaced persons and former prisoners of war not wishing to return to the Soviet Union also sought to avoid repatriation by various means. The majority of the Russians who found themselves at freedom as displaced persons strove to put as much distance between themselves and Europe as possible - beyond the Atlantic Ocean. However, this possibility didn't open right away but only in step with the deterioration of relations between the former Allies and the Soviet Union during the Cold War.

Back then, there was a negative attitude toward the Russians not only in the United States. For example, at first Argentina also issued an order to its consulates not to grant visas to people of Slavic origin - particularly to Russians. Only beginning in 1949-1950 - especially after the adoption of a benign law regarding immigration in the United States - did the camps for displaced persons begin to disperse.

Community organizations of Russian emigrants, which had been created back before the start of the Second World War, received government subsidies. For example Americans financed the Tolstoy Fund, which had been created in the United States in 1939 with the participation of B.A. Bakhmet'ev. Thanks to the assistance of these organizations, many Russians managed to save their lives. The Vlasovites that had escaped repatriation to the Soviet Union were in particular grateful to the Tolstoy Fund since many governments - including that of the United States - prohibited the resettlement of the Vlasovites in their countries.

In distinction from the many Russian organizations which were created with foreign financing but made their goal to help Russian refugees settle in the New World, the government agencies of the Western countries pursued primarily political and economic objectives. Moreover, the economic goals - to obtain cheap labor - took priority over the others. But however it happened, between May 1947 and 1952 approximately 213,300 Soviet wartime refugees were brought out of the Western occupation zones of Germany and Austria to other countries on the European and American continents. Canada alone accepted 38,708.

A commission under the direction of the then Soviet historian D.A. Volkogonov probably obtained a more accurate number. It determined that there were 504,000 refugees in the camps in Western Europe that didn't return to the Soviet Union.

However, even this isn't the end of the story. Their estimate does not include those who avoided the refugee camps altogether and thereby weren't counted in the statistics of displaced persons. This category was numerous. Approximately 300,000 people remained outside the camps. Thus, the number of those who didn't return to the Soviet Union varies markedly from official Soviet statistics and amounts to as many as 800,000 people.

In 1955 the new Soviet regime attempted to repeat Stalin's ploy and again tried to lure hundreds of thousands of emigrants into its nets. This time the action took place under the slogan "Mother Russia is calling you!" As we see, the propagandists hadn't bothered to think up anything new. The KGB or SMERSH didn't direct the campaign - as had been the case previously - but a Committee "For the Return to the Motherland", which was organized in Moscow under the direction of KGB General Mikhailov.

Once this Committee requested a "sensible" editor be sent to them from the Publishing Institute where I was working as an instructor. It send them a fine editor, but the woman only lasted two months in her new post even though she was being well-paid. Once I happened to bump into her and I asked her why she had left. She replied: "I've never seen more falsehoods in my entire life. I couldn't take it!"

When speaking about the return of the second wave of emigrants back to the Soviet Union in the 1950s, one thing should be said. They weren't condemned to the Gulag or forced to work as laborers at construction sites, but they also weren't given any particular benefits. One Leningrader, whom they'd allowed to return home, told me that when he returned he had lived for three years in an earthen dugout outside the city before he obtained a permit and was granted a 6-meter square room in a communal apartment in the city of Leningrad.

It is known how this widely-advertised campaign ended. Almost everyone that was able to do so returned back to those countries where they had been previously living before being lured back to the Soviet Union - where they had worked honorably and had acquired a normal human life.

In order to more fully understand what these so-called filtration camps were like (in their best possible light) in the early days of their organization in Germany, I will tell you about one of them that I once happened to visit. About 15-20 kilometers from the place where our artillery brigade was stationed, there was a filtration camp for women. Three officers climbed on their motorcycles and quickly reached the spot. There was no enclosure and no guard huts, barbed wire or sentries. It was a wonderland! We could hear only feminine voices and their singing. The streets all had Russian names. There were tidy little German homes with small gardens. Female Returnees were living in them.

At first, a so-called blockhouse had been set up on each street. Next to it was a plank deck with dining tables. Meals were served here. The women did everything themselves. They prepared the food and cleaned up afterward. There was an inspection once a day. The camp had a medical station and a bath house. Medical check-ups were conducted there, since without one departure for the Motherland was prohibited. Sometimes they showed patriotic films.

When darkness fell, Italian prisoners of war - whose camp lay next to the women's camp - would sing or whistle serenades. Someone, laughing, observed: "It's just like a Pioneer Camp!" A sentry soldier told us a lot about the place. We noted that he was unarmed.

We inquired of him: "What's possible here and what's impossible?" The soldier proudly replied: "For the victors, everything is possible!" But he cautioned: "Before the cavaliers present themselves to the damsels, they'd better first visit the command post."

The SMERSH officers received us with open arms. They eagerly told us about their facility, where approximately 5,000 female refugees were housed. They warned that the next time we better not come without cognac.

We tried to find out a thing or two. For example, why wasn't the camp guarded? How was the situation with rations? Did they hold the women long here in the camp before sending them back to the Motherland? Here's what one mustachioed Colonel obligingly told us: "Our contingent must acquire the complete confidence that the camp is already part of the Motherland! Where can they flee and why? There are checkpoints on all the roads and military units in all the villages and woods. The Americans won't take them back!"

He was dissembling, lying or he simply didn't know the truth! Soon all the "Pioneer Camps" adopted a new form - in the Soviet way. While we were talking, dinnertime arrived. Women were heading for the blockhouse with little buckets.

Suddenly I started in surprise: I spotted Vera, a pretty and engaging young woman I had met in a German home in the Sudeten who was the first to tell me that the war was over. Her face was now drawn - her eyes dull and unexpressive - and she was now dressed shabbily: second-hand clothes, worn-out shoes and nothing else. We met after dinner. Our conversation was not a happy one. I found out from her that after we had parted in the Sudeten, the new authorities had driven her out of the home where she'd been living the very next day - letting her take nothing with herself but something to eat. Where were they taking her? The Czechs after the war didn't stand on ceremony with the Sudeten Germans. After the war they exiled the Germans - approximately 2 million of them.

She was brought to this place, Vera told me, where she had revealed everything about herself - "cleansing the soul" - and once back in the Soviet Union she would "let the chips fall where they may." She told me her entire personal story. She was from the Crimea and she'd been working as a dishwasher in a German officer's mess in Balaklava where the Germans had built a submarine base: this saved her mother from hunger. Some German naval officer took notice of her. They began to meet. Soon he departed on a deployment. They brought him back half-alive with a badly-burned face. Vera helped take care of the submariner. Then he was assigned to a special hospital in Czechoslovakia where he would finish his treatments. The wounded officer brought her with him to Czechoslovakia as a nurse. He returned to duty after recovering his health, but never returned from his next deployment in the Atlantic. Vera began to look for work. She was hired as a housemaid of a rich Sudeten German who had fled with the retreating German army as the Red Army approached in 1945. That was when I had first met her.

I attentively listened to Vera's story. She could hardly hold back her tears. Sitting beside her, the entire time I felt somewhat awkward. I was forcing myself to try to find at least a few warm words of comfort for Vera. They wouldn't come. The entire meeting seemed somehow unnatural. Nevertheless, I returned the next day to the camp to spend more time with Vera. I brought her a quilted jacket, stockings and some new shoes. As she parted, she told me about the fate of her neighboring friend from the Ukraine who had hung herself. The poor woman had simply been unable to reconcile herself with the buried dream of living in the West.

By tradition, the entire camp gathered to see off the next party of women to the Motherland. The spectacle burned itself into my memory. It is difficult to describe. One had to see it. One had to have a deep sense of compassion to understand what was happening. Many of us, Red Army officers, over the years of the war had forgotten what compassion was. They formed the women into a column. With their little bags and handmade satchels slung over their shoulders, the formation moved off toward the gates of the camp. Honestly, I didn't notice that many of them had sadness in their eyes. The camp officers encouraged the women - trying to scatter their slightest doubts. "Girls," they said with a crafty smile, "everything will be fine!" Indeed, the "girls" believed them - or more accurately, wanted to believe them. A well-known song rang out in the air: '*Shiroka strana moia, rodnaia* ...' ['*My native country is broad* ...'].

On that day, for the first time I pondered the foul trickery of the authorities. Neither I nor my comrades said a word. Back then, we still didn't know a lot about how Mother Russia would greet its returning daughters who had been extracted from the Nazi hell by the victory of the Red Army. There were a lot of "stigmatized" women like Vera in the camp, as they were called for associating with the Germans.

The Encounter with the Motherland

As the trains approached the Soviet border, the eyes of the "Returnees" lost their sparkle and a cold fear filled them inside. They didn't ask for anything or make any demands on that same government - which had been unable to defend them - to save them from the enemy. Not in 1941, nor in 1942 or in 1943 or in 1944. It took the Red Army four-and-a-half years to liberate their native lands from the German occupiers.

As soon as the train reached the border, it was switched onto a side track. There, soldiers with dogs surrounded it. Having been counted off, the women were all formed up. Secret bundles were unloaded from the trains. Officers who met the trains broke the waxed seals on the secret papers. Immediately, orders rang out: this woman to the left; that one to the right while some were told to remain in place. Some were already led away under escort to freight cars with grilled windows that were waiting for them on different lines. That train set off at express speed to its scheduled destination. Others were forced onto a different freight train and had a long, long way to go across their native land aboard it. Both the "stigmatized" and the "clean" women couldn't guess back then that the majority of them were being sent into the Gulag system - to agricultural camps – where, as the government intended, they were to constitute the production basis for the food to supply the entire system of camps in the country.

Thirty years after the war when I was living in Moscow my neighbor, a retired colonel, told me about these camps. In the years after the war he had directed the Gulag's Agricultural Department. He was formerly an agronomist - a graduate of the agricultural Timiziarev Academy.

The camps, of which there were more than a hundred, annually provided up to 40 per cent of the "food" for the Gulag. The main cleverness of the conceived idea consisted in the following: The camps turned over everything done by the labor of the inmates to the local authorities. The government meanwhile supplied the Gulag with everything issued to it - right down to the last beet or carrot. Of course, in these agricultural camps the women lived better than those in the logging and mining camps, but they were still "*Zeks*" and were each serving 10-year sentences - if not longer - just like the men. What crimes did they commit for such a cruel fate? For betraying the Motherland, serving in the *Wehrmacht* or subordinating themselves to the "Master Race"? How could they have refused? Was it because some of them had slept with German officers or soldiers - after which they were contemptuously called "mattresses" [the Russian slang term back then for any woman who slept with a soldier or officer of the opposing side]? Perhaps it was because risking their own lives, they had aided captured Red Army men or Allied soldiers? Incidentally, let's stop and ask ourselves: didn't we - Soviet officers, political workers, soldiers, communists and non-Party members alike - sleep with German, Polish and Romanian women? Didn't the Soviet army - having entered German territory and while liberating occupied European countries from Nazi oppression - rape women, plunder both our own and foreign homes and pillage wherever we went? And how!

For a long time the command closed their eyes to the low crimes of the "victors" and most often sought to ignore them. They continued to do so until there was a rumble of clear disapproval from higher up. There are many examples, but here's one. One of the squadrons of General Oslikovsky's Guards Cavalry Corps in Hungary just had to be quartered in a nunnery. The Cossacks raped the nuns in a wild, drunken orgy. The entire army quickly learned about this event from the contents of an order... Were the officers ashamed? Nothing like it... they chuckled over it and joked about it. Well, what a stroke of luck for the men - nuns.

Let's return to the fate of the Returnees. They were dreaming of one thing: to return home; to press themselves against their mothers' breasts. After everything that they had endured, all the bitterness they had tasted down to the dregs, shouldn't they have been seated in carriages and not in cattle cars to be taken back to the Motherland - there to be greeted with music and a guard of honor as they do in democratic societies?

Isn't that, Brother, what you're saying you wanted?

"Drummers are marching in a file,
Beating their drums. The drummers themselves
are flaying the skins on them."

Berthold Brecht

13

The Fall Guys and the Devil[1]

"Fall Guys"

A "Fall Guy" is, well, a fall guy - whether he be a soldier or a Marshal; if he happened to take the bait of the *osobisty* [members of the notorious Special Departments in the Red Army] or SMERSH men [SMERSH was the organizational successor to the Special Departments in the Red Army]. I will cite the two following cases:

Two soldiers were conversing in an adjacent company. One said: "We fight and fight, but always to no avail." The other replied: "With the swill we're being fed, there's only one way out - to go over to the Germans and drink tea." Both soldiers were accused of traitorous attitudes and the result as always was well-known in such cases: a tribunal.

The other case involved Marshal Zhukov himself. After the war ended, the SMERSH Chief Viktor Abakumov flew into Berlin. There he immediately began to arrest officers and generals in the immediate circle of Marshal Zhukov, who at that time was the commander-in-chief of the Soviet administration in the Soviet occupational zone in Germany. Someone reported to the Marshal what was happening and he immediately summoned Abakumov. Their meeting proved to be difficult. Zhukov demanded that the SMERSH chief quickly free all the arrested men and to leave Berlin within 24 hours - and Abakumov complied. However, the fall guy Zhukov paid a costly price for his noble act. In 1946 Abakumov helped Stalin topple the Marshal from his lofty post.

I remember that at the front both officers and the soldiers sought to avoid the Special Departments - to keep out of its gazing eye. Alas, this institution didn't give the frontline men any peace and frequently reminded them of its presence.

If the commissars called upon us, the men at the front, to join the Party and to lead men into battle, then the Special Department officers always called upon the soldier or officer to sell their souls to the devil - appealing to their ardent desire not to allow enemies to undermine the strength of our country. Indeed these words were effective, if you will, stronger than patriotic words about serving the Fatherland or the repetition of Stalin's words: "The enemy will be smashed; victory will be ours!"

All of the Special Department's frontline activity, as a rule, occurred in secrecy beyond the knowledge of the division's other units. The chief of the Special Department - and after him the chief of SMERSH - was subordinate to the division commander, but sometimes there was a silent agreement between the commander and the Special Department. For example, in the 331st Rifle Division in which I served, I know that the general asked the Special Department not to touch any officers without his prior approval.

The Special Department officers, as a rule, appeared in public only on three occasions. Usually, as soon as the troops had seized a town or village, they would follow them into it. They believed their first duty was to hurry to arrest the burgomaster, village elders, policemen and anyone who assisted the Germans in any way including translators, cooks and waitresses in the officers' mess halls - in addition to the traitors who had betrayed communists and Soviet partisans to the Nazis.

The final German rear guard units pulled out of Rzhev early on the morning of 3 March 1943; the forward units of the 215th Rifle Division moved into the city in their wake. At this time an operational group of 10 Special Department men entered Rzhev. It was headed by the Senior Plenipotentiary of the 30th Army's NKVD Special Department, P.I. Konovalov. The group's assignment was to penetrate into Rzhev and to secure the office of the Municipal Head, V.Ia. Kuz'min.

Senior Lieutenant of State Security, A.Iu. Sinitsyn, climbed up onto the balcony of the two-story building on the corner of Communist and Kalinin Streets together with some sub machine gunners. He hoisted the Red flag over it. A second flag was raised on a steeple of the Pokrovsky Church.[2]

General Segal' in his memoirs relates how during the fighting in the Ukraine, while traveling in his armored car, he encountered the following scenes:

> … As soon as the attacking troops liberated a settlement, officers of the military tribunals would follow them into it. Through local citizens they worked to identify traitors of the Motherland - primarily policemen and village elders - arraign them on charges and sentence them to death…

Once he was present at an execution, which he describes for us:

> … Quite a lot of people gathered … Two vehicles drove up - one a closed truck, the other a pickup. Two traitors - policemen for the Germans - were led out of the truck and made to stand in the bed of the pickup truck, which was then driven to a point underneath the gallows' crossbeam. The tribunal chairman read out the sentence and with his assistance placed nooses around the condemned men's necks. The driver stepped on the gas pedal.

> One condemned man's rope broke. He fell to the ground. Soldiers, standing nearby, began to kick and stomp on him. Soon they ordered for him to be hung a second time...[3]

The second cause for Special Department officers to make an appearance was the event of the arrival of the next batch of replacements in the division. They came to our 673rd Rifle Regiment and pulled the new soldiers out of the formation and led them away. Once out of eyesight, they worked to recruit stoolies. The discussion was brief and God forbid the word "traitor" be mentioned. The entire conversation between the Special Department officer and the soldier would be much like the following:

> Officer: "We serve one cause – victory over the enemy. But among us there are people who think differently and their attitudes are of a harmful nature. You must expose them and thereby strengthen the power of our army.
>
> Soldier: "Excuse me, I'm … what? What can I do?"

Some would agree on the spot while others would remain silent as a stone - breathing heavily and trying to find some argument against the recruiting pitch which occupied a special, I would say, primary place in the work of the Special Department. After all, their command demanded that the Special Department officers have their own snitch in each squad, which means no less than 30 stool pigeons per battalion. This constantly caused problems: after each battle, only half of the initial batch of stoolies would still be alive - sometimes even fewer. This forced the poor Special Department officers to give their private recruiting pitches over and over again.

There existed another, higher category of assistants: "agents". These brethren were carrying out orders directly flowing from the NKVD. They would set up investigations of suspected individuals. Unfortunately, it did happen that both the agents and the snitches would go over to the German side and tell us over the radio how they had been recruited into the NKVD service and what had been expected of them. Shameful stories, but everyone remained silent about them.

They even had a confidential discussion with me. However, fortunately I was able to find a reason for refusing to cooperate with them: "Understand me, I'm the regiment's youth leader and if one of your or my little slips becomes revealed, that will likely be the end of my credibility in front of them. I would lose any trust I have among the young soldiers. They then wouldn't follow me into battle."

In response the major laughed and said: "You're being clever, lieutenant. But consider, dear friend, that it is better to befriend us than to teach us morals."

Usually there were three Special Department men in every rifle regiment. The division's Special Department consisted of 21 officers including the chief and his deputy, investigators, acryptographer and a commandant who had a platoon of sub machine gunners under his direction.

The third occasion when the Special Department would make a public appearance was usually, though not always, when the department chief would meet personally with an officer - starting with a battalion commander.

Once near Rzhev I picked up a German leaflet off the ground. Reading it, I laughed; it was painfully funny and clumsy. Not able to restrain myself, I read it aloud in the presence of two officers of the regiment headquarters. Usually we would receive a batch of replacements together and we knew each other well.

The next day I was summoned to see Colonel Razumovsky - the commander of the 673rd Rifle Regiment. He ordered everyone else out of the bunker and asking me to take a seat, quietly said: "How could you have acted so senselessly… you picked up an enemy leaflet and read it aloud? You distributed it. A trip before a tribunal ought to be the result. You're lucky that your officer acquaintance wrote his report to me and not to the Special Department."

Knowing that Colonel Razumovsky had served back in the Tsarist army prior to 1917 I asked him: "Can you imagine a similar situation, Comrade colonel, in the old Russian army?"

"Lieutenant," the regiment commander replied, "back then the Special Department hadn't yet been conceived. Now they exist and we're obliged to be more careful - and we must teach our soldiers that. I know you as a combat officer and that this is your first incident; I forgive you, considering your youth."

It seems that on that we parted. However, just two weeks passed when I was summoned to the Special Department. An enormous fellow met me - about such men we used to say: "He's seven *pud* [an old Russian unit of weight equivalent to roughly 16 kilograms] of lard and crap." Having seated me in front of himself, he gazed silently into my eyes for a long time - trying to prompt me to say something. Finally, he broke the silence: "What, you're teaching the soldier to go over to the Germans as if they feed turncoats chocolate and honey and let them go back to their women in the village?"

"Forgive me, Comrade major, let me respond."

"Well, speak up, speak up, lieutenant."

"You've likely read the newspaper *Krasnaia Zvezda*. A large article about counter-propaganda was printed in it."

"Of course I've read it; just don't wag your tongue at me."

"But this was Ilya Ehrenburg's article and I was behaving forthrightly! I was calling upon soldiers not to believe the deserters."

"You know, there is an old Russian saying: 'The eagle doesn't hunt flies.'"

"Comrade major, are you comparing me with a fly? I'm an officer of the Red Army!"

"You were …"

"How am I to understand you, Comrade major?

"Here's how: you acted like a real enemy propagandist."

"I don't understand you."

"Now you'll understand. Let me read something to you - what your own soldiers are writing about you."

The officer put on a pair of eyeglasses and read out a denunciation against me: "It seems that in a conversation with your soldiers you were repeating everything the deserters said the day after they deserted."

"Comrade major, you have a rotten assistant - a real bonehead. I repeated the words of the scoundrels, but I was calling upon the soldiers not to believe them! Yet your informant, or as you call him, your "witness" didn't write about this."

"We'll check," the major concluded the discussion with me, "We will see."

I stepped out of the Special Department drenched with sweat and with a heavy heart. I would have to be cautious. I thought: "It turns out that you have ears around you. The slightest stumble and you'll wind up in the devil's paws. That's what I've already heard one of the officers call the Special Department." Now I had seen the very Devil himself in human form. Why did he come after my head?

From that unforgettable day on until the end of the war, I, like many of my comrades, tried to keep my distance from the Special Department - and after 1943, SMERSH. However, twice more during the war I fell into their clutches, but thank God both times I managed to break free. I've already discussed these episodes in my memoirs.

The front teaches more quickly than any of the finest schools. It teaches you not only how to fight, how to suppress the fear of death; it teaches hatred for the foe and malevolence toward the idiot-commanders. It instructs despite all the different forms of ignobility. It is no coincidence that after the war, in the Soviet Union one year of service at the front was considered equal to three years of peacetime work experience.

Both the soldiers and the officers very quickly figured out who was who. Handfuls of soldiers are in the frontline and behind them are innumerable chiefs. The special penal companies hovered over the handful of soldiers, while the officers faced special assault and penal battalions. Behind them were the blocking detachments. A recent Russian publication presents data in its appendices about the number of men who served in the penal platoons, companies and battalions during the war.[4] According to its figures, 29 assault and 63 penal battalions were formed - as well as 1,102 penal companies and six penal platoons. Altogether at one time or another 727,910 officers and men served in them. This number is 5-6 times greater than the comparable number of men who served in German penal units. However, the handbook doesn't say a single word about the losses! Incidentally, it is known that somewhere up to 50-70 per cent of the officers and soldiers in the penal units were killed in action.

I myself, while participating in the fighting to liberate Minsk in 1944, watched as penal troops were thrown into battle against seven lines of German defenses. They broke through them all and cleared a path for the tank armies.

It should be noted that the Special Departments - and then (after April 1943) SMERSH - controlled the penal units. In each penal battalion and in each separate penal company there was a Special Department officer.

The front teaches honor and courage and an understanding of the nature of bravery - as well as of betrayal. With every passing year the strength of the Red Army increased; the soldiers acquired combat experience; the officers grew wiser and a bit more mature while the generals learned not only how to defend, but how to attack. Aviation divisions and armies appeared and mechanized corps, artillery divisions and tank armies. Yet there was still the art of fighting "at any cost" and the baleful influence of the Special Departments - and then SMERSH - on the army. The more closely we neared victory, the more each combat officer and Red Army soldier sensed their deadly presence.

No matter how big a hero you were - no matter how many times you'd been wounded or how many times you'd been decorated - you had no defense against the Devil. I don't recall a single case when soldiers attempted to defend a comrade that had fallen into its clutches. That goes without saying for the officers. In similar cases they sought not to intervene in events that were taking place in front of their eyes. Practically speaking, this meant they were turning over their troops for slaughter to the Special Department officers.

Oddly, victory blinded us frontline men. Many of us once again became simpletons. We forgot about the unspoken surveillance over each of us and the denunciations. So many honorable frontline soldiers and officers were killed - having forgotten this nefariousness with which Stalin's *oprichniki* surrounded us.[5]

In order for the reader to better understand what this "hell" was like, I will say that the life of the Red Army - from the soldier to the general - was under a magnifying glass. I will acquaint you with the recollections of other frontline men and women who fought near Rzhev.

Former, still living Special Department and SMERSH officers - not to mention contemporary FSB officers - complain far and wide that they are being smeared in the popular press and on the radio and television. In contrast, they assert that both the Special Department and SMERSH played an enormous role in the achievement of total victory. Was this so? As a rule, the defenders of the Chekists assert that their critics as a rule don't know the real truth and don't back up their accusations with documental evidence or the memoirs of veterans. Well then, I've decided to help these apologists and to familiarize the reader with the recollections of soldiers and officers about them during the war.

How can a man serve such a godless matter as denouncing one another and raise a hand against a comrade and live without a troubled conscience? No one talked about this aloud, but each of us at the front indeed reasoned this way. We castigated the snitches with hatred and sought to avoid them by any possible means, right up to murder.

In his memoirs, **Boris Polyakov** recalls:

> ... Once ... I dropped by the regiment headquarters, where the chief of the Special Department requested I come by to see him in order to put together a report plan. I quickly created one, but

meanwhile the *osobist* became interested in my German machine pistol that I had discovered in a German command vehicle that had been knocked out near Beyli back in February 1942. Scrutinizing the gun in his hands, the *osobist* said he was going to seize it as captured German property. I exploded with indignation and in an agitated tone I told him exactly what I thought of his conduct … Having blurted out every thought that had boiled up inside me, I rose and left his office - not neglecting to slam the door behind me. The repercussion to this incident didn't come right away.

On some later date, my platoon and I were returning from a training exercise; we were moving in an extended single-file formation along a narrow forest path. I was bringing up the rear. Passing through a small clearing, the point man picked up a German leaflet, read it through while on the move and passed it back to the man following him. In this fashion the leaflet passed down the chain of men and eventually reached me. I read it, tore it into pieces and threw them onto the ground and immediately forgot about it. There were a lot of leaflets lying around in this forest near the front - both ours and German.

On the next day I had reason to recall it. That evening my assistant platoon leader called me deep into the woods and showed me the draft of a report that he had found under the bunk of the soldier Tuchin. It laid out yesterday's incident with the leaflet in detail and in a generally accurate fashion, but without any extra discussion … Tuchin was a pedagogue with a higher education. Previously Tuchin had fallen asleep while on duty at a post. But it was wartime, and he was at the frontline. So he was put before a tribunal and threatened with being sent into a penal company. For some reason, his avoided this fate. No one knew about this. True, rumors had reached me that the Special Department had recruited him as a one of its stoolies and had directed him into my platoon. It has to be assumed that it was in order to put me under surveillance.

It was possible that a case could have been fabricated against me from Tuchin's report. It was forbidden to read German leaflets - although soldiers would nevertheless read them before using them to roll cigarettes and lighting up.

There were no consequences for me from this tip-off. Only after the war did I find out that the matter had been squelched at the initiative of the Regiment Commissar A.N. Sharevin. He had the unwavering esteem not only of our regiment, but of the entire division.

Such was the overall system of the atmosphere of pressure under which we all, the war's soldiers, lived at the front. Many postwar years of reflection often led me to the thought that I should consider myself lucky not only that an enemy bullet didn't strike me, but also that fate protected me against the tentacles of a totalitarian regime - under which we were all mixed up in that terrible game...[6]

* * *

The recollections of **Captain Ivan Meskovtsev**, a veteran of the 215th Rifle Division, regarding Ivan Maslennikov's diary:

> ... Officers and soldiers knew that any sort of note-taking (diaries) was forbidden. The Special Departments zealously kept watch to make sure no one kept a diary. To violate this ban meant to wind up in the SMERSH and this didn't promise anything good because nobody ever returned from there. Indeed, even the word itself was spoken with apprehension and a sense of mystery. We looked at anyone being escorted into the SMERSH office as a condemned man...[7]

The memoirs of artilleryman **P.A. Mikhin**, a gun platoon commander in the 32nd Rifle Division's 1028th Artillery Regiment:

> ... Once the Germans pinpointed our battery's position and a Ju-87 bomber came after us; it flew over the battery's front and released one bomb over each of the four guns... The soldiers, like startled sparrows, darted headfirst into their shelters but not one of the bombs exploded - though each one was right on target. Sergeant Khokhlov couldn't restrain his astonishment: "That's an ace for you! Perfect work! Four bombs and each one on target!" Each of us was thinking the same way, but we stayed silent. In those times it was dangerous to say such things out loud since you might be sent to the Special Department where they didn't handle our brothers with kid gloves. It was better to die in battle than to have any business with the SMERSH... The sergeant immediately checked himself and I made an effort to bail him out of the situation - deliberately disparaging the German pilot's achievement: "But after all not a single one exploded!"
>
> Several of the fellows - who hadn't yet shaken off their recent fright and had lost any caution over what could or couldn't be said - chimed in together: "What if they had exploded, though?"

> Some equally short-sighted men replied: "Nothing would have been left of us." Another one added: "And there would have been nothing left to bury."
>
> Just then, crews from other guns came running over - delighted that we'd been left unharmed by some miracle.
>
> "That has to be upsetting to the Germans with all the work they put into it and how masterfully it was conducted - yet all in vain."
>
> "And you're sniveling because you feel a bit sorry for them..."
>
> I interrupted this dangerous talk, which had to be reported: "So why didn't the bombs explode?"
>
> "God saved us," said the elderly Trofimov with conviction as he crossed himself.
>
> "God or not, but such a thing has never happened that all four bombs didn't explode," I said.
>
> "It's the anti-fascists' work," the battery's Party Organizer Romashov declared...
>
> Perhaps he was the one who was reporting on all the conversations in the battery in his political dispatches.
>
> An uncommon event in the war - a small scene with a representation of human feelings - but it so accurately illuminates the situation of the soldiers at the front. "Better to be killed, than to fall into the hands of the Special Department!"

P.A. Mikhin offers another story about the Special Department and its menacing presence in the Red Army. It is a story about the tragic fate of the brave scout Volkov, who was the commander of the battery's fire direction and control platoon[8]:

> ... With its [the battery's] support the company attacked the enemy infantry and occupied the German trench, but then it was forced to fall back 200 meters. At this moment communications were interrupted and Volkov couldn't support the company with the battery's fire. He, together with his scout and signalman, were cut off from their own forces. They hid in an empty German bunker and decided to wait until the onset of darkness. The Germans discovered them and a combat erupted. The scout was killed and Volkov was wounded in the arm... Exploiting the darkness, Volkov and his signalman scrambled out of the bunker and broke through back to their own lines... We greeted them as heroes. But

> a Special Department lieutenant arrived. He considered Volkov a traitor who had spent all that time in the enemy rear. Therefore he ordered two "pits" to be dug in the battery's position and to place Volkov and the signalman in them under armed guard. We were prohibited from communicating with them.
>
> The interrogation lasted for the entire day and that evening Volkov was sent to the Special Department under escort. I still remember the anguished smile on Volkov's pale face. I remember how it was distorted with bitterness and how his eyes were brimming with tears. He could barely refrain from bursting out crying (he'd been a schoolboy when he joined the Red Army). His own people had inflicted this umbrage upon him. We were sorry for Volkov, but back then there was nothing we could do for him. Before the war ended I wound up in tragic situations like Volkov's three times, but I was lucky. Each time communications were re-established and fending off the Germans, I made it back to my observation post. But in those awful minutes, I experienced the same fears and concerns as Volkov as our own guys retreated: the Germans are running past you and you're lying there without communications, pressed to the ground, pretending to be dead and fearing not death but being taken prisoner and what your commanders and *osobists* are thinking about you...[9]

All of us, the soldiers and the officers, found ourselves in Volkov's situation when the *osobists* equated heroes with traitors. The innocent men were executed, beaten, or sent into the special penal companies or battalions. I had approximately the same experience at Smolensk, but at an order from the battalion commander as the attack was ending, I left the German trenches together with remnants of a company.

However, in his own memoirs P.A. Mikhin tells of us his experience when he fell under the suspicion of the Special Department after a howitzer in his battery had a misfire and the shell blew apart the gun barrel:

> ... I ran up to the howitzer and was stunned. My eyes stared at the space beyond the gun shield where a 2-meter-long, elevated, menacing gun barrel was supposed to be. I was looking at a howitzer without a barrel! It was as if I was looking at a person without a head. The unimaginable loss struck me like a knife in the heart. Then a terrifying thought killed the pain of the loss: "What will happen to me?!" My sorrow over the loss of the howitzer was replaced with fear of responsibility...
>
> The members of the gun crew shook me out of my state of shock. They gathered around me and were shouting joyfully: "We're all alive, Comrade lieutenant!"

I came back to my senses. My happiness for my men offset the bitterness of the loss and my fear of my own fate. I felt a bit ashamed because I had thought first of the howitzer and myself - forgetting about the crew. But it was really not my fault that I had been trained that way: Die yourself, lose your men, but first of all save your guns!

"How did you escape with your whole skin, boys?" I responded, "It wasn't just a shell that exploded a meter away from you, but one ton of steel that blew into pieces right in front of you - and the whole barrel sent fragments flying all around!" But I thought to myself I had been lucky together with them. I didn't lose a single man; perhaps they wouldn't execute me and only send me to a penal battalion. Back then I didn't yet know that a penal battalion was a much worse fate than a quick death.

A lieutenant from the Special Department arrived at lunchtime on horseback. Together with him, also on horseback, loomed two guards armed with submachine guns. At first I was happy that the person who was going to conduct the investigation was not some grumpy old man, but someone my own age, but when the guest - without saying hello - carelessly saluted me and quickly introduced himself as Lieutenant Kapitsky, I tensed up.

"Where is the exploded gun?" Kapitsky asked sternly - addressing no one in particular. His black, penetrating eyes were looking past me - leaving me no hope for a friendly, confidential conversation… Kapitsky was wearing a freshly-pressed tunic, a crisp new leather belt and his spick-and-span trousers were perfectly ironed. The narrow tops of his gleaming leather boots clung tightly to the slender calves of his legs. Even the sub machine gunners that accompanied him looked like they had been plucked out of a candy box - standing in sharp contrast to my artillerymen, like the difference between new shiny nails and old, rusty, bent nails pulled out of a board. One could see that our "guests" never had to drag heavy howitzers from swamps and had never pressed their chests against the tall, dirty wheels of a howitzer.

The first order of business for the Special Department lieutenant was to scatter the crew of the destroyed gun at 30-meter intervals in different directions from the howitzer and order them to dig a fighting hole in which they were to sit. This was done so that the men could not communicate with each other and so that they would feel as if they were under arrest. While the crews were digging their earthen cells under the watchful eyes of the guards,

Kapitsky led me into my dugout and began the interrogation. I was the senior officer of the battery and was thus responsible for everything.

"Show me your weapon," was the polite request of the *osobist.*

I gave him my sub machine gun. Kapitsky silently laid it at his feet. Then he somehow quietly asked in an everyday tone of voice: "Why did the barrel of your gun explode?"

"Most likely, the shell had a defective detonator and it triggered the explosion prematurely when the round was still in the barrel."

"Or perhaps you forgot to remove the muzzle cover or there was dirt inside?" asked the detective venomously - who then tilted his head to one side and ostentatiously gaped, playing the fool.

"A gun is not a garbage bin for gathering trash; take a look at how well the other howitzers have been treated. Colonel Uriupon can also confirm this. He's just been here. As for the muzzle cover, it is still lying rolled up next to the gun."

The *osobist* stared fixedly at me in a threatening way: "You could have done all this afterwards. Perhaps you deliberately decided to put this gun out of action?!" I had never dealt before with the NKVD and I'd never been under investigation. Thus I couldn't imagine that they would openly ask such offensive questions.

"Today one gun is out of action, tomorrow another, and soon you'll see to it that the entire battery is out of action," the lieutenant continued - paying no attention to my outrage. "How many dead and wounded from the explosion?"

"No casualties," I declared with pride.

"How?! You deliberately put the crew under shelter before you blew up the barrel! Which means you spared your men so they wouldn't turn you in!" Kapitsky casually grabbed his belt, shifted his pistol around to his front and then sharply demanded: "Well, answer me, lieutenant! For what purpose and on whose orders did you blow up the gun?"

This question stunned and frightened me. The matter had taken a serious turn.

"Who are your partners?! Perhaps to blow up the gun, you tossed some sand down the barrel?!"

Such a charge was enough to have me executed. But I found a counterargument: "And just where in this swamp can you get sand?"

Over and over again I explained what had happened to Kapitsky at his demand. But the *osobist* needed a confession: "The round and the barrel have both been blown to pieces and this is a fact! You have no proof that the barrel was clean. The fact that you had no casualties only aggravates your guilt. Confess, and this will lighten your sentence. Think it over. Meanwhile, I'll interrogate the gun crews."

The lieutenant left - taking my sub machine gun with him. A guard began to pace back and forth in front of the entrance to the dugout.

Kapitsky spent a long time questioning the other men of the battery. He was especially thorough with the soldiers of the Number Three gun. When he returned to the dugout, I had nothing new to say.

"Something is becoming clear," he said vaguely - taking a seat in front of me. "Confess and tell me who your other accessories to the crime were."

"I've told you everything. Let's fire the rest of the rounds from this batch to see if there are any defective ones," I suggested.

"What?! You want me to blow up the other guns together with you?! You want to carry out an enemy order with my help?!" Kapitsky boiled over.

"Why would they explode if, according to your version, all the detonators are OK… and we'll clean all the other guns in your presence? We have to expend the remaining shells anyway; soon the infantry will be calling for our support."

"We're going to court-martial you, lieutenant, for the deliberate destruction of the gun, and you will not get away with this. You're going to accompany me back to SMERSH."

I knew that I wouldn't be coming back from the SMERSH. There, in the SMERSH, I had even slimmer chances of proving my innocence because they had to demonstrate success and show that they were doing an effective job. It's a bitter end to die from a Russian bullet as a traitor; it's better to be killed by the Germans.

The investigator - seemingly satisfied that all was clear and that my guilt had been proven - stood up and headed for the exit. At that moment something dawned on me: the fateful shot of the Number Three gun had been its second one! If the barrel had been dirty, it would have blown up with the first shot!

"But it was the second round!" I desperately shouted towards the departing *osobist.*

"Why does that have any significance?" Kapitsky shot back without turning around.

"No, listen, I'll prove that you are wrong, lieutenant!" I shouted at the top of my voice.

My shout and the improper use of the familiar "you" [Russians still distinguish between a formal 'you' (vy) and a familiar 'you' (ty); the latter is equivalent to 'thou' abandoned long ago in English. Using the familiar 'ty' in certain contexts can be insulting in Russian] upset the detective. He came back to put me in my place. He sat down and looked at me with a smirk.

I began my explanation: "If the gun barrel had been dirty or still covered, then the first round would have exploded in the barrel. But the first round had a properly functioning detonator and the discharge was normal. Why then did the second round explode prematurely if the barrel had already been cleaned by the first round and the cover had been torn off by the pressure, as you consider?" Then I triumphantly answered my own question: "Because it had a faulty detonator!"

Kapitsky became lost in thought … Then his face brightened up, he smiled and said: "You're a lucky man, lieutenant! Two shells were lying in the box: one normal and another with a faulty detonator. Plainly the limber gunner could have grabbed the faulty one first. Then the gun would have exploded with the first shot and you would have been executed! But here you're right - you are innocent. You should thank your luck."

That night, the whole lot of suspect rounds was taken away from the firing positions back to the ammo dumps. That was my close call with the Special Department…[10]

* * *

The veteran **Burlakov** recalls:

… On the following day after Rzhev's liberation, we discovered scattered leaflets everywhere. The Germans had produced them to look like Party membership card covers. One phrase struck my

> memory: "Bolshevism - this is not a theory or a body of knowledge, but 'organized crime'." The sense of these words was incomprehensible and foreign to me... Our commissars conducted explanatory work with us while the Special Departments zealously made sure that these leaflets were all gathered and destroyed. Indeed, speaking personally, the soldiers had no interest in these German papers. We had to fight.
>
> Only several decades later did I begin to ponder the meaning of those leaflets in light of why we entered the war so poorly equipped and poorly trained - and of all the blood that this cost us... All of this was readily apparent in the first years of the war on the Rzhev land...[11]

* * *

V.F. Khodosiuk, a former sub machine gunner in the 215th Rifle Division's 404th Rifle Regiment and a participant in the assault on Rzhev, recalls:

> ... Our commander was a good man - tall, solidly-built and kind - which could not be said about the political instructor, who was short, poorly educated and ill-tempered. He hated me because I constantly asked him all sorts of questions that he didn't like to answer and that he couldn't answer on the spot. For example, why was it forbidden to read the German leaflets? After all, we were reading them anyway. The Germans conducted a broad propaganda campaign. They were scattering their leaflets even behind the frontlines - red, white and blue ones. They all had one and the same message: "Come over to our side, the Red Army has been crushed." Below the leaflet, there was a space marked off by black ink, where it was written: "Tear off and save this pass. You will be fed and given work." For known reasons, we couldn't speak openly about them...[12]

The former nurse **Tat'iana Artemovna Motina** recalls:

> ... On 25 June 1941 I was already at the mustering point in the city of Nelidovo. There our horse-drawn Mobile Field Hospital No. 2297 was forming. All of our equipment was allocated among the wagons. We had 40 pairs of horses. I soon found out what the front was like near Smolensk. Blood, casualties and the moans of the wounded while constantly overhead were aircraft bearing black crosses - just like vultures that have sensed blood - that were diving on their prey with howling sirens. Human body parts, pieces of wagons and medical equipment were fly-

ing into the air. Everything became jumbled together back on the ground… At the end of October, the Germans encircled us and took us prisoner (at Viaz'ma), then drove us like cattle in the direction of Dorogobuzh. I managed to escape. Hungry and emaciated, I wound up among good people. I was then 21 years of age. They found some civilian clothes for me to wear. Then we left - having linked-up with cut-off troops that were moving back toward friendly lines… I was thinking that having regained my strength, I could make my way through the German lines back to my own people.

I was able to spend just a week with my parents behind German lines. However, one evening a neighbor woman came running up and said: "Run, Tat'iana, Germans are coming for you now. Someone squealed to them." I managed to escape… In February 1942, I finally managed to reach friendly lines together with a friend.

Immediately I was summoned to the Special Department, where I told them about all my adventures. Then they sent me to a special camp in Podol'sk where there was one officer - a junior lieutenant of the Medical Service. The detention conditions here were very harsh. For all practical purposes this was a confinement camp - or, as it was known back then, a filtration camp - where people were scrutinized and awaited their fate.

It is awful to recall all the things they were trying to pin on me. There were endless interrogations and a host of questions: "Why? Why didn't they kill you, but instead you wound up as a prisoner? How did you escape? How did you cross the frontlines?" They were both questions and unfounded allegations. To put it simply, they talked to me like I was a criminal. God forbid anyone wind up in such a situation.

There were people whose lot it was to receive long prison sentences. There was a constant flow of people through the camp - therefore many of them simply disappeared and we never knew their fates. After long torments, I was finally told that I was going to be sent to a penal battalion as a medic. Together with me many officers from the different branches of service were stripped of their ranks and decorations, issued the uniform of an ordinary private and sent to the front. That's how I wound up in a penal battalion, which was deployed in the area of the Semashko Rest Home near Rzhev.

We were to force a crossing of the Volga River. They told us: "Atone for your guilt with blood and then you will rejoin the reg-

> ular ranks of the Motherland's defenders." It was a surprise attack and we impetuously advanced in three echelons. Two of the waves managed to reach the opposite bank, but the Germans shot up the third one with machine-gun fire. Tormented cries, groans and swearing - coming from a fleeting hand-to-hand combat in the German trenches on the opposite bank - immediately rose above the sounds of the fighting. The Germans couldn't withstand the onslaught and retreated. We seized the grounds of the rest home and dug in to hold the bridgehead we had established.
>
> My assignment was to render first aid to the wounded and oversee their evacuation across the Volga. I could only do this work at night... The fighting was heavy; only a few of us remained in the battalion. For three months of combat I never took off my quilted jacket; never had a chance to wash up and seeing myself in a mirror once I was horrified - my hair had gone entirely gray. A blocking detachment followed us over all these days and was buttressing us with machine guns - of which we clearly didn't have enough. Our fellows fought courageously and were dying not because a blocking detachment was prodding us, but because one impulse was motivating all of us: to smash the aggressors.
>
> After the liberation of Rzhev, the pitiful remnants of the battalion were withdrawn from the front and sent to Moscow where we were given new uniforms; our ranks were restored - albeit with a demotion - but no one received their decorations back. I was assigned to a railroad battalion. My service in the Red Army ended in November 1945...[13]

However, the shadow of suspicion continued to hang over her for a long time to come. She was repeatedly summoned and told to keep silent about how she had wound up in the penal battalion, which aggravated her spiritual wound - the wound of an innocent person sentenced to a fate from which it seemed there was no escape. What was all this - pathetic and vain attempts to wriggle away from the executioners, or to get a fair hearing in front of the stern voice of the people?

F.S. Ivanov, a soldier in the Separate 149th Ski Battalion, recalls:

> ... I'd been cut down by shell fragments. I was badly wounded. I lay there, bloody and with mutilated extremities - constantly losing consciousness as I attempted to crawl. They found me the next morning and stretcher bearers picked me up toward evening. Five such heavily wounded men were collected. They took us in a vehicle to the town of Velikie Luki. The road consisted of log beams that had been laid down crosswise. I blacked out re-

> peatedly from the violent jolting as the vehicle moved along the corduroy road; whenever I came to, I heard the entreaties of the wounded men to stop to give them a bit of rest. The ambulance rattled along the road in a wild dance without stopping. It seemed as if there was going to be no end to this punishment. Most of the wounded men beseeched God to put an end to their suffering immediately rather than endure such tortures.
>
> Once at the hospital, as they were loading us onto stretchers, the driver walked up, fell to his knees and said: "Guys, forgive me. For God's sake, I couldn't stop; I have a strict timetable and if I hadn't returned in time - I would have been shot."[14]...

Oh, how little a soldier's life was worth at the front no matter what he was: an infantryman, a sapper, an artilleryman, a tanker...

There is one important matter which should not be avoided: this is grasping the essence of Stalin's Order No. 227 from 28 June 1942 which became known as the "Not One Step Back!" Order. The particular way it was perceived by the public is revealed in that title: "Not One Step Back!" This essentially meant, according to popular thought, that the artilleryman must never leave his gun under any circumstance; that a tanker had no right to abandon his tank and if necessary should burn together with it; and as for the infantryman, there's nothing to be said other than "Don't even stir!"

Commanders treated it differently: No retreat without authorization. If it was tactically advantageous to do so, however, or if the enemy had bypassed you then what should you do? Some commanders tried to be devious and feigned that they had been compelled to retreat, but if this occurred a tribunal awaited them.

Propaganda began everywhere to propagate the significance of sacrifice in the name of victory and dozens of "Matrosovs" appeared - including in our 220th Rifle Division; a soldier named Ivanov duplicated Aleksandr Matrosov's "deed".[15] Ivanov's name wound up on the front page of the newspaper *Pravda* and in a short time the entire front gave the names of 300 "Matrosovs".

In my own personal archive on this subject I've preserved a song the tankers used to sing, which they called their own hymn. With it I'll end the first part of this chapter.

Chorus:

It's a pleasure, Brothers, a pleasure

A pleasure, Brothers, to live.

It isn't fitting in the tank brigade

To grieve.

First Verse:

The first round struck the tank head-on

And laid the mechanic-driver in his coffin.

Repeat chorus

Second verse:

Then it cracked the turret

and wounded me with little fragments.

Repeat chorus

Third verse:

The turret man and radio operator my wounds do bind

While my vehicle burns off to one side.

Repeat chorus

Fourth verse:

Then I'm called to that Special Department

"Why didn't you burn together with your tank?"

Repeat chorus

Fifth verse:

I answer them: "Excuse me" and declare

That in the next attack I absolutely won't leave the fire.

Repeat chorus

"The Hunters Seeking Skulls"[16]

This devilry continued for the entire war. As the war advanced, it became ever crueler. With a terrible effect - like black storm clouds in the sky - it cast a malevolent shadow across the army's spirit. As an example I'll cite a conversation I had with the commander of an artillery battery at the end of 1943. Here's what the senior lieutenant said to me: "I stand at my gun and pray to God that he'll kill me sooner. I don't want to see the tragedy and death of my battery. They'll put me to death and there will be no one to answer for it..." What could I tell him in response?

Events in the Red Army took on a particularly deadly nature from the spring of 1943 - or more precisely, on 19 April - when it became known that Stalin had conceived the idea to create a new agency of intimidation both against his own people and against the opposing side. He called this agency "our own father" - the military counterintelligence agency SMERSH ("Death to Spies"). It was as if he was saying: "Look what we can do!"

So that no one in the Red Army, behind the frontlines or on occupied territory had the slightest doubts in the menacing name of the new agency or in its actions, the People's Commissar of Defense placed the trusted executioner V.S. Abakumov in charge of SMERSH. At the moment of his appointment as the SMERSH Chief, Abakumov was serving in the NKVD as Beria's deputy.

What was the essence of military counterintelligence? It isn't difficult to guess that Stalin created this special agency - subordinated to him personally as the People's Commissar of Defense - not to allow another 1941. After the Battle of Moscow and the German defeat at Stalingrad, the war entered a new, decisive phase. How the more confident commanders and indeed the entire emboldened Red Army would now behave - is it difficult to conjecture? SMERSH was created precisely in order to place the entire army under Stalin's firm control. But more importantly, in order to deal with those who as he believed had betrayed him in the first days of the war; to dispose of collaborationists who had betrayed Soviet power - especially in the Baltic republics; in the Ukraine; in the Crimea; and in Belorussia.

Abakumov - a protégé of the 1930s whose education had never progressed beyond the second grade, but who was a Communist Party member with fanatic inclinations who had beaten more than one general with his own powerful fists...

It is difficult to imagine, but true that more than a half-million people on the occupied lands of the Ukraine, Belorussia and the Baltic republics served in the *Wehrmacht*, in the S.S. troops or in the local enforcement agencies.[17] Stalin was determined to get even with them all.

This "office" was a three-headed entity. SMERSH in the Red Army was under the People's Commissariat of Defense and was directly subordinate to the People's Commissar, Stalin. A second SMERSH was organized in the Soviet navy and was subordinate to the Navy commander-in-chief. Finally, the NKVD also had a counterintelligence branch. The ranks of all SMERSH officers were equivalent to officers' ranks in the army and they wore army uniforms. All the Special Departments, which had previously been subordinate to the NKVD, moved under SMERSH control.

What was military counterintelligence to do? First of all, it was to secure Stalin's firm control over all the army. In the process, particular attention was to be given to the military commanders. The SMERSH officers, as practice demonstrated, splendidly coped with this task. There was not a single mutiny in the Red Army command. Having ended the war victoriously, the marshals and admirals obediently accepted humbling posts that had been previously thought up for them by the Supreme Leader.

As concerns the war years, according to the data published in the journal *Profil'* by the well-known political writer Leonid Mlechik, during the war SMERSH arrested 101 generals and admirals. Twelve of them could not endure the inquisitions and died; eight were released due to the lack of any evidence of a crime; 81 were convicted by the Military Collegium of the USSR Supreme Court or by a special panel.[18] To thwart so-called traitorous actions in the army, if you will, SMERSH also focused on the area where the Special Departments had previously shown great zeal (desertions, self-mutilations, defectors, distributors of hostile propaganda etc.).

The year 1943 was marked in the history of the war by not only the Battle of Kursk, but also the intensification of the vicious struggle between SMERSH and the *Abwehr* - the German military intelligence and counterintelligence agency. The dimensions of the secret war, led by German intelligence during the war years, had no equal in history.

After the failure of the *blitzkrieg*, in the period between November 1942 and the end of 1943 - in order to recover all that which had been lost - the Germans created an unprecedented network of intelligence schools, which annually graduated up to 10,000 agents, saboteurs and terrorists. Between January 1944 and May 1945, despite the defeats it had suffered, the German *Wehrmacht* continued to demonstrate the capability of conducting active combat operations. It was precisely in 1944 that the Germans created a special military agency the *Waffen S.S. Jagdverband* along the line of the German Special Services - headed by the S.S. General and special forces commander Otto Skorzeny - which was designed to infiltrate enemy lines, create confusion in enemy command and control and to conduct guerilla operations in the enemy rear.

The Germans had more than 130 intelligence, sabotage and counterintelligence teams of the SD and the *Abwehr* operational on the entire Eastern Front and more than 60 intelligence schools that prepared agents for dropping in the Red Army's rear. Four local stations of the German military intelligence were created in the occupied areas of the USSR: *Abwehrstelle*-Ostland, *Abwehrstelle*-Ukraine, *Abwehrstelle*-Sud-Ukraine and *Abwehrstelle*-Crimea. They worked to expose Soviet intelligence agents and members of the underground - as well as people holding hostile attitudes toward Nazi Germany - struggled against the partisan movement and trained agents for the *Abwehr*'s teams at the front. The *Abwehr* also established subsidiary stations, subordinate to the *Abwehrstelle*, known as *Nebenstellen* (Nests) in major cities occupied by the *Wehrmacht* that had strategic or industrial significance like Tallin, Kaunas, Minsk, Kiev and Dnepropetrovsk; these in turn had branch stations known as *Aussenstellen* in smaller cities convenient for deploying agents behind enemy lines.

In June 1941 *Abwehr Ausland* (Foreign Department) had established a special organ on the Soviet-German Front in order to organize sabotage, intelligence and counterintelligence work against the Soviet Union; it had the codename "Walli headquarters" - to which the *Abwehr* teams attached to Army Groups North, Center and South were subordinated. Each of these teams had three to eight *Abwehr* groups.

The *Abwehr* also had specially organized diversionary and sabotage units - the Brandenburg-800 Division and the Kurfürst Regiment - which carried out "special tasks" deep in the Red Army's rear areas. When carrying out an assignment the men of these units would wear Red Army uniforms, be equipped with captured Soviet weapons and would carry cover documents. In March 1942 S.S. leader Heinrich Himmler ordered the creation of a special sabotage, intelligence and espionage organization for the Eastern Front codenamed "Zeppelin".

From the very start of the war, Soviet counterintelligence conducted a specialized and secret struggle against all these German intelligence and sabotage agencies and units. This "secret war" intensified in 1943. Altogether between 1943 and 1944, SMERSH sent more than 2,000 operational groups and more than 8,000 agents across the frontline. Over the years of the war, Soviet military counterintelligence exposed 30,000 German agents, 350,000 saboteurs and 6,000 terrorists![19]

How should we regard these figures that were cited in the press? What do we know about the fate of the agents sent deep behind enemy lines? What were the results of their activities? What do German sources say? As concerns the German agents, saboteurs and terrorists the published numbers are quite dubious. They have not been substantiated in any concrete way. I assume that a considerable number of the "spies", "saboteurs" and "terrorists" that fell into the clutches of the Special Departments were Red Army soldiers and officers - as well as partisans - who were falsely branded as such.

I am not denying the heroism of the intelligence agents who actually did work behind the enemy lines. Honor and glory to them! Twenty-nine of them became Heroes of the Soviet Union. Several names of the heroes have been given in the press: Drobiazko, Bogdanov, Kozlov, Skorobogatov and others. Moreover, several SMERSH officers managed to penetrate the *Abwehr* and achieved significant results through their work as undercover agents.

According to information in the Soviet press, SMERSH rendered great assistance through its activities to the Red Army in the Battle of Kursk, in Belorussia - as well in the Iassy-Kishinev and the Baltic operations - again, according to the Soviet press. What was done by SMERSH with these aims and how it was done... this and much else remains classified.

Research conducted after the war into the work of the Special Departments in the period before the creation of SMERSH and after its appearance confirms what has been said above.[20] Political repressions in the Red Army in the first period of the war were primarily carried out according to Article 58.1(b): "Betrayal of the Motherland". According to research into the cases, approximately 90 per cent of those arrested by the Special Departments fell under the given article. We'll note that subsequently, after the war, many of them were rehabilitated. Unfortunately, you can't restore life to those people who were shot for their supposedly traitorous actions or attitudes. The rehabilitation of approximately 60 per cent of those arrested demonstrated that all of these individuals had been falsely charged.[21]

In the following period of the war - running from the latter half of 1943 until the end of the war - the tactical directives guiding SMERSH's work in the Red Army took on a new nature. In addition to betrayal of the Motherland, there was the new accusation of working for German intelligence plus the standard, hackneyed charges of sabotage and terror.

Practically all of the investigative cases belonging to the second phase of the war show that the SMERSH departments were striving by any means possible to carry out their assignments - to beat a confession out of the arrested servicemen that they had been recruited by German intelligence. The very same thing was happening in the partisan detachments, about which a lot of evidence has been preserved.

Instructive is the affair that came to light literally in the final month of the Great Patriotic War when our troops had already been fighting on German territory for some time. The events themselves that served as the material for the case stirred up by SMERSH actually occurred back at the end of 1944 when military intelligence agents came under suspicion: men, it would seem, who had been already checked repeatedly. On 17 September 1944 a group of the Reserve Front's intelligence officers boarded a transport aircraft in Lithuania, which was sent into German territory deep inside the enemy rear area. For almost four months, the agents - dressed in civilian clothes - successfully operated behind the German lines and transmitted important information to the front command. However, in January 1945 two of the clandestine agents - T.E. Lopatin and A.A. Zaitsev - were arrested by the German gendarme in some woods near the German city of Insterburg. After several interrogations they were held in a concentration camp in the city of Soldau (Dziadolwo) in north-central Poland.

On the eighth day of their internment, the experienced agents (one was a sergeant, the other a senior Sergeant) managed to escape the camp. Two days later they managed to link up with attacking Red Army units. However, the week-long imprisonment cost them quite dearly. The intelligence agents were held in a filtration camp for more than three months and then placed under arrest. On 8 April 1945 the SMERSH Chief of the Reserve Front, Lieutenant General Khannikov, confirmed the arrest warrants for Lopatin and Zaitsev. The text of each warrant concluded with the words: "Escaped a concentration camp under suspicious circumstances ... There is cause to suspect complicity with German intelligence agencies ... Subject to arrest and a search."

Three times before the end of April, a SMERSH investigator interrogated each of the arrested men. Each time after the prisoner recounted the same story about his brief time in the concentration camp and subsequent escape, the investigator said: "You're lying. Tell me how and when you were recruited and what assignments you received." However, the investigator was unable to obtain incriminating testimony from the prisoners: each man refused to confess to anything. The accusation of spying fell apart.

I believe that two unusual documents - attached to the archived investigative papers of the case - played a significant role in this: denunciations from two of SMERSH's secret informers. As a rule such documents are never attached to the investigative papers of a case, but instead are kept in the personal file of the informer as a record of his activity (or inactivity). However, in rare instances such denunciations wind up (apparently by mistake) in the files of the accused. It turned out that among a group of 11 military intelligence agents (which carried the code name "Chorus") were two secret SMERSH informers. Upon returning from a mission behind enemy lines, they would turn in detailed reports to SMERSH of their observations regarding the conduct and conversations of all the agents.

In the opinion of Konstantin Rozhkov, the SMERSH military counterintelligence organization created by Stalin directed its main efforts against so-called "anti-Soviet" elements: those officers and soldiers who expressed doubt in the infallibility of the Soviet system. He argues that this organization fought against internal dissidents in the Red Army.[22] It tried by any means to squelch dissent within the army. Is Rozhkov correct? In general, yes. Three facts support his conclusion. First is SMERSH's brutal and bloody reprisals in the years 1945 and 1946 against Russian former prisoners of war and Returnees. As a result of SMERSH's constant and at times dishonorable actions, more than a million Soviet citizens went straight from fascist slavery into Soviet prison camps.

As a rule, the press brings us facts and figures from the Chekists' side. However, there is not a word or even a half-word about how and what the Germans thought about SMERSH operations.

A curious fact, which is readily apparent and difficult to miss: SMERSH ceased to exist as soon as the repatriations came to an end - that is to say, in 1946. Ponder that for a moment. It turns out that one of the secret ideas behind Stalin's organization of military counterintelligence was to deal with the former prisoners of war. SMERSH did a lot as well in order to organize the secret services of East Germany, Czechoslovakia and other countries of the Socialist Bloc according to its own model. In addition, fascist concentration camps on German and Polish territory were preserved and now "enemies of Socialism" were serving out their sentences in them. Several years after 1945, Buchenwald still held up to 60,000 inmates - those who had fought against the Germans.

Certain contemporary sources maintain that in addition to the obvious successes in the struggle against foreign intelligence services, SMERSH during the years of the war acquired a sinister notoriety thanks to the system of repressions against Soviet civilians living in territory under the temporary occupation of German forces or who'd been sent into forced labor in Germany. There are also claims that the slightest suspicion of collaboration led to arrests and executions among both military personnel and civilians. Some authors assert that SMERSH was a continuation of Stalin's system of terror and suppression of dissent in the Soviet Union, and waver between categorizing it as an intelligence agency or as a tool of repression. For example, it is reported that between 1941 and 1945 nearly 700,000 people were arrested by Soviet secret services - of which approximately 70,000 were shot.

Investigations were more difficult to conduct under wartime conditions. Thus today one can read or hear that large groups of people were arrested illegally and that due to its repressive nature SMERSH made a 25-year sentence "standard" for many of the condemned; that not only those suspected of collaborating with the Germans received such sentences, but also former Soviet citizens who had returned to the Soviet Union from forced labor in Germany; that in order to monitor and control dissent SMERSH created an entire system of surveillance at the front and among the civilian population; and that SMERSH threats of punishment led to collaboration with the secret service and to unjust accusations against military personnel and civilians.

These conclusions of modern authors and others similar to them can be taken into evidence - though not in the case of unsubstantiated allegations offered in general phrases or citing pseudo-historical sources. Today, authors are striving to substantiate these allegations with evidence.

Often the SMERSH organs receive criticism for the work it conducted in the filtration camps. In 1941 I.V. Stalin signed a State Defense Committee decree regarding official vetting of those Red Army servicemen who'd been taken prisoner by the Germans or who had come out of encirclement by enemy forces. It was anticipated that this "filtration" would expose traitors, spies and deserters among them. By a Council of People's Commissars decree from 6 January 1945 Departments of Repatriation Affairs began to function in all front headquarters and involved the work of SMERSH officers. Collection and holding points for receiving and checking Soviet citizens who'd been liberated by the Red Army were set up. Such filtration work demanded not only the highest professionalism of the SMERSH officials, but also civilian courage. It was especially difficult to conduct such checks among former commanders and soldiers of the Red Army just released from German prison camps. To them, the SMERSH interrogations seemed offensive and unjust.

In its scope and extent, this SMERSH activity - in the words of the Soviet press - had no equals in history and this is true. Over the war years, approximately 10 million men and women passed through this vetting process - former military personnel, partisans, returning citizens and the enormous masses of people who'd been living under German occupation - and approximately one quarter of them were executed.

Here, for example, is what the soldier Aleksei Mikhailov has to say about his experience with this filtration process. He returned from German imprisonment at the end of October 1945 and immediately was sent to a filtration camp:

> ... All the [returning] prisoners of war were sent to Opukhlika Station where they were housed in dugouts. Formally we'd been assigned to the Gor'ky Division, but factually this was a filtration camp. Our SMERSH counterintelligence agency directed all the work there. The regimen was like a prison camp and we were fed like prisoners. One had to prove his loyalty, but most importantly, demonstrate that he'd been taken prisoner unwillingly. There was a sorting process going on and people were being sifted to differ-

> ent places: some to the Motherland, where they would become fully legal citizens of their own country; some to Kolyma to mine gold; others to the Siberian taiga to log timber. The slogan: "To each, his own" was again constantly looming in front of us...[23]

The Stalinist filtration process has no equal in the history of intelligence services or in the history of any other army. It left enormous scars in the lives of Soviet soldiers and darkened the entire postwar period of the Soviet people up to Stalin's death.

Often the question is asked: Was SMERSH such an effective system and did realities justify the creation of this organization? A lot of opinions exist regarding its effectiveness, but there can be no doubts that this was a frighteningly cruel system. This was true not only toward its adversaries, but primarily toward its own people. Any, even the most insignificant slip-ups were punished in the harshest manner. Stalin held SMERSH in his hands and placed intense pressure on the SMERSH officers.

Any officer sent behind enemy lines to carry out a mission was subject to re-checking. He was kept under suspicion: "Had he been recruited by the enemy?"

In any case any man who'd spent a long time behind enemy lines was automatically subject to the most careful scrutiny. They were trying to find out if he was still loyal or whether he had been turned by the Germans; whether he'd given them more information than required; or whether the Germans were using him without his awareness of that fact. It required enormous willpower to endure all this questioning. However, even after the vetting they might in any event declare you a "suspect". The leading SMERSH agent Aleksandr Ivanovich Kozlov - who was one of the prototypes of the main character in the films *Put' v Saturn* [*The Path to Saturn*] and *Konets Saturna* [*Saturn's End*] - served in the *Abwehr* and rose to the rank of captain even though the Germans knew he was a Russian. Passing through the sternest trials, he returned to the Motherland and was imprisoned. Later they gave him amnesty and created papers for him - declaring that between 1942 and 1945 he'd been a prisoner of war. His life and career were trampled underfoot. Instead of giving him the opportunity to pass along his invaluable experience to young agents, he labored in construction. Kozlov was remembered only somewhere in the mid-1960s. Hurrah! General Pavel Sudoplatov, the most famous organizer of diversions in the Germans' rear area, did 15 years of time and his sentence was not reduced during Khruschev's de-Stalinization process. He was not alone...

The first wave of rehabilitations began under Khrushchev. A tribunal of the Moscow Military District acquitted A. Kozlov in absentia. It even returned his previously "lost" Order of the Red Banner to him for the partisan struggle. Meanwhile, the KGB fashioned new papers for him so that the three years of his existence in the German intelligence service seemingly dropped from his biography. No matter how much you pestered the now elderly intelligence agent, you just couldn't get any precise information about his background and experiences from him. He lived his entire postwar life without any of the benefits allocated by the government to front-line veterans and rehabilitated people. Books were written and films were made about Kozlov, but formally he was known everywhere simply as a former prisoner of war.[24]

The fate of the intelligence agent Stefanovsky also proved to be harsh. After being dropped from an airplane on 22 May 1943 that had taken off from one of the airfields in Finland, the spy group - dressed in the uniforms of Red Army junior officers - landed in a wooded area that was in the zone of responsibility of an Arkhangel'sk Border Guard Unit. Stefanovsky and his accomplices presented themselves to the Border Guards as staff officers of one of the General Staff's departments who were carrying out a secret mission to select a location for the construction of a special facility. They needed to get in touch with Arkhangel'sk and Moscow urgently.

The Border Guards handed the "visitors" over to representatives of the Arkhangel'sk Military District. Under questioning in the villa of the district's SMERSH Counterintelligence Department, Stefanovsky and his "colleagues" talked about their mission. After discussions between the Chief of SMERSH's investigative branch in the Arkhangel'sk Military District - Mikhail Riumin - and officers that had arrived from Moscow, the agents agreed to cooperate with SMERSH.

Yet later even this intelligence agent was arrested and imprisoned. "What did they make me out to be? A spy dropped by the enemy." That's what Stefanovsky wrote about himself. This willing or unwilling confession speaks for itself. However, at the end of 1955 Stefanovsky managed to win an early release from prison. This happened during the wave of prisoner rehabilitations that occurred during Khrushchev's thaw. After securing his release, the ex-agent worked for a certain time in his former profession. After he returned to Moscow, he even distinguished himself in the pedagogical and printing fields.

Speaking about the successes of Soviet counterintelligence, in his book Sudoplatov writes:

… the *Abwehr* and Gestapo inflicted serious damage to the Soviet intelligence agencies. In addition to the deaths of valuable agents in 1941-1943 - as a result of the actions of the German counterintelligence - we lost the handlers of our agents in Smolensk, Kiev, Odessa, Khar'kov, Minsk, Kherson, Nikolaev…

Among those killed were prominent agents within the Soviet intelligence system. Practically speaking, our intelligence networks in Belorussia and in the Ukraine - as well as in the Baltic republics - were totally wiped out during the war.

The Smeared…

In recent decades the Kremlin's propaganda in Russia in every possible way is striving to whitewash the role of the NKVD agents, the SMERSH officers and the KGB agents during the war years and in the postwar period. From the total flow of mass information we can pick as an example a newspaper article by a certain Lozun'ko that appeared under the title *Obolgannye…* [*The Smeared…*].[25]

The author writes:

> ... There are few in recent years who have been subjected to such wide-scale stonewalling, humiliations and defamatory statements as the Chekists (the Special Department officers/ SMERSH officers/NKVD agents). Their role in the Great Patriotic War is being filtered through a primarily negative light. Most of the people are receiving their information not from documentary sources (archives or eyewitness recollections), but through popular culture, artwork and primarily through the "most important of the arts" -- films. Yet since the latter follow an expressly "anti-*osobist* (anti-NKVD) line, then the opinion about the counterintelligence agents (who were members of the Special Departments or SMERSH) and the military personnel of the NKVD follows accordingly. In contemporary film, there is a stock character - some SMERSH villain or NKVD miscreant - who is sitting out the war in the rear area (guarding prisoners, who are depicted as totally innocent people who have been wrongly charged) or serving in blocking detachments (the numerical strength of which, judging from the films, almost exceeded that of the operating army). Such films include *Moskovskaia saga* [*Moscow saga*], *Deti Arbata* [*Children of the Arbat*], *Kursanty* [*The Cadets*], *Pervyi posle Boga* [*First after God*], *Konvoi PQ-17* [*Convoy PQ-17*], *Na bezymennoi vysote* [*On a nameless height*], *Blagoslovite zhenshchinu* [*Bless the woman*], *Peregon* [*The Railroad Section*], *V iune 1941* [*In June 1941*]. Only Bogolomov's similarly-named film *V avguste 1944* [*In August 1944*] stands out as an exception among contemporary films and shows the work of SMERSH in a positive light...

In order to convince the reader that he is correct, Lozun'ko presents arguments in support of the Chekists:

> ... The Special Department officers (after April 1943, the SMERSH officers) worked to expose the pre-determinants of desertion and betrayal. If you watch the films mentioned above, the following impression forms: the more heroically that the officer and soldier fought, the more intensively the *osobisty* seek to undermine him - trying under some pretext to turn him into an adversary. But how was it in reality? Quite the opposite!
>
> So why did counterintelligence take Red Army men under special monitoring and launch investigations? Because a soldier or officer told an anecdote of an anti-Soviet nature or expressed a disloyal phrase in a fit of temper and so forth. They [the coun-

> terintelligence officers] were showing vigilance! However, as soon as a combatant demonstrated courage and loyalty to his oath, all suspicions about him disappeared...

Further the author provides examples to show that the *osobisty* always acted in just that way:

... The role of the NKVD agents in the Great Patriotic War was not restricted to carrying out purely specific, menial jobs. In fact, of course they weren't sitting out the wars in rear areas like modern popular culture shows us. This lie tarnishes the memory of many thousands of osobisty who were killed at the front and those veteran Chekists who honorably did their duty and have survived to the present day, but who should now be ashamed that they served in the NKVD.

> Someone had to cut it [desertion] off and conduct regular work to prevent it, by identifying potential panic-mongers and cowards...

[Lozun'ko goes on to offer a host of data from a dubious source - an article in a 1997 issue of the *Voenno-istoricheskii zhurnal* [*Military-historical journal*] written by I. Pykhalov]:

> Let's just say that already by 10 October 1941 657,364 military personnel - who had been cut off from their units and had fled the front - had been detained by the operational screens of the Special Departments and the NKVD blocking detachments (not to confuse these with the Red Army blocking detachments that were created following Order No.227)!
>
> Of this total, the vast majority of the men were sent back to the front. A total of 25,878 were arrested (1,505 as spies, 308 as saboteurs, 8,772 as deserters and 1,671 as cases of self-mutilation); of those arrested, 10,201 were shot. The counterintelligence agencies trained and sent more than 2,200 operational groups behind enemy lines - from which 4,400 vital radio messages arrived (including about the preparations for the Kursk offensive, which allowed the enemy attack to be anticipated). For example, in June 1944 alone 118 operational teams numbering a total of 7,000 men were operating in the enemy rear. The facts and archival information refute the broadly contrary thesis that the SMERSH named everyone - in particular those who had been enemy prisoners of war - "enemies of the people" without looking into the individual cases.
>
> For example between October 1941 and March 1944, 317,594 former prisoners of war had passed through or were at the time undergoing the vetting process. Of them, 223,281 (70.3 per cent) were sent back to the Red Army; 4,337 (1.4 per cent) to

> the NKVD's military escorts; 5,716 (1.8 per cent) to the defense industry; and 1,529 (0.5 per cent) were hospitalized. Just 8,255 (2.6 per cent) were assigned to penal companies or battalions and 11,283 (3.5 per cent) were arrested. With respect to the balance (61,394), they were still undergoing vetting in March 1944. It turns out that just a little more than 6 per cent of the men were subject to repression and the majority of these soldiers and officers had the possibility of reacquiring their rights through service in the penal units (see I. Pykhalov: '*Pravda i lozh' o Sovetskikh voennoplennykh*' ('*Truth and falsehood about the Soviet prisoners of war*'), *Voenno-istoricheskii zhurnal,* No. 5 (1997)).

[Author's note: these are dubious numbers from a highly questionable source].

> So does the oft-repeated assertion that people went from Hitler's prison camps straight into the Gulag correspond to the truth? No - according to Pykhalov. He cites data in the Russian Federation's State Archive, which show that as of 1 March 1946 4,199,488 Soviet citizens (2,660,013 civilians and 1,539,475 prisoners of war) had been repatriated - of which 1,846,802 had arrived from the zone of operations.

Lozun'ko goes on to talk about the NKVD combat troops that participated in battles and writes about the work of the Special Departments, of SMERSH and about the filtration camps. He then discusses the military counterintelligence service's struggle against the *Abwehr*.

The author confidently states that military counterintelligence agencies exist in every army. However, this assertion sounds naïve since for example neither the American nor the British counterintelligence agents behaved criminally - as was common in Soviet counterintelligence. The author doesn't mention the criminal role of the NKVD and the Special Departments during the blockade of Leningrad or talk about the criminal actions of the Leningrad NKVD agents.[26]

The author's conclusion about the more significant losses of NKVD troops and agents in the initial stage of the war isn't entirely accurate. I think that the NKVD's heavy losses are largely explained by the fact that many of them were executed both by their own side and by the Germans. All of the NKVD divisions – and even the 70th Army, served under the overall command of the Red Army.

The rehabilitation of NKVD, SMERSH and KGB officers and agents primarily occurred once Putin came to power. From year to year, ever more action thrillers in the spirit of James Bond are appearing on the shelves of bookstores. They as a rule are printed in large numbers with eye-catching covers; customers eagerly snap them up. Indeed, it is especially surprising that in these nearly primer-level detective books, ones about Abakumov - the omnipotent SMERSH Chief - occupy a special place.

As an example, I'll name several of these action thrillers which praise the heroic achievements of SMERSH officers (and of course their commanders) to the heavens. At the same time, all these books and articles contain the same reference to the 30,000 spies supposedly exposed by SMERSH.

Take, for example, Abarin's book. What is it about? The title itself answers this question: *Pobeditel' Abvera* [*The Conqueror of the Abwehr*] which is, of course, Viktor Semenovich Abakumov.

Such books all have catchy titles: *Zagadki Gimlera* [*Himmler's Riddles*], *Saturn* and *Smert' Saturna* [*Saturn* and *The Death of Saturn*], *Narkom SMERSH* [*The People's Commissariat SMERSH*], *Apostol* [*The Apostle*] and *SMERSH, budni riadovogo kontr-razvechika* [*SMERSH, the daily life of a regular counterintelligence agent*]. In all these books - or more accurately, in all this trash - there is the assertion in complete seriousness that Soviet military counterintelligence was the best in the world in the war years and that in 1944 it vanquished the *Abwehr*. Does the reader know that in February 1944 Hitler abolished the *Abwehr* and that its chief, Admiral Wilhelm Canaris, lost his post and was soon arrested before being hung at Hitler's order in 1945?

What can be said about the attempts to rehabilitate Abakumov? This "person", if it is possible to call him one, knew too much about what Stalin and the Party Central Committee were perpetrating. It is no coincidence that his final words before being shot were: "I will tell everything to the Politburo." The historian Kosterchenko has more to say about the work of this monster than anyone else.[27] We also advise the reader to get acquainted with Leonid Mlezhek's essay about General Abakumov.[28]

Forty years after Abakumov's conviction and execution, on 17 September 1997 the Russian Federation's General Procurator re-examined the sentence given to the general, dropped the charge against him of betraying the Motherland and replaced the death sentence with 25 years of imprisonment without confiscation of personal property. What will be hailed next? The legend about the hero is consolidating in the people - and besides the books, a documentary film about "the conqueror of *Abwehr*" has already been released as well as a photo album dedicated to him … Consider two famous anniversaries, one of which has taken place and one that is now looming in front of us: 2012 - the 200th Anniversary of Russia's Victory over Napoleon; and 2015 - the 70th Anniversary of Russia's Victory over Nazi Germany. From the books, films and photo album it follows that Abakumov is now a legendary figure. One of the books about Abakumov is entitled: *General Abakumov – vsesil'nyi khozian SMERSHa* [*General Abakumov - SMERSH's omnipotent master*].

Was that the case in reality? No! Stalin, the People's Commissar of Defense, was the omnipotent master of SMERSH over the three years of its existence. Stalin determined everything that SMERSH did. Let's ask ourselves: Could General Abakumov arrest anyone without the approval of the People's Commissar of Defense? He could not. Every deceptive radio game played against the Germans required the transmission of information deemed to be accurate on the surface. The General Staff prepared the contents. However, the People's Commissar of Defense gave it the stamp of approval before it was broadcast to the enemy camp. The fate of the Russian former prisoners of war was in Stalin's hands. Abakumov merely carried out Stalin's tyrannical purposes. This was so in everything: the dispatching of SMERSH agents into the enemy rear; the organization of the entire counterintelligence system; the establishment of the filtration camps; the harsh treatment of those returning from forced labor in Germany and the former prisoners of war… this entire terrible mechanism under the name of SMERSH - Stalin was the one who kept it turning and revolving from day to day.

The 2004 television mini-series *Shtrafbat* [*Penal Battalion*] particularly irritated the Chekists (and not only them), but to me it was a superb film which I watched with tears in my eyes. In contrast, here's how a film critic of the ultra-nationalist and anti-Semitic newspaper *Duel'* reviewed it:

> … Once on television I happened to see the movie *Shtrafbat*, which was concocted by film's pathological scum Volodarsky, Dostal' and Vaisberg (well, there you have it… once again they're all Jews!) Throughout my long life (and I've seen in it all kinds of immoderate crap), I've never before seen a more sordid, odious work about the Soviet people's Great Patriotic War against Fascism! I won't speak about the contents of this detestable film caper. I just hope Russian people saw it on TV and didn't have to pay to see this abomination by the rabid Jewish execrators. And I hope they rated it accordingly! It is only a pity that the actor Aleksei Serebriakov allowed himself to be drawn into accepting the lead role. However, in general such swinishness is a common practice (and a filthy one, of course) in the creative world…

What are you up to these days Sir NKVD member, Sir Special Department member, Sir KGB member? Strive to become "the most vivacious of all the living" - to earn the people's honor, love and respect - and to join the ranks of Red Army veterans. Start with just a confession!

Take at least a couple of steps back into your past; reveal the historical truth to people. Reveal your secrets and show us your heroic intelligence agents. Describe the history of the Soviet underground movement and write about those who were killed in occupation as a result of betrayal. Explain its grassroots nature in the war years; the time has long since come to tell the truth about the partisan movement. Weren't there principled and honorable procurators and military tribunals during the war? Of course there were, but what do we know about them? Yet they deserve to be known. Finally, explain how you justify your past - beginning from the first days of Soviet power.

Open your archives, which have likely long ago been covered with mildew. This, I assume, will resurrect the historic truth. After all - Sir NKVD, Special Department and KGB agents - the time has long since passed when the documents of our past should have been declassified. Of course, there might be some information of a super-secret nature. Well then, for God's sake just keep that information to yourselves. But as for the rest, why keep it secret? For example, what about the *Cheka's* archives? You know perfectly well that the fate of those *Cheka* romanticists from the first years of the Revolution was long ago sealed by Comrade Stalin.

Why don't you release into special archives those of your files that contain material from the Khrushchev and Brezhnev eras? Can't you allow anyone to approach your files relating to the cases of L.P. Beria and V.S. Abakumov?

Why are you keeping locked up in your bins - seemingly in perpetuity - the history of Stalin's war against his own peoples (1944-1946): the Crimean Tatars; the Kalmyks; the Turk-Meskhetins; the Kurds; the Kabardinians; the Chechens; the Balkarians and the Ingush? Just two facts regarding this...

In accordance with a Decree of the Presidium of the USSR Supreme Soviet and a Resolution of the Council of People's Commissars dated 28 December 1943 the NKVD executed Operation Nomad Camps to resettle persons of the Kalmyk nationality to regions of Siberia and the Far East. Altogether 26,359 Kalmyk families numbering 93,139 people were loaded onto trains, which delivered them to places of resettlement in the Altai and Krasnoiarsk Districts and the Novosibirsk and Omsk Oblasts. Unable to adapt to the new conditions, climate and diet that were untypical for their way of life, the Kalmyks were doomed to dying out. Only in 1954 were those still living allowed to return to their homeland.

The native people of Yamal - the Nenets - also shared the fate of repressed peoples. In November-December 1943 local Party, Soviet and *Cheka* organs provoked a demonstration by a group of Nenets, which broke up the collective farms - divided up the communal reindeer herd - and disappeared deep into the tundra. Bykov, his deputy Garanin and the Chief of the Yamal District NKVD Department Medvedev viewed this as a rebellion organized by German intelligence. The naval surveyor Pliusnin was subjected to torture by the NKVD resident in Yamal, who was able to extract from him a confession that he'd been recruited by a German officer who'd been landed by submarine and that they were to organize insurgent units among the local population.

A company of sub machine gunners was sent to Yamal from Omsk aboard aircraft. Having gathered the unarmed Nenets by a subterfuge, the soldiers opened fire on them: seven of the Nenets were cut down outright and just as many were wounded; the remaining reindeer herders were arrested and taken away to Salekhard before being sent into the Gulag. The instigators of this criminal "rebellion" scenario received medals: Bykov, the Order of the Red Banner; Garanin, the Badge of Honor; and Medvedev, the Order of the Red Star. Only in 1946 did the new leadership of the USSR Ministry of State Security reexamine this case in the course of the latest purge in the agency.[29]

Where did you conceal all the invalid veterans (the cripples) after the completion of combat operations? It is known that a portion of them wound up at Valaam and were buried there. But the remaining unfortunates: What did you do with them, where did you send them?

Few things about the filtration conducted in the country have been declassified. Some general numbers and isolated cases have surfaced! I'm convinced that the total number of 30,000 supposed "spies" captured in the war years was obtained by means of violence against people and the falsification of many thousands of criminal cases. Each and every one of them connected to this grinding machine must be re-examined - especially those of the former Russian prisoners of war.

Reveal the truth about the reprisals against the former Russian prisoners of war who escaped German imprisonment and joined the ranks of the French or Italian partisans. After VE Day and their return to the Motherland, the fate of these heroes was tragic - many of them following the notorious filtration process wound up in Siberia in forced labor camps!

So far there is no answer to the question: Why did "filtration" become so widely developed in the Baltic republics, in Belorussia and especially in the Ukraine? Without producing materials from your archives about the time of German occupation, there is so much left unsaid about the lives of Soviet people living under the conditions of the "New Order" established by the Germans. This is an acute problem of national history, which to this point has still not become a closed question …

Many of the military archives are still inaccessible and their most important files have been classified - for example those documents related to the conduct of the Red Army with respect to the civilian population of Germany. To this very day, historians remain dependent on the Ministry of Defense. While the mechanisms of governance during the time of Stalin and the Gulag have been widely revealed by documents, there is nothing similar with respect to the Second World War. Thus, in particular, Soviet-era myths about the war still circulate. Nevertheless, their discrediting is blocked not only by military officials - who take academic criticism as an "attack upon the Fatherland" - but also the present-day leaders of Russia who are manipulating nationalist sentiments.

To be taken prisoner during the Great Patriotic War was considered an act of betrayal. This, of course, is unjust; there cannot be any war that does not involve losses and prisoners from both of the adversaries. It is a different matter if one side suffers heavy losses and the other side does not. The fortunes of war fluctuate… we had a colossal numbers of prisoners taken by the Germans from encircled units during the war.

Finally Sir NKVD, Special Department and KGB members, isn't it time to open the archives related to the use of fascist concentration camps in order to detain opponents of Soviet rule in East Germany after the war?[30] For five years after the war ended, a total number of 60,000 prisoners were held in Special Camp No. 7 in East Germany. At least 12,000 of them died from starvation and diseases. A large number of these prisoners were sent on to the Soviet Union; later, only 5,500 returned to East Germany. After the final 8,000 prisoners were released in the spring of 1950, the camp was shut down.

I'll ask a few final questions of the present-day employees of the FSB (the KGB's direct descendant): Why were young children taken from Germany in the early postwar years and brought to the Soviet Union at the NKVD's order? What was their fate? Were any of them able to reconnect with their families? Did at least some of them return to Germany - now as adults? The newspaper *Argumenty and fakty* [*Arguments and facts*] was one of the first to report about this secret history with an article about one of the now grown men, Pavel Nikolaevich Shepelev.[31] Sixty years ago, as a young boy he'd been brought to a Soviet orphanage with a certificate stating: "Brought from Germany at the order of the NKVD". Indeed!

To the present-day "vainglory" of the "immortal" Chekists about their victory over the *Wehrmacht*, one can add a detailed, accurate story from a book by E.S. Fedorov. It came out in the city of Rzhev in 1994 in a small printing of just 300 copies.[32] Naturally, hardly anyone knows about it. Yet in its pages the picture of life under German occupation in the cities of Rzhev and Sychevka is shown. It portrays the highest honor and patriotism - as well as abominable treachery; such was life then. The book also discusses how Soviet intelligence agents were sent behind enemy lines and about the hasty and poor training they received - as a result of which many of them were killed. Such are the stated facts!

"To criticize one's country is to do it a service...
Criticism in short is more than a right;
it is an act of patriotism - a higher form, I believe
of patriotism than the familiar rituals
and national adulation."

Senator William J. Fulbright

14
Whose Victory?

Who won the war? Private Ryan or Private Ivan?

Ever since the film *Saving Private Ryan* by the American film director Steven Spielberg came out on American and Russian movie screens, mass media in the West and in the East have repeatedly discussed the relative contributions of Private Ryan and Private Ivan to the victory over Fascism.[1] Before diving into this unusual question, I'll briefly remind the reader about the film's subject. At first glance it is a simple film, but this is far from the case. In it, the American command learns that one American mother has received a telegram about the death of three of her sons on one and the same day. Her fourth son - paratrooper Private Ryan - is fighting somewhere in France. General George Marshall, having learned about this, sends officers to visit the unfortunate woman. They inform her of an order: to save James Francis Ryan (played by the actor Matt Damon). Soon a small Ranger detachment headed by Captain John H. Miller (played by the actor Tom Hanks) is sent through enemy lines to find and retrieve Private Ryan. The detachment reaches the airborne unit in which Private Ryan is serving and rescues him literally out from under enemy fire. At what cost? The entire detachment and Captain Miller are killed in action.

Let's ask ourselves: Was the given situation even possible in the Soviet army during the war years? Incidentally, this film is based upon an actual historical case and even the family's name is known. Spielberg's other films *Schindler's List* and *Amistad* are also based upon genuine historical figures and events.

Once Chekhov said, speaking about art: "One can lie in love; in politics; in medicine; and one can deceive the Lord God himself - there have been such cases.

But in art it is impossible to deceive." Did Steven Spielberg's film deceive the viewer in America or in Russia?

In order to answer this question, let's return to the film's subject. The film's final combat scene is tragic. Soldiers are dying. Each one understands that his final hour is at hand. Captain Miller and Corporal Upham are killed. Naturally a question arises: Were their deaths in vain? Obviously, this scene is the culminating moment of the entire film - evidence not only of human courage, but this scene also serves up a lesson on high morality!

The film ends with a scene at the Normandy American Cemetery amid a sea of white crosses. The tall, upright and no longer young Ryan is standing in front of Captain Miller's grave. He is weeping and reassuring himself that they didn't die, but ascended into heaven.

Saving Private Ryan is the first film about the Second World War that I saw after coming to America. It filled me with pride and tears and I'm not ashamed of the latter. I didn't see a single false scene in the film: everything was just as it was in the war!

What was the main idea expressed in the film? I think that it was about the value of each human life; it was in the name of this that both Russian and American soldiers fought with the fascists. However, for many years after the war and especially during the Cold War, the Soviet press sharply criticized the Soviet Union's former Allies for underestimating the contribution of the Red Army to the defeat of Nazi Germany. This criticism, which in many ways is unfair, continues even today. What explains it?

In both the United States and in Europe, many people still believe that John Wayne was Hollywood's main film hero during the Second World War and that Private Ryan saved Europe from Nazism. Dwight Eisenhower, the Supreme Commander of the Allied Expeditionary Force, expressed his overall assessment of the role of the U.S. army in the war: "The campaigns in the Mediterranean theater of combat operations and in Europe had no equals in the history of warfare; in the course of these campaigns the armies of the United States conducted operations that were unprecedented since the time of its creation in 1775."[2]

One American newspaper, on the 60th Anniversary of VE Day, published a column that stated:

> … As the great democracies widely celebrate the 60th Anniversary; as they commemorate the courage of the "G.I."… and the resolve of the liberators of Paris; the horror at the discovery of the concentration camps and everywhere - the brilliance of the American troops, one guest is always absent from the festive table. Among the speeches, one poor friend, about whom everyone is a little embarrassed, remains outside the door. This friend is the Soviet soldier Ivan. Yet it was he that threw down the swastika banner from the Reichstag!…

The English historian Anthony Beevor has noted that D-Day - the invasion of Normandy - cost the Americans approximately 10,000 soldiers and officers in casualties. Spielberg's film *Saving Private Ryan* showed how the Americans suffered such losses on this day - 6 June 1944. Yet as Anthony Beevor points out, they were fewer than the average daily losses suffered by the Red Army throughout the course of the entire Great Patriotic War! In these words, a serious change in the views of the West toward Ivan's role in achieving total victory is apparent!

In Russia, many citizens have the opinion that the main role in the defeat of the *Wehrmacht* belonged to the Red Army. It is based on the fact that more than 70 per cent of the German soldiers killed during the war were lost on the Eastern Front and that even after D-Day, the *Wehrmacht* kept the bulk of its divisions on the Eastern Front.

There is one more circumstance, however, and it should not at all be ignored. It has long been known that many Western historians and the press view the victory over Nazi Germany in the Second World War in a much broader context than Russian historiography does. In particular the Molotov-Ribbentrop Pact, which gave Hitler the green light to invade Poland and set the stage for the Second World War, must not be forgotten. Thus the heroism of the Soviet people and their enormous sacrifices that they placed on the altar of victory in the Second World War do not fully register in the Western mind. Though not disputing Russia's significant role in the defeat of Germany, it is not forgotten that Russia - together with Germany - essentially unleashed the Second World War with the signing of the Molotov-Ribbentrop Pact.

In response to such serious reproaches, the Russian sides brings up the Munich Agreement - one of the most embarrassing diplomatic episodes in British history - and one that Western historians have not treated kindly. Russia still stubbornly insists on its innocence in triggering the Second World War while neglecting Stalin's criminal record. By calling it the "Great Patriotic War 1941-1945" Russia draws a curtain over its own shameful and aggressive actions in 1939 and 1940 when it attacked Finland; forcibly absorbed the Baltic republics; stabbed Poland in the back and marched into Bessarabia and Northern Bukovina.

There is more: on the 70th Anniversary of the start of the Second World War (1 September 2009) Russian officials hatched a new explanation for the war's outbreak: it was all Poland's fault. In this interpretation, Poland in fact was the primary instigator of the Second World War. To bolster the case for this, the Russian Federation's FSB produced a special collection of previously secret documents regarding Poland's ties with Germany; about Göring's trip to Warsaw; about Poland's participation in a plan to share power with Germany in Czechoslovakia and so forth. This version, concocted by Kremlin ideologues, is a sheer fabrication and has the intention to distract public opinion away from the criminal Molotov-Ribbentrop Pact in 1939.

It is known that on the eve of the Anniversary of the beginning of the Second World War, the Council of Europe Parliamentary Assembly declared 23 August (the day the Molotov-Ribbentrop Pact was signed) to be the "Day of Remembrance of the Victims of Stalinism and Nazism". Incidentally, in a speech in Poland on 1 September 2009 at a commemorative meeting dedicated to the 70th Anniversary of the beginning of the Second World War, Russian President V.V. Putin was forced to acknowledge publicly that the pact was an "immoral fact".

In the past decade, substantial changes have taken place in the West in the evaluations of the Eastern Front's role in the Second World War. A striking example is a book review of Catherine Merridale's book *Ivan's War: Life and Death in the Red Army 1939-1945* (London: Faber and Faber, 2005) that appeared in May 2007 in the British newspaper *The Herald*:

> This is more than just a book: this is a rich, highly detailed and at times heartbreaking portrait of the archetype of a Russian infantryman - a man who cruelly suffered throughout the entire war (often not in the least at the hands of his own compatriots). The array of figures that measure the number of those who didn't return from the war - from the battles against the German *Wehrmacht* - is striking. Between 1939 and 1945 more than 30 million people of both genders were mobilized for the acting army and of them more than 8 million died in battle or from hunger and disease. The number of those killed among the civilian population is more than twice as great. Around 25 million people perished. The first years of the war were the most terrible. By the beginning of 1942, 2.7 million men had been killed on the battlefield; almost 3 million more had been taken prisoner. In the course of the war, the Red Army was destroyed and renewed at least twice. Approximately three-quarters of the soldiers that served in the infantry consisted of peasants, who didn't feel any great loyalty to the communist system; primarily - notes Merridale - the Soviet people who fought and died defending the Stalinist regime protected a tyranny. Ivan saved the Motherland, but was himself enslaved. He fought for his country, but not for freedom. Old soldiers who talked with Merridale said that the only positive experience that they had brought back from the war was that they had learned to value life more. It is sad, but these words appear to be a fully appropriate commentary on Ivan's decisive role in the bloodiest war in the history of mankind.

In the opinion of the British newspaper *The Guardian*, "In the struggle with Nazism approximately 40 Russian Ivans were killed for each Private Ryan that died." However the results are summed up; changes are taking place in the assessments of Western historians and military specialists.

Aleksandr Gennis, a publicist and journalist, expresses his own opinion regarding the multi-year argument over the role of Ryan and Ivan:

... Western popular historiography of the Second World War is undergoing a complete turnaround. Until recently it was for the most part focused on the combat operations of the Allies: mountains of books were published on all the battles on the Western Front from El Alamein to the Normandy invasion and the Battle of the Bulge. Such predominant attention to the combat operations of the Western Allies created an assurance among uninformed American readers that the Americans and the British defeated Nazi Germany. True, Western historians were always noting the heavy losses of the Soviet Union (which were incomparable with the Allies' losses) and sympathized with the tragedy that befell its citizens, but always plainly underestimated the role of the Soviet army in the victory...

Here's how Benjamin Schwarz, a reviewer of new books on Russia's role in the war, explains this in his survey article 'Stalin's Gift' published in *The Atlantic*:

> ... Churchill's chronicle of the Second World War, which has all but permanently fixed the contours of the conflict in the popular mind, deliberately downplayed the Soviet superpower's pivotal role in defeating the Axis. Since then, while scholarship advanced on, say, the Allies' Air War against Germany or the North African Campaign, it was stalled or warped on the Eastern Front. Soviet historians were forced to evade the many aspects of the conflict that the State deemed embarrassing. For their part, Western scholars, denied access to Soviet archives, relied on German records and the self-serving memories of German generals...

As Schwarz notes, the first to take a serious approach to the Eastern Front in the English language was the British historian John Erickson, who published a two-volume history: *The Road to Stalingrad* (1978) and *The Road to Berlin* (1983). The foremost American scholar on the Red Army in the Second World War is David Glantz, a retired U.S. army Colonel, who between 1989 and 2006 wrote 16 fundamental studies on the war on the Eastern Front; his output shows no sign of slowing down as he recently penned a massive three-volume study of the Stalingrad Campaign and is now producing an equally detailed study of the 1941 Battle of Smolensk.

In 2006, two British authors published two books of great historic and literary value: Anthony Beevor - together with the Russian translator Luba Vinogradova - released in English the great Soviet writer Vassily Grossman's frontline notebooks under the title: *A Writer at War*, which Benjamin Schwarz considers "the best eyewitness account of the Eastern Front in English." Schwarz also mentions the diplomat and historian Rodric Braithwaite's *Moscow 1941*, which provided a detailed description of life in the Soviet capital in those days as the Nazi army was approaching it - resulting in a battle for the city that cost 926,000 Soviet soldiers their lives.

I would like to linger on two books in particular that Schwarz mentions in his review article: Geoffrey Roberts' chronicle *Stalin's War* and a book by the well-known British historian Norman Davies, *Europe at War 1939-1945*. Davies, whose book was written with unexpected vehemence and a sharp sense of irony, directly condemns Americans for their narcissism. He makes a particular target of the American popular historian Stephen Ambrose, whose highly-acclaimed and top-selling books have convinced his compatriots that it was they who stopped Hitler. Regarding Davies' book, Schwarz writes:

> ... For four years, more than 400 Red Army and German divisions clashed in an unrelenting series of military operations over a front extending more than 1,000 miles (at its most intense, the war in the West was fought between 15 Allied and 15 *Wehrmacht* divisions). Eighty-eight per cent of the German military dead fell there; in July 1943 - in the decisive battle of the war - the Soviets permanently broke the *Wehrmacht's* capacity for large-scale attack at Kursk - "the one name" Davies properly asserts, "which all historians of the Second World War should remember."...

He goes on to argue:

> ... The Soviet war effort was so overwhelming that impartial historians of the future are unlikely to rate the British and American contributions to the European theatre as much more than a sound supporting role...[3]

In my opinion, this assertion is completely correct. However, it must not be forgotten that between December 1941 and August 1945 the Americans were simultaneously conducting far-flung land, sea and air campaigns against the Japanese.

Davies' conclusion about the decisive role of the Red Army in the victory over Germany leads him to another point - as Schwarz expresses it:

... the most odious criminal regime in Europe's history was defeated by an even more murderous regime, if numbers are the yardstick...

One despot defeated another despot. Incidentally, both Davies and Roberts plainly give preference to the Soviet despot. True, they both hold Stalin personally responsible for the terrible military catastrophe that befell the Soviet army at the start of the war, but they come to the conclusion that an enormous share of the credit in achieving the victory also belongs to Stalin personally.

Benjamin Schwarz sums up the positions of both authors in the following fashion: First, Stalin eventually put talented generals in command of the armies and gave them freedom of action. Secondly, he was personally involved in the leadership of all the different spheres of responsibility during the war years - from the remarkable industrial rebirth in the country after 1942 to the realm of high diplomacy. Roberts, in his book *Stalin's War,* goes further than Davies and declares:

> ... To make so many mistakes and to rise from the depths of such a defeat to go on to win the greatest military victory in history was a triumph beyond compare. Stalin... saved the world for democracy...

I believe that this is taking things too far in the other direction. Stalin didn't defeat Hitler; the victors were those people that Stalin ceased obstructing: the officers, designers, builders, and doctors - as well as those who are often forgotten in discussions of historical processes (the privates, lieutenants, nurses, penal battalion members, Claudia Shulzhenko, partisans, women working in the rear factories...[4]

Despite the cited facts, on the eve of the 60th Anniversary of VE Day, the Russian Duma voted to send a sharp declaration to the West - in effect stating that no one has the permission to re-examine the history of the war and again reminding Western scholars and officials of Russia's enormous losses in the struggle against the Nazi aggressors. In this situation it is useful to recall Cicero's ancient saying: "He who is so deaf that he doesn't even want to hear the truth from a friend is hopeless..."

Aleksandr Iakovlev, the prominent Russian democrat and academic, not long before his death in 2007 expressed his doubts about the official statistics on the losses of the USSR during the war. In his view, they were plainly understated and far from accurate. He gave his own estimate of the total number of those killed: more than 30 million. However, he believed that not even that number was conclusive and noted that some scholars believed that the number killed was in the neighborhood of 43-45 million. Iakovlev also verified that in the war years approximately 1 million Red Army soldiers and officers were executed by their own side. Most importantly, Iakovlev called for a halt to the discussion about whose contribution to the victory over Fascism was weightier.

Aleksandr Iakovlev stated:

> ... I read an American textbook about the Second World War. There was not even a mention of the Soviet Union in it; this is extremely immoral. However, on the other hand it is also immoral if someone among us says that we and we alone achieved the victory. The time has come to reckon with the facts of history: Victory was achieved by the coalition against Hitler. They could not have vanquished Hitler without us, nor could we without them...

This is correct from every point of view - including both from the moral and from the point of view of our future as a united mankind. But to be motivated by the point of who had the greatest number of war dead... in my opinion, this is even more shameful - a tawdry argument based upon counting corpses. Iakovlev noted: "One shouldn't disturb the dead, more or less... They can also avenge themselves; they also know how to speak."

To highlight casualties as the decisive factor of victory is both stupid and absurd. Incidentally, this thought is expressed often in the pages of the Russian press or uttered by Russia's leaders, which is atrocious and testifies to a careless attitude toward Ivan and also points to the ineptitude of the Russian military commanders.

Western historians often ask: "Why were other European nations able to fight differently; to minimize their own troop losses?" On the Eastern Front, hundreds of thousands of soldiers' lives were sacrificed to satisfy Stalin's demand to "fight for the sake of victory at any price"!

Somewhere between 60 and 70 per cent of the Russian population believes that the Red Army could have achieved victory without the help of its Allies. Is it possible to agree with such an opinion? Such a point of view - as it was in the past and as it is in the present - is based more on the Russian ignorance of many facts which have been hushed up or distorted by their official historians.

What does the Russian youth today know about that heroic time when America, Great Britain and Canada supplied the Soviet Union with weapons, ammunition and equipment through the framework of Lend-Lease? What do they know about the deaths of 6,000 Allied sailors as their ships plied the dangerous waters of the North Atlantic in order to deliver their loads to Soviet ports? What does the Russian youth know about the combat operations of the British pilots in the north; in the regions of Murmansk and Arkhangel'sk?

In contemporary Russia, do they truly understand what the "Second Front" means? The Allies devised their own strategy and chose to initiate operations against Nazi Germany in the Mediterranean theater, in North Africa, where Hitler had created the so-called Afrika Korps under the command of the talented commander General Rommel. Indeed, had Hitler been able to supply his forces in Africa with additional reserves, weapons and - most importantly - the necessary amount of fuel, it is likely that Rommel would have broken through into Egypt and Palestine.

After the Japanese attack on Pearl Harbor (December 1941), the United States was drawn into the Second World War with practically nothing. Between the two World Wars, the U.S. army had dwindled to approximately only 140,000 soldiers and officers.

Some publicists and historians - more frequently in Russia than in the West - adopt the following line of reasoning when discussing the Allied contribution to victory, as expressed by the Russian political commentator Leonid Rodzikhovsky:

> ... Well, [by the time of the Normandy invasion] the German viper was already dying and it didn't take much effort to finish it off; its main point was not to allow the Red Army to win on its own.
>
> Thus the landing in Normandy enabled an end to the Second World War and prevented a Third World War from breaking out. If the Red Army had tried to seize all of Europe, the Allies would not have allowed this...[5]

At the very least, this statement and such talk about the Second Front is rather flippant.

In the same article, Leonid Rodzikhovsky goes on to say:

> ... If we won the war on the ground - while the war on the sea had no decisive significance - then the Allies won the war in the air!...

Of course, doesn't this beg the question of whether or not the Allies would have even been able to open a Second Front in Europe and to render such an enormous quantity of aid to the Soviet Union via Lend-Lease if the German submarine fleet had not first been destroyed?

The German submarines, which had been prowling the oceans and seas freely right up until 1943, significantly complicated the Allies' efforts by restricting trans-Atlantic shipping. In 1942 alone, German submarines sank 1,027 of the Allies' ships. The German submarine fleet inflicted enormous damage on the Allied fleet - destroying thousands of ships, both military and commercial, with a combined tonnage of more than 14 million tons. At the beginning of 1942, it had become clear that a landing in Europe could only be organized by having first crippled the German submarine fleet in the Atlantic.[6] Nazi Germany entered the war with 57 submarines. Between 1 September 1939 and 4 May 1945 another 1,113 submarines were added to the German submarine fleet. Of these, 863 submarines took part in combat operations - of which 630 were destroyed.

The Allied operations in North Africa created the conditions for a successful landing in Europe. Over the course of 1942 and 1943 the United States transformed its industry in order to satisfy the ever-growing need for military resources by the Allies. In this period the American industrial capacities supported remote bases and operations in the Pacific Ocean, campaigns in North Africa and Italy, while simultaneously mobilizing the human and material resources for the invasion of Europe. All this time, the United States continued to deliver critical supplies to its Western Allies and the Soviet Union. This fact that the United States managed not only to provide for its own needs, but at the same time together with Canada and Great Britain continued to support the Soviet Union, speaks to the colossal industrial might of the United States at that time and also their allegiance to the Allied cause.

The mobilization and training of the large number of soldiers, sailors, pilots and Marines necessary for conducting the war with Japan in the Pacific - and for an eventual invasion of Europe - was a complex task and required time. In 1942 and 1943 the United States could mobilize and prepare a sufficient quantity of military personnel to conduct only smaller-scale landing operations. At the same time, the military operations in North Africa allowed the green American troops to gain vital combat experience and to find more gifted military commanders.[7] The intensive and thorough preparation for the unprecedented scale of the Allies' Normandy invasion required more than a year.

Finally, it should be remembered that in 1942 and 1943 the Allies were fighting a war in the Pacific where enormous forces were assembled - including ground troops and both naval and air fleets - in order to win back the territory that the Japanese had seized in the first few months of the war.

There is yet one more circumstance that official Russian historians often neglect. That is Lend-Lease itself - without which the Red Army would hardly have been able to overcome the crisis of 1941 and which facilitated an irreversible turning point in the war with the aggressors within one-and-a-half to two years.

Just why was the Red Army for such a long time unable to cope with an adversary - over which it had overwhelming numerical advantages in both men and combat equipment? I'll start with the factor of surprise, by which alone it is possible to explain the initial German successes. In Russia, historians and officials are unwilling to cite data that show on the very first day of the war the Germans destroyed almost 6,300 Soviet aircraft. This cannot be explained by surprise. It turns out that after the initial strikes, Stalin still had a sufficient number of aircraft in order to avoid such massive losses. Over the entire war, the Soviet Air Force's irrevocable losses in aircraft at the front amounted to approximately 75,200 combat airplanes. The *Luftwaffe* lost 5.6 times fewer combat aircraft - approximately 13,500. A similar correlation exists in the respective tank losses of the two sides. Meanwhile, the Red Army's irrevocable losses in officers and soldiers were almost 2 to 3 times greater than the *Wehrmacht's* losses.

I'd like to mention one more genuine contribution that the Allies made to the final victory: the destruction by their strategic air forces of all enemy possibilities to create an atomic bomb. This includes both a factory for producing heavy water in Norway and uranium mines in Saxony and Czechoslovakia - as well as demolishing the research center in Dahlem, near Berlin, where for many years the brilliant physicist Werner Heisenberg had led ultimately unsuccessful research into the making of an atomic bomb.

At times it is amusing to read commentary in the Russian press to the effect that the Germans surrendered their cities to the Allied troops over the telephone. The memoirs of Dwight Eisenhower, General Omar Bradley and Field Marshal Montgomery describe the stubborn nature of the fighting in Western Europe honestly and in detail. The German army fought in the West with the stubbornness of the doomed right up until the last days of the war. In many of their units there were S.S. fanatics who had the authority to shoot retreating soldiers.[8]

I haven't even mentioned yet the natural obstacles that the Allies faced; there were more of them on the Western Front than on the Eastern Front. Twice the Allies had to fight their way through lines of defensive fortifications that had been laid out and constructed with great tactical and engineering skill. As Eisenhower wrote: "In the annals of military history, the breakthrough of the West Wall or other lines of the Seigfried defenses will remain a shining page."

I'll now point the reader's attention to concrete facts... On the Western Front, the density of the German forces - including weapons and equipment - was more than twice as great as it was on the Eastern Front, which complicated and restricted the tactical possibilities of the Allied troops. Although they were never completed, the Germans in the West had the Atlantic Wall and the Siegfried Line - both of which consisted of numerous reinforced concrete bunkers and pillboxes - whereas in the

East the Red Army faced similar fortifications only in East Prussia. Having landed successfully in Normandy the Allies immediately ran into elite German forces in the difficult bocage country including an S.S. panzer corps, Panzer Group West, the 5th Panzer Army and others. Between D-Day and 11 August 1944 the American, British and Canadian forces lost 170,000 men in killed, wounded and missing. The German casualties of between 200,000 and 300,000 officers and soldiers over the same period were also heavy. The cited figures testify to the ferocious, bloody nature of the fighting between the Allied troops and the *Wehrmacht* in the West.

Immediately after the landing in Normandy, an S.S. panzer corps - which had been positioned in Poland - was transferred to the Western Front. This significantly eased the task of the Soviet forces in Belorussia. The urgent transfer of a significant portion of the *Luftwaffe's* fighters to the Western Front contributed even more to the success of Operation Bagration. On D-Day - 6 June 1944 - the Germans had 288 fighters in the West and 550 fighters in the East. Another 250 fighter aircraft were in the Mediterranean theater, in the Balkans and in Norway. Finally, 1,179 fighter aircraft were part of the Reich's direct air defense and fought exclusively against the Anglo-American strategic bomber raids. On 22 June 1944 - the day that Operation Bagration was launched - there were now only 441 fighters on the Eastern Front while their number had grown on the Western Front to 704. The corresponding numbers in the other theaters and in the Reich's defense were now 338 and 538 respectively. As German memoirists note (their testimonies were gathered into a two-volume book *Hitler Moves East* and *Scorched Earth* by Hitler's former personal translator Paul Schmidt and published under his pen name Paul Carrell), it was precisely the *Luftwaffe's* absence in the air - together with the Red Army's crushing superiority in tanks - that led to such a rapid disintegration of Army Group Center in July 1944. The Allies in Normandy had not quite a 10-fold quantitative superiority over the adversary in aircraft and a three-fold superiority in tanks. However, it is often forgotten that for the first few weeks of combat against the *Luftwaffe* following D-Day the Allied aircraft were still based across the English Channel.

Right up until the end of the war, supplies remained the main problem confronting the Allied armies in the West. Interruptions in the supply of fuel and ammunition often reduced the Allies' advantage. Once combat moved into Germany, every day American aircraft delivered 200 tons of supplies to the attacking armies.

The Soviet superiority on the Eastern Front in 1944-1945 was approximately the same as the Allies had in the West. The entire question lies in who used that superiority more effectively: the Allies - who suffered approximately the same number of killed as the German units opposing them and took more prisoners by an order of magnitude - or the Red Army, which expended 10 of their own soldiers' lives for each German soldier killed. Instructive is the correlation of the irrevocable losses of army officers on the Eastern Front from June 1941 until the end of 1944. Over this period 65,200 German officers were killed or went missing in action as opposed to 784,000 Soviet officers (excluding the political, judicial and administrative staff which was represented in the *Wehrmacht* by civil servants). This yields a correlation of 1 to 12.

The opening of the Second Front - to where a third of the German army reserves were diverted - played a decisive role in the Soviet successes of 1944 and 1945. Over this period the *Wehrmacht* on the Eastern Front was practically deprived of *Luftwaffe* support and any reserves when attempting to repel the Soviet offensives.

Unfortunately many Russians - especially the youth of today - think approximately the following: "When all the combat-capable *Wehrmacht* units were already ground down in the East, the crack Allied forces easily smashed the weak German formations in the West in 1944 and 1945. The main job had already been done by the Russians in the East."

The opening of the Second Front led to a fundamental turning point in the course of combat operations on the ground. Official Russian historians, when speaking about the Second Front, strive to reduce its significance down to nothing. So, its opening in 1944 supposedly had no influence on the outcome of the war?[9]

The Western Allies took on the main burden of the air war against Germany. Two-thirds of the *Luftwaffe's* irrevocable losses in personnel were suffered in combat against the United States army Air Force and the Royal Air Force. As concerns the war at sea, then practically the entire German, Italian and Japanese fleets were destroyed in combat against the Anglo-American navies and air forces.

Allied bombers hampered the growth in German military production, while essentially paralyzing, in particular, the realization of the German atomic bomb project, and in the last six months of the war achieved a 30-40 per cent reduction in German fuel output. By the end of 1944 rail transportation in Germany was essentially paralyzed. Under systematic Allied air attack, the German production of synthetic fuel fell from 316,000 tons in May 1944 to 17,000 tons in September. As a result, both the *Luftwaffe* and the German panzer divisions constantly lacked fuel.

In both Russian school textbooks and in solid academic treatises, the successes of the Red Army in the second half of 1944 are discussed without any sort of connection with the Allies' actions. Further, in academic - or more accurately, pseudo-academic - works of recent years, everything in fact is turned upside down. For example, in E.N. Kul'kov's, M.Iu. Miagkov's and O.A. Rzhev's 2001 study *Voina 1939-1945* [*The War, 1939-1945*] the authors state:

> ... The success of the Allies' landing Operation Overlord, which was launched on the Western Front on 6 June 1944 was made largely possible thanks to the operations of the Soviet Fronts in Belorussia...[10]

Apparently, the authors are counting upon the fact that no one will recall that the invasion of Normandy took place 16 days prior to the launching of the Soviet offensive in Belorussia.

It is not a coincidence that the only strategic offensive operation conducted by the Germans in the final year of the war targeted the Anglo-American forces in the Ardennes. The relatively shallow depth of the Western theater opened opportunities for achieving a decisive success in the course of a single operation, whereas the wide open expanses of the Eastern Front gave no similar prospects.

Incidentally, another Soviet legend is connected with the Ardennes - purporting that Stalin at Churchill's request pushed up the date of the Red Army's offensive in order to save the Allies. The start date was moved up from 20 January to 12 January 1945 - which is what he told the British Prime Minister. Only in the 1990s did historians reveal that according to Zhukov, the forces of the 1st Belorussian Front were ready to launch the offensive by 29 December 1944 and that 8 January 1945 was foreseen as the start date of the offensive, but because of bad weather that grounded flight operations, it had to be postponed. Meanwhile, in Churchill's letter to Stalin the Ardennes was mentioned, but there was only a request for information about the Soviet military plans; there was no "pleading" for help at all. Stalin then feigned his "willingness" to sacrifice the lives of Soviet soldiers for the sake of Allied interests - knowing full-well that the offensive would begin around 12 January anyway.

The former Nazi Minister of Foreign Affairs, Joachim von Ribbentrop, gave three main reasons for Germany's defeat: the unexpected resistance of the Red Army; the Lend-Lease supplies to the Soviet Union; and the superiority of the Western Allies in the air.[11] Could the Soviet Union have fought one-on-one with Germany without American benzene and aluminum; explosives and copper; radio equipment and Studebakers; rations; tanks; ships…?

The Allied bombing campaign of German territory during the war was costly. The British over the five years of the war in Europe lost approximately 12,000 aircraft - primarily bombers. The Americans suffered even greater losses since unlike the British, their Flying Fortresses and Liberators bombed targets and cities in Germany in daytime. The air war over Germany cost the Allies approximately 150,000 in killed, wounded, captured or missing in action. Each one of their heavy bombers cost more to produce than six fighters; the Americans lost over 1,000 Flying Fortresses. One of the reasons for these heavy losses was the fact that until 1944 the bomber armadas flew into Germany without fighter escort because prior to that time the existing American and British fighter aircraft lacked the range to fly into Germany and back again to their bases in England.[12]

A reader can obtain a lot of information about the Western Front from the memoir of the General Siegfried Westphal, who was an operations officer under Rommel during the Desert War before being appointed chief of staff under General Albrecht Kesselring in Italy. He ended the war as the chief of staff to General Gerd von Runstedt, so his entire war service took place in the West.[13] The general highly rates Churchill's plan to make a landing in the Adriatic, which might have hastened the end of the war. We learn that as a result of the destruction of the German railroad network due to the Allied bombing campaign, it took four weeks to transfer a single division from the Eastern Front to the Western Front; this was a trip that in 1941 had taken a week. The author notes that the influence of the Allied air forces did more to disrupt the balance at the front than did the "indecisive masses of Russian soldiers".

Westphal argues that the balance of forces tipped sharply in favor of the Allies with the entry of the United States in the war. He also examines the *Wehrmacht*'s battles with the American forces in March-April 1945 in detail.

Official Russian historians also strive to conceal the superiority of the German combat equipment - especially in the final stage of the war. The German King Tiger was not only winning the duels with the T-34s, but also with the latest Soviet heavy tank the IS-2. The Tiger's 88mm gun could penetrate the armor on the IS-2 at a range beyond which the IS-2's 122mm gun could destroy the German tank. The latest versions of the Focke-Wolf 190 fighter, which was often used as a fighter bomber as well, were superior to all of the Soviet fighters of that time in its combat and flight performance. The Germans also managed by the end of the war to put the jet fighter Me-262 into mass production - as well as the V-1 and V-2 rockets. Jet aircraft didn't appear in the Soviet Union until after the war and even this was largely thanks to captured German documents and German designers - as well as the subsequent theft of British and American technological secrets by Soviet intelligence. The situation was the same with the atomic bomb, rocket technology and the latest submarines; the Soviet Union simply copied the German submarines in its possession as the war ended.

The Red Army fielded no strategic air force in the war. It is no coincidence that after the war, special Soviet teams were collecting damaged Flying Fortresses and B-29s wherever they could find them - a fact that you won't learn in official Russian sources.

In the Soviet era we were taught in school that the heroic Soviet people defeated the Nazi monster - albeit it with some help from the valiant French pilots of the *Normandie-Neman* Fighter Regiment. I don't recall whether the schoolbooks mentioned the American assistance through Lend-Lease, but in any case the opening of the Second Front was discussed in almost an ironic sense as if Churchill and Roosevelt, whom Stalin asked to open a Second Front in 1942, finally managed to gather the strength to do it in the summer of 1944 when the defeat of Germany had already been decided by the victories of the Red Army.

It is a shocking story. Today in Russian schools, teachers tell their students the very same things that our students heard after the war. More precisely, teachers in Putin's Russia are compelled to repeat these Soviet-era myths and legends.

"Courage is a great virtue of the soul;
A people marked by it can be proud of itself."
N.M. Karamzin

15

How Generalissimo Stalin Stole the Victory

The War's main myth

In truth, the war's final day was a nationwide holiday. God only knows how much suffering the Soviet people had to bear and how many lives it had to sacrifice on the altar of victory. Unfortunately, even to this very day, Russian statistics on the war are far from truthful. One of the main reasons for this is that the Dictator took the credit for a victory that really belonged to the people - to the applause of his subjects. How did this happen?

The guns had barely had time to fall silent when a fanciful glorification of its main victor, the Generalissimo, spread across the country. The national press, radio and Party apparatus began fervently to redraw in its own ideological way the picture of the colossal military events that had just taken place. It turned out that "He" alone defeated Nazi Germany. Only "He" - like a genius - knew everything, anticipated everything and calculated everything. "He" worked out the ingenious strategy of victory. This myth continued to reign supreme in Russia until "He" died almost eight years after the war ended.

The former Russian Prime Minister, Iurii Primakov, asks: "How was Stalin able to assume the role of a 'Great Commander' and to become the hero of a contrived peace?" Then Primakov himself gives the answer: "He had already declared himself to be the hero and architect of the October Revolution and the hero of the [Russian] Civil War. Was he confident that this sleight of hand as well would be successful?"[1]

Please, if Stalin's vainglorious notion was the case then what did the frontline soldiers - from the marshals down to the platoon commanders and the millions of privates - do during the war? What about the Allies? We're all, each of us, on the periphery - banished from history!

We, the frontline soldiers and officers, were made to understand clearly that the war was a matter of the past. The State would concern itself with the dead; as for the rest of us, we were to think about the living. The most important thing was to get started on resurrecting the ruined country as quickly as possible. As regards the war, we were firmly to remember: "Stalin's 10 Blows" as the decisive factor in the victory. We were to banish completely any thoughts about 1941 and to memorize Comrade Stalin's book *O Velikoi Otechestvennoi voine* [*On the Great Patriotic War*].[2] Incidentally, I usually kept this book in the knapsack on my back. One day I pulled it out and discovered that a small shell fragment had almost completely penetrated it. I was lucky, as they say…

Meanwhile, the situation with the frontline soldiers and officers that returned from the war proved to be much more complicated than the Party bureaucrats imagined. They were saying that Stalin looked askance at the frontline soldiers; didn't love them; didn't trust them; and assumed each one to be a potential traitor. As Stalin himself knew, there were weighty justifications for this viewpoint.

"He" hadn't forgotten the war's beginning when as he believed the Red Army had essentially "betrayed" him. He was also aware of the popular saying that had appeared at the end of the war, to the effect that "Moscow's main blunder was that it had allowed Ivan to get a look at Europe and Europe to get a look at Ivan." How could he forget the Decembrist movement?[3]

Was the Leader mistaken in his notions about the frontline soldiers and officers? Those who spent the war at the front and survived and those who had seen Poland, Czechoslovakia, Austria and Germany no longer looked at life in the Motherland as they had before. Moreover, it hadn't taken a higher education to see that life in the capitalist European countries had been better than propaganda had painted it and better than their own lives back in the Soviet Union.

Most importantly, during the war people had lost their fear! They came back from the war as new people with a fresh perception of their surroundings; with new feelings and fresh ideas. They had gained confidence and, as the majority of them believed, the right to independent thoughts and actions.

The frontline soldiers had returned from the war with such lofty notions! We were the victors! From that point on, people viewed the war as the most significant event in their lives… Everything that had taken place before it and that would happen later was unimportant: both the good and the bad. There, at the front, life was entirely natural - sharpened by the close proximity with death. Indeed, it was there at the front that the soldier, for the first time in his life - freed from many of the fetters of the totalitarian system - felt like a human… one with a soul thrown wide open; who felt a lofty sense of joy! There, at the front, he understood that the Motherland was not the Kremlin, but his own home and family - and he would without fail defend them!

He courageously - often staring death straight in the face - wrestled back his native lands from the Germans, which had been so bunglingly and criminally yielded to them. Did the frontline soldiers understand who was at fault for so many tragic events, which might even have been avoided? As far as I recall - far from everyone, while some of us at times even sought ways to justify "Him". However, the dazzling triumph of victory didn't completely blind the eyes of many. They returned from the war with a chest full of the combat decorations they had earned; with dreams about a new, more sensibly organized life. Really hadn't so much blood been spilled for the sake of this?

It turned out differently. Few of those things, about which they had thought and dreamed so eagerly and happily, were realized.

The capital greeted the frontline soldiers with bells, joyous singing, music, bouquets of flowers and a sea of smiles. This entire cascade of sincere greetings and tears of joy excited the hearts of the victors.

However, very quickly, in the monotony of everyday life they began to sense that a powerful dissonance with their previous thoughts was occurring around them. Dark clouds were gathering. Why? Everywhere across the country, many official actions were demeaning the people - turning their hopes into illusions and converting yesterday's glory into a chimera, which led to moral decay in society.

After the victory over Hitler's monstrous regime, the frontline soldiers that had returned home with their very first steps collided with the most detestable aspects of Stalin's regime. Indeed, each time they realized that to a great extent these aspects were identical to the Fascism - with which they had fought for so many years and had eventually destroyed. Therefore, naturally, everything happening in their lives created a sense that the victory had been ambiguous - and this particularly affected the young. Why was this happening?

This question is like a thread and it is worthwhile to pull on it and to begin unraveling the entire spool. Then we will find out the truth about the numerous bungling and bloody battles which the American military historian David Glantz has termed "forgotten". This is because the truth about the causes of the Red Army's defeats was kept carefully concealed for many years.

The Party leaders didn't decide to calculate the first historic results of the war until 20 years after it ended. Of course, they did so in the idiotic spirit that predominated at the time. Over the course of 20 years - from 1973 until 1982 - the fundamental study *Ob istorii Velikoi mirovoi voiny* [*The History of the Great World War*] was published in 12 volumes. It is difficult to believe, but this colossal scribbling - the offspring of 300 scholars, generals and historians - proved to be nothing more than cheap propaganda riddled with falsified or contrived facts and events. I'll cite only one example.

Having believed in the seriousness of the authors' intentions for this publication, I signed up for it and gradually over time received all 12 volumes. However very quickly I realized the frivolity with which I had placed my trust in the compilers of this military encyclopedia. When the last volume came out, I gathered them all up and having neatly bound them up into a bundle, I took all the books to a bookstore. The seller, seeing what I had brought, broke out laughing and pointed at some shelves that were jammed with just the same book bundles that I had put together, but which had been brought in by other customers before me.

Following instructions from above, the official historians falsified various stages of the war. True, the Red Army's war consisted primarily of dictatorial reasoning; of the miscalculations of the Generalissimo and his brave and capable - but also endlessly cruel and glory-seeking - commanders who sent tens of thousands of men to slaughter to their certain deaths - even though this often could have been avoided. "Take a village at any cost": that was the typical wording of a military order of those years.

The highest sense of military duty led the soldier into the attack again and again. There were occasions when after a battle, a battalion had only a few survivors. In all honesty, my generation was a generation that was cut down like grass. Of every 100 men that entered the war, only three returned from it.

At directions from above, the veterans became the focus of the authorities' fixed attention. I'll give an example from my own experience. One day, Verukha came to see me. That's what we called the woman who tidied up the entrance to the apartment building where we were living. She led me off to one side and asked in a low whisper: "What's causing me to speak? They've been asking about you. They've been told to keep an eye on you." At first I was at a loss. It was very unexpected and unpleasant news. Regaining my composure, I gave a jesting response: "Tell them, mother, that I'm a fine fellow and that soon I'll become a crocodile." Verukha looked at me with curiosity and asked: "How so?"

The following morning I headed toward the Krymsky Bridge and having caught a moment when there was no one around me, I discarded a German officer's dagger and a collection of *Wehrmacht* medals that were wrapped in a washcloth into the water below. My comrade, Evgenii Prokhorov - with whom I was studying in the Publishing Institute - was unlucky. He had returned from the war with a trophy German Walther pistol. The fellow forgot to lock the door to the room where he was living. At that moment he was carrying out his monthly cleaning and greasing of the weapon. Without knocking, a neighbor entered the room; immediately freezing in place from the surprise, he began to praise Zhenia [the Russian diminutive of Evgenii] fulsomely for his courage. He knew that Prokhorov had been a scout during the war. Within a week, the scout was rounded up. In accordance with the law, he was given five years in a prison camp for the illegal possession of a gun.[4]

Many of the veterans returned with various sorts of souvenirs from the war: pistols, daggers and bayonets; assorted envelopes, postcards and stamps; coin collections; maps and officers' binoculars; beer steins, figurines, cameras, harmonicas... the list is endless. One soldier came back from the front with his *smertnik* - the little wooden case that held his identification information. During the war, his comrades had told him repeatedly to get rid of the thing - believing that it would bring him to the attention of the Grim Reaper.[5] However, the soldier had survived - though he was wounded twice.

The security organs regularly reported up the channels about the weapons seized from former soldiers. However, it was impossible to keep track of everything. I'll cite a curious case that I heard about. Prior to the seizing of the Reichstag, 60 flags were made so that one could be raised over the building as a sign of the victory. These flags were distributed among all the battalions that were approaching the building in Berlin. One of these banners went missing: an officer had stolen it and when he returned to the Motherland he sold it to a local museum as a "Victory Banner". The affair was uncovered and the former lieutenant was arrested together with the museum staff official who had split the proceeds from the sale.

In the initial postwar years, Iurii Bondarev's novel *Tishina* [*Silence*] came out. The book was popular. It seemed that a new frontline writer had appeared and was talking about the fate of a young man, who had brought back a pistol from the war, having paid a heavy price for its use in life. Bondarev wrote a lot of books. I liked his novel *Batal'ony prosiat ogon'* [*Battalions request fire*] most of all. It became the subject of a film. Unfortunately, the author turned out to be a nefarious, power-hungry fellow who played a far from noble role in the years of perestroika.

The war had still not ended, but at Stalin's personal direction the SMERSH officers - with the help of the political organs - combed through the frontline trenches seeking "counterrevolutionaries". It is hard to believe, but many brave, experienced frontline soldiers were taken away in the victorious year of 1945 because in the opinion of the command they were too independent and had become obstinate, proud men. To that I will add that I don't recall a single case where any of the commanders, commissars or soldiers spoke up on behalf of their combat brother.

In the Political Department where I served they came for a private, Simka Kuziaev, who loved to tell anecdotes. During the search of his personal belongings they found a diary. The chief of the Political Department, Colonel Shilovich, assembled all the officers and warned: "Don't get involved!"

Toward the end of the war, an earthshaking event happened with Red Army men stuck in the Gulag. Suddenly they were all freed, handed rifles and sent off to take part in the final assault on Berlin. Few of them survived. However, after the war, authorities tried to track them all down and send them back into the Gulag to serve out the rest of their sentences.

At the beginning of demobilization (1946), a secret directive was issued that banned veterans from settling wherever they wanted after the war. All those demobilized from the Red Army - regardless of rank or title - were obliged to return to wherever they were residing at the time they were called up for service. In this fashion, primarily, Stalin managed to scatter millions of people across the country who might have otherwise coalesced into a resistance group. Peasants had to return to their villages, which prevented the flight of rural youth to the cities - not to mention the capital.

I'll share with the reader how this directive affected my own life. I was demobilized in June 1946. I traveled to my parents' place in Moscow and several days after my arrival I set out for the district police department in order to obtain my civilian passport. It was said about this document: "Without it you're a bug, but with the paper you're a person!"

In the Soviet Union, without this piece of paper you couldn't find work; you couldn't get married; you couldn't bury your father or mother; and you wouldn't be accepted by a university. Meanwhile, let's recall how our great poet Vladimir Maiakovsky praised the "hammer and sickle".

As I was preparing to head to the police station, I had donned my officer's uniform (though without the shoulder boards) and pinned all my Orders and decorations to it. The result was a respectable iconostasis.[6] The police officer didn't pay it the least bit of attention. Having read my application, he leaned across the table and handed me the text of the decree - and then after I had read it, he asked: "Where were you when you were called up?"

"In Kyshtym," I replied. Without letting me have a chance to add that I had been there by sheer coincidence, he decisively announced: "Then that's where you're going. There they'll give you a passport, register you and assign you a place to live." That seemingly ended our conversation. To all my entreaties, he only silently nodded at the text of the decree that was lying on the table.

I returned home a bewildered victor. My appeal to the city police headquarters ended with the same rejection. I'd been given the bum's rush. What was I to do? I talked with my parents. They promised to help. True, just a week later they told me to go again to see that same police officer. Just a day later I received a spanking new Soviet passport and then I was registered at my father's place of work and became a citizen of Moscow.

About 10 years later my mother revealed the secret of my passport's "magical" appearance. It turned out that the passport registration officer of our apartment building was intimate with the police officer at the passport desk. She asked my mother to bring her two bags of potatoes from the market; in return, she would arrange a passport for me. My mother carried out her "request" - for the sake of which she had to pawn her wedding ring.

When my mother approached the passport registration officer to report that "everything was in order" the gal told her: "Don't blame my Anisim. He's a gentlemanly guy, but his bosses are forcing him to behave this way: too many Jews are simply overrunning the capital. Your son, although a Jew, is a worthy fellow." What could my mother say in response to that?

Like a Bolt from the Blue

The war was gradually receding into the past. People, those who could, were getting readjusted to life in the peacetime that had finally arrived. The peasants - having laughed and cried together with their mothers, fathers and grandparents - resumed their "old" accursed collective farm lives again. What were the villages like in the first postwar years? Twenty or 30 years after the end of the war, such so-called "village writers" as V. Rasputin, V. Belov and F. Abramov described it accurately…

Numerous courses for mastering the most necessary professions opened across the country. In-service technical correspondence courses were developed, which offered the equivalent of both secondary and higher education. Secondary schools for adults opened. Millions of veterans were forced into the system of political education.

The country was devastated. Much has been written about this. Three million German and Japanese prisoners of war labored to rebuild the shattered cities and villages. Former Russian prisoners of war and thousands of guest workers gathered into labor battalions worked in the most difficult sectors.

I'll discuss briefly my own first steps after demobilization from the Red Army. I enrolled in the Moscow Correspondence Institute of Publishing[7] in the Department of Editing. Why correspondence? I intended both to study and to work. However, my father told me: "As long as I'm able, I'll help you. The main thing is for you to study and master a profession as quickly as possible. You've earned this right." So I strove to study.

My studies at times could be compared to a marathon. I mastered subject after subject in course after course and passed exams ahead of schedule. I attended lectures at the university and listened to presentations of major scholars in the Polytechnic Museum. But I spent most of my time in those years at the oldest library in Moscow - the "Historic" on Starospassky Lane. Precisely at 9:00 A.M. I would enter the "Historic" building - together with the first patrons - and I was among the last to leave it at the end of the day.

For three years I read the best books of the world and Russian literary classics. My favorite writers were Stendahl, Balzak, Thomas Mann and, of course, Pushkin and Gogol. I began to put together my own library, but this proved to be unbelievably difficult. The bookstores of the time sold primarily propaganda literature devoted to praising the Party and Stalin. Back then you could acquire an excellent book only on the black market, but I didn't have enough money for that. I was lucky; I was able to purchase my first book (a collection of Chekhov's stories) on the cheap from a drunkard.

Later I found out that a publishing center that published millions of books had been created in Leipzig - one of the centers of German printing. This is a special topic.

I managed to pass two courses a year. Back then, that was permitted for particularly zealous students. Thus I graduated from the Institute in 1950 after three-and-a-half years of study. In my final year of studies prior to the government exams, I managed to find work as a Junior Editor at the *Promstroiizdat* [short for Industrial Construction Publisher]: there was such a publishing house back then.

Over my years of study at the Institute I became friends with other veterans, Isak Sokol'sky and Tolia Konopel'kin. We spent many hours together, studied together and at times worked together as night watchmen on Kuznetsky Lane - where a Moscow store of subscription publications was located - so that we could be first in line when it opened for business and sign up for books. For example, we could sign up to receive Lermontov's three-volume work or V.I. Dalia's dictionary. In order to earn a little something (to help the home, purchase books or tickets to the movie or theater), the three of us went to work at nights loading trucks with vegetables; took part in crowd scenes at a movie studio in Moscow; and removed trash and leaves from parks and boulevards. We began to get things published in the *Moskovskii Komsolets* newspaper and busied ourselves with translations from the German language. Initially I often went to Moscow's flea market and sold everything that I had brought back with me from the army: my overcoat, my warm cap, my boots, my belt and the Leica camera I had obtained in Germany.

Sudden changes arrived in the life of veterans in 1946. At first they abolished the cash supplements and material benefits due to Order recipients. For example, roundtrip travel aboard trains or steamships had been free. This event agitated the minds of people and gave rise to assorted rumors. Everyone understood the State's difficult economic situation after the war. The government should have appealed to us honestly and openly - confident that not one veteran would have opposed the measure. Moreover, it should have been a voluntary measure - possibly even temporary. There should always be honorable legal and moral connections between the government and the people. In the given case, Stalin's decision was unprincipled; that's what many of my comrades believed. As a sign of protest, many of the veterans stopped wearing their Orders and medals - including me.

On 23 December 1947 Stalin "suddenly" canceled the official celebration of Victory Day - including the holiday for workers. Authorities said: "The country must be rebuilt and we must not be diverted by fireworks, ceremonies and salutes... and time shouldn't be wasted on meetings and trips to battlefields". That's how they explained, as always, Stalin's "wise" decision. For almost 20 years, the Soviet Union didn't note Victory Day on the government level. This doesn't mean that we forgot our shining day - 9 May. People gathered after work wherever it was possible: in parks, on sidewalks next to busy streets, outside the city, on riverbanks and of course in homes around the kitchen table. The newspapers on this day would print the recollections of individual veterans - primarily, of generals. Of course, in this holiday edition there would be a portrait of the Supreme Commander and the journalists would savor the victories, but there wouldn't be a single word about the defeats - just as if there hadn't been any. In this fashion, an increasing number of new "blank spots" appeared in the history of the war - topics or events that were never mentioned or discussed.

The radio would play songs from the war years and intone excerpts from the works of M. Sholokhov, A. Tvardovsky, A. Tolstoy, and I. Ehrenburg or K. Simonov's verses. A great amount of air time would be dedicated to the Generalissimo and endless songs and verses about "Him" would be played.

That's how we lived for almost two decades - without an official holiday to mark Victory Day. In 1965, however, the new powers in the Kremlin recollected the day: L.I. Brezhnev returned their holiday to the victorious people. In this year in honor of the 20th Anniversary of the Victory, a new medal was created - "For victory in the Great Patriotic War" - with an image on it of the Generalissimo. Many of us wouldn't wear it.

It is known that on this 20th Anniversary, L.I. Brezhnev met with veterans of the 18th Guards Army in the Central Theater of the Soviet army; during the war, he had led the 18th Guards Army's Political Department. During this meeting he called the veterans "the country's gold assets". We never heard such words from Stalin, or surprisingly, from Khrushchev either. It isn't clear why N.S. Khrushchev didn't restore the official holiday on 9 May - especially after the XX Party Congress and his complete seizure of control over the Party and the government.

In the initial postwar years, an unthinkable event that saddened the heart occurred right in front of my generation's eyes. At that time in Moscow one could see many armless, legless or sightless war invalids around the intersections of major streets; at the entrances and exits to subway stations; and on suburban commuter trains. They were dressed in tattered clothes. Those without legs moved around with the use of self-made wooden scooters. The government neglected its war invalids.

On one ordinary day, these former frontline soldiers - who were now human "stumps" - suddenly disappeared. Where did they go? The press was silent - as were those in power. Who ordered these unfortunate people - many with combat decorations - to be cast adrift for all practical purposes? I heard one high-ranking bureaucrat, who was drunk at the time, blabber aloud something like: "Praise God... They've cleaned the city of these drunken freaks!" Whenever I heard a similar expression, I would immediately have the thought: "It is possible that these 'drunken freaks' lost their arms or legs while defending Moscow."

It was also whispered that across the country all these invalids had been rounded up on the same day and hour and, at government expense, sent off to the Valaam Islands in Lake Ladoga near Leningrad where a special hospital had been set up. This is simply impossible (there were too many war invalids across the country to be housed on the islands - though it is true that a number of the invalids were put away on Valaam). But where did all the rest of them go? All this was done involuntarily without any publicity. I will discuss the fate of these war invalids in more detail in a later chapter.

Fragmentary evidence about the terrible fate of the Russian former prisoners of war - as well as the situation of the "Returnees" - tormented the frontline veterans. Stalin dealt cruelly with eyewitnesses to his own disgrace in 1941. We knew little, or more accurately, almost nothing about it. For long years, this subject - both under Stalin and after him - was totally closed to study or discussion. Even to the present day Russia has still not fully opened the archives, which might give us a picture of those tragic events in the past.

A.I. Solzhenitsyn should be given credit as the first of the Russian writers to write about Stalin's agreement with the Allies regarding the forcible repatriation of Russian prisoners of war to Russia - and about the Vlasov movement. However, his monumental *Gulag Archipelago* didn't appear in the Russian language until the beginning of the 1990s. In the West, books that talked about the Russian prisoners of war and the Vlasov movement were published back in the 1950s. Since then an entire library of studies, collected archival material and memoirs have been published.[8]

The 30th Anniversary of the Victory was a major event. From this period, the term "*frontovik*" ("frontline soldier") was replaced by the word "*veteran*". The government began to award veterans with food benefits. We were given "veterans' booklets". Factories began to be built to produce prosthetic devices; workshops for making orthopedic shoes were opened - and at last crutches of various sizes began to appear in drugstores.

Army and divisional Veterans' Councils were created. For two years I was a member of the 220th Rifle Division's Veterans' Council. What did we do? We sent out birthday greetings to surviving veterans of the division; worked to bring veterans together in Moscow on Victory Day; and visited schools where we talked to the children about the war. We drove to Minsk to celebrate the 30th Anniversary of the Belorussian capital's liberation. In 1961 we visited the city of Elets, where in 1941 the 220th Rifle Division was formed. At a meeting with the veterans, the local military commissar told us that out of the division's initial formation of 20,000 men only 40 were still alive.

Our former division owes a lot to one man: Vasilii Ragulin from Lugansk (previously Voroshilovgrad). Vasilii spent almost 18 years searching for the surviving veterans of the 220th Rifle Division. He contacted them by mail. On 9 May 1975 at his invitation, 146 former soldiers and officers of the 220th Rifle Division journeyed to Moscow. We arrived at a park, which at the time was the Central Military Museum. There was an officer in a military uniform standing on a stage in the center of the park holding a placard in his hands: "I'm Vasia Ragulin".

It is difficult to express what happened next. Everyone rushed to Vasia, tossed him into the air, hugged him and kissed him - unable to hold back their tears.

From that day on we gathered every year in Moscow. Alas, at each new reunion, fewer of our fellow soldiers showed up. The elimination of the government benefits that had come with some of the government's decorations became the first manifestation in the official debasement of the veterans. At first - particularly in the 1960s and 1970s - we couldn't imagine that the "era of gratuities" would end with the complete devaluation of the decorations. The combat decorations became virtually worthless and nothing more than children's playthings. They sold on the black market for pennies. The government began to distribute honors for years of service in the army. For 15 years of service, you got the Order of the Red Star; for 20 years of service, the Order of the Red Banner; and for 25 years, the Order of Lenin. During the war, these had required feats of combat heroism to obtain.

Next - in order somehow to quiet the indignation of the veterans over the awarding of the Order of Victory to the General Secretary of the CPSU's Central Committee, L.I. Brezhnev -surviving veterans were all given a more honorable Order for frontline soldiers: the Order of the Patriotic War. According to the decree about awarding the Order of the Patriotic War -1st or 2nd Class - they were given to all veterans who had the medal "For military service"; "For the victory over Germany"; or "For the victory over Japan"; or who had documents that certified they'd been wounded in the war.

The Order of the Patriotic War, 1st or 2nd Class: during the war years this had been the most honorable Order among the fighting men. Only those who actually served at the front could receive this Order. Not even staff officers of a division headquarters that was involved in combat could receive it. Thus it is no coincidence that many frontline veterans declined to go to the local military enlistment office to receive this "medal".

It is a shameful fact that must be mentioned: in 1947, KGB officers were awarded combat decorations for the murder of the author Solomon Mikhoels. Lieutenant General Tsavan received the Order of the Red Banner, while Colonel Shubnikov and Lebedev - as well as Senior Lieutenant Kruglov - each received the Order of the Patriotic War 1st Class. Similar criminal cases of the use of combat decorations in Stalin's times were often kept secret from the people.[9]

Much failed to happen after the war - much, very much, that the soldiers and officers thought about and dreamed about in the trenches, was not to be. I'll summarize what some of those things were based on soldiers' conversations. First of all, life in the village - and this meant the transfer of at least partial ownership of land to the peasants (or more often, the full return of the land taken from them by the Bolsheviks after 1917): They wanted the liquidation of the collective farms and the reduction of taxes on the peasant households. The bureaucrats argued: "Bah, what don't the peasants want!" One of the peasants in the trenches once boasted: "For that holy cause I'd take off my boots and slowly set off in bare feet across the freshly plowed land. And it, the soil, as if newly reborn, would cheer up and gently awaken under my feet!"

The men of faith - and there were a lot of them among the men at the front - believed that they'd be able to worship freely again. The educated soldiers and officers speculated about the approach of a liberal era; about the end of repressions - a transition "from fear to freedom." In response to them, the bureaucrats growled: "Bah, what don't the intellectuals want!"

A little about rural life after the war

The village in the initial postwar years was on the verge of death. Over the war years the soil had to a great extent become unfertile; fields had gone fallow or had become choked with weeds. There were no tractors or vehicles. If just one gaunt horse still remained in the village, this was considered a blessing.

Not many of the men returned from the war: just one or two men to each village - and some of them had lost arms or legs. Both those and the others were considered heroes - the "leading men in the village".

The village had no electricity; the peasants lived just as their forebears - illuminating their cottages with wood shavings, or else someone might have a kerosene lamp. Later I found out that of the 5,000 reestablished district printing offices, 4,500 were using manual printing machines.

The "primary labor element" in the villages consisted of females. All of the difficult rural work fell on the shoulders of the women. The men assumed leadership positions and comprised the first detachments of the new rural bureaucracy (collective farm chairmen, Party organizers, members of the collective farm management, tractor brigade leaders, warehouse directors, etc.). In a word, it was just like the saying: "One with the plow, seven with spoons."

People were living a hand-to-mouth existence. During the war, the villagers had given everything they had - not that they had much - but nevertheless they gave whatever they could to the front. Now after the war during the planting season or the harvest, the women took on the work that had once been done by horses or machines. There might be one cow to 50 homes and at times there would be nothing to feed it.

The question often tormented me: What happened to all that wealth that was transported back to the USSR from Germany - supposedly as reparations? It is known that over the years 1945-1947, 600,000 horses were taken out of East Germany and shipped back to the Soviet Union - among them heavy draft horses from Holland as well as more than a half-million head of cattle and almost a quarter-million tons of wheat.

Whom to ask: "Where did all this great wealth go?" Was it distributed among the villages? Not quite. Many of the cattle and horses died en route.

Incidentally, there were some villages under German occupation where the land retained its former appearance and where the men, women and children didn't go hungry. The norms set for agricultural requisitions established by the German army were lower than the villagers had faced on the collective farms under Soviet power. Although the Germans kept the collective farm system on the occupied territory, their main desire was to see rich harvests. There was silence about this fact after the war - and that silence continues today.

Disillusionment

Stalin decided to spit on the hopes of the frontline soldiers and reestablished the basics of life in society as it had existed before the war. What did he fear? Why didn't he accommodate the people who deserved a happier fate after saving the Soviet Union and securing a victorious conclusion to the war?

Why hadn't Napoleon liberated the Russian serfs from slavery? Why didn't Hitler liberate the Russian peasants from the collective farm yoke or opt to create education systems on the territory they had seized in Russia, the Ukraine, the Baltic nations, and in Belorussia that were tailored to the specific nationalities? Why was he afraid to arm anti-Stalinists and instead of this chose to eliminate more than 2 million Russian prisoners of war? These difficult questions for my entire generation arose already in the years immediately after the war. Even to this day, these questions remain without answers. However, one thing is clear: neither the one nor the other dictator was capable of acting differently or less cruelly.

Having returned the nation to its prewar past, Stalin again doomed millions of people to poverty, a semi-famished existence and a lack of proper housing. People lived in barracks, cellars or in so-called communal apartments. Most of the people received miserly wages. Starting in 1946, the Party cracked down on the society's spiritual life. The process of active degradation of science and education began.

The Big is seen from Afar

Already in 1945, Stalin banned anything to be written or published about the military events. The interesting, little-known recollections of A.M. Vasilevsky and G.K. Zhukov have been preserved, which permit one to understand the Supreme Commander's attitude toward the historiography of the just-completed war. For many years, Vasilevsky refused to take up the writing of his memoirs. He wasn't alone. Aleksandr Mikhailovich supported his stance with valid arguments - in particular the fact that soon after the war I.V. Stalin had expressed his disapproval of memoirs. Back then, Vasilevsky had presented the Generalissimo with two books of recollections. One was a collected volume entitled *Shturm Berlina* [*The Storming of Berlin*], which had been compiled at the time when G.K. Zhukov was still in Germany in his post as the commander-in-chief of the Soviet Military Administration.

Superbly executed, the large-sized book of almost 500 pages with numerous illustrations was published in 1946. The authors wrote about how they had carried out the storming of the Third Reich's capital and shared with the reader what they had seen, felt and experienced. Among the memoirists were soldiers, non-commissioned officers, officers and generals. The illustrations were made on the basis of wartime sketches by combat artists of the Grekov Studio: L. Golovanov, A. Kokorin and N. Sokolov.

As A.M. Vasilevsky recalled later, when shown the book Stalin said that: "it was too soon to write memoirs immediately after the great events when there still hadn't been time for passions to cool - and that there wouldn't be the necessary objectivity in these memoirs." Stalin's comment is understandable. Obviously, he believed that the memoir literature might shatter his exalted status of the Supreme Commander.

What Stalin said to Vasilevsky was enough to ensure that the doors to book publishers and journals were for a long time closed to veterans - the heroes of the Great Patriotic War. In the initial postwar years, only one thing was permitted: the glorification of the Dictator - thanks to whom the Party and the Soviet people were able to crush the fascist aggressors and save the world from the monster of Nazism.

There is still another little-known historical episode. In 1946, after G.K. Zhukov's return from Germany, Stalin directed the Chekists to keep a vigilant eye on the Marshal. Soon they reported back to Stalin where Zhukov kept his documents and what those papers contained.

A short time later Stalin phoned the commander and asked him: "What, are you preparing to write a history? That isn't necessary. Let historians be busy with that task after we're all dead." Some of Zhukov's wartime documents were simply pilfered and the Marshal never saw them again.

N.A. Voznesenky's book *Voennaia ekonomika SSSR v period Otechestvennaia voina* [*The war economy of the USSR during the Patriotic War*], which came out in 1947, cost the author his head.[10] Not one marshal; not one general - not to mention any military historian - was permitted to write about the war, but if he glorified the Generalissimo… well, as you please! Here's one example: historians back then contrived to depict the tragedy of 1941 as a shrewd defensive strategy. Moreover, it was categorically forbidden to publish books by Western historians or generals on the history of the war.

The Generalissimo exclusively took over the right to assess the victory. At Stalin's direction, all the archives that contained wartime documents and materials about the war were closed to the public.

What did Stalin fear? It was as if information from domestic authors - much less Western authors - might confuse the minds of Soviet readers. After all, from the very first postwar years we were nurtured on the examples of Stalin's victories which did not include the bloody failures of 1941-1942. Thus, the best books about the Second World War - written in the West - weren't available to the Russian reader until the glasnost' period and the end of censorship in the 1980s and 1990s: that is to say, 30 to 40 years after they had first come out. Here are several examples: Albert Speer's memoirs (40 years after the original publication), Kurt von Tippelskirch's 1951 book *History of the Second World War 1939-1945* (44 years after the original publication) and Erich Manstein's *Lost Victories* (29 years after the original publication).

The fate of B. Mueller-Hillebrand's book *The German Ground Army, 1933-1945* is not without interest. It was translated into the Russian language and published by two major publishers: Inostrannaia literatura (1956) and Voenizdat (1976). However, in both editions censors removed any mention of the participation of Soviet people in the war on the side of the *Wehrmacht*. In 2002, an unexpurgated version of the book was finally published in Russian.

There is still another surprising example. Former German commanders, participants in the Rzhev epic, published more than 50 books in Germany about their combat experiences. What do we know about them? One of them wound up in Rzhev by coincidence. In the early 1990s a group of Rzhev citizens spent some time in Germany and returned home with a book by the former German commander of the 6th Infantry Division, General Horst Grossman, entitled: *Rzhev – the Cornerstone of the Eastern Front*. Local historians, ethnographers and journalists Oleg Kondrat'ev and Leonid Myl'nikov in 1996 - 40 years after the book's original publication in German - published Grossman's book in the Russian language in a small number of copies.

In the Foreword to the Russian-language edition of Grossman's book, there are the following words:

> … More than a half-century has passed since its [the Battle of Rzhev's] conclusion. Unfortunately, the truth about the Battle of Rzhev still largely remains untold. Military historians are silent about it…

Honest and sincere words, filled with anguish over their long-suffering city.

There is silence around the Battle of Rzhev, but not only around it alone. Many battles are "orphans" that were omitted from the "Pantheon of Glory - the Legendary and Invincible", erected by Russian historians back in the 1950s and 1960s. A striking fact: in the four-volume series on the Great Patriotic War published in Moscow in 2001, just try to find honest lines about the Crimean catastrophe; about the dramatic battles for Khar'kov; about the Rzhev slaughterhouse; about the surrender of Kiev; about the destruction of entire armies and other "unpleasant" events in the war.

One of the reasons for such absurd stubbornness consists in the unwillingness to reject the false, so-called histories of the Great Patriotic War that were written in the Stalin, Khrushchev and Brezhnev eras with official blessing. In addition, there was no desire to diminish the names of I.V. Stalin and the celebrated Soviet marshals and generals. Meanwhile, weren't they themselves obliged to tell the truth about how everything actually happened? They didn't; neither did Zhukov, nor Konev, nor Leliushenko - the main commanders in the fighting for Rzhev. In their memoirs that they published after the war, they all adroitly sought to avoid the entire, unpleasant episode in their military records - the defeats and the murder (it can be called nothing less) of tens of thousands of soldiers and officers at the Rzhev-Viaz'ma salient. At the same time there is nothing less logical than a history - from which some or another events and facts have been erased at the behest of top officials. To restore the truth isn't such a simple task - especially many years later.

A never-before-seen thing has happened. It is an old truth that victors write the history. Well, Russia shunned a real history of the Great Patriotic War. In this case it was the defeated, and not they alone, who began to reconstruct the historic truth about the war in the East.

It is said that after the war, having become the Minister of Defense in 1955, G.K. Zhukov gave a green light to the former military commanders and the historians to create a national military historiography. Work groups were established at the General Staff under the leadership of famous generals in order to produce works that summarized the experience of the largest military operations. After N.S. Khrushchev summarily removed Zhukov from all his posts and sent the Marshal into retirement, the historians changed course and set to work to create a new official history of the war. G.K. Zhukov later wrote: "It is impossible to read what they cooked up. It [the official history] must be written all over again." Now after so many years, a brand new official history won't come out!

For almost six decades since the war's end, mountains of books have been published in Russia on the basis of this essentially "contrived" official version: fundamental multi-volume works, encyclopedias great and small, monographs, text books and reference books - with which several generations of Soviet people and officers have grown up. Meanwhile it is well known that any half-truth is more dangerous than a lie because it is always easier to spot a lie than a half-truth. Over all the years of postwar censorship, which held sway for more than 40 years, I can recall only one coincidental breach of the official silence: an effort to tell the truth about the tragedies of 1941. This was Alexander Nekrich's famous book *June 22 1941*: *Soviet Historians and the German Invasion*, which created a sensation. After the book came out in 1965, the talented academic-historian lost his job and then he was kicked out of the country.

"Patriotism mustn't blind us:
Love for the Fatherland is an act
Of clear judgment, not blind passion."

N.M. Karamzin

16

Comrade Stalin's Return

The Round Dance around Stalin's Spirit

Is it true - as historians maintain - that one of the main political conflicts in contemporary Russian culture is the conflict with our own past? A reader's understanding of this viewpoint can be obtained through the materials of an international conference that took place in Moscow on 5-7 December 2008 on the subject: "Studying the History of Stalinism". This event was extraordinary - and not only for Russia alone. Representatives of 86 different universities, institutes and other scholarly organizations took part in the conference - which was attended by more than 260 Russian historians and scholars and 96 of their counterparts from around the world. The conference became a major event in academic life that year and received a great deal of public attention. It was an audacious challenge to authority. Indeed, although the presentations were largely of an academic nature and there were no angry words addressed to those guilty of Stalinism's resurgence in contemporary Russia, its results testified to the fact that the government has failed to carry out its duty before society. It has been unable to acknowledge and overcome its own criminal past, which cost Russia 50 million human lives.[1]

In the preamble to the conference's program, the alarm and concern of scholars from around the world was clearly expressed "about the broadening chasm between the scholarly and the everyday view of the dictatorship's essence, which makes plans for the authoritarian modernization of society popular."

I want to acquaint the reader with Arsenii Roginsky's report, entitled: *Remembrance of Stalinism.* It was recognized as brilliant according to the general opinion of everyone attending. In his presentation, Roginsky precisely outlined the contemporary status of Stalinism in Russia.

Recent sociological surveys (2008-2009) indicated that 53 per cent of the Russian people have a positive view of the role of Stalin in contemporary history. In 1988, only 12 per cent of the respondents had considered Stalin a significant world leader - more than four-and-a-half times fewer.[2] In his address to the conference, Andrei Sorokin - the director of the Ruslen Publishing Company - called this trend "a catastrophe". Characteristically, around 50 per cent of the respondents don't believe Stalin was a tyrant.[3]

The director of the Russian Federation's State Archive, Sergei Mironenko, has an interesting opinion. He believes:

> ... Our society isn't ready to receive the truth or to learn the truth about our own history. From my point of view, this phenomenon still hasn't been adequately studied and is insufficiently understood. What was Stalinsim? Why is it so enduring in our society? Why does Iosif Vissarionovich Stalin occupy such an honorable place among government figures? To a great extent, it seems to me this is a result of a contradiction. The more we criticize, the more we expose - the more positive the effect. [However] the Russian citizen, the Russian person, doesn't put much credence in any sort of revelation...

It is difficult to agree with this interpretation of Stalinism's evolution. It is likely that the cause of Stalinism's return to respectability consists in the powerful influence of the Kremlin-directed mass media on the population.

What explains the main reasons for such a sharp resurgence of Stalinism in Russian society? Why has the figure of Stalin become such an idol to a significant portion of Russian intellectuals and the youth?[4] I would like to ask why Russian television has made Stalin one of Russia's main symbols.

We'll note that Stalinism's resurgence particularly occurred on the eve of anniversaries -the 50th Anniversary of Stalin's death in 2003 and the 60th Anniversary of Victory in the Great Patriotic War in 2005. It was in this period, first and foremost, that Russians accepted the return of Stalin to his former pedestal. Monuments and stelae were erected in commemoration of Stalin in the Russian cities of Cheliabinsk, Volgograd, Ishim, Krasnoiarsk, Orel and Kaliningrad - as well as in the Iakut city of Mirnyi. Russian citizens began to rename streets, squares, parks and boulevards after Stalin - or more accurately, they began to display placards with Stalin's portrait over them that displayed Stalin's name. Stalinists completed the release of Stalin's collected writings in 17 volumes and went to further extremes to commemorate Stalin. However, the main point here is that people didn't want to begin to learn the truth about Stalin. Instead, the myths about the "Great Creator of a powerful Soviet State"; the "Great Statist"; the "Great Humanist"; and the "Great Manager" struck their fancies.

Scholars in the East and the West are alarmed that the mythologizing of Stalinism is becoming increasingly popular in Russia. This concern was voiced rather seriously by most presenters at the international conference on Stalinism. Aleksandr Drozdov, the director of the First President of Russia Boris Yeltsin's Foundation, spoke up for continuing work on the subject of Stalinism. One of the most significant results of such work, in his view, should be the legal formalization of a process of de-Stalinization. Andrei Sorokin, Helen Carrere D'Encausse (a Russian specialist and the Permanent Secretary of the Academie Francaise) and the Russian TV and radio host Nikolai Svanidze were all united around the view that the most important thing to do today would be the complete termination of discussions about Stalin in Russia.

What has actually happened in Russia which has so actively influenced the thinking of Russians and their changing views towards Stalin's role in the history of the State? The conference participants - and in particular Arsenii Tarkovsky - attribute these changes to the gap that has arisen between the academic perspective on Stalinism and the everyday understanding of that concept in the public mind. I believe that this gap is more a consequence than a cause. I'll attempt to define the main reasons for the mythologizing of Stalinism and its recent increase.

Putin and the "New" Russia

First of all Russian citizens often refer to Stalin not by his name, but by the label "Russia's Boss". It sounds, if you will, loftier than "Stalin" - who as a rule during his life was called "the Boss" or "the Father of Peoples" or "the Authority" (by Chekists). Yet how did an ordinary former KGB lieutenant colonel by the name of Putin earn such a lofty title: "Russia's Boss"?

In 2008, a book came out in Great Britain under the title of *Putin and the Rise of Russia*. It was written by a German historian, Michael Stuermer, who had worked as a foreign policy advisor to Germany's Chancellor, Helmut Kohl. The author has met with V.V. Putin on numerous occasions.

The greater part of this book is devoted to the author's recollections about his discussions with Putin. He is attempting to answer the question: "Did Putin's presidency actually lead to Russia's rise?" According to the author Putin managed to increase the nation's well-being but he has been unable to achieve his primary goal, which was stable economic growth. In essence, Russian prosperity has depended almost solely on its role as an energy-producer and the country has benefited from the high prices for oil. Stuermer describes Putin as a calculating man with guarded manners who is quite cognizant of his own power and whose "eyes like a laser beam… examining everybody to determine whether friend or foe."

Further on, Stuermer describes the political system put in place by Putin as a mixture of authoritarianism and democracy. Significant elements of an autocracy are plainly apparent and Stuermer believes possibly that they are strengthening and becoming more important. However, according to the author one can also say that Putin's Russia has elements of a democracy and believes it is a mistake to perceive Russia today as a recreation of the Soviet Union; in reality, it has moved far from the Stalinist Soviet Union and become a completely different country. Even so, Stuermer sees no circumstances under which Russia might one day become a Western-style democracy.

Is the author correct in his assessment of Putin? Stuermer views the rise of Russia as due to Putin. However, Russia under Putin's Presidency has moved ever further away from genuine democracy. He has liquidated many democratic institutions in the country - which had been founded by Gorbachev and Yeltsin before him - and has put in place a new model of power based upon autocratic methods of government. Putin as president has hardly elevated Russia. More accurately, in the eyes of world public opinion, he has lowered the country. In a short period of time he managed to spoil relations with America and Great Britain; pick fights with the Ukraine and the Baltic countries; proved unable to normalize relations with the countries of the former Soviet republics; and finally, unleashed a war against Georgia and seized two of its autonomous republics (Abkhazia and South Ossetia). I'm not even talking about how complicated Russia's relationships with the European Union and NATO have become. Condoleeza Rice, the former US Secretary of State, called such behavior in Russia's foreign policy a manifestation of "paranoia".

Putin overturned many civil freedoms - strengthening his own personal power at the expense of others. Starting in 2000 the Kremlin began to take control over Russia's independent television stations, which subsequently became subservient and obedient. It began muzzling the mouths of political opponents; expelling foreigners from the country; persecuting non-government organizations that were critical of Putin's administration; and it abolished the competitive election of governors - replacing it with a system whereby the Kremlin appointed the regional heads. Public discussions in Russia lost their former lively and freewheeling nature. Freedom of speech became largely restricted to online communications. The State finances 95 per cent of the radio and television stations and through them broadcasts pro-Kremlin information across the entire country. In Russia, only a single semi-free radio station, Ekho Moskvy, still exists.

However, assertions that Russia is returning to its Soviet era are an exaggeration. The former nightmare of Soviet rule doesn't exist - and not only because Russians have obtained access to food products and foreign goods. Putin's Russia is a cautious and cunning autocracy - a system where the political realm is strictly controlled, but which has a pressure valve to release built-up steam in the form of freedoms in everyday life. Internet access in Russia is practically limitless and there are a great number of cell phones in the hands of the Russian people; the pursuit of financial wealth has become an organizing and guiding ideology and trips abroad are now a normal occurrence. Under the old regime, these were considered a threat to government stability.

The new power has been built upon the remnants of the foundations of Stalin's regime. Over eight years of Putin's presidency, we never heard from him a balanced assessment of Stalin and his terrible epoch. He didn't take a single step or say a single word against Stalin and his criminal regime. At the same time, his positive comments about Stalin have become well-known.

In confirmation of what I've just said, let's turn to an electronic publication entitled: '*Prezident Rossii V.V. Putin, 8 let raboty*' ['*President of Russia V.V. Putin, 8 years of work*]. It came out in Moscow at the beginning of 2009 in the form of a set of three discs that contained more than 150 hours of audio and video clips. The set contains an enormous amount of information - including all the legal acts adopted under Putin - 426 archived files of his main speeches and 28,000 photographs. Going through all this material, one cannot find a single trace of a critical remark regarding the Stalinist past. Incidentally, none of Russia's rulers after Stalin - neither N.S. Khrushchev, L.I. Brezhnev, M.S. Gorbachev, B.N. Yeltsin nor V.V. Putin – enacted any legislative acts directed at condemning Stalin's crimes or the dictatorial nature of his regime.

I'll cite only a few examples from President V.V. Putin's speeches. He once stated: "We will not allow the past to seize us by the sleeve..." Russians, having heard these words from their president, right away grasped what he was driving at and immediately supported him. Putin set about rehabilitating Soviet-era symbols - including the Stalinist national anthem (albeit with different words) - and the public display of a red banner with depictions of Lenin and Stalin on it. He resumed military parades through Red Square and exalted Stalin's role in the Great Patriotic War. This new policy direction also included a corrective in the course that the historiography of the Great Patriotic War should take. Scholars should return to a focus on the successes and achievements of the Red Army and the Soviet system that led to the Great Victory, and not strive for a balanced study of the war's history with all its plusses and minuses. Scholars who have disregarded this directive have lost their jobs or suffered other personal repercussions.[5]

Even at the outset of his presidency, during a trip to Warsaw Putin declared: "The Russian people will never put Stalin in the same league with Hitler. It is impossible to compare Stalin with Hitler, who was a Nazi."

It has long been known and proven that Stalinism was no better than Nazism. What price the Katyn Forest massacre; the forced relocation of nationalities deemed "suspect" from their native lands; the punishment of the former Russian prisoners of war; the Molotov-Ribbentrop Pact and Stalin's role in the launching of the Second World War - and all the shameful, cruel events associated with the secret protocols to this criminal pact?

On the eve of the 60th Anniversary of Victory Day the American president, George Bush, and other major political figures in Russia and the West urged Putin to condemn the Stalinist past publicly and to begin the life of the country from a "clean page". Putin rejected these calls and, unexpectedly for the entire global community, gave his speech to the State Duma wherein he declared: "The break-up of the USSR was the greatest geo-political catastrophe of the 20th century." His words shocked the world - as if the Soviet system based upon its Stalinist foundations was even better than the current regime.

In the opinion of David Satter, a former Moscow correspondent and expert on Russia and the Soviet Union, this "nostalgia for the past" wasn't harmless and "ignores the fact that the Soviet Union was just as much a terrorist country as Nazi Germany, but it is also a rejection of that which Hannah Arendt called the 'all-penetrating socialized stupidity'". Within it lies an inability to recognize that the truth about the past is extremely important; in reality, in this recognition lays the best hope for a worthy future.

Russian society by and large supported the speech of its president in the State Duma. This flowed from the widespread opinion among the Russian people that a "firm hand" at the helm of the ship of State was needed and that "the Great Captain" Comrade Stalin created a system strong enough to destroy the Nazi regime.

History has pronounced its own judgment on the Dictator: the State, which was constructed according to his designs, quickly fell apart. More than 60 years passed from the time of his death and the country never reached the quality of life available in its European neighbors - including that in "vanquished" Germany. The Soviet regime attempted to explain that this was due to the past war, but failed to explain why the vanquished were living better than the victors.

The Russian public longs for Stalin as the embodiment of a firm hand in the leadership of the Great Empire. During the 60th Anniversary itself, Putin's Government did much to exalt Stalin as the Generalissimo. There was a ceremony to unveil a commemorative plaque in honor of "the Great Commander, the Victor over Fascism". At V.V. Putin's behest, the Russian Government Treasury minted 500 silver coins bearing an image of Stalin.

Just imagine if a West German chancellor had unveiled a memorial plaque in honor of Adolf Hitler and authorized the *Bundesbank* to mint 500 or even 1,000 coins with Hitler's image on them. How would the world have reacted to these acts? It would have shuddered at the thought of the rehabilitation of Nazism.

Reading the materials of the international academic conference on Stalin and Stalinism, I ran into the following phrase: "Putin and Medvedev are not Stalinists." Following it, there was an argument in support of this statement. It turns out that each of them on a single occasion visited a monument to Stalin's victims. Well, isn't that something special?!

Instead of welcoming the conference in Moscow - and I'm not speaking about making a personal appearance - on the day of the conference's opening a search was conducted in the offices of the *Pamiat'* organization[6] and valuable documents were removed from it. I believe this could not have occurred without Putin's prior approval. Thus from the very first minutes, the scholars from the West and the East received a warning: don't get smart with the Russian authorities, but if you're thinking about making jokes at its expense do it in a low voice. Be obedient, little ones! Otherwise... That's how it indeed happened.

If you will, the above is a brief sketch of the system that Putin has put into place over the eight years of his presidency. Under it, the objective study of Stalin, Stalinism and its consequences and legacies has faltered. Attempts to study Stalinism had been undertaken during Gorbachev's and Yeltsin's presidencies. However, with the economic growth and the appearance of the new great power ambitions under Putin, these efforts came to nothing. On the wave of rising patriotism in Russia, the history of the country is being rewritten once again. Anything that doesn't contribute to the image of a bright, heroic past remains in the shadows. The participants of the Moscow conference - among whom there were approximately 100 well-known experts in the field of Stalinism from around the world - in fact stood in opposition to just such tendencies.

Power and the People

Upon assuming power, Putin took several actions to weaken democracy in Russia during his tenure as president. He turned the upper chamber of the Russian Parliament, the Council of Federation, into an obedient institution made up of representatives that came from among the regional governors that Putin himself now appointed. Elections to select these executive heads of the Russian regions had been terminated in February 2005. The president thereby was able to weaken the independence of the Russian parliament (the State Duma). Beginning with the parliamentary elections in December 2003, using his control over the pro-Kremlin Party *Edinaia Rossiia* (United Russia) - of which he was the chairman - he secured a parliamentary majority in the Duma with two-thirds of the seats. The other political parties, not connected with the Kremlin, were consigned to the backbenches. The Kremlin uses its control of the mass media to promote *Edinaia Rossiia* and the Kremlin's line while other Party leaders have very limited access to television or radio. The independent liberal parties have been weakened and now operate under much more restricted conditions and in a much more confined political space than they had enjoyed in the 1990s.

When Mikhail Khodorkovsky was arrested and sentenced at Putin's direct order, it was an unambiguous signal to anyone else who thought to take an opposition role in the political arena against Putin. Opposition now exists only on the very periphery of Russian political life.

In April 2007, in his annual message to the Federal Council, Putin made an appeal to xenophobic nationalism - warning that the West was conspiring to undermine Russia's sovereignty. He declared:

> ... The flow of money from abroad - used for the direct meddling in our internal affairs -is rising. Not everyone likes the stable, progressive advance of our country. There are those who, adeptly using pseudo-democratic phrases, would like to return to the recent past: some, in order with impunity to vandalize the national wealth and to plunder people and the State as they did before; others, in order to deprive our country of economic and political independence...

Soon thereafter the Kremlin expelled the Peace Corps from the country; closed the Organization of Security and Cooperation in Europe's mission at first in Chechnya and then in Moscow; and forced the non-governmental organization Internews-Russia, which specialized in increasing the professional qualifications of Russian journalists, to close its offices - accusing its director of embezzlement.

Putin and his team simultaneously shelved reforms that were capable of strengthening other branches of power. The justice system still remains weak and when discussions touch upon important political questions, the courts turn into an auxiliary instrument of presidential authority (as happened in the course of the struggle with NTV [the Independent Television Company][7] and Khodarkovsky's trial). Attempts were even undertaken to strip one of Khodarkovsky's lawyers, Karin Moskalenko, of her license to practice law.

Many of Putin's defenders, including several Kremlin officials, are no longer even bothering to give the appearance that any democracy exists in Russia - not even a "sovereign" democracy or a "managed" democracy. They maintain that the retreat from democratic norms and values has allowed the government to address the citizens' needs more effectively.

It is known that the USSR under Brezhnev, who was the first to open and develop the Tiumen' oil fields, earned approximately $300 billion in oil sales. However, all this money was senselessly wasted in the arms race with the United States. The Soviet Union lost this competition and the Ural and Siberian forests became the final resting place for thousands of outdated tank models.

Putin proved to be wiser and more far-sighted than L.I. Brezhnev. He didn't listen to the entreaties of the military commanders - who never seemed to have enough money for the latest tanks, cannons, ships and aircraft. Enormous amounts of the dollars earned through oil sales were diverted into the government reserves to pay off the country's debts, while some of these earnings were allocated to raise pensions and increase the welfare of Russian citizens.

It is impossible to explain all these actions simply through Putin's good fortune, as the global press at times tries to depict it. Yet at the same time, the opinion that Vladimir Putin's campaign against democracy is bringing Russia stability and causing it to flourish is today becoming generally accepted. Whatever the success achieved by Putin's autocratic rule, these achievements would have been much greater in a democratic system.

What of the people? The people are silent. It had no choice but to spit on democracy once the authorities began to pay wages regularly and to increase pensions once in a while. When the opportunity to earn *baksy* [bucks] became available; when foreign goods and foodstuffs appeared in stores; and when they were allowed to travel abroad to wherever they wanted to go and whenever they wished, most people were willing to remain silent about political matters.

Despite Putin's temporary success, a cluster of unresolved problems still remain in Russia. Social services are in a sorry condition and corruption has become totally rampant. Social services have become so infected by dishonesty and irregularities that patients are forced to pay bribes to doctors for treatments and surgeries and parents are forced to cough up money for their children's admission to schools and to ensure good grades. Corruption has spread to higher education.

Most tragic in Putin's Russia is the complete lawlessness as a result of the regime's politicization of all the courts. But the people tolerate even this - seeing it as an unpleasant necessity. One of the clearest examples of the unlawfulness was the trial of Vladimir Khodarkovsky - one of Russia's wealthiest and most talented men - and the government's destruction of his famous and most effective company in Russia at the time, Yukos. By right the district court in Moscow, where the trial of Khodarkovsky took place, began to be called a "kangaroo court".

Putin's so-called "sovereign democracy" is full of examples of government retaliation against those who refuse to toe the line. The well-known historian and writer Boris Kuznetsov, the author of numerous accurate and honest books about the Great Patriotic War and Doctor of Historical Sciences, wrote an article that displeased the authorities. The institute, where he was working as a senior research fellow, received a phone call from the Kremlin. On the following day the institute director summoned him and recommended that he tender his resignation. The institute is dependent on the Kremlin, from which it receives government financial support. That was it: a prominent specialist and gifted man lost his job. Of course this is no totalitarian regime - under which he simply would have received a prison sentence or been shot.

In yet another flagrant case, Gavriil Popov, a Doctor of Economic Sciences and a prominent economist, wrote an objective and truthful book entitled: *Pravda o voine* [*Truth about the war*] for the 60th Anniversary of Victory Day. Not a single Moscow publisher wanted to touch the book. Gavriil Popov was forced to travel to America with a copy of the manuscript. In the course of two weeks, the New York publisher Liberty published it. I acquired a copy. Returning to Russia, Gavriil Popov was stopped at the border - together with 160 copies of his book. Without any explanations, officials confiscated every single copy of his book.

Yet another example: every autumn, "Russia's Boss" vacations in Sochi. At the end of his vacation, he always gathers the chief editors of the leading mass media. Typically 50-60 people arrive in Sochi in order to hear Putin's latest instructions. In 2008, now as the Russian Prime Minister, he organized an analogous meeting where the Editor-in-Chief of Ekho Moskvy, Aleksei Benediktov, who adopted a liberal (i.e. anti-Kremlin) position on the Russian-Georgian conflict, received harsh criticism. Benediktov attempted to defend his position, but Putin angrily hurled the following words in his face: "You're not a liberal, but a foe! Indeed, you'll have to answer for your incorrect actions."

There are many more examples I could cite if you wished. One can imagine the position of the average Russian in a system where justice is not blind.

The thought that Elena Bonner expressed in her interview with Radio Svoboda on the eve of her 85th birthday is seemingly convincing: "I dream of a different people in Russia." Is this great woman correct? Both yes and no; yes in the sense of that old truth that "any people get the government that they deserve." No, because Russia has never had and does not have a public demand for democracy and freedom. It is no simple task to free itself from its many centuries of serfdom and bondage. Let us remember that Russian peasants were freed from serfdom just a little more than 150 years ago. Soviet power didn't bring freedom and democracy to the workers, the peasants or the intellectuals. Stalin enslaved Russia for 30 years. For example, the collective farm peasants between 1932 and 1974 had no domestic passports and consequently they were bound to the villages in which they lived.

Specters of the past

A single apparatus has remained intact in its operation - albeit with numerous superficial name changes - throughout all of Soviet history and on into contemporary Russia: the ChK, GPU, NKVD, KGB and finally the FSB. Vladimir Vladimirovich Putin came from its ranks: the "Despicable Lieutenant Colonel" as the well-known human rights defender and publicist Vladimir Bukovsky called him.

President Putin has elevated the role of the latest incarnation of the State security apparatus - the FSB (Federal System of Security) - like no Soviet or Russian leader before him. Not even Stalin permitted himself to do what Putin has done. He has placed the FSB not only above the State itself, but also over all of the parties - including his own *Edinaia Rossiia* Party. Most of the Russian business elite today consist of former KGB/FSB officers.

"Russia's Boss" never misses a single anniversary event in the life of the FSB - taking advantage of them to meet with his Chekist comrades over bottles of champagne. This includes the day celebrating Felix Dzerzhinsky - the first director of the Bolshevik secret police - which the Chekists honor together with the president, or the day commemorating the former KGB Chairman Yurii Andropov, who held this post for 15 years. At Putin's direction, the Russian Ministry of Communications releases an annual set of stamps under the title: "Honorable Chekist". For example, in 2002 a set of stamps celebrating Vsevolod Balitsky was released as part of this series. He was a man who committed abuses and outrages in the Kiev ChK; in the middle of the 1920s he was appointed Chairman of the Ukraine GPU. He took part in organizing the 1931-1933 famine in the Ukraine and was executed in 1937 during Stalin's Great Terror.

For his part, Yurii Andropov conceived two new techniques in the KGB praxis: consigning dissidents to mental institutions and forcibly expelling others from the country. In addition, he created special departments within the KGB responsible for "ideological control" over the people. Political murders occur more frequently in the practice of the FSB.

Who are these victims? Why are people being killed? We can find, I believe, the most accurate answer to these questions in an article published back in 2007 in the newspaper *Novaia gazeta* under the title: "Kak v Rossii sovershaiut ubiistva v interesakh gosudarstva" ["How homicides are being perpetrated in Russia in the interests of the State"]. The government has assumed the role of killers!

According to this article, the Russian special services have created a parallel structure for carrying out extrajudicial sentences. The article rests its case on a document in the possession of *Novaia gazeta*, which is a secret directive to the Russian special services that sanctions murder "in the interests of the State".

Igor Korol'kov, an analyst on the staff of *Novaia gazeta*, published excerpts from this directive back in 2002 in the *Moskovskie novosti* [*Moscow News*]. However, the events connected with the murders of Anna Politkovskaia and the former FSB Lieutenant Colonel Aleksandr Litvinenko - as well as the attempted poisoning of Egor Gaidar - help us take a fresh look at this document. As Igor Korol'kov writes:

> ... The document... is naturally against the Constitution, the norms of criminal law and any ideas that we may share about a State where extrajudicial punishments are not possible...[8]

This controversial document carries no signature or seal of secrecy, which leads one to doubt its authenticity. However, the man who passed the document to the journalist informed him in words that it was signed by Hero of Russia Colonel Seliverstov and that he had removed the classification markings while photocopying the document so that, as he put it: "Journalists wouldn't have any extra problems."

This supposedly secret instruction, which consists of 70 pages, explains much that has been happening in Russia over the last 15 years. It consolidates dozens of terrorist acts - conducted in Russia and abroad - under a single strategic plan.

In an interview with the *Novaia gazeta* analyst, Colonel Seliverstov claimed that he had never signed any documents similar to the one in question, but declared: "The one who passed this document to you has perpetrated a State crime." Instead of meeting with the analyst, Seliverstov sent a man who presented himself as an "Officer of the Competent Agencies". He attempted to persuade Korol'kov that the document itself was not criminal, just as a knife originally wasn't intended as a murder weapon. The unidentified man explained: "The entire question is how the instrument is used; a knife can also slice bread." He persistently urged Korol'kov not to publish the document or else "the same difficulties might arise as did for Pas'ko and Nikitin." Grigorii Pas'ko and Aleksandr Nikitin were former Navy officers who were accused of divulging State secrets. Experts on the special services that the journalist consulted about the secret document observed that such a document could not appear without a more general directive at the government level. This coincided with the statement made by the man who passed Korol'kov the copy of the document: He revealed that there was a secret government decree in the process of development - under which this secret instruction was compiled. Further, the unidentified informant stated that the secret government decree's creation was linked to the country's first deputy prime minister at the very beginning of the 1990s, Iurii Skokov.

Putin constantly bombards Russian citizens with frightening messages; following Stalin's example he likens Russia to a besieged fortress. "There are enemies, enemies, enemies everywhere!" Putin shouts and the political establishment falls in line behind him - echoing his messages. Stalin, who conceived the term "enemy of the people", used it to terrorize the public. Putin has adopted the term "enemy of Russia" - and "enemies of Russia" should be killed. Allow me to cite several examples on this subject:

Igor' Domikov: a *Novaia gazeta* journalist. He spoke up against the abuse of power in Russia. In the year 2000, unknown men beat him to death; the killers have not been identified.

Zelimkhan Iandarbiev: former acting president of the Chechen Republic of Ishkeria between 1996 and 1997 and General Dudaev's assistant.[9] Living in exile in the Qatari capital of Doha, he was killed by a bomb planted in his sall-terrain vehicle. The killers were caught and turned out to be three military intelligence officers stationed in the Russian Embassy. One was released due to diplomatic immunity but two were put on trial, found guilty and sentenced to death. At the request of the Russian Government, the death sentences were commuted to life sentences in prison. On 23 December 2004 Qatar agreed to extradite the prisoners to Russia where they were to serve out the rest of their sentences. However, the agents received a hero's welcome and soon disappeared from public view…

Iurii Shchekochikhin: an outstanding journalist, who in his final years worked for *Novaia gazeta.* The FSB could never forgive him for exposing the widespread network of informants in Russia. He constantly spoke out against corrupt officials. He was a true democrat. His last fight was his bombshell article published under the title: 'Chernaia tamozhnia' ['Black customs offices'] in *Novaia gazeta.* It was about a racket being run by customs officials and FSB officers. They were deliberately placing lower values on large shipments of furniture arriving from abroad, which allowed them to reduce the import duties. A prosecutor opened a case against them. Iurii Shchekochikhin, a deputy of the State Duma, received threats and was warned not to stick his nose into other people's affairs. The journalist refused to drop his coverage of the case. In 2003 he was poisoned by some unknown culprit or culprits. The investigation into the case was closed and the killers were never found. A prosecutor ordered the *Novaia gazeta* editorial board not to conduct its own investigation into the entire matter. Iurii had been poisoned in the Kremlin Hospital. An investigation into his murder ended with no charges being filed.

Anna Politkovskaia: a fearless woman and a talented, honest journalist for *Novaia gazeta* who wrote many articles against the banditry of the Russian officials in Chechnya. She published three books: *Russkii dnevnik* [*Russian diary*], *Putinskaia Rossiia* [*Putin's Russia*] and *Za chto?* [*For what?*]. They were published with unbelievable difficulty in limited print runs - partially at her own expense. In the West they were published in large numbers and received high praise. One can call this fragile woman a fighter against Fascism. In 2006 she was murdered by unknown persons in the entrance to the building where she lived. Her body was found in an elevator; after a long delay, arrests were made in the case. Eventually three men were charged with directly aiding Politkovskaia's killer - though an FSB colonel suspected of playing a leading role in the organization of the murder was never charged due to insufficient evidence. After a rare jury trial, all three men were acquitted of Politkovskaia's murder in February 2009. Before the trial even ended, Stanislav Markelov - a lawyer who investigated many of the abuses documented by Politkovksaia - and a freelance contributor to *Novaia gazeta* named Anastasia Baburova were murdered in a double shooting on 19 January 2009. A new investigation of Politkovskaia's murder has been opened.

"Yet we asked for no honors
Or expect decorations for what we did.
For us, Russia's overall glory
Was the soldier's award."

G. Pozhenian

17
Stricken from Memory of the War

Now I want to discuss Stalin's criminal offence - which still hasn't been fully revealed. A year after the Great Victory, more than 100,000 crippled invalids - armless and legless - at Stalin's order were sent away to remote locations of the country. This was done so that they wouldn't besmirch the pompous laurels of the Generalissimo with their poverty and appearance.

Wait for me and I'll return

The third year of the war was under way. In cities and villages, thousands and thousands of families were being overwhelmed with an increasing number of somber death notices. Disabled soldiers were returning home from the front: one-armed, one-legged, epileptic, blind, deaf and mute with faces showing the effects of severe burns - not a single war had ever known such barbarism.

O, grief! Mothers were crying, grandfathers and fathers were heavily sighing: "*Voina – ne mat' rodna* ['War is not a dear mother']. Every single misfortune from it is accursed." As a rule though, the invalids were welcomed warmly: "God showed his mercy - a man very much alive has returned."

War had flared up everywhere on Russia's vast expanses and elsewhere. Its readily understandable adversities were joined by incomprehensible woes. In the process - on a never-before-seen scale - families began receiving notes that were not entirely clear at first glance: "Your husband (or son) has gone missing."

What to make of such news? A man isn't a needle; he was a soldier! Where are his combat comrades, where is his platoon or company commander? Was he taken prisoner? Did he join the partisans or is he lying low somewhere behind German lines? An enormous expanse of Soviet land was still under German occupation. Mothers and wives went running to the military enlistment centers and wrote letters to the units in which their children or husband was serving, or turned to local authorities for answers. Old men reminded: "Such things didn't happen in the 1905 War or the First World War. Newspapers printed the names of the killed and wounded. But now there is only silence."

There was one more supplement to the unhappy news: the missing became ever larger in number. They went uncounted.

Did the Soviet people know the truth at the time? Were they aware of the cruel catastrophe at the front in 1941; about the destruction of the acting Red Army in the first weeks of the war; about the capture of millions of Red Army soldiers and officers; about their terrible fate in the German camps in the fall and winter of 1941-1942; or about the mass executions of commissars, communists and Jews? Not many were…

Bells began to ring! An alarming outcry began: "What have become of the defenders of the Fatherland - our sons?" The old men kept silent and advised: "Don't torment yourselves; have patience and wait." However, here's the obstacle that arose out of all this: the Generalissimo banned the word "prisoner" from public use. Having parted with his conscience at some point in his past, the Supreme Commander issued directives that stated: "We have no prisoners - only traitors."

The verb "to wait" somehow imperceptibly became the faith and hope of the people - to which one of the best frontline poets of the war, Konstantin Simonov, successfully responded. He wrote the marvelous verse "Wait for me and I'll return …" The literary bureaucrats greeted this verse with disdain. In these lines there was no heroic pathos; no patriotism; no rabid hatred of the foe … all those things that in the war years formed the foundation of Soviet propaganda. They saw in them only schmaltzy doggerel.

It isn't known how Simonov's poem became known to Stalin. He immediately saw its enormous power - capable of elevating the fallen spirits of the nation as a result of the Red Army's endless reverses at the front. He seized upon Simonov like a magic wand - capable of saving his exalted status. An order immediately went out: publish the author in the main Party newspaper *Pravda*; print his verse in all the central and frontline press and disseminate it. Don't spare any paper!

Very quickly, the poem entitled: "Wait for me and I'll return …" - made famous by a mortal god - became a unique lifebuoy. Millions of people grasped it. The verse was rewritten out by hand, memorized and recited in the morning and at bedtime just like a prayer. They particularly comforted human souls when letters showered down from hospitals: "Come pick up your invalid son." There were so many of them!

Only 40 years after the end of the Great Patriotic War did the first official estimate of the number of war invalids appear in a book released by the Russian Ministry of Defense in 1993 under the editorship of Colonel General Krivoshein. Here are the cruel statistics: A total of 3,798,800 men were discharged from the Red Army due to age, illness or wounds. Of these, 2,576,000 were invalids - including, we'll note, more than 450,000 armless or legless men. Horrifying numbers! Not a single war has known such a number of soldiers left totally disabled. The cited figures force one to ponder them and allow the confident assertion that a significant number of the wounded were a result of the Stalinist strategy and tactics of combat operations - to achieve victory "at any cost" - which were accompanied by the complete failure to hold commanders responsible for the enormous casualties.

Was Marshal Zhukov actually speaking the truth in his conversation with D. Eisenhower? He once informed the American general that Soviet commanders often sent soldiers into attacks across known minefields. One can only guess how D. Eisenhower took Zhukov's information. If any American commander had acted just once in that way, he would have immediately been relieved of his post and sent before a court martial panel.

It has long been known that invalids of any war are unloved - neither by the victors or the vanquished. For the former they are evidence of a difficult victory and the ineptness of commanding officers; for the latter they are a bitter reminder of the defeat.

I think that it will be interesting to the reader to become familiar with a document taken from the FSB archives. It gives a picture of the lives of invalids in the initial postwar years. An article by a Ph.D. Candidate in History, A.I. Vol'khin, entitled: 'Operativnaia rabota territorial'nykh organov NKGB sredi invalidov Velikoi Otechestvennoi voiny v 1943-1945' ['Operational work of the territorial organs of the NKGB [People's Commissariat of State Security] among invalids of the Great Patriotic War in 1943-1945'] contains an excerpt from this document. In its own way this unique article is interesting first of all not by its contents, but by its place of publication and the author's post. The article was published on the official website of the Federal Security Service. Thus, the author's point of view to a certain extent reflects the position of this agency. Moreover, the author exclusively uses materials from the Central Archives of the Russian Federation's FSB.

Permit me to cite an extended excerpt from this article:

> ... In the war years, in the rear regions of the Soviet Union - especially in rural areas - invalids were returning from the front in an uninterrupted stream. Their presence genuinely complicated the operational situation in places. From the year 1943, information began to arrive systematically in the USSR NKGB about the rising tension in a number of rear regions connected with adapting invalids to the new housing, social-political and psychological conditions of life. Disorganization, hunger, diseases and the in-

difference and abuse of local authorities: all this has given rise to widespread anger and the dissatisfaction of the invalids, who have at times adopted a destructive attitude. There are also data about the presence of traitors and German intelligence agents among the invalids.

In connection with this, the USSR NKGB in the course of 1943-1944 sent through the channels of [its] Second Branch a number of directives to the local organs of State Security demanding that through their network of agents they make a study of the processes occurring among the war invalids. The task was given to keep Party and State organs informed about shortcomings in job placement work (and the rendering of necessary material and medical support to invalids of the war) and to expose and arrest the organizers of anti-Soviet activity - the traitors and the agents of enemy intelligence organs. Implementing the directives' instructions of the central apparatus, the NKGB conducted surveillance of the work of hospitals and the local councils and organs of social security on questions of medical service; of job placement for the invalids; of the timely arrangement and payment of pensions and allowances to them; and of the real assistance [to them] in resolving housing problems.

Agent surveillance of the contingent of invalids of the Patriotic War was set up: traitors; German intelligence agents; and people who engaged in anti-Soviet agitation, sabotage and wrecking were exposed and arrested. For example, the Uzbek SSR NKGB kept up-to-date records on 554 war invalids - the majority of which had been taken prisoner by the Germans. More than 30 invalids were arrested by this same NKGB organ for various crimes. The Krasnodar NKGB District Bureau over the month of 1944 alone exposed 103 invalids who had formerly been prisoners of war and had returned to the Soviet rear under suspicious circumstances. The Molotov NKGB Oblast Bureau arrested 13 war invalids for anti-Soviet work. Analogous measures were taken by the NKGB bureaus of the Udmurt Autonomous Soviet Socialist Republic; the Krasnoiarsk District; and the Novosibirsk, Smolensk, Briansk, Chita, Vologda and other oblasts.

In the reports from the territorial organs of State Security, various forms of anti-Soviet work were recorded - the initiators of which were invalids of the Patriotic War. The most widespread manifestation of their socio-economic dissatisfaction was speeches against the collective farms. In Molotov Oblast, war invalid K. called upon the collective farmers to stage an organized protest against collective forms of labor. In the Sharypov region of Krasnodar District, invalid M. - who was working as a collective farm Chairman - according to agents' information deliberately delayed the execution of plans for grain deliveries to the State and conducted anti-Soviet agitation among the collective farmers (designed to bring about the collapse of the collective farm). In September 1944, M. - in the presence of a group of collective farmers - said: "After this war a good life will come; kulaks will return from exile and will demand the return of their homes and property that were previously taken from them. Thus now it is necessary bear down even more on our households and personal gardens for no matter how much we work, everything will go to the State and we'll again be sitting through the winter hungry." M. was arrested.

Isolated cases of group protests with the participation of war invalids against collective farm leadership were assessed as especially dangerous for Soviet authority. In the village of Kozhevo in the Komi Autonomous Soviet Socialist Republic, a "Union of War Invalids" consisting of a group of military servicemen who had returned from the front after being wounded was organized by T. - a former major in the Red Army. Meeting in the apartment of Guards Private A., the invalids conducted anti-Soviet discussions. Slanderous inventions spread among the collective farmers in connection with the dissolution of the Comintern and the opening of churches - and they agitated for the dissolution of the collective farms. A group of former kulaks - "wreckers of collective farm production" - headed by invalids of the Patriotic War A. and K., was arrested in the Churachinsk area of the Chuvash Autonomous Soviet Socialist Republic by agents of the NKGB's District Department. An investigation established that the accused persons composed and presented a slanderous statement in March 1944 at a regional committee meeting of the VKP(b) [All-Communist Party (Bolshevik) in which they accused the board of directors of a collective farm of abuses. Then on their own - without the knowledge of the village Soviet and collective farm board of directors - they arranged a meeting of collective farmers at which they removed the collective farm Chairman Party member Osipov from his post and selected a new board of directors headed by A. At a collective farm gathering, A. "brought slander against the local communists" and K. "threatened collective farm Chairman Osipov with murder". At his arrest, a revolver was seized from K.

Threats and the carrying-out of terrorist acts on the part of invalids of the Patriotic War are noted in many of the reports from the local NKBG organs. In October 1944, collective farm Chairman Zakharov was murdered in the Krasnoufimsk region of Sverdlovsk Oblast. The murder was done by war invalid T. - a machine-tractor station tractor driver who had in the past been put on trial for hooliganism. T. was characterized as an idler; a violator of labor discipline who regarded the demanding Zakharov hostilely. In the Chekmagush region of the Bashkir Autonomous Soviet Socialist Republic, K. - a war invalid and the deputy chairman of the collective farm "Udarnik" - engaged in the theft of collective farm grain and tried to persuade a group of collective farmers to murder the chairman under the pretext of the necessity of halting the expropriation of grain by the State. In Orel Oblast, war invalid N. wounded the secretary of the rural council Sukhorukovaia with a Finnish knife because she incorrectly filled out documents for his brother - as a result of which his brother was mobilized for the Red Army. At his arrest, N. declared: "It's all the same to me now ... to be free or in prison." In the Koverinsky region of Riazan Oblast, in October 1944 Borisov - a Communist Party member who was an invalid of the Patriotic War and the chairman of the collective farm "Vozrozhdenie" - was murdered by a shot from a revolver. Through an investigation it was established that the murder was committed by a group of war invalids who were plundering collective farm property and violating labor discipline. In the Krasnodar Territory's city of Eisk in July 1944, a group of war invalids beat up police officers at the marketplace. Having gathered a crowd of up to 400 men in the street they chased the policemen with shouts of: "Smash the City Executive Council so that we'll be allowed to trade".

It must be noted that terror and the terroristic attitude of a portion of the invalids of the Patriotic War fully accords to the logic of the military-political life of the country in the 1930s and 1940s, which gave rise to a mass psychology of conflict.

The difficult living conditions of the families; cases of abuses by local responsible individuals in the service sector; the crudest violations of the laws when granting allowances and pensions; rejections of petitions; official red tape; the failure to provide tax benefits; and much else: these are several of the antecedents that provoke war invalids to commit crimes. In addition an intensive process of social dissolution was occurring among them. A portion of the war invalids - who'd been tossed onto the roadside of life - engaged in speculation, got drunk and made nuisances of themselves at marketplaces and were drawn by criminal elements into swindling, thefts and banditry which had an immediate effect on the situation of public security in the country.

In the years 1943-1945 a situation formed in the country where it became impossible to solve the problem of invalids of the Patriotic War who were inclined to anti-social forms of conduct by repressive measures alone on the part of the government, while the mechanism of the socio-economic adaptation of them to the conditions of peaceful life were still only being worked out.

Special efforts of the NKGB's territorial organs were concentrated on exposing and unmasking war invalids who were simultaneously agents of the German special services. In Molotov Oblast's city of Kizel, M. - born in 1915 and a former candidate member of the Communist Party and war invalid - was arrested. An investigation had established that in 1941 - having been taken prisoner by the Germans - he had escaped the prison camp and spent some time living in Smolensk where he was picked up by the police during an identity check and recruited by a Special Service officer, Wagner. M. maintained observation over the conduct of the Smolensk population and reported to Wagner on those suspected of taking part in the struggle against the German occupiers in return for monetary awards…

Guided by directives of the GKO [State Defense Committee], the USSR SNK [Council of People Commissars] and the TsK VKP(b) [Central Committee of the All-Communist Party (Bolsheviks), the territorial organs of State Security set up agent surveillance of the contingent of invalids of the Patriotic War with the aim of revealing harmful elements among them; of strictly suppressing any anti-government manifestations coming under Article 58 of the 1926 RSFSR Criminal Code. In connection with the expanded interpretation of Article 58.10 (anti-Soviet propaganda and agitation), a portion of the invalids was unjustly held criminally responsible. Simultaneously, informing the Party and Soviet organs about the contradictory processes that were occurring among the war invalids - and the shortcomings and abuses of local organs of authority in the matter of arranging facilities for invalids - the NKGB organs attempted to eliminate the present tension among the latter and to improve the moral-political situation in the USSR's rear regions…

Good grief! Not a single kind word addressed to the former frontline soldiers who were now invalids. Despite the difficulties of the postwar period in the life of the country; despite the red tape, departmentalism and oppressive atmosphere of the Stalin regime, war invalids of the so-called 2nd and 3rd Categories returned to peaceful life and as far as they were capable, lived and worked honorably.

War invalids of the so-called 1st Category - the disabled (armless, legless, or blind) - wound up in the most difficult position. The Soviet State, obliged to look after its defenders at the front, was unready to care for the invalids - especially in such an enormous number as proved to be the case. Instead of serious support - including housing, medical assistance, rehabilitation and material aid - Stalin's regime for all practical purposes abandoned tens of thousands of war heroes to the whims of fate.

Of course, when the war ended the country was in a difficult situation. It was devastated. Millions of citizens were living in dugouts, barracks, cellars or were crowded into communal apartments. The people were consuming the final remnants of the food supplied through Lend-Lease. Entire cities, mines, factories, schools and hospitals had to be rebuilt from the ground up. The national treasury had been totally drained. All this is known and understandable. But among the entire sad list of postwar obligations, in the first place was the Soviet State's sacred duty to look after the fate of the war invalids. During the war, the Soviet Government had issued several lengthy decrees about aiding the invalids. Not a single one of them was carried out. Here is just one example: Of the 35 homes for invalids planned by 1950, only four were eventually constructed. The country had only two homes for invalids when the war ended.

In 1948 I was studying in the Moscow Publishing Institute by correspondence. One day the wife of a war invalid, who had lost both legs in the war, appealed to us (the former frontline soldiers who were now students). He had just enrolled to study in the Institute, but he needed assistance. His name was Kolia and his wife's name was Lusia. They had been in love with each other even before the war when they had been fellow classmates. Lusia waited for Kolia through all the years of the war and didn't reject him when he returned as a cripple. By the time she had made her appeal to us, she had graduated from the Medical Institute and had become a doctor.

We helped Kolia. Every week we took turns traveling to his home - bringing him our lecture notes, which we explained to him in detail. We taught him to write reviews; took dictation together with him; discussed his essays with him; and helped him with the textbooks. Kolia successfully graduated from the Institute and began to work as an editor at the publishing company *Znanie* [Knowledge]. We cherished and loved this fellow. However, unquestionably Lusia was his main pillar of support in life. She "scrounged" a pair of prosthetic legs for him and taught him to walk with their assistance. She procured medicine for him; she fed him and gave him drink as if he was her child - and when special vehicles for invalids appeared in the 1960s, she set him up behind the steering wheel of one. Cheerful, kind: that's how I remember Lusia. The birth of a son, Aleksei, became the greatest joy in this family.

Unfortunately, the fate of many war invalids - especially the disabled and the blind - proved to be much less fortunate than Kolia's. Some of them simply had nowhere to go after the war: their villages had been put to the torch during the war or their childhood homes were now ruins. The war brought great tragedy to others: their other family members didn't survive the war. Many of the cripples opted in their helpless conditions not to return to their families. To be sure, they were primarily counting upon government assistance. But the government abandoned all these unfortunate men - in their 20s who had lost their youth irretrievably in the war and had become helpless - to the streets.

They wandered from city to city homeless and became beggars - adding to the country's poverty. Kind craftsmen fashioned a means to move around for those left without legs. They knocked together several boards into a little platform and attached little wheels to it.

Many of these invalids' families had official death notices for them - or word that they'd gone missing in action - and were continuing to wait for their return. Meanwhile they were moving through marketplaces in carts; propelling themselves with wooden poles; or hobbling around on crutches or crudely manufactured prosthetic legs. They wandered wherever the road would take them and crowded the train stations and streets near movie theaters, bakeries and beer stands.

They were begging - drinking away what little money they received only then to resume their begging… appealing with outstretched hands to passersby. A host of recollections about crippled accordionists and blind people clinging to sighted people have been preserved. They would sing sad songs and then again extend their hand for handouts. Here is one such mournful story, told to me by a friend:

> … I grew up in Moscow in the Iakimanka District. There, a peg-legged man spent every day at a beer stand. There were a lot of alcoholics back then. The peg-legged man had been badly disfigured in the war, but he was always wearing a jacket with his Orders and medals. He only had one leg; one arm had been amputated at the elbow and he had lost his other arm entirely. He was blind. Every morning his mother would bring him in a cart with wheels on it and leave him at the beer stand. Then, of course, everyone plied him with beer. Once I became an unwilling witness to an old woman who walked up to him and asked: "Sonny, perhaps you can ask someone to finish you off?" He answered her: "Mother, I've never once asked. Indeed, no one wants to take such a sin upon themselves." This scene has always remained in my memory…

It was the month of May 1946

On one spring night, an evil deed was perpetrated: various dates are given for it, but dating it isn't important. Here's what is known… In May 1946, NKVD officers and specially selected police detachments rounded up the war invalids in all the major cities of the country. They picked them all up one after the other wherever they were taking shelter, threw them into paddy wagons and took them to train stations where they were placed in special rail cars with bars blocking the windows and sent off to remote areas of the country.

Before being banished to internal exile, it was explained to the stunned cripples in flowery language: "This is being done for your benefit. You will be living with dignity as befits victorious heroes! You will be well-treated and fed - and receive medical help!"

Russia has an old saying: "Whoever has shame also has a conscience." The Blackshirts (how else can those villains be called who have no fear of God's wrath?) pounced on the unfortunates at an order from above without any shame or conscience.

What does a person never have enough of other than the capability to distinguish a truth from a lie? Some of the young disabled veterans believed the explanations they were given: "See, the government has had second thoughts and has remembered us."

A few dramatic lines of verse have been preserved on this matter:

Stand up at full height

When one no longer has legs

Clasp a hand

When one has nothing to clasp.

There are no more words

We are no more

Only one thing has remained:

Victory! Our victory!

Where to settle, albeit under lock and key, the absolutely helpless disabled and the blind in a country that had been devastated by war? Where to exile tens of thousands of people forever? Someone came up with a devilish idea: to place the invalids in monasteries that had been empty for a long time. Monasteries that had been famous in Russia in olden times - Kirillo-Belozersky, Goritsky, Aleksandro-Svirsky, Valaamsky - became asylums for the war invalids that had been expelled from the cities. How similar this conducted "operation" was to an analogous event in Nazi Germany when at Hitler's order, they dealt with "defective" Germans who were spoiling the appearance of the Aryan race!

Understandably, the mass "cleansing" of war invalids from the cities couldn't take place entirely unnoticed. If they asked, Soviet people were told that the victorious State could no longer tolerate the poverty of the invalids. It was going to take care of its defenders. Not everyone believed them. They were shouting and rushing to block the tracks. Lord, what could the totally disabled have done?

Stories of eyewitnesses to those events have been preserved. Here is one of them, as told by Iurii Andreevich Bagrov, an old policeman who has spent his entire life in Kiev:

> ... I was seven years old when we came back to Kiev from evacuation. We were living in a building near the Bessarabka neighborhood; my school was not far from there. Around the Bessarabka right up to the "Second Bessarabka" where now the Sports Palace stands, there were "lockers" along the roads – stalls - where the collective farmers sold produce. Invalids, primarily legless ones in carts, loved to gather around these stalls. They played card games for small wagers like Blackjack, Thirty-one and Skat. They also ran shell games. They weren't stealing, but to empty the pockets of some peasant in a card game or shell game was considered a virtue. When it became cold, the invalids spent the nights in earthen bunkers they had dug along the Sobach'e Trail (near Lesi Ukrainki Street). If one of them didn't want to bed down there or was unable to go there for the night, he would sleep beneath one of the stalls.
>
> One day when I was walking home from school, I lapsed unconscious and dropped from hunger. Mama had either lost her ration cards or someone had stolen them from her, so we went hungry. When I came to, I saw a hand in front of me offering me a piece of bread and I heard a voice say: "Eat, kid, eat." That's how I became acquainted with an invalid, Uncle Grisha, as I called him. "Uncle" was only around 19 or 20 years old and he had lost both his legs in the war. As Uncle Grisha fed me the bread, he said: "Kid, whenever you're walking home from school, drop by here, OK?" So I began to go see Uncle Grisha every day. I would take a seat next to him on a stone (he would obligingly spread something over it for me and remark: "Just so you don't get prostatitis") and I would watch as he played cards. Once, when I dropped by to see him after school, Uncle Grisha told me without tearing himself away from his card game: "Here you are, kid" and stretched out his hand to me, which was clutching something. I still recall this partly melted sticky toffee which he had obtained somewhere for me. It was the first piece of candy I ever had.
>
> So, for the next several months I would go to see Uncle Grisha after school. I found out that he had lost his legs in the Korsun-Shevchenkovskii pocket. In 1943 he was 17 years old and he had been conscripted along with thousands of other young shavers and without even being handed a weapon, he was thrown

into this slaughterhouse. They told him: "You'll get your weapon in combat!" He wasn't even issued a uniform; they didn't want to waste it on this cannon fodder. Later, after the hospital and demobilization, he didn't return home to his village. He knew that a superfluous mouth to feed in a peasant family was a terrible burden. Only one who works lives. Each and every day, around 400 of these invalids gathered in the Bessarabka. They played, drank and sometimes fought among themselves. They didn't fear anyone - these young men in their 20s - because they'd long ago lost everything. They respected only one local police officer - who himself had served in the frontlines of the war and had been wounded - and as the invalids would say, he was "one of their wave." They couldn't tolerate the throngs of dapper "frontline men" that strutted around with one or two Orders on their chests. They called them "Michurinists". I asked: "Why 'Michurinists'?" Uncle Grisha replied: "Because while we were fighting, they were sitting it out in the far rear eating Michurin pears."[1]

It was the month of May - just one year after the victory. It was a time of hunger, but also interesting; I had an older friend. Once, just like always, I arrived in the Bessarabka after school and before even reaching the customary place I was struck by a strange, alarming silence. It was eerie and quiet; even the sellers were speaking in a half-whisper. At first I didn't understand what was going on and only after a bit did I notice… there was not a single invalid in the Bessarabka! Later, I was told in a whisper that the night before the [security] organs had rounded up all the Kiev invalids, packed them aboard trains and shipped them off to Solovki[2] without any charges; without any trial or investigation just so they wouldn't "discomfit" citizens by their appearance. It seems to me that the invalids primarily prompted the hostility of those who had actually sat out the war in rear headquarters. Rumors went around that Zhukov himself had personally organized this action…[3]

Further, Bagrov added to his childhood recollections:

…At this time several thousand invalids all over Kiev were shipped off. They didn't touch invalids that were living with their families. The "purge of invalids" was repeated several more times. However they were sending the invalids back then to "homes", which incidentally were also much like prisons. From then on, there were never any more invalids in the parades. They were simply swept out of the way like an unpleasant memory. So the Motherland

> never again recalled its best sons. Even their names slipped away into oblivion - this, when much later those invalids still alive began to receive benefits, rations and similar goodies. Meanwhile those - the legless and armless young men - were simply buried alive at Solovki. If the invalid had a wife, no one touched him. Incidentally, in just this way by a sudden marriage, many were saved from repressions back then. Fortunately there were a lot of unattached and heartbroken women at the time - more than a million. Only unmarried invalids and beggars, which incidentally at the time was a natural way to earn a little money for bread, were subject to being exiled...[4]

Allow me to cite another short recollection of an eyewitness:

> ... In my childhood in the city of Tula, I saw a lot of such men wearing Orders and with an outstretched hand; also those without legs on makeshift padded pedestals. An upside-down cap was attached to a plank for donations. There was one such man - loud, who cursed vociferously and inveighed against the authorities - near the market. This was now after Stalin's death. By evening he would be laying as drunk as a skunk. Later somehow they all disappeared at once; all these cripples and the blind men who would walk along the passenger rail cars with an accordion - together with a sighted person - and the shell-shocked deaf veterans with such incommunicable torment on their faces. Only one-armed and one-legged men remained. I had two such kinsmen. They passed away naturally, but prematurely. I suppose the truth is hidden somewhere. They whisked them away out of eyesight and where they took them I do not know.
>
> I was in the city on short visits. I lived in a village outside Tula. There we had our own "stream" of vagrants that would pass through begging. They were searching for family members and friends - from the Urals to the West and back again. They walked from one end to the other. None of them had money. Our area in Central Russia was an intersection of the paths they took. We would give them something to eat. Our home was on the outskirts of our village and a lot of them would come by our place. I would bring them something to eat and drink...[5]

Yet the newspapers; the families; the army; writers and historians were all silent - not a single word or half-word. The people didn't speak up for their children. More exactly, everyone back then had been reduced to servile obedience. Only the Boss back then said aloud what was on his mind. It seems to me that he was thinking the following: "They lost an arm or leg - that's war. We didn't start it. They've forgotten about their oath; about the Motherland that raised them. They're wagging their tongues; they're cursing Soviet power, the swine! Yet Soviet power cares about them more than their own mothers. They've smeared their own victorious country!"

There is so much cynicism, guile and crap in such thoughts! Looking back on that difficult time for the country after the war, naturally a question arises: Could Stalin have acted differently or, more accurately, should he have acted differently?

Let's reckon a bit over this together, dear reader. Really, couldn't the Supreme Leader have sent the returning war invalids back to rear hospitals for additional treatment and rehabilitation for a short period of time - say, one or two years? Really, was the Supreme Leader incapable of forcing the local Party and State bureaucrats to come together with the city and village councils to look for possibilities and ways to assume the responsibility to aid the war invalids? Really, couldn't the Supreme Leader have ordered the army to take some of the responsibility for caring for the war invalids?

At the time, I was still serving in the Red Army. Our division was stationed in the city of Suma in the Ukraine. I'm confident that having received such an order we could have done a lot, quite a lot, for the war invalids.

Unfortunately, there are few who know in detail about the sad fact I've related. The subject was closed for many long years and was shameful for the country. I'll add that it has been little studied. The forced round-up of the war invalids and their exile to backwater places - as remote as possible from the country that was "rejoicing over the victory" - was the simplest solution for Stalin's regime.

Gradually the Soviet Union recovered from the cruel war. However, poverty and begging in the cities never fully disappeared and veterans and war invalids comprised a significant portion of this lumpen proletariat. It turns out that the mopping-up operation implemented against them in 1946 wasn't complete. It is also possible that a fresh wave of invalids appeared - men who'd been discharged from hospitals after the war directly out into the streets.

> In the mid-1950s, as mentioned in the recollection above, a second mass "operation to liquidate poverty" took place; that's what it was called, but in fact it amounted to a repetition of the first sweep through the cities to round up and send away war invalids. Before I speak about this second operation, I'll cite a document that has been preserved - an inter-office memorandum from G.M. Malenkov to N.S. Khrushchev:
>
> ... The USSR MVD [Ministry of Internal Affairs] is reporting that despite the measures it has taken, such an intolerable sight as begging still continues to have a place in the major cities and industrial centers of the country. In the second half of the year 1951, 107,766 panhandlers were detained by the police in the cities and on the railroads - followed by 156,817 in 1952 and

182,342 in 1953. War and work invalids comprise 70 per cent of the total number of detained beggars. The organs of social security and local Councils of Workers' Deputies are paying insufficient attention to the work to prevent and liquidate poverty, and are poorly handling the organization of housing for the beggars in homes for invalids and the elderly.

The struggle against panhandling is also complicated by the fact that a certain portion of the impoverished invalids and elderly reject being sent into homes for invalids, while those who have been placed in them often voluntarily leave them and return to begging on the streets. By the order from the Presidium of the USSR Supreme Soviet "On measures of the struggle with anti-social and parasitic elements", it was foreseen to send those individuals who engage in begging - who shun socially useful work and lead parasitic lifestyles (as well as those vagrants who have no job or place of residence) - to special settlements in a remote area of the USSR with their obligatory enlistment in labor activity. However, the police organs cannot broadly use this order in the struggle against begging because a majority of the beggars are not capable of working or are aged and don't fall under the decree's jurisdiction. Moreover, the investigation and checking of documents on these people requires holding them under arrest for a lengthy period of time, which wasn't foreseen by the law. As a result of the causes indicated above, the number of people who engage in begging remains significant while in certain places it is not only not falling, but is even growing… In order to prevent the voluntary departure of inmates from homes for the invalids and the elderly who don't desire to live there - and to deprive them of the opportunity to engage in begging - a portion of the existing homes for the invalids and the elderly should be converted into homes of the closed type with special regulations.

Minister of the MVD

S. Kruglov.[6]

This document is not only gloomy, it is also cynical. The Minister of Internal Affairs is comparing war invalids to "anti-Soviet elements" and is proposing to put them away in boarding homes of the "closed type".

To this point little is known about the removal of the invalids from society and their forced expulsion from the cities. By that time the first invalid homes had appeared and some invalids went to them - but really, in the tens of thousands?

Unfortunately, the military leadership of the country - including Zhukov - as well as the other glorified marshals and generals, didn't lift a finger to help their former troops.

One of the most well-known places where the war invalids were exiled was Valaam Island, where already for a long time an enormous monastery complex had been standing empty. More is known as well about the fate of those invalids who were exiled to Valaam because this island - located in Lake Ladoga 200 kilometers from St. Petersburg - also happened to be a major tourist attraction. Thanks to the guides and tourists who from time to time penetrated the closed zone where the invalids were living, a few fragments of evidence about how the unfortunates lived and died have nevertheless reached us.

The Mournful Road to Valaam

War invalids were held on Valaam Island from 1946 to 1984. Many of the tourists who spent time on the island in Soviet times didn't even imagine that somewhere quite nearby them was a closed zone where war veterans, many of them armless and legless, were living in monastery facilities practically in total isolation. They'd been brought there by force like prisoners.

Those left disabled by the war were dying on Valaam from day to day due to unendurable anguish and their extreme debilities. A few of them attempted to break out of the inhumane conditions and to run away - their frozen bodies were found on the lake's ice, across which they'd tried to reach the mainland.

A detailed story by Aleksandr Zak, one of the tourists, has been preserved. It is entitled "Breakout on Valaam". It describes an event connected with the desire of a crippled war veteran who had lost both his arms to steal aboard a tourist steamship and to escape the island. He prevailed upon a sailor to hide him for 300 rubles. But prior to departure, a security guard arrived on the dock and demanded that the concealed "*Zek*" be handed over or else he wouldn't allow the ship to sail. Aleksandr Zak recalls how the invalid, loudly sobbing, disembarked. What do we know about the security of these closed zones - which even the guides were not permitted to enter? Almost nothing. Nevertheless it did happen on occasion that isolated, unrestricted individuals, guides and tourists made it into the closed zone.

The appearance in 2003 of a short 70-page booklet entitled *Valaamskaia tetrad'* [*Valaam notebook*] was a lucky break.[7] Its author, Evgenii Kuznetsov, had been a guide on the island in the 1960s and 1970s and had worked there for 15 years. His recollections of the war invalids are staggering and unique. They disclose many secrets about this inhumane "experiment" with the war heroes. In Kuznetsov's book, his discussion about the life and death of the maimed war veterans occupies only a few pages. It is impossible to read them without a lump in the throat. Allow me to cite them in full:

> ... Already at the end of February 1940 it became clear which way the war [the Winter War between the USSR and Finland] would go. Within the monastery they urgently began to prepare for a large evacuation. Everything that could be saved from pillaging and destruction (crosses, icons, the library, the archive and

some of the bells) were loaded onto sleighs and on the night of 28 February (fearing a Soviet air attack), the column moved out across the ice of Ladoga toward the mainland in the direction of Lakhdenpokh'ia. They were able to overcome many kilometers across the uneven ice - in pitch-blackness and frigid temperatures - and by dawn they reached the shoreline. Twelve of the elderly remained laying lifelessly in the sleighs. Next the column moved on to the city of Joensuu where all manners of ordeals awaited them. The Finnish Government wanted nothing to do with the monastery; the Republic of Finland, already exhausted by the war, was attempting to deal with a wave of approximately 300,000 refugees from the territory conquered by the Red Army. Nevertheless, that year the monastery managed to buy some land: Pallineme's Estate (named for the lake that surrounds it) and began to make its new home there. A new monastery arose. It received the name "Novo-Valaamskii" ["New Valaam"].

But what about the islands? At first the archipelago remained uninhabited. Then our forces arrived and by September 1941 a school for naval apprentices and a training school for Baltic Fleet boatswains had been set up there. In October 1941 the archipelago was again abandoned. In the war years a small Finnish garrison was stationed on the islands. However, in 1944 - after the signing of a secret agreement between the USSR and Finland - the garrison left the islands without combat according to an order. The territory once again passed to the Soviet Union and the islands were again uninhabited. Yet in 1950 - pursuant to a decree of the Supreme Soviet of the Karelo-Finnish Soviet Socialist Republic - a home for war invalids and a home of labor were established on Valaam and in the buildings of the monastery complex. Now, that's quite a facility!

The question, likely, asks itself: "Why here, on an island, and not somewhere on the mainland?" After all, it would be simpler to supply it and cheaper to maintain if not isolated on an island. The formal explanation is that there was already a lot of housing, utility rooms, businesses (one firm of which is still functioning), arable land for household plots and fruit tree and berry gardens present on the island. But the unofficial, real reason was that here hundreds of thousands of invalids (without arms; without legs; homeless and those engaged in begging around train stations; on trains; on streets; and a lot of other places) wouldn't be a painful eyesore in front of the victorious Soviet people. Well, judge for yourselves: they were wearing Orders and decorations on their chests, but were left to beg for handouts near bakeries. That's unacceptable! Get rid of them whatever it takes; but where to put them? How about in former monasteries on islands! Out of sight, out of mind. In the course of several months, the victorious country swept its streets clean of this "blemish"! That's how such poorhouses arose in the Kirillo-Belozersky; Goritsky; Aleksandr-Svorsky; Valaamsky; and other monasteries - or more accurately in the ruins of monasteries; in the pillars of the Orthodox faith that had been destroyed by Soviet power. The Country of Soviets punished its invalid-conquerors for their loss of limbs; for the loss of their families; their livestock and native homes - devastated by the war. It punished them with meager services, isolation and hopelessness. Anyone who wound up at Valaam instantly realized: "This is it. There is no longer any way out. Ahead lies the silence" - of an unmarked grave in a neglected monastic cemetery.

Reader! My obliging reader! Can we comprehend today the degree of bottomless, utterly overwhelming despair that gripped these people at that instant when they first stepped onto the island? In prison, in a terrible Gulag camp, the prisoner is always warmed by the hope of being released to resume a different, less bitter life. There was no escape from this place. The only way out was the grave - just like a death sentence. Can you even imagine what sort of life went on behind those walls? I saw all of this right next to me for many years. Yet it is difficult to describe - especially when their faces and eyes with their inexpressible smiles… the smiles of souls who have seemingly been condemned forever for something - seemingly begging for some sort of forgiveness -appear in my mind's eye. No, this is impossible to describe; impossible, likely, also because when recalling all this, the heart simply stops - your breathing becomes labored and an impossible confusion - some sort of clot of pain, arises in your thoughts! Forgive me…

I will say only that they cleaned out everyone and their mother - so to speak - and even those without one. The matter reached the point that many brought half-liter glass jars (for the gruel) with them to meals in the Dining Hall. There weren't enough aluminum pans! I saw this with my own eyes. To a question of any one of them: "Shall I bring you something back from Petersburg?" as a rule we heard in reply: "If I could only have a small tomato and a piece of sausage, or even just a piece of sausage." Whenever my children and I - having been paid - arrived at the village (as the former central monastery building has now begun to be called) and purchased 10 bottles of vodka and a small keg of beer, just what wouldn't start up! In wheelchairs, on trolleys[8] or on crutches they would hurry to the meadow at the Znameskaia Chapel where there was a dance floor - for legless invalids! Just think of that! There was also a beerhouse here. A banquet would begin! Each would get 100 grams [about 3.5 fluid ounces] of vodka and 100 grams of beer and after that a slice of tomato and a piece of cheap boiled sausage… my God, have the most refined gourmands been able to sample such pleasures of the table!? Then how their eyes would soften; their faces would begin to brighten and those terrible excusatory, guilty smiles on them would disappear.

With what resolve, with what hunger for a holiday (anything that diverted them from their drab lives was in fact a holiday) they would "hurry" to the tourist pier more than 6 kilometers from the village to get a glimpse of the arriving beautiful, well-fed, well-dressed people. Sometimes they had a chance to exchange just a single phrase with them. It was an opportunity to see life. Allow me to repeat that they reached the pier, again, in wheelchairs, trolleys and on crutches; only the "aristocracy" (those who in some way or other had some money) could permit themselves to reach the pier aboard skiffs. Of course, using oars - but if by motor (an old, 2-cylinder that coughed with every cycle) - this was already a genuine luxury. There was nothing like today's Mercedes 600 limousines that frequent the island! No comparison!

Back then, it was completely impossible to show this poorhouse in all its "splendor" to the tourists. It was categorically forbidden not only to lead groups to there, but even to point out the road leading to it. For this, employees would be punished with dismissal from work and even KGB interrogations. Nevertheless now and then someone would slip through and walk there, but of course only alone or in small groups of three or four people. Then one had to see the upset faces of these people when they returned - their shock from what they'd seen. It was particularly terrible to meet women of a certain age who'd lost men at the front - especially those who'd received not a death notice, but the notification "missing in action". After all, some of them had been undertaking genuine pilgrimages around all these institutions trying to locate their husbands, sons or brothers. This phenomenon was quite familiar to my generation: many invalids had taken the courageous decision and had voluntarily doomed themselves to this nightmare if only not to be a burden to their families.

> Two lives were going on separately back then on Valaam. One: the Home for Invalids - impoverished, sad and detached. The other: the tourists' world - jocular, exciting and not only well-nourished, but even with extravagances…

Human nature has been so adapted as to be capable of conforming to any improbable arrangement in the desire for life. However, this is only on its surface. What do we know about the inner feelings of the unfortunates and their "benefactors" - about which Kuznetsov speaks so honestly and justly? Almost nothing. Nevertheless, through the crumbs of available evidence we'll try to get a glimpse into the war invalids' lives on Valaam Island. I'll cite several recollections that supplement Evgenii Kuznetsov's own.

Arkadii Beienson relates:

> … At the end of the 1980s I no longer saw the invalids themselves (in 1984 they'd been returned to the mainland) and having returned home, to Moscow, I didn't bring back anything from that trip other than that very horror that literally lingered in the air. I managed to spend some time on Valaam again a couple of years later. My wife and I arrived aboard the motorboat *Kabargin* on a one-day excursion. The tour guide, who led us around the island, spoke in general terms about the history of the Valaam Monastery and mentioned the "particle of spiritual light", which each person should take away from this place. I looked at the churches that had been rebuilt and that were under reconstruction; heard about the widely developed activity of the Russian Orthodox Church on the island; and I couldn't shake the feeling that everything taking place now was only a fine layer of gilding concealing that which should never be expunged from the history of the island - or which they are seemingly trying to conceal. To a direct question about the invalids, the tour guide (organized tours to the island are monopolized by the Valaam Monastery's Pilgrimage Service) answered evasively - saying that yes, it's no use crying over it; there were such, but that the "invalids were being punished for destroying the shrines and for bombing the monastery during the war with Finland." That was all. Naturally, this didn't satisfy me, and having returned home, I went to the Internet.

There are practically no traces of those who died in poverty and physical impairment on Valaam. A participant on a film school excursion to the village of Svetlana and Valaam Island observed: "On Valaam they almost never made headcounts of 'these inva-

> lids'. They died in the hundreds, but at the Valaam Cemetery we found only two leaning pillars bearing... numbers. Nothing remained of them; they all went into the ground - leaving behind no monument to the horrifying experiment of a human zoo park on a Soviet island of Dr. Moreau." Incidentally, on the matter of this remark: "they died in the hundreds"... While listening to the reluctant response of the tour guide about "God's punishment", I noticed an old man - by his appearance a local resident - who was plainly listening in on our discussion. From his apparent age he looked to be possibly an eyewitness to those events, so separating from the group I quickly went over to him. He really was a local resident and moreover, an invalid who had lived in that very same Home for War Invalids and who had avoided being sent back to the mainland due to "family circumstances": he'd gotten married. From him I learned that although the first batch of war invalids had been brought here back in 1950, electricity reached the place where they were living only in 1952. There were no lights and the premises were unheated so the majority of those "hundreds" in fact died in the first two years. In the summertime, the "samovars" and "briefcases" [cruel Russian slang for people with no arms or legs or only one limb] were suspended - sometimes in pairs - in baskets from trees in the woods. There were occasions when no one remembered to retrieve them... and the nights in Karelia are cold even in the summertime...

Here is another piece of Valaam testimony from A. Berevkin that I found on the Internet:

> ... The first time I was on Valaam, several buildings and churches had been returned to the monastery and its slow reconstruction had begun. I lived in the monastery for about a month as a laborer (there is such a practice in monasteries; one can live and work there for a while). Once, I glanced into a window of one of the monastery's outbuildings. There was a dark, narrow corridor cluttered with buckets, wash basins, some sort of boxes, piles of rags and what appeared to be several small jail cells lining the walls of the corridor. Old men, blind and silent, were sitting on stools or lying on beds in these filthy, small cells. There was little light and an odor of a premise that had long been unventilated wafted from the cages. At first I thought that this was some sort of prison and that the cells accommodated some kind of exiles. However, a bit later when I asked a monk why these old, haggard men were in the monastery he replied without any evasion that they were war

> invalids that had been exiled to this place soon after the war at Stalin's order...[9]

Quite a few similar stories have been preserved. Taken altogether, to a certain extent they allow one to recreate a picture of the virtually imprisoned life of these former defenders of the Fatherland. A female cook in the Home for War Invalids on Valaam has left behind curious evidence:

> ... In a red building - at one time the monastery hospital, but now a communal residence for the local civilian population - we walked down a high, vaulted corridor that was filled with clutter and the smell of cats and knocked on a timeworn wooden door. One of the old women was half-reclined on a bed while the other was sitting at a nightstand looking out the window; beyond the window the September sun cast its golden light on the freshly painted cupolas of the monastery. One of the old women relates:
>
> > "Here there were aged invalids who'd lost one or more limbs, war invalids and elderly invalids from prisons. They'd come to see me at the Dining Hall, totally soused (I was the person in charge while my sister worked for 17 years in the shop as a storeroom clerk and as a sales clerk) and demanded: 'Give me more; it's owed me!' But how could I give them more? It was strictly rationed... Once the following happened to me: an invalid physically assaulted me in the kitchen - a stout man with a prosthetic leg. But you couldn't touch them, or they'd slap you with a lawsuit! I screamed. The deputy director came in and gave him such a blow that he went flying! But nothing came of it; the invalid didn't sue him because he sensed that he was in the wrong.
> >
> > And how they worked! The doctors prescribed them physical labors while those who were unable just lay around. At the Nikolsky Hermitage, there were "idiots" without arms; without legs - they lay in baskets. Some without permission traveled to Sortovala on the mainland; they'd take seats on a steamship and go there. Once there, they'd go on a bender and sprawl about. What was the police to do? They'd send them back to us."
>
> Her friend, Maria Prokhorova, confirmed: "Yeah, they'd lie in a basket; there weren't any hospital trolleys then and they were brought to Nikolsky where we'd look after them. Well, they'd eat a little, sleep a little... they were, you know..." - and Maria

> twirled a finger next to her temple. When we were departing, the director of a local club (Kseniia Emmanuilovna, who helped us a lot) told us that when she arrived on the island in the 1980s and entered the main Cathedral she sensed some improbable, ghastly energy everywhere throughout the building - in the atmosphere. The horror was virtually palpable. It was perceptible in the air...[10]

A short commentary from the newspaper *Vesti Karelii* casts a bit more light on the subject of these invalids:

> ... Recollections of that Valaam also remained with the director of the Karelian State Regional Natural History Museum, Mikhail Gol'denburg. What he witnessed at 10 years of age stuck in his memory for the rest of his life. The island was literally crammed with invalids. He says: "On such, you know, pads; some on crutches; well... there was quite a lot of disabled men. They were literally everywhere - and well, you know, a certain state of depressive shock remained."...

The monastic life returned to Valaam at the end of the 1980s while the residency for invalids was transferred to the mainland - to the Olonetsky area. Some of the staff also moved here. Among them was the residency's paramedic Liubov' Shcheglakova. Now she is working to help analyze the archives and is rehabilitating the names of those who never in fact entered the history of the Great Patriotic War.

Liubov' Shcheglakova says: "Each case is unique; each man his own story. The people were deprived of attention and now it seems that we're a little late because none of them are still living... and relatives don't know, perhaps, where their fathers and sons have been buried."

How many veterans in total were on the island? Where had these men fought? A lot of questions remain. However, the first lists of the former residents of the Valaam Home for Invalids in the nearest future will enter the public domain.

"Petr Ivanovich Antonov: wounded in combat in defense of the USSR..."

"Ivan Fedorovich Gordeev: wounded in combat in defense of the USSR..."

In the archive there are dozens of veterans' individual cases. Now their names by right will become part of the country's military history.

I can't help but ask the question: "Is that so?"

The most cheerful, joyous recollections reveal that a few young invalids - even those with severe disabilities - found females among the staff to love them and got married. In such cases they took them into the communal residence, which became the occasion for weddings. Children were born. Some of them, having grown up, chose to remain on the island. Whether there were many such idyllic cases we don't know.

The most forbidding place on Valaam is the cemetery. The graveyard is just a 10-minute walk from the renovated Cathedral. Enormous marble crosses - under which lie the five founders of the Valaam Monastery - stand next to a small church. Right here, behind a low fence, there are several thousand more graves spread out among the thickets of birch trees. In addition to local residents, Soviet soldiers who were killed in the Second World War found their final resting place here - as well as several hundred Finnish soldiers. Former inhabitants of the Home for Invalids of the Great Patriotic War - starting in 1950 - also lie here.

The majority of graves are unmarked. Here and there among the mounds stand unpainted log posts, to which a tablet has been nailed that bears a family name and an iron star. That's how the Motherland thanked those who poured out their blood for it: first it hid them out of eyesight on a Lake Ladoga island and then erected a monument to them in the form of a log post and a bit of metal. In distinction from the monastery's grave sites, the graves of the veterans reside in dense thickets and are overgrown not only by grass, but also trees. The cemetery wasn't even spruced up for the 60th Victory Anniversary - although the victory was commemorated on the island quite pompously.

Among the neglected graves, a small monument to Hero of the Soviet Union Grigorii Voloshin stands out. At the front he lost his arms, legs, hearing and speech. Grigorii Andreevich spent 29 years among such invalids on the island. The relatives of the Hero of the Soviet Union learned of his fate only in 1994. Later a monument was erected in his honor at the Igumensk Cemetery.

Autographs of the War

One of the most valuable autographs of the memory of the Great Patriotic War invalids belongs to the talented Russian artist, Gennadii Dobrov. A graduate of the Surikov Art Institute, he was a student of the well-known Soviet artist Kibrik. Dobrov created a series of portraits of veterans who'd been left disabled by the fighting. The artist's pencil recorded on paper the faces of these people - the breasts of which displayed their combat decorations for many succeeding generations and their ancestors.

In the martyr-cripples - who'd been sent to die on the island - the artist saw striking spiritual strength; captured their sorrow, but at the same time their continued pride for honorably carrying out their soldier's duty.

In 1974, almost three decades before the appearance of Evgenii Kuznetsov's *Valaamskaia tetrad'* [*Valaam notebook*], the artist went to the island and spent more than three months locating models to sit for him. It was then that he created his first portrait. Six years later, he had completed a series of 40 "Pages of Sorrow" - as he called his Valaam portraits.

Take, for example, one of these portraits: a blind woman - almost without a face. She had fainted from the shock of the news about the war's start and had fallen directly into a hot oven. Her husband, whom she loved to distraction, had the previous day been sent to the Brest fortress and her heart hadn't tricked her - he was killed on the first day of the war. The blind woman with the face badly scarred by flames sang folk tunes to Dobrov in a motif known only to her. They struck the artist and remained in his heart; he remembered them for the rest of his life.

"I was the only artist", says Gennadii Dobrov, "who approached the subject of the war from an unexpected direction. The bureaucrats were frightened: 'Have you ever seen depictions of armless and legless people at an exhibition? There was a reason why they were banished from eyesight. You had to infiltrate the island on the sly.' Secretaries of the Union [of Artists] visited my studio, examined my work and said that I was a fascist; that I enjoyed the view of other people's sufferings and that as long as they had the authority, I'd never be seen at any exhibitions."

Indeed, his portraits were never on display! Yet the masterfully-drawn portraits of the martyr-invalids - who by some miracle survived the war and life in the Homes for Invalids - "had the last word": thousands of people in Russia and the West have seen them. But the public reaction, like circles in water, later dissipated.

It would seem that the sad story of the war invalids would inspire the writers' pen and provoke angry lines from them. Alas, this hasn't happened. "A tale of a real person" doesn't matter. Who would remember this literary vaudeville? Even after Gennadii Dobrov's portraits, writers - the "engineers of human souls" - could find no place for the so-called "invalid subject" in their output. This indifference can be explained - and possibly even to a certain extent justified - during Stalin's time and while Soviet censors existed. But later... please, I don't understand. However, nevertheless there were three writers in all of Soviet literature who weren't afraid and responded to the forbidden subject: Viktor Nekrasov, Iurii Nagibin and Mikhail Veller. Two of the three named writers though, only described the life of a war invalid but didn't touch the tragic - and at the same time shameful - history of their mistreatment after the war. Only Mikhail Veller ever so slightly revealed the truth. This, just think, is the only example in all of Soviet Russian literature.

The frontline writer Viktor Nekrasov in his tale *V rodnom gorode* [*In my native city*] talks about the postwar lives of the disabled veterans. His hero relates:

> ... My biography has come to an end. Now, some sort of hogwash has remained. I was a pilot, you know - and not a bad one. I had eight [enemy] aircraft to my credit. This after just somewhere around eight months; I started at Stalingrad. I was also a Komsomol member and thought of joining the Communist Party. But now what? I've got a stump; I'll never fly again and I was kicked out of the Komsomol. I knock about around cities on some kind of frigging slippers. An invalids' workshop in Rostov makes them - good ones with buckskin leather soles. I ship them to Khar'kov; to Odessa; and to this place: you can always get by with a prosthetic leg - no one will stop you. But three guys, these slick operators, impound them. That's how I live: I earn a bit and drink it away; earn a bit more and again drink that away. You say that's a blessing. Nothing like it! I can't grow another leg...

The story, in particular, talks about how the Soviet officials treated the invalid soldiers after the war. The maimed soldier-conquerors couldn't find decent work; weren't given acceptable housing; and the invalids didn't have quality prosthetic limbs.

Iurii Nagibin, in his tale 'Terpenie' ['Endurance'] - which was published in the journal *Novyi Mir* - describes a journey to one of the northern islands where he sees invalid soldiers on the wharf:

> ... One couldn't say about the cripple that he stood or sat; he propped himself up like a log and on either side of his truncated, broad-chested body - with the thick, dark leather sewn on the bottom - stood handcrafted wooden "extenders" that looked like old cast-iron presses which he used to propel himself. His neighbor, also legless but a bit older and not as stoutly built, was on a cart with little wheels. He dealt in scrounged, soggy Kazbak and Belomor cigarettes and drank away the proceeds together with winos in beer halls, watering holes, stairwells and gloomy apartment hangouts; or together with trashy - though at times simply unfortunate - widowed women or with thieves who adapted the invalids to their craft; and he would squabble, raise hell and fight...

Alas, Mikhail Veller's short piece '*Samovar*' sharply stands out. It is difficult to read such words as "We're samovars" without agitation. As the author explains:

> ... An invalid who has no arms or legs is called a samovar. This is likely because what you get is some sort of a freak with a spout down below. We've already been here for many years now. Our families think we died long ago. This is a secret hospital for such invalids. We really don't know where we are. There are rather a lot of such places around the country. They are located far from inhabited areas and roads, concealed from human eyes and completed isolated from the outside world. They are not included in any summaries or accounts and are not mentioned in any reports. People give the appearance that we don't exist. However, it is clear to anyone that we are here...

There is still one more prominent figure. In 1998, the film *Bunt palachei* ['*The Revolt of the Executioners*'] came out on the screens of the country. It didn't receive wide distribution and it didn't run for very long. In fact, I watched it over the Internet.

It is an unusual film. It tells about an unexpected encounter after the war in one of the Gulag's camps between a former combat officer and one of his soldiers - now legless - who'd been brought to the camp to be executed. The officer, now an executioner, stands up to defend the war hero - his former soldier - and attempts to save him. Of course, this is an artistic creation of the filmmaker Zemel'. One can quibble with aspects of it. For example, they didn't execute invalids and combat officers of the regular army didn't serve in the Gulag system. Even the encounter itself between old combat friends seems contrived. But these things aren't important. The most important aspect from my point of view is that the film touched upon the subject of war invalids, which was so unpleasant and prickly for the Soviet authorities.

If you will, this is all that domestic Russian culture has devoted to the history of the invalids over the entire postwar period in the matter of exposing the truth about the lives of the disabled veterans of the war. Russian historians have also been uneager to study the given subject. However strange it seems, military historiography has also been silent about them. I searched the Internet sites dedicated to literature of the Great Patriotic War and found hundreds of names and book titles. But alas! It is as if wars take place without leaving behind mutilated and maimed survivors.

To the present day, only a handful of enthusiasts study this forbidden subject. One of them is the historian and genealogist, Vitalii Semenov. Apparently, after reading *Valaamskaia tetrad'* and visiting the cemetery on the island, in 2003 Vitalii Semenov headed to Valaam again but now not for purposes of tourism. He managed to write down the recollections of many of the surviving, old residents of the Home for Invalids. As a result of his inquiries he managed to gather documentary evidence of the death of 50 veterans, which is far from a complete list. He also was able to collect evidence on the number of invalids who had lived on the island. According to him, in January 1951 there were 901 invalids located here; in December of the same year, their number had dropped to 876. In 1955 there were now 975 invalids on Valaam, but later their number steadily decreased: 812, 670, 624… in December 1971, as documents showed, there were 574 invalids living on Valaam. Of course this is fragmentary and incomplete evidence, but it also presents an interesting historical question: Where is the data on invalids for the preceding and subsequent years? They are tucked away in archives and are inaccessible. There is also far-from-complete evidence about the number of invalids at their other points of exile.

After Valaam, the historian took up the study of the Galitsky Home for Invalids. It was located in the Goritsky Monastery, where primarily veterans from Leningrad and Leningrad Oblast were sent. According to documents that Semenov has been able to locate, in 1948 there were 747 invalids here. The study of archival materials revealed that this Home for Invalids was transferred to Cherepovets in 1972. The Goritsky Monastery's papers are partially kept there and partially stored in the archive of Vologodskaia Oblast's Department of Social Security. Here is what Vitalii Semenov said about his searches:

> … At first the staff of this institution seemed to meet me half-way and even helped me establish one-and-a-half-dozen names of invalids who passed through the Goritsky residence - as well as

> mentioned an analogous special institution, located in a different place, in Vologodchina-Andoga. However, there the department head had placed a ban on further research - supposedly according to the law about personal records; without the agreement of descendants of the dead, it is forbidden to disclose information about the deceased since this is a violation of their descendants' rights. Thus it is necessary first by some highly improbable means (perhaps with the help of extrasensory perception?) to find the descendants of a person unknown to me and only then ascertain his first and last name! There is no logic here and in reality it turns out that local authorities are the ones who must engage in resurrecting the memory of everyone who fought. However, to this point in time they're not showing the least bit of activity in this regard. Only after several sharp letters from me addressed to the oblast chief did the situation seemingly change for the better. At the end of July I received an official letter which informed me that at the order of the Nizhegorod governor, a work group had been created to perpetuate the memory of those military personnel that were disabled in the fighting on the fronts of the Great Patriotic War who had then lived, died and were buried on the territory of Vologda Oblast...

Two lamentable institutions were in Vologda Oblast: the Goritsky Monastery at Kirillov and one in Andoga (Kaduisky District). During its existence the Goritsky Home for Invalids served 454 invalids of the Great Patriotic War - according to the chief of Homes for Invalids of the Vologda Department of Social Security - from 21 December 1955. But how many of them died in Goritsky and were then buried in a forest cemetery where now there is not the slightest sign of them?

Today, when so many years have passed, people react variously to the actions of the authorities - undertaken by them in the 1940s and 1950s to exile people in Homes for Invalids. After all, people were sent into them without their consent. It was compulsory and a resident could leave such a closed facility only through death. The question immediately arises: Would it have been better if these people had ended their lives as beggars in an enclosure? However that may be, these people lived the rest of their hard lives under medical observation - although that was indeed meager. They were being fed in a famished country and people at least sought to tend to them.

To the present day, their grandchildren and great-grandchildren have been trying to find at least the slightest bit of information about their ancestors who were considered missing in action or killed, but then after so many years they suddenly find out that their grandfathers or great-grandfathers survived the war, but had been left severely disabled and their lives came to an end far from home. However paradoxical it may be, they continue to search for them.

On 24 March 2010 the Russian newspaper *Rossisskaia gazeta* published an essay by Svetlana Tsygankovaia entitled: 'Valaamskaia bessrochnaia' ['Valaam's eternity']. Here's an excerpt from it:

> ... In 1964 the Home for War Invalids moved to the village of Vidlits, which is in Olonetsky District. None of the former frontline soldiers are still alive. However, thank God, in the residency they've decided to resurrect the names of the veterans and to study their archives. The Paramedic Liubov' Shcheglakova is engaged in this work: she herself was born on Valaam; began working in the Home for Invalids while it was still on the island; and remembers many of the invalids. "Previously there was not such attention to the war veterans," says Liubov' Pavlovna Shcheglakova; "They lived like ordinary people. Of course, all sorts of things happened: drunkenness, fights and deaths. Sometimes they donned their medals; I remember this."
>
> "Where did their decorations and documents go?"
>
> "I don't know. In the archives they've found the Red Army booklet for one of them."
>
> The collective farmer Stepan Danilin had been mobilized for the front in August 1941 out of the Priazhinsky area of Karelia. Three years later he was discharged due to disability. He returned home without a leg where Stepan's wife and two small sons were waiting for him. How they greeted the invalid and what happened next is unknown.
>
> For the remaining residents of the Home, there are practically no frontline documents or references about their decorations. In order to identify the participants of the Great Patriotic War, one can only turn to their year of birth and medical notes about their treatment; there it is documented if the individual was wounded at the front. Primarily these were people who were severely shell-shocked, blinded or who had lost upper or lower limbs. Ivan Kalitarov, 1924 year of birth, whose right side was paralyzed after a severe wound at 36 years of age, was found frozen to death 10 kilometers from the road to Valaam Island; it is assumed that he was trying to reach the mainland across the ice. They found him a month after he went missing. Mikhail Kholodnyi, 1920 year of birth, had suffered atrophy of his lower extremities, while Matvei Kotov had lost a leg. Vasilii Men'shikov, a former officer, after the war attempted to live in the city; rented a corner of a private home and worked, but medical problems emerged and he wound up on the island. War invalid Ivan Gorin left behind a wife and

> children in Petrozavodsk. Once a year, his spouse wrote a letter to the institution's administration asking how her husband was doing and complaining that he wasn't writing back. They repeatedly informed her that her husband was healthy and had promised to write. A year later the woman would again send a letter, but for some reason she never came for a visit. The one-way correspondence ended in a small stack of papers, which was found in the frontline veteran's archive file, on which was printed: "Inform so-and-so at the indicated address that Gorin has passed away."
>
> "So far we've established the identities of 47 residents," the paramedic of the Vidlits Home for the Aged and Invalids Liubov' Shcheglakova told *Rossiskaia gazeta*; "We're continuing the work."
>
> But even today, letters arrive in the village from various cities in which people are requesting assistance in finding their relatives. Thus far in response to their appeals, we haven't been able to find anyone...[11]

Time is putting ever more distance between us all and the war - and we are forgetting those distinguishable and bloody traces of the old battles that are disappearing. War invalids have long since fully disappeared from our streets and most of them are no longer living. What does the current generation of Russians know about Stalin's crime against the war heroes after the war ended?

In all likelihood, we'll never find out all the names of the thousands of ruined human lives. By the way, is my pessimism possibly exaggerated? God grant that I'm proven wrong.

A Known Fact?

At the end of July 2009, the well-known radio station Ekho Moskvy broadcast the following discussion as part of its series '*Imenem Stalina*' ['*In the name of Stalin*']:

> **Natella Boltianskaia**: "Comment upon that monstrous fact when at Stalin's order after the Great Patriotic War, invalids were forcibly exiled to Valaam; to Solovki; so that they - armless and legless heroes of the war - didn't spoil the celebration of the victory with their appearance. Why is so little said about this now? Why aren't their names known? After all, it was just these people who paid for the victory with their blood and wounds. Or is it also forbidden now to mention them?"
>
> **Aleksandr Daniel'**: "Well, what's there to say about this fact? It is a known fact - a monstrous one. It is completely clear why Stalin and the Stalinist leadership expelled the veterans from the cities."

> **Natella Boltianskaia**: "Hmm, was it really because they didn't want the holiday look to be spoiled?"
>
> **Aleksandr Daniel'**: "Absolutely so. I'm certain that it was out of aesthetic considerations. Legless men on trolleys didn't fit that artistic production, so to speak, in the style of socialist realism into which the leadership wanted to convert the country."

According to historian Aleksandr Daniel', one of the participants in the discussion, the fact of the expulsion of the war invalids from the cities was well-known and there was no need to comment upon it. Is that so?

Unfortunately, history has preserved precious little evidence about the lives and deaths of an entire generation of invalids - exiled at Stalin's order into oblivion. We have here the so-called invalid residences, but in reality the "reservations"; the "concentration camps"; the "Homes for Invalids of the closed type"; the "leper colonies" - as people variously refer to the places - into which the disabled veterans of the war were sent.

As a rule, almost all of the information about the invalids that has reached us today is based on publications by the tour guide Evgenii Kuznetsov, the artist Gennadii Dobrov and the historian Vitalii Semenov. To be sure, there is one nuance that is characteristic for all these authors. They speak about the war invalids who lived on the island after the opening of the so-called Home for Invalids. The home for invalids and labor! We have no information at all about the first wave of unfortunate young people in their 20s that were exiled. It is complete darkness!

Moreover, the recollections of the cited authors are of a fragmentary nature and leave many questions unanswered. For example, during the first sweeps in the 1940s tens of thousands of disabled veterans were "hounded down" and exiled. Where were they sent; where did they live and die? Only the names of the ancient Russian monasteries - where hundreds of disabled veterans were consigned - are known. I've listed them here in this chapter. Yet these few places couldn't have held all the tens of thousands of exiled war invalids. Where, then, were the remaining asylums of the exiled? We don't know!

There is evidence that some of the invalids were sent to Solovki. However, there are no reliable records about this. There is also a cruel story that has circulated that supposedly the legless, the armless and the blind were shipped off to the North and loaded onto barges which were then sunk and the invalids left to drown. Whether such an abomination really took place, we don't know. There is simply no reliable evidence.

Vitalii Semenov presents fragmentary data on the numbers of the contingent in the Home for Invalids on Valaam between 1952 and 1971. But where is evidence about the early contingent? There is none. Almost nothing is known as well about the personnel who worked in the monasteries. What type of people were they; how did they help the patients survive? We know almost nothing about the medical service rendered to the invalids. Thus far we know little about the custodial guards at these so-called special facilities.

To the present day thousands of personal records on the veterans; their passports; their military tickets; and Orders are stored and gathering dust in archives - and access to them is tightly closed. Hasn't the time come for Russia to de-classify these archival records? The known fact is that not a single message from the invalids themselves - who were driven into inhumane conditions from where the cemetery was the only way out - has reached our times.

There is evidence that having wound up on the island in the monastic "mansions" - which were hastily cleaned and prepared to receive the *"Zeks"* - the arriving inmates collapsed into wild terror, died one after the other and even committed suicide. Was this really the case? We don't know.

What happened more frequently: Did the invalids laugh or cry? We don't know.

What did they think about, talk about or reminisce about? We don't know.

Did they turn to faith and become religious? We don't know.

It must have been difficult to reconcile oneself to a hopeless existence; to absolute helplessness and to endure the conditions of a life in prison to which they'd been consigned. Undoubtedly, these people asked themselves and each other more than once or twice about why they were being so cruelly punished.

Astonishingly, we have evidence that these invalids wore their combat Orders and medals and were proud of them. Possibly, this is because they considered their past military service as the most important period in their lives.

Did they believe in miracles after the world surrounding them faded away forever? We don't know.

The First Names

On 10 July 2011 the Moscow and All-Russian Patriarch Kirill and a Karelian delegation opened a Memorial in the memory of the soldier-invalids of the Great Patriotic War on Valaam. It was dedicated to those who had lived on the island in the Home for Invalids between 1950 and 1984 and who had found their final resting place there.

The Memorial includes a large Eastern Orthodox cross and seven black granite slabs - upon which the last names of 54 of Valaam's invalid veterans have been engraved. The opening of the Memorial in the Igumensk Cemetery of the Valaam Monastery was the result of cooperation between the monastery and the Sortovala Area's Council of Veterans of Karelia.

After giving a requiem prayer, the Patriarch stood next to the cross and appealed to those who had gathered for the ceremony:

> ... This was not any kind of Home for Invalids, but an ordinary prison camp... I well remember the people, in whose memory this cross has been raised. They were people who had received the most burdensome disabilities in the Great Patriotic War. Many of them didn't have arms or legs, but likely they were most torment-

> ed by the fact that the Motherland - for the freedom of which they'd given up their health and even their lives - didn't consider it possible to do anything better for them than to send them here; to this cold island rather distant from the community of victors... I think that our entire country, our entire people, should know about today's event so that remembrance of the victory would always be accompanied by a prayerful remembrance of the heroes who gave up their lives for the Motherland or received the most severe disabilities - including those who in fact didn't receive the care and support of those who bore the responsibility for the fate of our country back then. That's the callousness, the obduracy and hypocrisy upon which the people were nurtured. Today we are overcoming with great difficulty the weighty consequences of the past decades. God grant that we never again make such mistakes...[12]

Spoken openly, but far from completely - finally the Russian Orthodox Church remembered them. For this, thank you: better late than never.

Incidentally, there is a question that must not be avoided: Why did they engrave only the last names of 54 invalid veterans? Aren't now many more names known who are worthy of this honor?

We will send to all of them - the heroes of the Great Patriotic War who went into oblivion not by their own choice - our warm words of love!

Afterword

Had I been on the island on the day of the unveiling of the Memorial, here's what I would have said:

The words of the Most Holy are only a drop of the truth. They have avoided questions of responsibility for what was done; how can we absolve the State of its great sin by praying? It is obliged to confess before those soldiers left undone by the war; before their fathers and mothers - then, finally, within a year place the historical truth of what was done in full view. However this truth came about, it must become the property of the entire society! Oh, just one more thing: a trifle. It would be desirable to construct a memorial on Poklonnaia Hill in Moscow which would display the names of all of those ruined against their will. At the same time, here would be the place as well for an exhibition of artist Gennadii Dobrov's 40 "Pages of Sorrow".

18

When Will the Last Soldier be Buried?

First I'll acquaint the reader with the official Soviet/Russian data on the losses of the Red Army in the Great Patriotic War. The total irrecoverable losses of the Soviet armed forces amounted to 11,444,100 men. When calculating the so-called demographic losses of military personnel, we must subtract the number found still alive after the war - 1,836,000 men who returned from prisoner of war camps and 939,700 men who were called up a second time on liberated territories who had previously been listed as missing in action - from the total irrecoverable losses.[1] Thus, the Red Army's official losses can be determined as 8,668,400 men killed or missing in action.

The largest portion of this figure consists of missing in action. According to documents, they amount to 5,059,000 men. Not all of these men were taken prisoner. The results of research into archived documents of the German *Wehrmacht* command give evidence that approximately 450,000-500,000 of this total number were either killed; escaped captivity, but remained on occupied territory; or joined the partisans while 4,599,000 wound up as German prisoners - of which only 1,836,000 returned to their homeland after the war. Another 200,000 men emigrated after being released from German prison camps while the rest died in German captivity.[2]

Twelve-and-a-half million officers and soldiers ended the war in the Red Army. On the 64th Anniversary of VE Day in 2009, only 900,000 of these men were still alive in all the republics of the former Soviet Union. Of these, 450,000 were living in Russia. In Moscow there were 274,000 of these veterans. However, among them only 47,000 were former frontline soldiers. What do these figures signify? That with each passing year the number of living frontline veterans of the Great Patriotic War is dwindling. By the 70th Anniversary, unfortunately very few of them will remain in Russia. But who are the rest of these so-called veterans who were not among the 47,000 former frontline troops? It was strange for me to see middle-aged men walking in the column of veterans while watching a 9 May 2009 television program about a Victory Day Parade in Omsk - especially given that the average age of the genuine Great Patriotic War frontline veterans is now 85 years.[3]

Even though nearly 70 years have passed since the end of the Great Patriotic War, the remains of more than a million soldiers and officers who were killed in the war have still not been buried.[4] The State has failed to carry out its plain duty to the defenders of the Fatherland: to locate them and given them proper burials. Indeed, this is not just a tragedy for millions of their mothers and fathers, sisters and brothers, wives and children, grandchildren and great-grandchildren, but also a tragedy of the entire Red Army.

There has long been the saying: "The war isn't over until the last soldier has been buried." However, Russian history has never known such a disgrace. The remains of soldiers and officers who were killed but never buried rest in forested tracts; by brooks and streams; in lowland swamps; and where vanished villages once stood. People are searching for and finding bullet-riddled helmets, half-decayed machine-gun belts, rusty sapper spades, tin cans - and next to them human bones covered with dirt and foliage. A multitude of cartridges, shell casings, rifle bayonets and soldiers' remains are being found in abandoned and partially filled-in bunkers and trenches; in enormous bomb craters; in clearings and beside highways… they lay in heaps in roadside ditches. They are found in places of long-ago battles; in forested gullies and beside lakes and in piedmont ravines. These skulls and bones have been lying without ceremony under a shallow layer of earth ever since the war. Even in the initial years after the war, Ivan Pereverzev's quatrain was passing from hand to hand:

O, Motherland, not in a cemetery
In a prominent city or next to it
The saintly bones of the men
Lay scattered across the land.

During the war, as a rule the recovered dead were wrapped in canvas tent halves before being strewn with green branches and covered with a shallow layer of soil. A wooden plank or short wooden post would be driven into the ground - upon which the following information would be written with an ink pen: the name and nationality of the fallen soldier, his year of birth and his home address. In addition, the date and place of his death would be noted and the area where his grave was located. Many former places where fighting took place were never tidied up in full measure; never swept clear of unexploded shells and mines, which after the war often caused civilian deaths and injuries.

According to information from the Russian Ministry of Defense's Military-Memorial Center, there are approximately 30,000 military burial sites on Russian territory which hold the remains of more than 7 million soldiers and officers of the Red Army. The names are known of only 2.5 million of them - while the rest were buried unknown.[5]

Some of these mass grave sites remain on desolated, depopulated territories. Monuments were raised to mark them immediately after the war and in the 1940s and 1950s; some were crafted from gypsum or crushed marble - non-durable materials. Meanwhile, those made of metals were pilfered in the 1990s. Even the world-renowned Monument to the Soldier-Liberator in Treptower Park nearly collapsed after 60 years of rust and neglect. But the most important thing lies not in the decay of monuments and markers erected in the past.

Those who search for these grave sites note that graves were prepared and the fallen buried (and bullet-riddled helmets placed around the grave). But when you returned to the site a month or so later, you could no longer find it because it would be overgrown with chest-deep orach. The grave site was no one's concern. More often there was utter desolation. In 2005, in connection with the 60th Anniversary of VE Day, the authorities paid attention to the war's cemeteries and began sprucing them up.

The Russian Government annually spends $1.5 million to rehabilitate and tend to military burial sites. Unfortunately, this is still too little. The German Government annually spends 20 times more for this purpose.

"No One is Forgotten" (lyrics from a song)

In the latter half of the 1960s, a movement was born in the Soviet Union which was unique for a totalitarian State. Older schoolchildren, students and young workers voluntarily formed into search teams and in their free time they would drive out to the places of former battles and moreover did so at their own expense.

As a rule - and this is natural - this movement's beginning was connected with frontline veterans who by some miracle had survived the war. They were constantly tormented by the thought that their former comrades remained unburied and that frequently their remains were left lying on abandoned former battlefields. Moreover, no one was showing any concern about them. Here and there obelisks and fraternal graves appeared, but everywhere - where this cursed war took place - the Russian land was strewn with the unburied remains of fallen soldiers.

Most often, these enthusiasts on their own sought to bring the government's attention to this horrible state of affairs. They knocked on the doors of the offices of Party and government bureaucrats and wrote letters to all the authorities - asking one and the same question: "Why, even though quite a few years had passed, did their military comrades remain unburied and how could such a thing have happened"? These attempts to jog the Party's and State's conscience, as a rule, ended with empty demagoguery. The frontline generation for a long, long time had lost any faith in Party and Soviet power. However, tired of the useless fuss and bother, many of the people realized that they could only count upon themselves to accomplish anything.

The veterans recruited the young into a movement of searchers - as the young men and women who were given the task of searching for remains of the fallen were called. Virtually all of them were their children, grandchildren and great-grandchildren... Their once isolated, disorganized teams have given rise today to an entire army of searchers in contemporary Russia - and the words: "We are searching for people, not bones" has become their slogan.

The young people are deeply convinced that they are doing an important and necessary job - conserving history. The searches are attempting to retrieve the names and fates of the "missing in action" from nothingness.

In 2004, the Union of Search Organizations was formed in Russia: the most wide-scale youth association in Russia. It has more than 100,000 members - patriots from dozens of republic, district and oblast search organizations.[6]

The names of the war's heroes, such as Aleksandr Matrosov and Zoia Kosmodem'ianskaia, are widely known. But what do we know about the fate of soldiers whose feats belong to ground that was soaked with their blood? Years have passed and a new generation of youth is overhauling the truth of the war; the truth of those who were listed "missing in action". The search for the unburied remains of the defenders of the Motherland has become the driving force in the lives of many of Russia's young citizens.

The searcher's task involves not only heavy physical labor, but also entails major psychological mood swings which combine the overcoming of apprehension; the understanding of their responsibility to the living and the dead; the joy of a successful search; and the bitterness of failure.

The youthful searchers ask themselves: "Who are these men and women who died for us? Or more accurately: "'Who' or 'What' are they - people or things?" This duality, between individuals and their skeleton remains, is sharpest of all. In their work, each searcher travels along an edge separating the world and human relations from the world of inanimate objects. Constantly, from day to day - coming across that which remains of an individual who was killed 60 years ago - the searcher begins to exhume objects… never forgetting for a moment that these once made up living people. This duality constantly haunts them.

"It seemed to me," writes a 16-year-old girl, "that from the very beginning I understood that these were people who were at one time living, but nevertheless it didn't seem like that. On the final day of excavation, for a brief second I pondered what I was washing in the river. These were the bones of people who in general hadn't been much older than me. These people were once walking on this earth, but now they were no longer. And at this moment I couldn't keep working. I sat like that for not more than three minutes, but to me those minutes seemed oh so long."

Here's another perception shared by an 18-year-old searcher: "Sometimes it was hard. When you imagined that these arms and legs were feeling pain and what the brain inside this skull was thinking… What were these guys thinking about and recalling in the last minutes of their lives?"

The conscience of young people who are normal in their moral development cannot escape this duality. There are also, of course, others: those who indifferently smash a human skull because they never developed a sense of at least involuntary queasiness or unease at the sight of what remains of someone else's death. This indifference is a clear sign of apathy toward someone else's life and there are also so-called *chernye* [black] searchers who seek to locate grave sites only to pillage them for relics that they can sell.

Prior to 1988, the honorable search work was conducted by totally independent groups of enthusiasts with their own effort and money. The infrequent sponsor donations - and more often the personal means of the participants - allowed them to conduct only small-scale expeditions without any official permission at their own responsibility and risk.

In March 1988, the first All-Union gathering of the search team leaders took place in Kaluga. A Coordinating Council was established - headed by a former veteran, the journalist Iu.M. Ikonnikov. Expeditions were conducted in the region of Miasnoi Bor. Over 800 people from 15 cities of the Soviet Union took part in them. Together, they found and gave proper burial in a military cemetery to 3,500 sets of remains.

These first large-scale search expeditions caught the authorities' attention. For the first time, the Ministry of Defense rendered substantial and direct assistance to the enthusiasts with means and equipment.

The work in Novgorod Oblast in 1988 enabled them to find a location for staging 1989's "Keeping the Watch of Remembrance". This pompous ceremony had previously been staged at majestic memorials in cities under direction of the Party and Komsomol organs and the army. It was considered that by staging this ceremony, full tribute was being given to all the war dead. Then suddenly in the autumn of 1988, the name "Miasnoi Bor" - which had previously been unknown to them - appeared in the lexicon of the functionaries. The result of the joint work of hundreds of searchers stunned them with its unexpected results and tragic element. It was decided to stage the next "Keeping the Watch of Remembrance" in 1989 precisely in Novgorod Oblast in the village of Miasnoi Bor.

Search work was not only conducted in Novgorod Oblast. Fifty oblasts of the former Soviet Union were in need of search surveys and particularly Smolensk, Briansk, Kaluga, Tver' (Kalinin), Leningrad, Murmansk, Pskov, Kursk, Vitebsk, Kaliningrad and other oblasts where heavy fighting took place.

In April 1989, 1,500 searchers came together in Miasnoi Bor. Over 10 days of work, another 3,400 sets of remains were exhumed and reburied; 89 of the remains were identified. The 1990 "Keeping the Watch of Remembrance" was held in Smolensk Oblast. Over 10 days of work, 1,200 searchers located and reburied 3,320 sets of remains of soldiers and officers who were killed in the 1941-1942 Viaz'ma encirclements and in the 1942-1943 Sychevka Operation - and 52 of the remains were identified. The next "Keeping the Watch of Remembrance" took place in 1991 in Tver' Oblast. Search expeditions continued later as well. The search organizations - strengthened materially and morally - took on new, large-scale expeditions. The searchers gained skills and experience. In just Miasnoi Bor alone, searchers have found and given proper burial to a total of more than 30,000 soldiers and officers who fell in the Great Patriotic War.

By the 50th Anniversary of VE Day, the government's interest in search work had grown. The General Staff of the Soviet army issued a directive for the Soviet army to help the search organizations by "...giving the search formations worn-out uniforms and equipment." It is a pity that the reader can't picture their condition!

The searchers say: "We hardly are able to bury everyone: We paid too high a price for victory and a lot of time has passed as well, but we're trying to do everything within our strength - though to be sure, subsequent generations will have to complete the task."

I'll cite a few articles from the News.com website for 2007 about the work of search expeditions:

> ... In Murmansk Oblast, a ceremonial reburial of the remains of 130 soldiers of the Polar Division - 10 of which were identified - took place on Saturday in the Valley of Glory. Among the remains were those of Soviet pilot Dmitrii Shatiuk, which were found by Norwegians in the wreckage of an airplane that crashed on Norwegian territory. The airplane was salvaged from a swamp. The pilot's remains were delivered to Murmansk Oblast.
>
> During the war, there was savage fighting in the Valley of Glory for Kol'skoe Zapoliar'e, which is located 80 kilometers from Murmansk on the western coast of Kol'skii Harbor. Traces of the German fortifications and trenches - and the bunkers of Soviet troops - still exist. Altogether, 72,000 soldiers and officers of the Red Army perished on the territory of Murmansk Oblast, while over 32 years of search work in the Valley of Glory, approximately 15,000 have been found and reburied...

Here is another article:

> ... Searchers have uncovered nine fraternal graves. In the same place, a separate grave was found which contained the remains of Colonel Kurdriashov - a cavalier with two Orders of the Red Banner - who was the commander of the 267th Composite Division. He was killed on 17 December 1942 during Operation Little Saturn. Even in his grave, the division commander was holding a sabre in one hand and a compass in the other. In the course of the search work, members of the "Don" team found the remains of 65 Soviet soldiers...

Just several lines, but they reveal one more of the sad pages of the war which became known thanks to the letters of the searchers.

In April 1942 after the *Stavka's* ill-considered order to seize the city of Viaz'ma, three divisions of the 33rd Army under the command of Lieutenant General Efremov wound up encircled northwest of Iukhnov. In large groups and in groups of just 2-3 men, the troops sought to reach the mouth of the Vor' River and above it along the course of the Ugra River where the 43rd Army was striving to create a corridor with the aim of freeing the encircled men. However, everywhere the Germans met them with dense fire. It was impossible to break out.

A battalion of the 43rd Army - suffering enormous casualties and blanketing the Ugra and the adjacent forests with the corpses of Russian soldiers - also couldn't break through to the encircled elements of the 33rd Army. The famished, exhausted encircled troops took a desperate step: crafting crude rafts from logs, they dropped them into the river and laid down on them. Some no longer had the strength to search for logs so they simply lay down on floating chunks of ice (the ice on the river had just broken up).

It was the middle of April and it was cold, windy weather. The men attempted to lay motionless in their water-logged coats and combat blouses. It was unimaginably difficult to endure the five to six hours they had to spend on the rafts, but they had to suffer more than the torture of the cold. German trenches stretched along the banks to the left and right and the enemy quickly realized that the bodies lying motionlessly on the ice chunks and rafts were not corpses, but desperate Ivans - and they were alive. Target practice began. It was about 100 meters to the targets. The Germans were enjoying themselves and from their trenches one could hear outbursts of laughter while the Russian soldiers were doomed to death. Thus they died - powerless to change the situation.

No one knows precisely how many of them there were: possibly hundreds. It is known that the German target practice lasted for around a week. A few men, barely alive, were lifted from the ice in the sector of the 43rd Army's 53rd Rifle Division. After passing through the scrutiny of SMERSH, they were returned to active duty. But what about the rest? Where are their remains? The majority of the bodies were left in the river. The current carried them downstream until they became stuck on little islands.

There was one large island located near the command post of the 43rd Army's 53rd Rifle Division where a lot of the bodies purportedly accumulated. An aerial photograph of this island was taken in April 1942. This photograph was scrutinized and knowing its approximate location, a search was launched. The results were meager, but interesting. At first earthenware fragments were encountered - beneath which the searchers came across fishing sinkers that were crafted from stones with a hole drilled through the center of them. Suspicions arose in the searchers about the great age of the findings. With further digging, they found fragments of human bones. A cheekbone fragment was of a coal-black color both on the surface of it and in the cross-section. It was possible to assume that the remains were connected with the time of the Great Standoff on the Ugra River when Ivan III faced down Akhmat, Khan of the Great Horde, in 1480. But there was nothing to indicate that the searchers had found what they were seeking. This was no "Island of Death".

The search was resumed the following year. Now a tall, black cross stands on the edge of a field and next to it rest the remains of 1,500 soldiers which were found in the surrounding forests by searchers of a historical-archeological institute. Thus the searchers have gradually been reconstructing page after page of truth about the past war - and this, if you will, is their great contribution.

Frequently, a question like the following is raised by the searchers: "Why, given such a large quantity of the remains of fallen soldiers that has been found, hasn't it been possible to establish their identities - which means we've been unable to locate their loved ones or descendants?"

I think that there are three main reasons. First, too much time has passed since these men died and it has obliterated many human traces. Second, in September 1942 the People's Commissar of Defense issued Order No. 376 "On the Withdrawal of Identification Medallions from the Red Army Supply." I tried to find out why such an absurd - in essence - order appeared, but I was unable to learn why.

Let's recall that many soldiers didn't hurry to use the *smertnik* [literally, "someone condemned to death"] - the nickname that these identification medallions received among the soldiers. Especially the older soldiers believed a *smertnik* was indeed a token of certain death to any man who wore one. In the war, I also chose not to wear a medallion. As far as I recall, the medallions were not waterproof. Thus, they were virtually worthless. As a rule, in the opinion of the searchers, even the medallions that they've found were frequently used by the soldiers to store thread, a needle, small photographs, pencils or bits of soap.

I'll familiarize the reader with one story from the life of the searchers. Three years ago the promising journalist of the Balakovskii Television Company of Saratov Oblast, Oleg Erokhin, couldn't even imagine that he'd ever become a searcher. The last will and testament of his grandmother changed his entire life. When she was dying, Mariia Fedorovna told her grandson about the puzzling disappearance of his grandfather in 1942. Some believed that Fedor Pirogov had been struck down by a random bullet while others believed that he'd been taken prisoner by the Germans and had become a spy. Oleg's grandmother told him just before her death: "Your grandfather was always an honorable man. I know he died as a hero. Find his gravesite and bury my beloved together with me."

Erokhin got in touch with an acquaintance who worked in a Novosibirsk search group. "It wouldn't be too much to ask to make a film about us," she said to Oleg - and without stopping to think he agreed. Having filmed the searchers, Erokhin himself soon joined them.

Erokhin relates: "I'll never forget how the searchers found the daughter of one of the fallen. The father of this village woman, who went missing in action, was considered a traitor. To her, this was simply slander. When we told this woman how her father had been killed and showed his grave to her, she burst into tears. Then the entire village came to her to beg forgiveness."

Oleg returned to Saratov Oblast as a changed man. He created a search group called "Nabat" and headed it.

Says Oleg: "And you know, before the authorities didn't welcome the search work at all; an unspoken taboo had been placed on it. It was believed that all the fallen had been buried with honors. The rest were either former prisoners or traitors. But people were continuing to find fields that were strewn with human bones and the remains of parachutists hanging in trees. They began to demand explanations."

After all his experiences, Erokhin began to take eager part in the search for fallen soldiers and made more than a few discoveries. Recently, Oleg Erokhin discovered the remains of a 20-year-old soldier. His identity was established from an ordinary aluminum spoon, in which the fellow had inscribed his name. The uncovered spoon had been penetrated by a bullet. On it was the inscription "V.P. Terent'ev". Oleg explained that this private had been called up from Leningrad Oblast. He found the soldier's relatives in order to reveal to them that Terent'ev had not been a traitor, but he'd been killed defending his Motherland!

"But what about your grandfather?" his mother reminded him. "You've found so many men while he's still lying somewhere unknown?" So Oleg set out in full search for his grandfather. However, it turned out to be practically impossible to find any trace of him.

Erokhin relates: "I knew only that my grandfather was a native of Kabardino-Balkariia. I began to dig further and ran into a dead end! The records of the local military enlistment center had been irrevocably lost or destroyed. I appealed to the FSB. There I was told: 'Be tough and prepared for the fact that your grandfather was on the lists of traitors.'"

Oleg was advised to search for the "files" on Pirogov in the NKVD archives. There was the belief that Erokhin's grandfather had been captured, and later a member of the German special services with his name had infiltrated the Red Army. But like his grandmother, Oleg didn't believe this. He made his way to the NKVD archives. On a list of 38 names, Erokhin didn't find that of his grandfather. Then he formed his own hypothesis. He listed all the regiments that had been formed back then in Kabardino-Balkariia. Step by step he gathered information about them. During the war, one of the regiments had been sent to the Ukraine. Then Erokhin remembered that once his grandmother had told him about how she'd traveled to Russia from the Ukraine with a 1-year-old daughter. He looked up the archives of the "Ukrainian" regiment and found the name of Pirogov!

It turned out that Oleg's father had wound up in a pontoon bridging battalion, which was billeted in the hamlet of Skita near present-day Volgograd. He was assigned to work on constructing a pontoon bridge at a river crossing and disappeared on 13 May 1942. But Erokhin managed to find another combat report in the regiment's archive dated 16 August 1942. It mentioned that the body of Fedor Pirogov had been dragged out of a river. On 13 May he'd been killed by a bombing attack and the river's current had carried him away. The soldier's remains became lodged on the river bank only on 16 August. However, they were able to recognize that they belonged to Pirogov. Thus Oleg proved that his grandfather was not a traitor, but had been defending the Motherland and had died with honor. He wasn't buried in a grave, but in a nearby shell crater. Oleg Erokhin's discovery shocked his entire family.[7]

In recent years, Russia's Ministry of Defense has detached an entire battalion to assist the searchers in the Leningrad Military District. Why only one and not two or three? Why didn't the Red Army right after the war ended send entire regiments to search for the remains of fallen soldiers and officers? Why did the Orthodox Church remain on the sidelines from this noble, sacred matter? If it was difficult to answer these questions in Stalin's times, then God himself has ordered this job to be finished.

According to records of the Russian Ministry of Defense - as Colonel Igor' Presniakov reported on 20 April 2009 - it was storing approximately a million decorations which hadn't been given to frontline honorees in due time. Many of them had already died or it was difficult to determine their new place of residence. Over the years since the war ended, the Ministry of Defense had been able to find a total of 253 veterans - to which they had presented 256 decorations… a blatantly unique fact![8]

Two Cemeteries: One War

There are two different cemeteries: at one, Soviet dead are buried while the remains of *Wehrmacht* soldiers lie in the other. All-German cemeteries appeared in Russia in the 1990s - 45 years after the end of the Second World War. In the following 10 years, 25 German cemeteries have been opened.[9]

I want to focus on one of them. On a large field covering more than 12 acres - located 100 kilometers from Saint Petersburg - a Peace Park and a cemetery for 40,000 German graves was created next to the village of Sologubovka. The opening of this, if you will, largest cemetery for former adversaries took place on 9 September 2000.[10] A large cross stands on a pedestal in the center of the grounds. The same sort of cross stands over the Russian military cemeteries in Germany. Just to one side, a granite monument depicting a woman with an infant in her arms: the work of the German sculptor Yrsa von Leistner. Her fiancé went missing in action on the Eastern Front.

In the autumn of 1941 the Nazis entered Sologubovka and issued an edict: "Unauthorized individuals are forbidden to reside in the village. Report to the Kommandatura on the appearance of outsiders." A woman, Ul'iana Fenagina, the mother of four children, was living in this village. One evening, a stranger knocked on the door of her home and asked to spend the night there. He was a Russian. Under the risk of a death sentence she let him in, gave him a change of clothes and fed him… in the morning he left and reported her to the Kommandatura. He was a Russian traitor who was working for the Gestapo.

Eyewitnesses of those times remember that her infant daughter was brought to Ul'iana in jail so that she could breastfeed her baby. Subsequently the woman was shot in front of the eyes of the entire village. Several days later, her infant daughter died from hunger. The story of the execution of Ul'iana Fenagina was revealed at a Nuremburg Trial as evidence of a military crime. The Church of the Assumption of the Mother of God in Sologubovka served as a hospital during the war. Hundreds of German soldiers died of their wounds in the church cellar. Today, where bunks for the wounded once stood, there are now bookcases holding "Books of Remembrance" in which the names of all the Germans who were killed in Russia are listed.

The Church of the Assumption in Sologubovka was rebuilt only in 2003 by contributions from German citizens. Father Viacheslav Kharinov became the church's priest and ever since he has been endlessly accused of walking with a censer among the graves of adherents of a different faith and of preserving "Books of Remembrance", which list the names of fascist aggressors in the church's cellar.

In response to these comments, the priest wrote the following:

> ... What should be the attitude to a foe after a war? What is ecclesiastic peace-building? I believe that war is the most implacable form of sinful intolerance of fellow man. This intolerance is easy to incite on the level of the mutual relations between two governments or nations: "Kill the German"; "A gypsy is subhuman". In the Church's peace-building, the superficial isn't as important as in the secular world...
>
> There are conflicting passions in every man and sins break him down - and this is the main reason for all wars. It is important to expose not only the impermissible aspect of war, but also its immoral, sinful nature.
>
> My position with respect to the fallen Germans is no more or less than that of a Christian. The body of the deceased must be given to the soil no matter what sort of person he was in life. Of course it is possible to carve up the foe's remains, riddle them with bullets, burn them with napalm and pulverize them into the tiniest atoms. But all the same the Lord will raise everyone up on Judgment Day, place them in front of Him and each will have to answer for his sins. Why should we substitute ourselves for the Lord God? A heathen attitude toward the body of any man is impermissible: both the soul and the body of each living person were created by God with equal love.
>
> Every person has a specific limit of moral fortitude and if it is exceeded, then irreversible consequences will set in. A man who has witnessed brutality will never emotionally reconcile himself with the foe. So then he puts his trust in his own will and reason and in the mystical sensation of the need for achieving peace in his heart. It is hard to forgive. But forgiveness doesn't mean reconciliation with evil. One must know how to be courageous and stout-hearted; to speak both about the senseless atrocities of the Germans and the unjustified cruelty of our soldiers.
>
> Germans are coming to Sologubovka and crying over the graves of their compatriots. I visited Russian military cemeteries in Germany together with our veterans of the war. We convinced ourselves that the graves of our soldiers are in very good condition. That is to say that you will not surprise the Germans with the cemetery here

itself. They are more touched by the fact that we can forgive; that there is a place where they can commemorate their own kinsmen. Completely different sorts of people are coming. One monk visited - a remarkable fellow - simply an elder, but as one could see immediately a man who had lived an honorable, cheerful life. He came to find the grave of his brother. A staggering story emerged. It turns out that his brother was a deeply religious man and dreamed of the monastic life, but he was sent like cannon fodder to the Eastern Front. Meanwhile my conversation partner had held completely different life plans. His brother's death changed his entire life; he realized that he must do something for him. He became closer to the Church. In fact, in the end he entered a monastery. "I'm a monk because my brother was unable to become one," he told me. He cried when we found his brother's grave.

The German cemetery and the Peace Park in Sologubovka is a peace-building project between Russia and Germany - made real by the contributions of ordinary people. This is the most important thing!

The tragedy of the war and the moral problems connected with it were fully revealed to me when I began to study the Sologubovsky Church. The Germans were planning to demolish the church in order to lay down a direct road to the cemetery. I had to speak up on behalf of the church (which at the time was actually in ruins) and to persuade them of the need to redesign the German cemetery. I said to the Germans that within 50 years the cemetery would be neglected and unkempt if this place wasn't commemorated by rebuilding the church as a monument of reconciliation between the two peoples. The fact that the Germans were involved in its destruction during the war was another reason for the joint reconstruction of the church.

Reconciliation over Graves

It is impossible to avoid discussing the story of the origins of the German cemetery in Rzhev. Years passed before it was possible to create it. Former Communist Party functionaries spoke out against the cemetery's organization. They held meetings, appealed to authorities, wrote disgraceful leaflets and fostered anti-German moods among some of the veterans. However, they were unable to achieve their goal.

Surviving adversaries were united in their desire to honor the German officer Ernst-Martin Rhein and his fellow soldiers from Eastern Westphalia who were killed 60 years ago in the bloody fighting around Rzhev. The casualties on both sides were colossal: tens of thousands of killed, wounded and missing in action. Back then, his fellow soldiers believed that Rhein had been killed in action. However, many decades later they found out by coincidence that their commander had survived the war and had spent years in a Soviet prison. They invited him to join the Veterans' Association that had been formed in 1977. In the last days of September 2002, the veterans - led by Ernst-Martin Rhein - again visited the old battlefields; this time in order to participate in the opening of a modest German cemetery there.[11]

In May 2002, Erich Fornholdt from Gutersloh sent a letter to the city of Rzhev's Council of War Veterans, which contained the following words: "We want to extend a hand of reconciliation to you. Through mutual acquaintanceship and an exchange of opinions, we should strengthen peace." Thus a mutual correspondence started up. A year later, the first meeting took place in Rzhev. It wasn't easy for the Germans to hear the stories about the suffering of the Russian civilians under German occupation. At the same time, the Russians discovered how German soldiers saved one or another family from an inevitable death by starvation. The revelations contributed to better mutual understanding.

Inspired by the positive results of two trips to Russia, members of the association and of a number of other societies created the Rzhev Stewardship Committee - choosing Ernst-Martin Rhein as its director. With time, representatives of the postwar generation - primarily educators and doctors - contributed to the work of the Committee. The exchange of delegations became bi-lateral. Guests from Rzhev - war veterans, German-language teachers, students, doctors and historians - repeatedly visited Gutersloh, Verl, Bonn and other German cities. Impressions from these trips changed the world view of the Russians.

Student exchanges and inter-school collaboration lay at the basis of partnership ties between Rzhev and Gutersloh. Many German-language instructors from Russian schools took part in methodological seminars in Germany and their best students studied in German schools. The Stewardship Committee collected and delivered teaching aids, books and furniture to Rzhev schools that were worth several tens of thousands of Euros.[12]

An annual German-Russian youth camp takes place near Rzhev. It is financed by the German War Graves Commission. Within the framework of humanitarian assistance, the Stewardship Committee supplied Rzhev hospitals with more than 200,000 Euros' worth of medical equipment, bandaging materials and syringes.

In 2002, a German military cemetery opened in Rzhev. At its opening, Ernst-Martin Rhein gave a speech, in which he stated: "We have waited long for this day, we - the Germans who survived the Battle of Rzhev. Those close to the fallen, who are located among us, are grateful to fate that they lived to see the day of this cemetery's dedication." In the name of the Rzhev Stewardship Committee he thanked all the Russian friends who, having taken up the idea of reconciliation and peace, continued to support it to the present day - refusing to yield to the attacks and accusations of the opponents.

Rhein continued:

> ... The majority of our comrades died here. The cross and every stone marker remind us today about them. From today, the Christian cross must preserve this recollection. When they fought, they didn't know what crimes were being perpetrated in the rear against the Russian people: These unimaginable crimes were an abuse of your country's traditions and culture. We are ashamed of this... Appearing here, we again recall the Red Army men who attacked our positions in hundreds - often in wave after wave - and who fell wounded or dead under our automatic weapons and artillery fire. It was just these scenes from the past that strengthened within us the desire to search for ways to communicate and reconcile with the adversary; with which we had one time fought. It is these memories that give us strength for our joint work...

At a crossroads not far from the town of Gutersloh, stands a signpost: "To the Rzhev monument!" The farmer Karl Nyhus-Obermann erected a monument on his land to his fallen comrades of the 58th Infantry Regiment and to the soldiers of the seven Soviet rifle divisions who were positioned opposite his regiment. After the joint laying of a wreath, a Russian veteran walked up to the German veteran and said: "Once we fired at each other. Now we are old and don't have long to live. We'll work together so that such a thing isn't repeated!"

My next topic is by itself a surprising story from wartime Rzhev. It is hard to picture a *Wehrmacht* soldier among the ruins of the city of Rzhev at the height of the fighting with a notepad and pencil in his hands. But there was such a soldier. The artist Franz-Josef Langer captured the war in his artwork; in letters to his wife and in his diaries. In May-June 1997, 86 works of Langer went on display in an exhibition hall in the city of Rzhev. In them the artist depicted Rzhev under German occupation. This exhibition generated the enormous interest of the city's citizens - especially among the elderly. Some of them brought live bouquets and laid them next to the sketches.

Franz-Josef Langer as an artist was obliged to celebrate the victorious campaign in the East in his creative works. But with the agreement of his commanding officer he produced not complete scenes, but landscapes and simple Russian faces. After all, this was also a portrait of the war: adults and children; prisoners and civilians; faces that reflected the hardships of war; the pain of humiliations; and the hope for the future.

In other sketches Langer captured views of the city - badly damaged by war. Here a half-destroyed church, the cemetery next to it, with leaning crosses rising above a blanket of snow. There the standing chimneys of burned-out homes rising skyward. Toward heaven! Above the temporal earth; the war; the horrors and death, which men in uniforms sow. Langer painted and drew not once in a while during lulls in the fighting, but also under Soviet artillery barrages and aerial bombings.

In letters to his wife he wrote that the landscape and the views of the city were constantly changing. He would plan to make a sketch of some building, but would find it already destroyed when he arrived there. He drew constantly. He had only one choice: to draw or to kill with a weapon in his hands. Thus in letters to his wife he requested that she send him more pencils and paints. He had to endure the envy and hostility of comrades because of his privileged position.

The military unit in which Langer served was surrounded at Bobruisk in the summer of 1944 and completely destroyed. The artist avoided death or being taken prisoner. That April, he had been sent back to Germany for exhibitions of his pictures in several cities. Thus his creativity saved his life.

Langer's letters, diaries and artwork might have remained unknown to postwar generations if not by the will of fate. His son Hans-Peter discovered them underneath floorboards of his father's home during renovation. The artist himself passed away prior to the first exhibition of his art in Rzhev.

What is the "Memorial to German Soldiers in Rzhev" like? We're speaking about land, which is indeed within the city limits, but which is located behind a brick factory and a gas station. Its dimensions are merely 287 by 100 meters. In the center of it is a small plot enclosed by a low fence where a metal cross stands.

In 1998, the association *Voennye memorial* [*War Memorials*] and the German War Graves Commission put on a joint display in the city of Rzhev entitled: "Reconciliation over Graves". At this Russian-German exhibition, photographs of analogous "consolidated German cemeteries" established in Russia were on display. There, the already prepared plan for the German cemetery in Rzhev was presented. Residents of the city visited the exhibition - including veterans and representatives of youth organizations.

"Do we have the right to lay flowers on our graves as well?" Nothing better characterizes the normalization of Russian-German relations in the understanding of the people than this question from a newlywed couple on the day of the German cemetery's dedication in Rzhev on 28 September 2002...

One of the major German burial sites recently opened on a little more than 12 acres of land in the Gagarin [formerly Gzhatsk] and Smolensk areas of the oblast, where during the war more than 120,000 soldiers and officers of the *Wehrmacht* fell in battle. This cemetery was opened with unbelievable difficulty because of the protests of local residents whose memory retained marked traces of indignation at the Nazi atrocities. It was precisely in the Gagarin area, in the years of occupation, where the Germans constructed eight concentration camps. In 1943, in the village of Chertovo, 439 peaceful residents were burned alive. In the former Karmanovsky District, the German soldiers torched the entire village of Leushino.[13]

There is another major German military cemetery in the village of Besedino in Kursk Oblast. In the area of Kursk during the war, the *Wehrmacht* suffered enormous losses - more than 200,000 soldiers and officers.[14] The remains of all the German soldiers buried in Orel, Voronezh, Tula and Briansk Oblasts were transferred here.

The Germans ordinarily bury the remains of their fallen soldiers in cartons measuring 50 by 80 centimeters with one set of remains in each carton. In Russia, searchers bury the remains of the dead in caskets with up to 10 sets of remains in each casket. When the German troops were "masters" of the occupied territory, in wartime photographs one can see their cemeteries: birch crosses in our cities and towns, in our fields! With German precision they plotted these burial sites on staff maps and plans and were strictly pegged to the location. According to orders, when retreating, almost all of the German cemeteries were demolished by them and leveled to the ground. For preservation - how paradoxical! On this subject, the German command issued a special order. It is worth hearing it today: "Resurrect your cemeteries!" and by their maps and plans, when regaining territory the German troops would quickly locate and resurrect them if this proved necessary.

How many Soviet soldiers and officers died in the Great Patriotic War? This question has been hanging in the air for a long time. It, as they say, touches many historians to the quick. They are increasingly criticizing the official 1993 data. Russia created a special commission in order to try to obtain a more precise figure for the military losses and to come up with final figures.

In the opinion of Russia's Ministry of Defense, it is hardly worth expecting large discrepancies between any new data and the existing figures.[15] I think the Russian generals are badly mistaken. Numerous facts point to this - primarily those connected with the searchers' work. In Russia; in Smolensk and Tver' Oblasts alone, in recent years the number of remains of fallen Red Army soldiers found by searchers - as well as investigations into the archives - have been increasing the previous estimates of the military dead by 5,000 to 6,000 per year.[16] With increasing frequency, historians are giving different figures for the number of Red Army soldiers who perished in the Great Patriotic War.

The graves of Russian soldiers – There are a lot of them around the world

Russian (Soviet) burial sites - as a consequence of the Second World War - are located in 49 different countries. With some of them (Germany, Austria, Hungary, Spain, Mongolia, Poland, Romania, Slovakia, Finland, the Czech Republic and Japan), agreements have been signed about the mutual support of memorials, cemeteries or fraternal graves to keep them in good condition. These agreements include such terms as research into archival material that reveals the fate of military personnel who were killed in action or died in an enemy prison camp; the reburial of remains; and the care of the grave sites in cemeteries. Of all the Soviet military burial sites, 95 per cent happen to be in these countries. How are these agreements being observed? Naturally, first of all we're talking about Germany. The remains of more than 500,000 soldiers and officers of the Red Army have been buried in German soil.[17]

Our veterans who visited these sites were shocked: all the graveyards were in pristine condition. It is known that even during Hitler's time in power, the Germans never touched Russian gravesites. Moreover, many of them buried our dead soldiers and even left their names on wooden crosses that marked the grave. We saw these old graves. Even today, inscriptions such as "Unknown", "Soldier Goncharenko" or simply "Soldier Ivan" remain on them.

Remembrance can't be measured in monetary units. But the means devoted by the country that lost the war to keeping up the military memorials are impressive. The German Government spends 25 million Euros each year on the tending of military graves; 1 million Euros a year goes just to caring for the memorials in Berlin in Treptower Park, Tiegarten and in Pankow. That these means are expended on their designated purpose is easy to see when visiting Germany.

In the very center of Berlin - with immediate access to the Brandenburg Gates and the Reichstag Building - stands an 8-meter-high statue of a Red Army soldier on a tall pedestal. Also part of the Tiegarten War Memorial's design are two Soviet T-34 tanks that guard the entrance to the memorial - on the grounds of which 2,500 Red Army soldiers are buried. The cut granite and marble of the curved stoa were taken from the ruins of the Reich Chancellery and bear the inscribed names of Heroes of the Soviet Union buried there.

Another Soviet war memorial (Schönholzer Heide) is located in the National Park in Berlin's Pankow District. The bronze sculptures on the right and left portals of Schönholzer Heide depict the Soviet people fighting and grieving. At the end of the park is a statue of a Russian Mother Earth weeping over her sons and behind it, a large obelisk that contains an Honor Hall. In the soil of this park lay the remains of 13,200 Soviet soldiers.

Finally, the best-known of the Soviet war memorials in the German capital is the Treptower War Memorial, which features an iconic bronze statue of a Soviet soldier with a lowered sword cradling a young German child in his left arm. In the arched dome of the mausoleum beneath the statue, there is an inlaid inscription in mosaic: "Glory to those who died for the Soviet people!" There are also the words: "Glory and gratitude to the Heroes of the Soviet Union, who fell in the struggle against Fascism. We accept the banner that they have handed to us." For over 65 years, the Germans have not censored these lines and each year on Victory Day they bring flowers to place on the staircase leading up to the monument of the Russian soldier.

The German War Graves Commission, which was founded in 1919 (nearly 100 years ago), plays an enormous role in the search for remains and giving them proper burial; the upkeep of gravesites and cemeteries; and the maintenance of the memorials. Today this public organization numbers approximately 1.5 million members. Many of them, as a public service, volunteer to take care of a cemetery in their free time. Only 10 per cent of the War Graves Commission's activities are financed by the government budget; most of its revenues come from voluntary donations and citizen endowments.[18]

The primary slogan of the Commission is: "Reconciliation over the graves of the fallen is work in the name of peace." The tidy, well-groomed burial sites of Soviet soldiers throughout Germany are confirmation of the sincerity of these words. You will not encounter here abandoned Soviet graves overgrown with head-high grass and with inscriptions erased by the passage of time; burial grounds that look like dump sites or gravestones defaced by vandals. The Germans take literally the words: "No one is forgotten and nothing is forgotten," which long ago became an empty phrase for many former "Soviet" people. They carefully look after the graves of both their own and others in equal fashion and lay flowers on them on days of remembrance. The nationality of the dead has no significance. The graves of the war's victims are protected by special law under the code: "Keep eternally".

National and international youth camps - the participants of which look after the military burial sites - annually bring together thousands of young people from around Germany and other European countries. Altogether, there are 3,600 such cemeteries on German territory.

Since 1996 work has been underway in Germany to compile a "Book of Remembrance". In its 1st Edition - which came out in 2002 - and in the 2004 2nd Edition, the names and fates of 60,000 Soviet officers who were German prisoners of war are given. Now a 3rd Edition is being prepared, which will list the names and fates of more than 900,000 Soviet soldiers and sergeants. This will allow the possibility to establish the precise location of up to 80 per cent of the burial sites in Germany of Soviet prisoners who died in captivity. The German Government and the War Graves Commission are jointly financing the project. This is just one tiny aspect of the soldier's fate that has been recorded in the "Book of Remembrance".

German authorities have decided to open one of the largest archives in the world - containing the personal files of 17.5 million victims of Nazism - to researchers and scholars. In accordance with the 1955 Bonn Accords, access to this archive was closed for 60 years but now this decision will be reviewed. The archive consists of various documents which the Nazis pedantically compiled and collected in the concentration camps and forced prisoner labor sites - and on displaced persons. This collection also contains the postwar documents of the Allied Powers on refugees. To this point only the International Red Cross has been able to use these records in order to assist anyone who is searching for relatives and who lost contact with them during the Second World War.

Since 1945 - with the assistance of the archive in Bad Arolsen - the Red Cross has replied to more than 11 million inquiries from 62 countries. They were submitted by relatives of people who went missing under the Nazis. The archive has also been used in order to assist a former forced laborer in Nazi Germany obtain compensation.

The initial publications discuss the unimaginable atrocities of the Nazis. I'll give one example. In the *Totenbuh* [Death Registry], kept in the Mauthausen concentration camp in Austria, on 20 April 1942 a gift of the camp commandant to Hitler on the occasion of the Führer's birthday is described with particular precision. Three hundred Russian prisoners of war were specially selected for execution in honor of the "great event". Each prisoner was subjected to the so-called *Genickshuss*: a single shot to the back of the head from a pistol muzzle placed against the base of the skull.

On each line of the list of the executed, the name and number of the prisoner is pedantically indicated - as well as the date and place of birth.[19]

In Germany's Westphalia there is a small town called Stukenbrock. Not far from it on the grounds of a fraternal burial ground stands a modest monument - beneath which rest the bones of 65,000 Soviet prisoners of war who died in the *Stalag* 326 death camp. How many towns and villages became known to the world as a result of such a dreadful presence! Auschwitz, Buchenwald, Dachau, Mauthausen, Salaspils, Stukenbrock...[20]

Among all the European countries, the most graves of Soviet military personnel are located in Poland: the graves of almost 1.2 million soldiers and officers of the Red Army - as well as Soviet prisoners of war and Soviet citizens driven into forced labor. There are 648 Soviet military cemeteries in Poland. Soviet and Russian soldiers of two epochs are buried in Boleslawiec [formerly Bunzlau]. In the center of the cemetery - where 718 Heroes of the Soviet Union and officers who fell at the end of the Second World War are buried - stands a monument to the Russian military commander Mikhail Kutuzov, who died in this city in 1813 during Russia's war with Napoleon.

New Russian war memorials and cemeteries are being created in places where tens of thousands of Soviet prisoners of war died at Bogusz and Kosowka. Searches are being conducted for burial sites of Russian soldiers who were killed in earlier military conflicts - and in particular the almost-700 cemeteries from the time of the First World War and a cemetery from the period of the Napoleonic Wars. Altogether, specialists believe that the remains of approximately 2.5 million Russian and Soviet internees and civilians are buried in Polish soil. Near Lodz, 6 kilometers from the city, 4,000 sets of remains are buried in a fraternal grave - of which only one has been identified.

Poles are devout Catholics. Their faith doesn't allow them to leave the dead unburied. On days of commemoration, they light candles over each grave - tens and hundreds of candles.

From Poland we'll move to northern Europe - to Finland and Norway. The people of these countries keep alive the memory of the fallen Russian soldiers.

In Norway, in October 2004 the 60th Anniversary of the liberation of Eastern Finnmark from the Nazis was widely observed. As a result of savage fighting during the Petsamo-Kirkenes Operation in October 1944, Soviet troops drove the *Wehrmacht* forces out of Sør-Varanger and created the conditions for handing authority over to the legitimate Norwegian Government. The liberation of the rest of Norway came much later: the last German soldiers surrendered to the Allies in May 1945. On 25 October, to mark the date of Kirkenes' liberation, wreathes were laid at the monument to Soviet soldiers in the memorial cemetery Vestre Gravlund in Oslo and officials gave speeches that were appropriate for the occasion.

The historian Marianne Neerlann Suleim researched and wrote a doctoral dissertation entitled: '*Sovjetiske krigsfanger i Norge*' ['*Soviet prisoners of war in Norway*'], which was published in 2005. She established that there were once 93,318 Soviet prisoners in Norway which were held in concentration camps across the country. The majority of these were Red Army soldiers who'd been taken prisoner elsewhere and shipped to Norway from other countries, but there were also 9,000 Russian civilians among the detainees including old men, women and children. As a result of starvation and the slave labor, 13,000 prisoners died. The figures for the victims are enormous, but all the same they are much lower than those of the concentration camps in Poland. This is largely due to the Norwegian people: despite the prohibitions and even the threat of being shot, they managed to bring food to the "Russian" prisoners.

The Soviet prisoners of war who died in prison - and later, those soldiers and officers who fell in the battles to liberate Norway - were mostly buried in churchyards and local cemeteries near the military and civilian sites built by the Germans. However, they were also frequently buried in undeveloped land and in mountainous areas that were difficult to access. In the spring of 1951, the majority of burial sites from Kirkenes to Bronnoysund were closed and the remains transferred to one fraternal grave. On Norway's Tjøtta Island, an obelisk was raised and a memorial park established; there, 7,551 dead were buried in a fraternal grave - of which only 823 were identified.

In the historiography of Finland, a persistent image has formed of a country that pursued a course independently of Nazi Germany. It is believed that the Finns, in distinction from the Norwegians, didn't turn over their Jews to the Germans and treated prisoners of war in a fully humane manner. Eight Austrian Jews, who had fled to Finland in 1938 and requested political sanctuary, were in fact handed over to the Gestapo in 1942 by the Finnish Government and seven of them died in Auschwitz. Finland later publicly expressed its official regret over this incident and financed the construction of the kibbutz Yad Hashmona ("Remembrance of the Eight") in Israel. However, in November 2003 the Finnish writer, historian and journalist Elina Sana cast doubt on this official version of events in her book *Luovutetut: Suomen ihmisluovutukset Gestapolle* [*Deported: Finland's Extraditions to the Gestapo*], published in 2003. As her research found, during the Second World War the Finnish Government in fact turned over 2,892 Soviet prisoners of war to Germany - among which were 75 Jews. The majority of these deportees were either executed or died in German concentration camps.

Sana observed that the Finnish Government displayed excessive zeal in turning over the prisoners of war - "over-fulfilling" the plans imposed by the Nazis. Sana's research was based upon Finnish records and German military archives - as well as on interviews with the deportees that were still alive or their relatives. As became clear, the Finnish Government was exchanging the Soviet prisoners of war in exchange for members of the Finno-Ugorsky peoples that had been seized by the Germans. In addition, Sana showed that of the 64,000 prisoners that were languishing in Finnish concentration camps, almost one-third perished; such a percentage of losses is only slightly below that of the "model" Nazi death camps.

The Finnish authorities devoted 2 million Euros to conduct a three-year research project headed by the General Director of the country's National Archives, Jussi Nuorteva. The start of the Commission's work was announced by Nuorteva in Jerusalem in 2005. He observed that the analysis of several thousand documents about the prisoners of war would require painstaking work and take a lot of time.

The official website of Finland's National Archives contains information that the project is anticipating not only the study of the fates of the prisoners of war that were held in Finnish camps or were among those deported to Germany; the project must also shed light on the fate of those were returned to Soviet authorities after the war ended. However, even after the completion of the work on the project it will be impossible to say that the lists of all those victims of deportation will be published. In 2005 the Commission adopted the decision not to publish the lists in order to guard personal information or because of the "sensitive nature" of these documents.

That the recent historical research upsets many Finns is an indisputable fact. However, the efforts to preserve the country's positive image at any cost will hardly be crowned with success.

One more example from Western Europe: 865 Soviet soldiers are buried in the Netherlands at the Amersfoort Russian Memorial War Cemetery. This unique burial site is called the *Russisch Erevald*, or Russian Field of Honor. Although officially it is located within the city limits of Leusden after a recent change in city borders, the cemetery was in the city of Amersfoort since its founding in 1947-1948 and it still carries the name of Amersfoort.

The 865 remains buried at the Russian war cemetery in the Netherlands came from three sources. The first set comes from Soviet prisoners of war who'd been held in a German concentration camp - formally called the Police Transit Camp Amersfoort, but which was better known as *Kamp Amersfoort* - just outside the city. Of the 35,000 people that passed through this camp, 101 were prisoners of war from the Soviet Union. Of these, 24 died from starvation, tortures or physical exhaustion while the remaining 77 men were shot on 9 April 1942. Later, on 28 March 1946 they were reburied with honor in land next to the Rusthof Cemetery - which was not far from *Kamp Amersfoort* - and became the Amersfoort Russian Memorial War Cemetery.

The second set consists of the remains of 691 former prisoners of war who were liberated from German concentration camps by American troops, but who died in hospitals from diseases and emaciation. These men were initially buried in the Netherlands American Cemetery in the village of Margraten, but in 1947 - at the initiative of the Americans - their remains were moved to the Amersfoort cemetery as part of their policy to separate the remains of non-Americans from the Americans. Since the largest burial site of Soviet soldiers in the Netherlands was in the city of Amersfoort, it became the destination of the remains of all the Soviet soldiers which had been buried in Margraten.

The third set of remains consists of 73 former prisoners of war who were voluntarily or forcibly serving the *Wehrmacht* when they died, or were laboring at German work sites. They had been buried in various places around the Netherlands, but were later reburied in the Field of Glory.

The Russian Memorial Cemetery (Soviet Field of Glory) officially opened on 18 November 1948. In 1956 Netherland's Ministry of Defense transferred this Memorial to the jurisdiction of the *Oologsgravenstichting* (War Graves Foundation). In 1962 the simple name tablets were replaced by limestone gravestones with engraved inscriptions.

On 4 May 1975 an obelisk was unveiled at the Russian Memorial Cemetery. The monument was crafted in the Soviet Union out of white Armenian marble. The obelisk is a 10-meter tall column which bears the inscription: "Glory to the heroes. To the soldiers of the Soviet army, who died in the struggle with the German aggressors in the period 1941-1945". Many of the buried here are considered "missing in action in the Motherland."

In 1998, the Dutch journalist Remko Reiding received a proposal from his newspaper's chief editor to try to find the relatives of the soldiers buried in Leusden. That which started as a journalistic investigation for Remko became his moral duty. He realized that if he couldn't bring the matter to a close now, then it would never happen.

Remko and his wife Irina have been conducting the search along two directions: finding supplementary information about the buried soldiers from the archives and an immediate search for relatives of those for whom they already had additional information.[21] By the year 2000, after devoting almost all his work time to this project and several trips to Russia at his own expense, Remko Reiding had been able to establish that eight of the men whose remains rest in the Soviet Field of Glory had been officially listed as "missing in action" and he was able to locate and inform their surviving wives, children and grandchildren that their soldier was no longer missing.

Years are passing. Alas, time stops for no one! The still-surviving veterans are becoming fewer and fewer. With agitation and pain they recall the nightmare of the war years. It is impossible to forget it until their final hour.

The world around us is in constant motion, but the fortress of the human spirit remains unchanged. The modern generation enjoys many new rights in Russia. But it doesn't have the right to forget what was done by those people who fought and died for their Motherland.

I want to end with a few lines by the poet Robert Rozhdestvensky:

We recall them all by name

With grief we recall our own

This isn't for the fallen!

This is for the living!

Beautifully said! But this must be not only for the alive, but also for the dead! Isn't that so?

Endnotes

Introduction

1 Editor's Note: This is a well-known reference to the 10 successful offensives, launched by the Red Army in 1944, which ultimately drove German forces out of Soviet territory. The term was first mentioned by Joseph Stalin in a November 1944 speech at a meeting of Moscow's Soviet deputies on the 27th Anniversary of the Bolshevik Revolution. The reference quickly became "Stalin's 10 Blows" - giving Stalin sole credit for the successful offensives.

2 Editor's Note: Aleksandr Matrosov, according to Soviet sources, in February 1942 threw himself against an embrasure of a pillbox - thereby blocking the machine-gun fire and allowing his comrades to advance. Matrosov was posthumously awarded the title Hero of the Soviet Union and his feat was widely acclaimed in the newspapers. Like many other Soviet-era stories from the war, the facts of Matrosov's self-sacrificial exploit have been questioned by contemporary scholars and challenged by revisionists.

Chapter 1

1 *Ia eto videl: Sbornik soldatskikh vospominanii* [*I saw this: Collection of soldiers' remembrances*] (Moscow: Izdatel'stvo Vremia, 1965)

2 *Ibid.*

3 *Ibid.*

4 Charles Burdick and Hans-Adolf Jacobsen [ed.], *The Halder War Diary, 1939-1942* [Novato, CA: Presidio Press, 1988), 410-413 [Translator's note: Gorbachevsky is actually using the Russian translation of Halder's war diary. Where possible, I am using the English-language version. However, it appears that the Russian version is complete, while the English-language version has been condensed. In cases where there is no corresponding existing English translation, I have used my own translation from the Russian.]

5 Kukryniksy was a collective name given to three cartoonists with a very distinctive style: Mikhail Kupriianov, Porfiri Krylov and Nikolai Sokolov. The name "Kukryniksy" itself is a composite of the three names. They became very famous in the 1930s for their caricatures lampooning Adolf Hitler, Benito Mussolini, Heinrich Himmler and Joseph Goebbels.

6 Ortenberg, *Iul'-dekabr' sorok pervogo. Rasskaz-khronika* (*July-December of '41: A narrative tale*) (Moscow: Sovetskii pisatel', 1984), pp. 10-11.

7 Podol is an old city district in Kiev

Chapter 2

1 To Soviet citizens, Stalin's appeal was striking because of his choice of words. He wasn't addressing "citizens" or "comrades" or "workers and peasants" – he addressed the people as his "brothers and sisters".

2 Editor's note: *SMERSH* is a Russian contraction for '*Smert' shpionam*' ['Death to spies']. This was the counter-intelligence department in the Red Army charged with investigating, arresting and often executing anti-Soviet partisans, saboteurs, spies, deserters and people accused of collaborating with the Germans.

3 Editor's note: Max Amann (1891-1957) was the head of the Reich Press Chamber during the war. During the Third Reich, Amann became the largest newspaper publisher in Germany after appropriating or closing down newspapers that did not demonstrate whole-hearted support for the Nazi regime. He had been the publisher of Hitler's *Mein Kampf.*

4 The existing English translation of this passage from Goebbel's war diary can be found in Taylor, *The Goebbels Diaries, 1939-1941: The historic journal of a Nazi war leader* (London: Hamish Hamilton Ltd., 1982), 444-447.

5 Ibid., p. 447.

6 Churchill, *The Second World War, Vol. 3: The Grand Alliance* [Boston: Houghton Mifflin Company, 1950], p. 316. The author is using a Russian translation of this volume.

7 V.D. Danilov, 'Stalinskaia strategiia nachala voiny: plany i realnost' ['Stalin's strategy of the war's start: plans and reality'] Otechestvennaia istoriia, No. 3 (March 1995). Now available in Russian at the website http://hronos.km.ru/statii/2003/danilov.html.

8 Editor's note: In October and November 1940, the USSR and Germany discussed the potential entry as a fourth member of the Axis. The negotiations included a two-day conference in Berlin between Soviet Foreign Minister Molotov, German Foreign Minister von Ribbentrop and Adolf Hitler. On 25 November, the Soviet sides sent a proposal on this matter to which Germany never responded. See John Lukacs, *June 1941: Hitler and Stalin* (Yale University Press, 2006), p. 65.

9 Editor's note: This view that Stalin was preparing to attack Germany and that Operation Barbarossa was a preemptive invasion has become a subject of heated debate in Russia - with scholars and popular historians arguing for and against it. As one cogent example of the contrary view that Stalin had no intentions to attack Germany, see B. Kavalerchik and L. Lopukhovsky, *Iun' 1941: Zaprogramirovannoe porazhenie* [*June 1941: A Pre-programmed defeat*] (Moscow: Yauza/Eksmo, 2010).

10 Author's note: This episode was deleted by the censors in the first edition of Zhukov's memoirs.

11 Editor's note: On 14 June 1941, the Soviet newspapers published a now famous (or infamous) TASS communiqué, which attacked rumors that there would soon be war between the USSR and Germany, and that Germany had presented territorial and economic claims to the Soviet Union. These rumors were denounced as "nothing but clumsy propaganda put out by forces hostile to the USSR and Germany and interested in the promulgation of war." Many believe that this communiqué was written by Stalin himself and that it was intended to give Nazi Germany a chance to make its own denials about the possibility of an early war. Because of this communiqué, the German invasion which came so soon after was all the more

stunning to the Soviet people. Immediately following the release of this communiqué, orders went out to the Red Army to relax the alert status, move back into camps and to move armored vehicles into tank parks.

12 K.A. Meretskov, *Na sluzhbe narodu* [*At the service of the people*] (Moscow, 1969), p. 209.

13 On these days Zhukov had been located with the Southwestern Front.

14 For the full text of this letter, the existence of which has not yet been proven, see David E. Murphy, *What Stalin Knew: The Enigma of Barbarossa* (Yale University Press, 2006), pp. 256-258.

15 Mark Solonin, 23 iiunia: 'Den' M' [23 June: 'Day M'] (Moscow:Yauza/Eksmo, 2007), p. 506. An English translation of this letter, which I have used, can be found on the Internet at http://personal.ashland.edu/~jmoser1/hitler.htm.

16 V.D. Danilov, "Stalinskaia strategiia".

17 Iurii Afanas'ev, *Drugaia voina* [*The other war*] (Moscow: RGGU, 1996).

18 Mark Solonin, *23 iiunia: 'Den' M'* [*23 June: 'Day M'*] (Moscow: Yauza/Eksmo, 2007).

19 Iurii Fel'shtinsky, "Chitaya knigi 'Ledokol' i 'Den'-M' Viktora Suvorova" ["Reading Viktor Suvorov's books '*Ledokol*' and '*Day-M*'"] *Vestnik*, No. 26 (2007).

20 Mark Solonin, *Ogonek*, No. 23 (2006).

21 Ibid.

Chapter 3

1 Actually, all of the German aircraft were unserviceable – Author's note.

2 Editor's note: Those readers interested in reading how the author was wounded during a human-wave assault can refer to his memoirs *Through the Maelstrom: A Soldier's War on the Eastern Front 1942-1945* (Lawrence, KS: University of Kansas Press, 2008).

3 Editor's note: Though not a professional military historian, Svetlana Gerasimova, a long-time staff worker and local historian with the Tver' State Consolidated Museum, wrote a history of the long campaign to recapture the city of Rzhev from the Germans and to reduce the Rzhev salient. It was published in 2008 under the title *Na podstupakh k Moskve: Rzhevskaia bitva* [*On the approaches to Moscow: the Battle of Rzhev*]. An English translation of this title has been published by Helion as *The Rzhev Slaughterhouse: The Red Army's Forgotten 15-month Campaign against Army Group Center, 1942-1943* (Solihull, 2013).

4 Editor's note: The Cathedral of Christ the Savior in Moscow was a famous city landmark and the tallest Orthodox Church in the world. Sitting on the banks of the Moscow River not far from the Kremlin, Stalin ordered its demolition in order to use the space as a location for a new Palace of the Soviets. On 5 December 1931 the Cathedral was dynamited. Construction of the Palace was interrupted by funding problems, flooding and the war. The flooded foundation hole later became the world's largest open-air swimming pool. In February 1990, the Russian Orthodox Church received permission to rebuild the Cathedral. Construction was plagued by controversies, but the completed Cathedral of Christ the Savior was consecrated on 19 August 2000.

5 Editor's note: This was Stalin's famous "No step back!" order, issued on 28 July 1942 which promised a military tribunal for unauthorized retreats and created penal bat-

talions for officers and penal companies for junior officers and soldiers. Moreover, the order directed that each army establish blocking detachments, which were authorized to shoot anyone fleeing the battlefield or displaying cowardice or panic.

6 In connection with the turnaround in the overall situation at the front in 1943, the need for these blocking detachments subsided. They were dissolved in the autumn of 1944.

7 Editor's note: For those interested, Petr Mikhin's superb memoir, translated into English and published by Pen & Sword in 2010 under the title *Guns Against the Reich: Memoirs of an Artillery Officer on the Eastern Front*, gives another gripping description of the terrible combat outside of Rzhev in the summer of 1942, including his own view of the "Valley of Death".

8 V. G. Soshnev, *S veroi v Pobedy* [*With faith in Victory*] (Moscow: Voenizdat, 1982), pp. 94-96.

9 All of the information on the battle for Bel'kovo, Svin'ino and Kharino are based on the materials of the Rzhev Regional History Museum - as well as in I.Z. Ladygin's and N.I. Smirnov's book, *Na Rzhevskom rubezhe* [*On the Rzhev line*] (Rzhev, 1992), pp. 63-74.

10 The author is referring to D.D. Leliushenko's memoirs, *Moskva – Stalingrad – Berlin – Prague*, published in Moscow by Voenizdat in 1985.

11 Before taking command of the 220th Rifle Division, S.G. Poplavsky had commanded the 185th Rifle Division, which took part in the First Rzhev-Sychevka Operation.

12 "War writes off everything" – this was a widespread expression in the Red Army, often used cynically to justify plundering, destruction of property, violence against civilians and high casualties.

13 F.W. von Mellenthin, *Panzer Battles* (University of Oklahoma Press, 1956; reprinted by Konecky & Konecky), p. 295.

Chapter 4

1 Vera Aleksandrova, 'Vokrug Fronta' ['Around the front'] *Sotsialisticheskii vestnik*, No. 21/22 (December 1942); 'Na obshchestvennom fronte' ['On the Public Front'] *Sotsialisticheskii vestnik*, No. 7/8 (April 1943).

2 Within a half-year, K. A. Koshman would become a regiment commissar. For his courage and heroism during the forcing of the Neman River, he would be awarded the title Hero of the Soviet Union. After the war he graduated from the Military-Political Academy and served in the army until his retirement.

3 S.M. Shtemenko, *General'nyi Shtab v gody voiny* [*The General Staff in the war years*] Volume 1 (Moscow: Voenizdat, 1968), pp. 123-124.

4 Boris Livanov was a popular actor with the Moscow Art Theater who played the role of Gorlov in the *The Front*. Obviously, Vsevolod Ivanov did not admire his performance in the play.

5 Editor's note: Tartuffe was the central character in Moliere's play of the same name - a man who exaggeratedly feigned virtue.

Chapter 5

1 G.K. Zhukov, *Vospominaniia i razmyshleniia* [translated as Zhukov, *Reminiscences and Reflections* (Moscow: Progress Publishers, 1985)], Vol. 2, p. 35; I.S. Konev, *Zapiski komanduiushchego frontom* [*Notes of a front commander*] (Moscow: Golos, 2002), p. 121.

2 D. Volkogonov, *I.V. Stalin – politicheskii portret: Triumf i tragediia* [*I.V. Stalin – a political portrait: Triumph and tragedy*] Vol. 2, part 1 (Moscow: Izdatel'stvo Agenstva pechati Novosti, 1989), p. 299.

3 This statement can be found in Zhukov, *Reminiscences and Reflections*, Vol. 2, p. 62.

4 Zhukov, *Reminiscences and Reflections*, Vol. 2, p. 110.

5 S. A. Gerasimova, 'Pervaia Rzhevsko-Sychevskaia operatsiia 1942 g: novaia datirovka' ['The 1st Rzhev-Sychevka operation of 1942: New dating' in *Sbornik nauchnykh trudov* [*Collected research studies*] (Tver' State Consolidated Museum), pp. 105-110.

6 Svetlana Gerasimova's full-length study of the campaigns to liberate Rzhev has been translated into English and was published by Helion & Company in August 2013 under the title *The Rzhev Slaughterhouse: The Red Army's Forgotten 15-month Campaign against Army Group Center.*

7 *Sbornik 'Rzhevskimi dorogami voiny'* [*Digest 'Along the Rzhev roads of the war'*] (Rzhev, 1982), pp. 20-23.

8 David Glantz, *Zhukov's Greatest Defeat: The Red Army's Epic Disaster in Operation Mars 1942* (Lawrence, KS: University Press of Kansas, 1999). The author has used a Russian translation of this book published in Moscow by Izdatel'stvo AST-Astrel in 2007.

9 H. Grossman, *Rzhev: Kraeugol'nyi kamen' vostochnogo fronta* [*Rzhev: The cornerstone of the Eastern Front*] (Rzhev, 1996), p. 130.

10 See Zhukov, *Reminiscences and Reflections*, Vol. 2, p. 86.

11 N. Belov and T. Mikhailov, *Rzhev 1942:Bitva za vysotu 200: voenno-istoricheskii ocherk* [*Rzhev 1942: The battle for Hill 200: a military-historical essay*] (Tver', 2000), p. 41.

12 As cited by A.J.P. Taylor, *The Origins of the Second World War* (Simon & Schuster, 1996), p. 251.

13 Field Marshal Erich von Manstein, *Lost Victories* (Novato, CA: Presidio Press, 1984), pp. 280-281. The author is using a Russian translation of von Manstein's memoirs of the war, published in Moscow by AST in 1999.

14 These numbers originally come from Hans Essmaier, a former staff officer in the Ninth Army's 26th Infantry Division. They can be found (in Russian) in E. Fedorov, *Pravda o voennom Rzheve: Dokumenty i fakty* [*The truth about wartime Rzhev: Documents and facts*] (Rzhev, 1995), p. 217.

15 The official data can be found in G.F. Krivosheev (ed.), *Grif sekretnosti sniat: Poteri vooruzhennykh sil SSSR v voinakh, boevykh deistviiakh i vooruzhennykh konfliktakh XX veka* [*The seal of secrecy has been lifted: Losses of the armed forces of the USSR in wars, combat actions and armed conflicts of the XX century*] (Moscow: Voenizdat, 1993).

16 *Rzhevskaia Pravda*, 8 March 2000.

17 Upon giving the authorization to abandon Rzhev, Hitler insisted not only that the remaining bridge over the Volga River be blown up, but also that he be able to hear the demolition.

Chapter 6

1 D. Ortenburg, 'Iul'-dekabr' sorok-pervogo: rasskaz-khronika' ['July-December of 41: a chronicle tale'] *Sov. pisatel'* (1989), p. 16.

2 N.S. Khrushchev, *Krushchev Remembers* (Boston: Little, Brown & Company, 1970), p. 187. The author is using the original Russian version of Khrushchev's memoirs, but I have employed Strobe Talbott's translation from the English-language version.

3 The author is using the Russian-language version [Halder, *Dnevnik boevykh deistvii*] which differs from its English-language version due to editing decisions. The figures for German casualties up to 3 July 1941 given in the English version are in the 6 July 1941 entry [Halder, *The Halder War Diary 1939-1942* (Novato, CA: Presidio Press, 1988), p. 453.], but these are slightly higher the figures that the author cites: 54,000 total losses (2.14% of 2.5 million), including 724 officers.

4 Beshanov, *1942 – god uchebnyi*, pp. 23-24.

5 As cited by Beshanov, *1942 – god uchebnyi*, p. 608.

Chapter 7

1 N.G. Semenova and Iu.V. Dorod'ko, *Mnogolikii antistalinizma i nichevo, krome pravdy* [*Multi-faced anti-Stalinsim and nothing, except the truth*] (Moscow, 2006), p. 1

2 A.I. Mikoian, *Tak bylo: Razmyshleniia o minuvshem* [*As it was: Reminiscences of the past*] (Moscow: Izdatel'stvo Vagrius, 1999),

3 N. Zlobin, 'Trumen' ['Truman'], *Kontinent*, No. 10 (2001), pp. 13-14.

4 Ibid.

5 Editor's note: There are two passages in the Bible that speak positively of what could be considered ideal Communism. Specifically, Acts 2: 44-45 states: "All that believed were together, and had all things in common; and sold their possessions and goods and parted them to all men, as every man had need." Acts 4: 34-35 states: "There was not a needy person among them, for as many that owned lands or houses sold them and brought the proceeds of what was sold and laid it at the apostles' feet; and distribution was made to each as any had need."

6 Editor's note: The original Soviet State security agency was called the Cheka - a contraction of the words '*Chrezvychainaia komissiia*' or '*Extraordinary Commission*'. Agents became known popularly as Chekists, which has been applied to State security agents ever since.

Chapter 8

1 Editor's note: *The Reference Guide to Russian Literature* by Neil Cornwell and Nicole Christian (Routledge Press, 1998) has this to say about Koz'ma Prutkov: "Koz'ma Prutkov, the fictitious writer and bureaucrat invented in 1852 by Aleksei Tolstoy and his cousins the Zhemchuzhnikov brothers, is one of Russia's most humorous literary creations. … "Author" of a wide variety of plays, poems, sayings and anecdotes, Prutkov is best remembered, however, for his absurd aphorisms - many of which immediately entered the Russian language and have retained their popularity to this day.

2 Mr. Roosevelt, who was host at a luncheon, said that he and I always referred to Stalin in our secret telegrams as "Uncle Joe". I had suggested that he should tell him this privately,

but instead the President made it into a jocular statement to the company. This led to a difficult moment. Stalin took offence. 'When can I leave this table?' he asked in anger. Mr. Byrnes saved the situation with an apt remark. 'After all,' he said, 'you do not mind talking about 'Uncle Sam', so why should 'Uncle Joe' be so bad?' At this the Marshal subsided, and Molotov later assured me that he understood the joke. He already knew that he was called 'Uncle Joe' by many people abroad and he realised that the name had been given in a friendly way and as a term of affection." Winston Churchill, *The Second World War: Triumph and Tragedy*, Vol. 6 (Houghton Mifflin Company, 1953), p. 345.

3 Biographical index: Harry Lloyd Hopkins, available at http://www.hrono.info/biograf/bio_g/gopkins.html.

4 Vladimir Pechatkov, *Stalin, Roosevelt i Truman: SSSR i SShA v 1940-x g.g.* [*Stalin, Roosevelt and Truman: the USSR and USA in the 1940s*] (Moscow: Terra – Knizhnyi klub, 2000).

5 Cordell Hull, the Secretary of State in the Roosevelt Administration, entered history as the founder and organizer of the United Nations - for which he received the Nobel Peace Prize.

6 Aleksandr Gennis, 'Pir vo vremia chumy' ['A feast during a plague'] *Zvezda* No. 10 (2000). A copy of this article is available in Russian at http://magazines.russ.ru/zvezda/2003/10/genis.html/.

7 P.P. Sokolov and B.L. Tsybulevsky (eds.), *Sbornik dokumentov "Tegeran-Yalta-Potsdam"* [*Collection of documents "Teheran-Yalta-Potsdam"*] (Moscow: Izdatel'stvo "Mezhdunarodnye otnosheniia", 1970).

8 Vladimir Pechatnov, *Stalin-Ruzvel't-Trumen: SSSR i SShA v 1940 g.g. Dokumental'nye ocherki* [*Stalin-Roosevelt-Truman: the USSR and USA in the 1940s. Documentary essays*] (Moscow: Izdatel'stvo Terra – "Knizhnyi klub", 2006), pp. 342-343.

9 Churchill, *The Second World War: Triumph and Tragedy*, Vol. 6, p. 351.

10 Gavriil Popov, *Voina i Pravda: Tsena pobedy* [*War and truth: the cost of victory*] (New York: Liberty Publishing House, 2005).

11 P.M. Dembitsky, 'Sud'ba plennykh' ['The Fate of Prisoners']

12 Hoffmann

13 B. Kuznetsov, *V ugodu Stalinu* [*In Stalin's favor*] (New York, 1993).

14 These figures are from the Russian Federation's Ministry of Defense in 2005. According to the data of the Russian historian G.F. Krivosheev, during the Great Patriotic War a total of 3,396,400 Soviet soldiers and officers went missing in action or were captured by the Germans. Of these, 1,836,000 eventually returned to the Soviet Union, while 1,783,000 didn't return (they either perished in German captivity or avoided repatriation). However, these figures are disputed and provoke doubts.

15 The four-volume work by Vladimir Bashev, *Vlasov*, has been completed and will soon be published.

Chapter 9

1 I have found much of the American version of events surrounding the link-up between American and Russian troops in Vilen Liulechnik, 'Vstrecha na El'be. God 45-I' ['Meeting at the Elbe: Year 1945'] *Mezhdunarodnyi russkii zhurnal*, No. 5 (May, 2009).

2 S.Ia. Lavrenev and M.M. Popov, *Krakh Reikha* [*Downfall of the Reich*] (Moscow: Izdatel'stvo AST, 2000), pp. 247-274.

3 Ibid.

Chapter 10

1 Valentin Falin, 'Bez shturma Berlina, Rossiiu zhdala by tret'ia Mirovaia voina' ['Without the storming of Berlin, a Third World War would have awaited Russia'] *Novaia istoriia*, 23 March 2005. Available in Russian on the Internet as of 2010 at http://anti-orange.com.ua/article/hystory/66/7709.
2 Lavrenov and Popov, *Krakh Reikha*, pp. 159-189.
3 British Broadcasting Corporation, 'The Allies: The Frustrated Triumph', a program aired on 21 August 2009.
4 Dwight Eisenhower, *Crusade in Europe* (Garden City, NY: Doubleday & Co. 1948; Johns Hopkins Paperback Edition, 1997).
5 Zhukov, *Reminiscences and Reflections*, Vol. 2 (Moscow: Progress Publishers, 1985), p. 397.
6 Iu. N. Erofeev, 'General, voshedshii v istoriiu' ['A General, who has entered history'] *Nezavisimoe voennoe obozrenie*, 24 November 2000.
7 See in particular David Irving, *Apocalypse 1945: The Destruction of Dresden*, 2nd Ed. (Focal Point Publications, 2007). [Again, Boris is citing the Russian translation of this work.]
8 Eisenhower, *Crusade in Europe*, p. 396.
9 Ibid.
10 The materials of the polemics surrounding Valentin Falin's article can be found in the article 'Za nashu i vashu Pobedu. Spory o vtoroi Mirovoi voiny' ['For our and your victory. Arguments about the Second World War'], which can be found on the Internet at http://www.strana.ru/05/01/19/3588/245786.html.
11 As of 11 April 2011 Hasting's article can be found on the Internet at http://www.dailymail.co.uk/debate/article-1209041/Operation-unthinkable-How-Churchill-wanted-recruit-defeated-Nazi-troops-drive-Russia-Eastern-Europe.html.
12 Eisenhower, *Crusade in Europe*, p. 399.
13 Sir Bernard Montgomery, *The Memoirs of Field-Marshal the Viscount Montgomery of Alamein*, K. G. (London: Collins, 1958), p. 271-272.
14 Ibid., p. 277-278.
15 Ibid., p. 279.
16 Ibid., p. 280.
17 Ibid., p. 331.
18 Ibid., p. 332.
19 Ibid., p. 331.
20 See G. P. Kynin's article, 'Sekretnaia telegramma I.V. Stalina D. Eizenkhaueru nakanune bitvy za Berlin' ['I.V. Stalin's secret telegram to D. Eisenhower on the eve of the battle for Berlin']

Chapter 11

1 These *Sovinformburo* reports are reproduced here in abridged fashion. The listing of liberated Czech cities has been deleted by the author.
2 Sources give varying dates regarding the preparation and initiation of the uprising. By 7 May 1945 however, more than 30,000 people were involved in it.
3 S.K. Buniachenko was a former member of the All-Communist Party (Bolshevik) from 1919 and had served in the Red Army. He graduated from the prestigious

M.V. Frunze Academy of the General Staff. As the commander of the 59th Rifle Brigade in November 1942 he surrendered to the Germans and was placed in a prisoner of war camp in Kherson. Here, having found out about Vlasov's appeal, he declared his desire to join the Russian Liberation Army. At first he was an instructor in schools that prepared the army's officer cadres, and then he fought in France. For his services, he was decorated by the Germans with three medals and one Order. After the decision to create the RLA 1st Division, he was appointed as its commander and in a short period of time he brought its strength up to 20,000 men.

4 The SMERSH agents hunted down and executed Vlasov's men throughout the city of Prague.

5 The Czech National Council consisted of 12 members - eight of which were communists.

6 Andrei Pugovkin, 'Gorech' istoricheskoi pravdy' ['The Bitterness of historic truth'] *Zvezda*, No. 7 (July 2003).

7 Editor's note: Radio Praha in 2004 conducted an interview with Antonin Sun, a member of the Czech resistance movement and Jan Masaryk's last secretary, which at the time of writing was available at http://www.radio.cz/en/section/czechs/calling-all-czechs-calling-all-czechs-the-prague-uprising-remembered. In the interview, Mr. Sun states: "The Vlasovs - that was a part of the German army made up of Russian soldiers who were imprisoned by the Germans and who turned sides. General Vlasov was ill at the time [of the Prague uprising] but he sent General Buniachenko and really they helped us for two days. We had practically nothing left. Without their help I do not know what would have happened."

Chapter 12

1 Editor's note: "Zek" is a Russian slang word for a prisoner or forced labor camp inmate. It is derived from the Russian word "*zakliuchennyi*", or "inmate", which in formal documents was often abbreviated as *z/k*, or "zeh-kah" as it would be pronounced in Russian.

2 Author's note: Sauckel was found guilty of war crimes and crimes against humanity at the Nuremburg Trials and sentenced to death. He was executed by hanging on 16 October 1946.

3 V.N. Zemskov, 'Repatriatsiia sovetskikh grazhdan i ikh dal'neishyaya sud'ba' ['The repatriation of Soviet citizens and their subsequent fate']

Chapter 13

1 Just who is "the Devil"? There are a lot of mentions of him in the Bible. Under the word "Devil", a person who maliciously lies, a foe or an enemy is implied. The word "Satan" is synonymous.

2 I.Z. Ladygin and N.I. Smirko, *Na Rzhevskom rubezhe* [*On the Rzhev Line*] (Rzhev, 1958), pp. 120-123.

3 Friedrich Segal', *Shkola muzhestva i blagorodstva* [*The school of courage and nobility*], 2nd ed. Revised and expanded. (Riga), pp. 43; 82-83.

4 I. Nykhalov, A. Pyl'tsin, A. Vasil'chenko et. al. *Shtrafbaty po obe storony fronta: Voenno-istoricheskii sbornik* [*penal battalions along both sides of the front: A military-his-*

torical handbook] (Moscow: Yauza/Eksmo, 2007). The handbook contains data on all the assault and penal battalions - as well as the separate penal companies and platoons (as well as the dates of their formation).

5 Translator's note: The *oprichniki* were Ivan the Terrible's notorious secret police - responsible for the torture and murder of his internal enemies.

6 See Boris Polyakov, 'Kogda podozrevalsia ves' narod' ['When the entire nation matured'] in *Eto bylo na Rzhevsko-Viazemskom platsdarme* [*It was in the Rzhev-Viazma staging area*] Book II, a compilation of recollections, (Rzhev, 2000), pp. 90-93.

7 Ivan Maslennikov, 'Stroki, napisannye voiny' ['Lines written by the war'], in *Eto bylo na Rzhevsko-Viazemskom platsdarme*, pp. 25-50.

8 Translator's note: Though I have chosen to use the translation "fire direction and control platoon" for the original Russian *vzvod upravleniia*, in the Red Army this platoon was responsible for more than controlling and directing fire. It also scouted enemy positions to identify targets and was responsible for maintaining communications between the battery observation post and its firing positions. My thanks to former Red Army artilleryman Isaak Kobylyanskiy, who has penned his own memoirs that have been translated into English under the title *From Stalingrad to Pillau: A Red Army Artillery Officer Remembers the Great Patriotic War* (University Press of Kansas, 2008), for explaining to me the responsibilities of the *vzvod upravleniia*.

9 Mikhin's accounts can be found in *Rzhevskaia bitva: Srazhenie za Polunino* [*The Rzhev battle: the fight for Polunino*] A collection of articles and materials (Tver': Izdatel'stvo Russkaia provintsiia, 2001), pp. 149-157.

10 Petr Mikhin, *Guns Against the Reich: Memoirs of an Artillery Officer on the Eastern Front* (South Yorkshire: Pen & Sword Books Ltd., 2010), pp. 22-27.

11 See Burakov's contribution in *Eto bylo na Rzhevsko-Viazemskom platsdarme*, Book One, p. 49.

12 Essay, 'Ognevaia pamiat' moia' ['My fiery memory'], pp. 99-107.

13 Leonid Malyshev narrates Tat'iana Motina's story in "... Vy luchshe les rubite na groby" ["... You better cut down the forests for coffins"] in *Eto bylo na Rzhevsko-Viazemskom rubezhe*, Book One, pp. 86-89.

14 Foka Stanislavovich Ivanov, 'Poslednii boi' ['The Last Battle'] in *Eto bylo na Rzhevsko-Viazemskom rubezhe*, Book Two, pp. 119-122.

15 Editor's note: Aleksandr Matveievich Matrosov was a Soviet infantryman in the Second World War who on 22 February 1943 reportedly threw himself onto the embrasure of a German pillbox - thereby blocking the fire of the machine gun inside, for which he was posthumously honored with the title Hero of the Soviet Union. Other Red Army soldiers were called upon to emulate Matrosov's self-sacrificing example for the greater cause of victory. Later, any man who voluntarily sacrificed himself in battle was called a "Matrosov".

16 This is what former Soviet soldiers and officers call those who served in the SMERSH or those who after the end of the war at Stalin's order disposed of people seen as insufficiently loyal to Soviet power.

17 S. Drobiazko, *Vtoraia mirovaia voina, 1939-1945: Vostochnye dobrovol'tsy v Wermakhte, politsii i SS* [*Second World War, 1939-1945: Eastern volunteers in the Wehrmacht, police and SS*] (Moscow: Izdatel'stvo AST, 2000), p. 3.

18 *Spravka: Istoriia sozdaniia i deiatel'nosti SMERSHa* [*Handbook: History of the creation and activity of SMERSH* (Moscow: RIA Novosti RU, 2008)

19 The Soviet newspaper *Krasnaia zvezda*, 21 June 2005.
20 *Profil'*, June 2004.
21 Viacheslav Zviagentsev, *Voina na vesakh Femidy: Voina 1941-1945 goda v materialakh sledstvenno-sluzhebnykh del* [*War on the scales of Themis: The 1941-1945 war in the materials of investigative official matters* (Moscow: Terra-incognita klub, 2006).
22 Konstantin Rozhkov, "SMERSH – kontrrazvedka ili orudie ustrashnenie?" ["SMERSH – counterintelligence or a weapon of intimidation?" - transcript of a BBC Russia broadcast from 16 April 2003 available at www.BBC.russian.com
23 See A. Mikhailkov, 'Chto bylo, to bylo' ['It was what it was'] in *Eto bylo na Rzhevsko-Viazemskom rubezhe*, Book One, pp. 118-129.
24 Valerii Kuznetsov, 'Pod znakom 'Saturna" ['Under the sign of 'Saturn"], *Stavropol'skaia Pravda*, 22 February 2008.
25 A truncated version of Sergei Lozun'ko's article can be found at http://www.news2000.org/print?a=%2f8365 (17 August 2009).
26 Nikita Lomagin, *Leningrad v blokade* [*Leningrad in the blockade*] (Moscow: Izdatel'stvo Eskmo and Yauza, 2005).
27 G.V. Kosterchenko, *Taina politiki Stalina: Vlast' i anti-semitizma* [*Stalin's secret policies: Power and anti-Semitism*] (Moscow: Izdatel'stvo "Mezhdunarodnye otnosheniia", 2003. The index contains 38 references to the name "Abakumov".
28 Leonid Mlezhek, 'Leningradskoe delo' i drugie dela generala Abakumov' ['The Leningrad Affair' and other of General Abakumov's matters'] *Profil'*, No. 21, 6 May 2006.
29 *Tomenskii kur'er*, 24 October 2006.
30 Hasan Husseinov, "Sachsenhausen: Two crimes in one museum"; an Internet article posted 11 December 2001 at http://www.dwworld.de/popus/popup_printcontent/0,,444981,00.html.
31 Svetlana Kravchenko, 'Pribyl iz Germanii v Rossiiu po prikazu NKVD' ['I arrived in Russia from Germany at the order of the NKVD'] *Argumenty i fakty*, No. 21 (1997).
32 E.S. Fedorov, *O voennom Rzheve: Dokumenty i fakty* [*On wartime Rzhev: Documents and facts*] (Rzhev: Proizvodstvenno-poligraficheskoe predpriiatie, 1995).

Chapter 14

1 A. Minkin, "Ch'ia Pobeda? Esli u nas budut prapravnuki – chto oni ponimat' o voine? I chto oni budut znat'?" ["Whose Victory? If we have great-great grandchildren, what will they understand about the war? And what will they know?" Available on the Internet in Russian at http://www.mk.ru/numbers/1960/article56220.htm
2 Dwight Eisenhower, *Crusade in Europe*, translated into Russian under the title *Krestovyi poxhod v Evropu* (Smolensk: Rusich, 2000), p. 502.
3 Author's note: Davies' figures aren't totally accurate.
4 Editor's note: Claudia Shulzhenko was a songstress much beloved by the Red Army soldiers - much like Vera Lynn to the British soldiers. Remarkably, she gave more than 500 concerts in blockaded Leningrad.
5 Leonid Radzikhovsky, 'Voina za zhizn' i voina za svobodu,' ['The war for life and the war for freedom'] *Rossiiskaia gazeta*, 4 June 2004.

6 Karl Doenitz, *Nemetskie podvodnye lodki, 1939-1945* [*German submarines, 1939-1945*] (Saint Petersburg: Izdatel'stvo Poligon, 202), pp. 172-173.

7 See the Russian Internet article "Ob anglo-amerikanskoi istoriografii Vtoroi mirovoi voiny" ["On the Anglo-American historiography of the Second World War"], available at http://historic.ru/books/item/f00/s00/z0000025/st060.shtml

8 Eisenhower, *Krestovyi pokhod*; Viscount Bernard Law Montgomery, *Memuary fel'dmarshala* [*A Field Marshal's Memoirs* (Moscow: Izdatel'stvo Izograf and Eksmo, 2004). This is the Russian translation of Montgomery's *The Memoirs of Field Marshal Montgomery*.

9 See, for example, V.A. Shestakov, M.M. Chernov and E.E. Viazemsky, *Istoriia otechestva XX veka* [*Twentieth Century History of the Fatherland*] (Moscow: Prosveshchenie, 2000), p. 233.

10 E.N. Kul'kov, M.Iu. Miagkov and O.A. Rzheshevsky, *Voina 1939-1945* [*The War 1939-1945*] (Moscow: Olma-press, 2001), p. 125.

11 Joachim von Ribbentrop, *Vospominaniia i poslednie zapisi* [*Memoir and final notes*] From his personal papers, published by Anneliz von Ribbentrop. (Moscow: Mysl', 1996).

12 Andrei Morozov, 'Neizvestnyi vtoroi front' ['The unknown Second Front'], *Nasha Istoriia* [*Our History*], No. 11 (November 2004).

13 Siegried Westphal, *Germanskaia armiia na Zapadnom fronte* [*The German Army in the West*] (Moscow: Izdatel'stvo Tsentrpoligraf, 2007). This is the Russian translation of Westphal's memoirs, which were published in the English in 1952 under the same title.

Chapter 15

1 Iurii Primakov, 'Stalin v roli velikogo polkovodtsa: udobnyi mif' ['Stalin as the Great Commander: a convenient myth']; a column posted to the World Socialist website on 13 December 2005.

2 A collection of Stalin's early wartime speeches, radio addresses and orders that was published during the war, this book went through six editions and more than a million copies were printed.

3 Editor's note: The Decembrist movement was a group that largely consisted of young Russian officers who had been exposed to Western culture and ideas after serving in Europe in the campaigns against Napoleon. Inspired by such ideas as constitutional monarchies, representative democracy and other liberal ideals they and other young noblemen staged an uprising against Tsar Nicholas I that was quickly crushed.

4 Evgenii Prokhorov served three years of his sentence, returned home, completed his education at the Publishing Institute and defended his dissertation. Later he taught textual studies at Moscow University.

5 Editor's note: *Smertnik*, literally a man condemned to death, was the nickname given by Russian soldiers to their equivalent of the dog tag. In 1941, soldiers were instructed to wear small wooden cases that were suspended around their necks by string or cord. These little cases carried a strip of paper inside that contained personal identification information like name and birthplace. These little cases were crudely crafted and not weatherproofed, so the information inside often quickly became illegible. Many soldiers - particularly the older ones - refused to wear them

because of the superstition that anyone wearing one was marked for certain death on the battlefield. In 1942, Stalin abolished the use of these *smertniki*.

6 Editor's note: This was the Russian nickname given to the impressive display of medals that officers usually wore due to the Russian fondness for combat decorations. Brezhnev in particular showed this proclivity.

7 In 1960 the Moscow Correspondence Institute of Publishing merged with the Moscow Printing Institute.

8 Joachim Hoffmann, *Vlasov protiv Stalina: Tragediia russkoi osvoboditel'noi armii 1942-1945* [*Vlasov against Stalin: The Tragedy of the Russian Liberation Army 1942-1945*] (Moscow: Izdatel'stvo Astrel', 2009). This is a Russian translation of Hoffmann's 1984 book, *Die Geschichte der Wlassow-Armee* [*History of the Vlasov Army*].

9 G.V. Kostyrchenko, Tainaia politika Stalina: Vlast' i antisemitism [Stalin's secret policy: Power and anti-Semitism. (Moscow: Izdatel'stvo Mezhdunarodnye otnosheniia, 2003), p. 392.

10 Editor's note: Nikolai Voznesensky was formally in charge of the Soviet economy during the war.

Chapter 16

1 Materials of the Moscow conference; see Khlevniuk's address to the conference.

2 These results are according to the Levada-Center - formerly the All-Russian Public Opinion Research Center in Moscow - which conducted the surveys.

3 Iurii Afanas'ev, 'V rossii idet reabilitatsiia stalinizma, demokraticheskie instituty – muzhliaki' ['The rehabilitation of Stalinism is underway in Russia; democratic institutes are hoaxes'], available at http://newsru.com, 19 May 2006.

4 Marietta Chudakova, 'Stalin polzet vverkh, kak stolbik rtuti' ['Stalin is rising like a column of mercury'] *Gazeta "Grani"*, Issue 326, 2007.

5 Editor's note: This includes such scholars as Valeriy Zamulin, author of the prize-winning book (in English) *Demolishing the Myth: The Tank Battle at Prokhorovka, Kursk, July 1943: An Operational Narrative* (Helion, 2011), and Lev Lopukhovsky, author of the title (in English translation) *The Viazma Catastrophe 1941: The Red Army's Disastrous Stand against Operation Typhoon* (Helion, 2013). Both historians have lost their jobs for writing books that didn't adhere to Soviet-era myths, but instead took an objective look at their respective subjects.

6 Editor's note: *Pamiat'* (*Memorial*) is an international society headquartered in St. Petersburg that is dedicated to recording and drawing attention to the victims of Stalinism and monitors current human rights in Russia and other post-Soviet States. Its own stated aim is to eliminate the legacies of Stalinism and to promote democratic values and government based on the rule of law.

7 NTV [Nezavisimoe televedenie – Independent Television] was a company founded by Boris Gusinsky in 1993 that quickly attracted the top Russian television journalists and news anchors of that time. An independent voice and often a sharp critic of Russian Government - especially of the Second Chechen War, Vladimir Putin and his *Edinaia Rossiia* Party - it provoked a fierce reaction from Putin's supporters. Soon, a criminal investigation was launched against NTV and charges were filed against Boris Gusinsky. On 14 April 2001 NTV was forcibly taken over by the State-owned Gazprom Media - after which its leadership was replaced and many of its top journal-

ists left. Soon, its weekly news commentary program and other news programs were terminated.

8 A complete English-language presentation of Igor Korolkov's article in Novaia gazeta has been posted on the website http://www.freerepublic.com/focus/f-news/1775306/posts by a user with the handle JadeEmporer. The original Russian article itself is available at http://www.newsru.com/russia/11Jan2007/ng.html

9 Editor's note: Iamderbiev is a far less admirable figure than the other victims mentioned by the author. Ianderbiev was implicated in the October 2002 Moscow theater hostage crisis. He was placed on Interpol's most-wanted list and also was added to the United Nations' Al Qaeda and Taliban Sanction Committee's blacklist of Al Qaeda suspects. He was in the Middle East to raise funds to support the radical Chechen faction the Special Purpose Islamic regiment, which was responsible for the Moscow theater takeover.

Chapter 17

1 Editor's note: Ivan Vladimirovich Michurin was a famous Russian geneticist who made major contributions in the development of genetics and was one of the founding fathers of scientific agricultural selection. He developed many fruit hybrids including apple, pear, cherry and other hybrids which were cultivated in the Soviet Union.

2 Editor's note: Solovki - or the Solovetsky Islands in the White Sea - is the site of a famous old monastery complex, but also of the Sovetsky Special Purpose Camp - one of the first Soviet labor camps that later became a prison before being transformed into a naval base. The Orthodox Church reestablished the monastery in 1992.

3 Author's note: Zhukov never had any connections with the NKVD.

4 This story is available on the Internet at http://www.badnews.org.ru/news/kak_v_sovetskoj_rossii_unichtozhali_invalidov_vov/2011-01

5 Account available on the Internet at http://www.contrtv.ru/forum/index.ph

6 Document available on the Internet as of 13 September 2011 at http://forum/ixbt.com/post.cgi?id=print:55:63

7 Evgenii Kuznetsov, *Valaamskaia tetrad'* [*Valaam notebook*] (Saint Petersburg: Izdatel'stvo Krug, 2003).

8 Translator's note: These trolleys were not like hospital gurneys. Typically, they were crudely fashioned carts made out of plywood and mounted on casters. However, at the time the USSR had no casters so ordinary ball bearings with a ½ to ¾ inch diameter were used. The legless invalid would use "*tolkachi*" or "pushers" to propel the trolley over the ground. Others preferred not to use the trolleys and instead used the *tolkachi*, which had wide bases, as short crutches to move along the sidewalk or ground. I want to thank author Peter Mezhiritsky for this information, who well remembers the sound of these trolleys and the sad sight of these disabled veterans from his childhood in postwar Kiev.

9 Available on the Internet as of September 13 2011 at http://www.center-rne.org/new.php?id=1255379013

10 Available as of December 2011 on http://ostrovforum.net/showthread.php&t=2000

11 Available as of 11 June 2011 on the website http://www.rg.ru/2010/03/24/valaam.html

12 Available as of September 13 2011 on the Internet at http://ptoday.ru/city///-news/2731-memorial-pamyati-frontovikov

Chapter 18

1 Editor's note: Soviet casualty data distinguish between "total irrecoverable losses" - which includes killed, mortally wounded, non-combat deaths from diseases and accidents, prisoners of war and missing in action - and "demographic losses", which excludes men listed in the latter two categories who were later found alive.
2 Available at time of writing at www.News.ru.com/Russia/15 nov.2002
3 Available at time of writing at www.Grani.ru, 9 May 2009.
4 According to data from the Russian "Book of Remembrance", as sited by Oksana Korneva in her online 'Polevoi dnevnik' ['Field journal'] at www.okorneva.ru at time of writing.
5 Aleksandr Babalin, 'Batal'ony bez vesti propavshix, trebuiut vozvrashcheniia is nebytiia' ['battalions of the unidentified fallen demand being returned from the unknown'] *Nezavisimoe voennoe obozrenie*, 18 June 2006.
6 *Soiuz poiskovykh ob'edinenii* [*Union of Search Organizations*], No. 2 (Kazan: Gazeta "Otechestvo", 2002).
7 Irina Golovinova, 'Rekviem' ['Requiem'], available at time of writing at http://www.requiem.ru/cemetery/doc148/
8 *Nezavisimoe voennoe obozrenie*, 11 May 2009.
9 http://www.News.com, *Novosti RossiįI*, 25 July 2007.
10 Irina Golovina, 'Rekviem: Novoe kladbishche v Sologubovke' ['Requiem: New cemetery in Sologubovka'], available at time of writing at http://www.requiem.ru
11 *Soiuz poiskovykh ob'edinenii*, No. 2.
12 *Ibid.*
13 *Novosti Rossii*, 25 July 2007; available at time of writing at http://News.com
14 The online article 'Na Kurskoi duge pokhoroniat tysiachi nemetskikh soldat' ['Thousands of German soldiers are being buried at the Kursk bulge']; available at time of writing at http://www.Grani.ru
15 'Nikto ne zabyt?' ['No one is forgotten?'] Vremia novosti, no. 46, 20 March 2009.
16 Svetlana Gerasimova, *Rzhev 1942: pozitsionnaia boinia* [*Rzhev 1942: A positional slaughter*] (Moscow: Izdatel'stvo "Iauza – Eksmo", 2007), p. 237.
17 Maksim Iaroshevsky, 'Rossiia provodit uchet svoikh voinskix zakhoronenii za rubezhom' ['Russia is conducting a count of military graves abroad']; available online at time of writing at http://www.svobodanews.ru/Article/2007/05/04/20070504161018277.html
18 'Mogila vsekh pomirit' ['The grave reconciles everyone'], 2000. Annual No.18-19 (365), 11-17 May 2007
19 'The S.S. archive reveals the horrors that the Nazis created', *The Independent*, 6 July 2006.
20 'Tsvety dlia Shtukenbriuka' ['Flowers for Stukenbrock'], available online at time of writing at http://nauka.relis.ru/25/0210/25210076.html
21 'Sovetskoe Pole Slavy' ['The Soviet Field of Glory'], available at the time of writing at http://www.soldat.ru/search/f_glory/annotation.html

INDEX

INDEX OF PEOPLE

INDEX OF PLACES

INDEX OF AMERICAN MILITARY UNITS

Army Groups:

Armies:

Divisions:

INDEX OF GERMAN MILITARY UNITS

Army Groups:

Armies:

Miscellaneous / Other:

INDEX OF SOVIET MILITARY UNITS

Fronts:

Armies:

INDEX OF MISCELLANEOUS TERMS

Related titles published by Helion & Company

The Viaz'ma Catastrophe. The Red Army's Disastrous Stand Against Operation Typhoon
Lev Lopukhovsky (edited and translated by Stuart Britton)
ISBN 978-1-908916-50-1

The Rzhev Slaughterhouse. The Red Army's Forgotten 15-Month Campaign against Army Group Center, 1942-1943
Svetlana Gerasimova (edited and translated by Stuart Britton)
ISBN 978-1-908916-51-8

Demolishing the Myth. The Tank Battle at Prokhorovka, Kursk, July 1943: An Operational Narrative
Valeriy Zamulin (edited and translated by Stuart Britton)
ISBN 978-1-906033-89-7

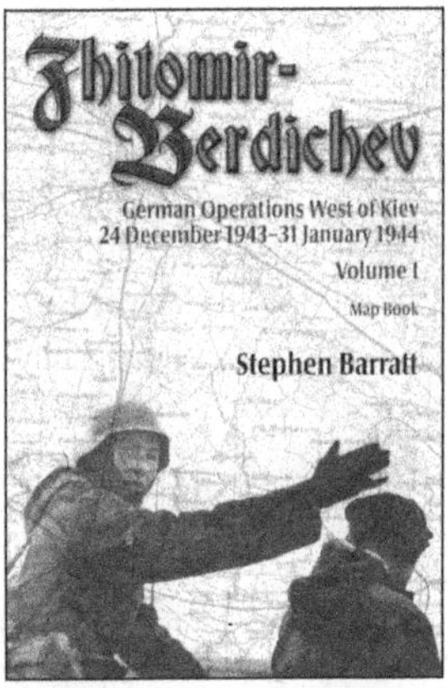

Zhitomir-Berdichev. German Operations West of Kiev 24 December 1943-31 January 1944 Volume 1
Stephen Barratt
ISBN 978-1-907677-66-3

Zhitomir-Berdichev. German Operations West of Kiev 24 December 1943-31 January 1944 Volume 2
Stephen Barratt
ISBN 978-1-909384-10-1

HELION & COMPANY
26 Willow Road, Solihull, West Midlands B91 1UE, England
Telephone 0121 705 3393 Fax 0121 711 4075
Website: http://www.helion.co.uk
Twitter: @helionbooks Visit our blog http://blog.helion.co.uk